# The Continuing Works of Christ

# The Continuing Works of Christ

## Exposing Unbelief

Second Edition
Revised and Expanded

Art Mathias

Wellspring Publishing
ANCHORAGE, ALASKA

Wellspring Ministries of Alaska
P.O. Box 190084
Anchorage, Alaska 99519-0084
907-563-9033
e-mail: akwellspr@aol.com
Website: akwellspring.com

ISBN: 0-9720656-5-2

Cover by C. Ruby Designs

# Contents

# Foreword

It is my joy to make a few comments on the teaching of Dr. Art Mathias. Recently he led a seminar at Auburn Heights Baptist Church where I have had the privilege of being pastor for eighteen years. To meet him in person and to discern his humble spirit, combined with his gifted revelations of the Word of God, has been one of the highlights of my ministry. One of the deacons of the church whispered to me during a teaching session, "Pastor, this will do more for our church than any teaching or preaching we have experienced and he never raised his voice." I whole-heartedly concur with my deacon's assessment of the teaching of Dr. Art Mathias.

We are mixed in our congregation in philosophy of doing church. Many come from a traditional Baptist background and many are more open in worship and doctrine. Art's ministry blessed across the spectrum and brought a spirit of unity as we were taught the Word of God in simplicity and power.

When I first was exposed to this teaching, I had a testimony of the Spirit that this is of God. I so wanted our people at Auburn Heights to hear this truth from God's Word. I have attended four Bible colleges and seminaries. I have earned a Doctorate in Ministry Degree and was never exposed to the truths Dr. Mathias teaches in his seminars and books. It is one of my prayers for young pastors to get this truth of God's Word and share it with their churches.

About two years ago I was diagnosed with rheumatoid arthritis. I can tell you from someone who is not just reading and teaching these truths, but applying them to my own life, that I am grateful for God's grace to bring me in contact with this gifted man of God.

There is integrity in this man's ministry, which is why I'm so privileged to recommend his books and if you can ever sit at his feet and absorb the wonderful truths of God's Word, you will understand why I have written these words.

Wayne Scarborough, Sr.
B.MIN., M.DIV., D.MIN.
Senior Pastor, Auburn Heights Baptist Church
Phenix City, Alabama

# Acknowledgments

I have spent years studying the Scriptures and working with people but there is much that I do not know. I learn and borrow from others constantly. God's truth comes from God Himself but I try to acknowledge those from whom I have learned.

I want to thank Dan Mace, the author of *Unmasking: Dispensational Theology and The Mystery of The Iniquity*, for help in developing portions of this book. I have used some of his work with his permission.

In Parts One and Three I have used several "lists" that come from the *Dake Study Bible*.

Several months ago as I was seeking God for more, He led me to a study of the Hebrew roots of Christianity. The Pastor of El Shaddai Ministries, Mark Biltz, challenged me to learn more about the cultural context of the Bible. He encouraged me to read and study several books which have greatly blessed me. This has been and still is one of the most exciting and challenging studies that I have done.

# Special Author's Note

In this book and my other writings I often talk about sin. At Wellspring Ministries we look at sin in a different light. When we learn that we have a sin, we shout "Hallelujah." We shout Hallelujah because we have learned about something that is separating us from God that we can deal with. Proverbs 26:2 teaches that the curse does not come without a cause.

If we go into condemnation, guilt or anger, we have only given Satan another victory. These are his tools. God comes to us in conviction, asking us to repent and forgive, so He can forgive and cleanse us of all unrighteousness. Satan wants to keep us in bitterness, anger and condemn us forever. Satan hates us and God loves us.

Learning that we have a sin is finding an answer. When we find the answer, then we can deal with it in repentance and forgiveness, and then find freedom and God's rest.

# Introduction

I have spent many hours contemplating the title of this book. I wanted it to express my experience and the truth of God's word. "The Continuing Works of Christ" expresses the fact that the works and miracles of Jesus are for today. His power, love and compassion have not changed. Let me explain.

In 1997 I became very ill. I questioned and blamed God for the disease. I cried out and asked "Why? Why me? Are you there God?" as many of us have. I was taught and believed a theology that nothing could happen to me that was not approved by God. "God is in control," therefore the disease had to be His will and He was testing me for some unknown purpose.

The doctors told me that I was going to die within two years and in that struggle and crying out to God I discovered the truth (see Part Two for my testimony). God the Father is love. He does not test us with disease any more than we would test our children with a calamity or disease. We serve a risen Lord who has power over sin and Satan, and He gave that power to each of us. If we will use that power, we do not have to remain defeated and hopeless victims. We do not have to cower in the corner afraid of the devil. We are not just puppets in the game of life. Christianity is not fatalism, it is victory in Jesus.

I was taught by college and seminary professors that the works of Jesus were necessary to substantiate the Scriptures but now that we have the written word, miracles are no longer needed and that is why they don't happen anymore, or only happen very rarely. These same professors also taught that the "gifts" or "manifestations" of the Holy Spirit recorded in I Corinthians 12 also ceased with the last of the original apostles.

Now, I have come to believe that all of the "works of Jesus" are for today. I believe that the miracles and signs and wonders that Jesus and His disciples performed in the gospels and the book of Acts are vital and necessary for today. The "works of Jesus" are a display of the Father's character, righteousness and love.

But, His miracles and works do not happen very frequently in today's world. Why not? In the first part of this book we explore this question by looking at unbelief and the doctrines of most of our churches. God proclaims over and over again that He has not changed. He is the same yesterday, today and forever. Therefore we must have changed.

Each of the doctrines that are discussed in this book are taught in most of our churches. I thought they brought me hope and security. Instead they really gave me defeat and hopelessness, and brought unbelief into my life. They brought a hopelessness that I did not even understand. I was deceived and did not know it. I was consumed with sins such as resentment and anger and did not know it.

What are God's purposes on this earth? The purpose of the Old and New Covenants has always been to bring God's own righteous character forth on the earth through the lives of His people. Jesus states this very plainly in what we call the Lord's Prayer in Matthew 6:10. In this prayer Jesus instructs us to pray "Thy kingdom come. Thy will be done in earth, as it is in heaven." Why would He teach us to pray this way if it were not God's will for it to happen? Under the Old Covenant, Israel was to be God's representative to the nations. Under the New Covenant, the church, which includes all believers, Jew or Gentile, are to be God's representatives to the nations and with the empowerment of the Holy Spirit our responsibility is to bring the Lord's will to the earth as it is in heaven.

His will is not a mystery. He has expressed it throughout Scripture. I believe that His foremost will is for everyone to choose salvation. The Father's love, grace and mercy have no limits. Scripture tells us that it is not His will that any should perish (II Peter 3:9). I believe that He has called and chosen every human from the foundation of the earth and that He wants each of us to also choose Him and experience His righteousness.

Isaiah 62:1-2

"For Zion's sake will I not hold my peace, for Jerusalem's sake I will not rest, until the righteousness thereof go forth as brightness, and the salvation thereof as a lamp that burneth. And the Gentiles [nations] shall see thy righteousness all the kings thy glory: and thou shalt be called by a new name which the mouth of the Lord shall name."

Isaiah 61:11

"For as the earth bringeth forth her bud, and as the garden causeth the things that are sown in it to spring forth; so the Lord God will cause righteousness and praise to spring forth before all the nations."

Why is God looking for actual, tangible, visible righteousness? First of all, because it brings Him glory: "Let your light [conduct] so shine before men that they will see your good works and glorify your Father which is in heaven" (Matthew 5:16). Second, because the fruit (manifestation) of righteousness destroys the kingdom of Satan. Imputed righteousness (Justification) is invisible; no one can see it! Only manifested righteousness (our actual works) can destroy the works of darkness. When we choose to believe, God counts or imputes our choice to believe as righteousness. This is only the beginning of our walk with God (see the topic of Eternal Life).

Proverbs 4:18

"But the path [way, or conduct] of the just is as a shining light, that shineth more and more unto the perfect day."

Isaiah 60:21

"Thy people also shall be all righteous: they shall inherit the land for ever, the branch of my planting, the work of my hands, that I may be glorified."

Isaiah 61:3

"To appoint unto them that mourn in Zion, to give unto them beauty for ashes, the oil of joy for mourning, the garment of praise for the spirit of heaviness; that they might be called trees of righteousness, the planting of the Lord, that he might be glorified."

Philippians 1:9-11

"And this I pray, that your love may abound yet more and more in knowledge and in all judgment; That ye may approve things that are excellent; that ye may be sincere and without offense till the day of Christ; Being filled with the fruits of righteousness, which are by Jesus Christ, unto the glory and praise of God."

Is it the fruits of righteousness that bring praise to God and bring the nations to Him? What are these fruits? Are they evident in Christianity today? Should they be? Of course they should be. The real question is, "why aren't they?" If God's will was being done on the earth as it is in heaven then the fruits of righteousness would be evident.

Many teach that since we have accepted Jesus as our Savior, all past, present and future sins are automatically forgiven and will never come to judgment. They believe that they have nothing to fear on the Day of Judgment, except maybe losing a few rewards. Is this true?

Many theologians teach that salvation is through grace alone, plus nothing, thus replacing the concept of salvation by grace through faith (Ephesians 2:8, James 2:17). They also teach that since it is by grace alone we do not play a role or have a choice in our salvation. Is this accurate? Is salvation by grace "alone" without any conditions or choice on our part? Does this make God a respecter of person and turn His grace into nothing more than a license to sin? It is faith, not unmerited favor that produces holiness and obedience to God. If we truly believe God, we will show our faith through our obedience. Actions speak much louder than words. If you really want to know what you believe look at what you do (obedience). Unbelief is manifested in disobedience.

Is salvation unconditional, irreversible and final? I Timothy 4:1 says: "Now the Spirit speaketh expressly, that in the latter times some shall depart from the faith, giving heed to seducing spirits and doctrines of devils...." But doesn't the Scripture teach that we are "eternally secure" in Christ? Absolutely! As long as we are in a vital relationship with Him. As long as we have not turned our backs on Him. As long as we have not chosen to do our own thing while alive on earth. Nowhere does Scripture teach that we are secure regardless of how unfaithful we are to Jesus.

Sanctification is a word or concept that we rarely hear today. Those who do teach sanctification usually teach a three-part sanctification. First, we are called and set apart by God. Second, it is good to sanctify ourselves in our experience and daily walk in this life, yet we are told that it is good to obey, but not really possible or vital to our salvation. And third, we will attain "ultimate sanctification" or Christ-likeness only when we are in heaven. We cannot be "holy as He is holy," or Christ-like in this life. Is this teaching true?

Why would God tell us to be Holy as He is, if it were not possible? Why would He tell us that if we obey Him, we will receive His blessings and if we do not, we will receive the fruit of our disobedience if it were not possible to obey? Why would Jesus tell us to be Christians or Christ-like if it were not possible? Has God played a mean trick on us?

The reality is that we live in a time of rampant religious deception. We as Christians need to stop looking at all the religious confusion "out there" in the world. Our problem is not the cults and new-age beliefs. The error that affects us is not the error that comes from outside the church but the false doctrines taught in our churches.

This is not a new problem. The book of Romans addresses both the legalism of the believing Jews, and the view of believing Gentiles that they did not have to obey, which were causing confusion. First and Second Corinthians deal with false apostles in the Church. Galatians deals with more legalism brought into that church by other Judaizers (legalists).

Second Thessalonians addresses false teachers who were teaching people in that church that the Day of the Lord was at hand. Second Peter deals with false teachers who had come into the Church promoting false liberty. The liberty they were encouraging was the liberty to sin.

Second and Third John deal with the spirit of antichrist that was already at work in the churches. The book of Jude is a direct attack against those who had come into the fellowship and were "turning the grace of God into lasciviousness [sin]." He reminded them of what God did to the angels, to Sodom and Gomorrah, to Cain, Balaam, Korah and the people of Israel who had sinned.

Satan is not a funny little character in a red suit, carrying a pitchfork. He is a fallen archangel, one of the most powerful beings in the universe. He is a master deceiver who knows Scripture better than we do. He comes to us as an angel of light, masquerading as a minister of righteousness, quoting the Word of God. He can deceive an entire church if the believers are not diligent. Too many Christians ignore him or view him as a lion with no teeth or claws. But Paul did not view him this way.

Is it possible that these and other deceptions are prohibiting the continuing works of Christ in our lives? Is it possible we have fallen prey to another trick of the devil?

Is the kingdom of God or Heaven only a future event? Why did Jesus command us to pray "Thy kingdom come. Thy will be done in earth, as it is in heaven" (Matthew 6:10), if that isn't what the Father sent Him to demonstrate in His ministry, and what He taught His disciples to do? Yet most of us have been taught that the kingdom of God is only a future event and that the ministry of Jesus was only for that day. Are these teachings correct?

In this book I will examine these and many other questions first, from the Scriptures; second, from the fruit of the teaching; and third, from history.

When we interpret the Bible there are three principles that we must understand and use. First, our beliefs and doctrines must be provable by Scripture. Only the Scripture is the final word. Secondly, I Corinthians 2:4 says, "And my speech and my preaching were not with enticing words of man's wisdom, but in demonstration of the Spirit and of power." Any teaching that is grounded in God's word will bring forth good fruit. The power of God, His nature and His righteousness will show through. Thirdly, history will also show the truth of the teaching. God has not changed. He is the same yesterday, today and tomorrow. His precepts have not changed. If it is true today, we will have seen it in the past. Conversely, if it was true in the past, it is true today.

Also, Scripture is alive. It has an application for the time it was written, an application for today and an application for the future. The book of Haggai is an example of this. Haggai, speaking on behalf of the LORD, told the people that they were suffering because they had not rebuilt the LORD's house. They had "cieled" houses (finished, with roofs) but He had none. Under the old covenant, the LORD dwelt in an actual dwelling or temple. Under the New Covenant, He dwells in us. We are His house. The past, present and future application is the same: rebuild His house by cleansing ourselves of all unrighteousness, and making a place worthy of our LORD.

We must always remember that God is love. He is the giver of every good and perfect gift. If it is not good and perfect, it is not from Him. He wants to walk in the cool of the day with each of us as He did with Adam and Eve. He seeks a personal relationship with each of His children. Never forget that God is a God of relationship. He is goodness, righteousness, and holiness. He cannot and will not violate His nature. Neither can Satan violate his.

Put on your thinking hats and let's study together, keeping in mind these principles.

# PART ONE

# The Biblical Basis for the "Continuing Works of Christ"

**WHAT ARE THE "WORKS OF CHRIST"?**
Let's begin by defining the "Works of Christ." What "works" did the Father send His Son, Jesus, to do? It is very important to understand that it is the Father that sent Jesus. In this fact we learn the heart of the Father. God the Father is not a "mean bad dude" waiting for an excuse to punish us. The first purpose or "work of Jesus" was to show us the Father. We can define who God the Father is, what His kingdom is, and what His will on earth is by looking at Jesus and what He did. Jesus said:

"If I do not do the works of my Father, do not believe me..." John 10:37-38, 14:11

"...He that hath seen me hath seen the Father..." John 14:9

"I and my Father are one." John 10:30

"If you had known me, you should have known my Father also." John 14:7

"...For this purpose the Son of God was manifested, that He might destroy the works of the devil." I John 3:8

God the Father sent Jesus to heal and deliver and save everyone, whosoever will, all who would believe. This is the nature, will and love of the Father. Our understanding of who God the Father is and what His will on earth is should and must be formed by who Jesus is and what He did. If it is not, then we have fallen into a trap set by the devil.

This is vital to understand. God is good! He always has our best interest at heart. Sadly this is not what is normally taught or believed. Instead we hear "I am just like Job, God is testing me with this disease." God does not test us with diseases or other calamities any more than you would test your child with cancer to see if he really loved you.

Let's study further to learn more of the Father's heart. Isaiah 61 is a prophetic passage of what the Messiah was being sent to do.

Isaiah 61:1-4

"The Spirit of the Lord God [the Father] is upon me; because the Lord [the Father] hath anointed me to preach good tidings unto the meek; He hath sent me to bind up the brokenhearted, to proclaim liberty to the captives, and the opening of the prison to them that are bound; To proclaim the acceptable year of the Lord, and the day of vengeance of our God; to comfort all that mourn; To appoint unto them that mourn in Zion, to give unto them beauty for ashes, the oil of joy for mourning, the garment of praise for the spirit of heaviness; that they might be called trees of righteousness, the planting of the Lord, that He might be glorified. And they shall build the old wastes, they shall raise up the former desolations, and they shall repair the waste cities, the desolations of many generations."

In Luke, Jesus Christ quoted this passage and claimed that He was the Messiah, the One sent by the Father to do these things.

Luke 4:16-19

"And He came to Nazareth, where He had been brought up: and, as His custom was, He went into the synagogue on the sabbath day, and stood up for to read. And there was delivered unto Him the book of the prophet Esaias. And when He had opened the book, He found the place where it was written, The Spirit of the Lord is upon me, because He [the Father] hath anointed me to preach the gospel to the poor; He hath sent me to heal the brokenhearted, to preach deliverance to the captives, and recovering of sight to the blind, to set at liberty them that are bruised, To preach the acceptable year of the Lord."

These passages show us that Jesus was sent to do several things:

1. Anointed to preach:
    (1) The gospel to the poor (the destitute, needy). The Gospel is the "good news" that if we will repent, obey and abide in Him, He will abide in us and give us eternal life with Him (John 8:31, John 15:7-8).
    (2) Deliverance to captives in sin, sickness, and death (Acts 10:38, Ephesians 4:8-10, Hebrews 2:14-15).
    (3) And proclaim the acceptable year of the Lord, but not the "day of vengeance" until His second coming.

2. Anointed to heal:
    (1) The broken in heart, mind, soul, and body (Acts 10:38, Isaiah 61:1-2, Luke 4:18-19).
    (2) The blind in body, soul, and spirit, those in darkness (Matthew 4:16, Luke 1:79, Luke 2:32, John 1:4-9, 3:16-21, 8:32, Acts 26:18, Colossians 1:13)
    (3) The bruised, the completely crushed and shattered in life, the oppressed and broken (Isaiah 58:6-14, Mark 5:1-20, Luke 13:16)

3. Anointed to destroy the works of the devil:
    (1) Jesus did this by casting out demons from people thus delivering them from the disease and bondage of Satan.
    (2) He paid the full price for our sin by His death on the cross, giving us a way to be cleansed from all unrighteousness.
    (3) The most important work of Jesus was the Father raising Him from the dead,

because it is in His life that we have the power over the devil.

(4) Because He is alive, Christians have the Holy Spirit living in them. Believers are the temple of God in the New Covenant (I Corinthians 3:16). The New Covenant gives us the power over the devil and his works, because we are now new creatures. Old things are passed away and all things are new (II Corinthians 5:17).

The Ministry of Jesus, while He was on the earth, was a ministry of first teaching people to repent because the (internal) Kingdom of God was at hand. Then He cast out demons, healed broken hearts, and healed all manner of sickness and disease. In doing this, He demonstrated the love of the Father and set the example for each of us to follow.

John 20:21-22

"Then said Jesus to them again, Peace be unto you: as my Father hath sent me, even so send I you. And when He had said this, He breathed on them, and saith unto them, Receive ye the Holy Ghost."

Jesus is sending His disciples with the same impartation of power and the fullness of the Spirit that the Father gave to Him (John 7:37-39; John 14:12; John 17:18; John 20:21; Luke 24:49; Acts 1:4-8; Matthew 18:18). This passage very clearly teaches that, if we are His disciples, we are to go in the same power and authority that was given Jesus by the Father. We, as His disciples, are to do the "works of Jesus." We are to do the "works of Jesus" for the same reason that Jesus did them, to demonstrate the love of the Father.

In John 10:37-38 Jesus says, "If I do not the works of my Father, believe me not. But if I do, though ye believe not me, believe the works: that ye may know, and believe, that the Father is in me, and I in him."

This is an incredible statement by Jesus: "...though ye believe not me," if you cannot believe me for who I said I am, "believe the works: that ye may know, and believe, that the Father is in me, and I in Him." Jesus is saying that His word and works both prove that He is the Christ, that the Father is in Him and that they are One.

Jesus does not put down those who believe because of the testimony of His works. It is His will that all should come to know Him, whether by His word or His deeds. The "works of Jesus" are just as necessary today as they were then to show His righteousness. Today the "works of Jesus" are manifested through His disciples just as they were in Acts.

Why do we see so few of His works today? Some teach that since we don't see them manifested today, they must have passed away. Why build a doctrine on our failures? Why not examine ourselves to see what has changed? Has God changed? Of course not, He is the same yesterday, today and tomorrow. He has not changed His purpose or His will or His nature. The only thing that has changed is you and me.

# UNBELIEF

In His ministry Jesus over and over again healed people in body, soul and spirit. In fact He healed all that came to Him. I can only find two passages where healing did not happen. Let's examine these to find out what prevented Jesus from doing the works that He was sent to do. This issue is the same today as it was in Nazareth.

In Mark 6:4-6 Jesus returns to His hometown of Nazareth from an incredible ministry trip where He performed many miracles and says to them: "A prophet is not without honour, but in his own country, and among his own kin, and in his own house. And he could there do no mighty work, save that he laid his hands upon a few sick folk, and healed them. And He marvelled because of their unbelief. And He went round about the villages, teaching."

Jesus "could do no mighty work" in His hometown because the people did not believe. It is not that He didn't want to teach and heal and save everyone. He did. But the unbelief of the people prevented Him. Even God cannot and will not override our free will.

John 12:40

"He [Satan] hath blinded their eyes, and hardened their heart; that they should not see with their eyes, nor understand with their heart, and be converted, and I should heal them."

It is God's will that everyone see with their eyes the truth of God, that everyone's hearts be soft, so that everyone can understand His love for us, so that everyone can be converted and healed. But He cannot and will not override our free will. It is His will that none perish (I Timothy 2:4, II Peter 3:9, John 3:16).

We minister to many people who are unable to read the Scriptures. They fall asleep, cannot concentrate, or do not remember or understand what they read. In doing these things the devil steals our faith because faith comes by the hearing and hearing by the Word of God (Romans 10:17).

The devil wars against us by making us blind and deaf and dumb spiritually. Though we have read in the Scriptures that we are to cast out demons and lay hands on the sick, in Jesus' name, we either do not do it, or do not believe that they will recover. We may have believed that God can heal "if it is His will" but not that He will heal. It is always God's will to heal (Psalms 103) and to say "if" is a statement of unbelief.

Even if we know all truth, it is of no value, if we do not "do" it. We are commanded in Scripture not just to be hearers of the word but doers. The Word of God only works if we do what we are taught. If we do not "do" the Word, we are in unbelief.

When Jesus came down from the mount of transfiguration, a father who had a sick son approached Him. This event is recorded in Matthew 17, Mark 9 and Luke 9. If you read the early verses in these chapters you will see that Jesus was descending from the mountain in each account. Along with other similarities we know that it is the same event told by three different writers from the perspectives given by the Holy Spirit for our edification. Let's read each of these accounts and notice how Jesus dealt with unbelief.

Matthew 17:15-20

"Lord, have mercy on my son: for he is lunatic, and sore vexed: for ofttimes he falleth into the fire, and oft into the water. And I brought him to thy disciples, and they could not cure him. Then Jesus answered and said, O faithless and perverse generation, how long shall I be with you? How long shall I suffer you? Bring him hither to me. And Jesus rebuked the devil; and he departed out of him: and the child was cured from that very hour. Then came the disciples to Jesus apart, and said, Why could not we cast him out? And Jesus said unto them, Because of your unbelief: for verily I say unto you, If ye have faith as a grain of mustard seed, ye shall say unto this mountain, Remove hence to yonder place; and it shall remove; and nothing shall be impossible unto you."

Mark 9:17-25

"And one of the multitude answered and said, Master, I have brought unto thee my son, which hath a dumb spirit; And wheresoever he taketh him, he teareth him: and he foameth, and gnasheth with his teeth, and pineth away: and I spake to thy disciples that they should cast him out; and they could not. He answereth him, and saith, O faithless generation, how long shall I be with you? How long shall I suffer you? Bring him unto me. And they brought him unto him: and when he saw him, straightway the spirit tare him; and he fell on the ground, and wallowed foaming. And He asked his father, How long is it ago since this came unto him? And he said, Of a child. And ofttimes it hath cast him into the fire, and into the waters, to destroy him: but if thou canst do anything, have compassion on us, and help us. Jesus said unto him, If thou canst believe, all things are possible to him that believeth. And straightway the father of the child cried out, and said with tears, Lord, I believe; help thou mine unbelief. When Jesus saw that the people came running together, he rebuked the foul spirit, saying unto him, Thou dumb and deaf spirit, I charge thee, come out of him, and enter no more into him."

Luke 9:38-42

"And, behold, a man of the company cried out, saying, Master, I beseech thee, look upon my son: for he is mine only child. And, lo, a spirit taketh him, and he suddenly crieth out; and it teareth him that he foameth again, and bruising him hardly departeth from him. And I besought thy disciples to cast him out; and they could not. And Jesus answering said, O faithless and perverse generation, how long shall I be with you, and suffer you? Bring thy son hither. And as he was yet a coming, the devil threw him down, and tare him. And Jesus rebuked the unclean spirit, and healed the child, and delivered him again to his father."

It is very interesting to note that Jesus healed this boy by casting out a spirit. The father said his son was a lunatic and had a dumb spirit. When Jesus cast the spirit out,

He called it a foul spirit, an unclean spirit, or a dumb and deaf spirit in the different passages. The demon caused:

1. A mute condition (Mark 9:17, 25)
2. Deafness (Mark 9:25)
3. Foaming at the mouth (Mark 9:18, 20)
4. Fits (Mark 9:18, 20, 26)
5. Gnashing or grating of the teeth, in rage (Mark 9:18)
6. Pining away, lifelessness, complete exhaustion (Mark 9:18, 26)
7. Prostration (Mark 9:20)
8. Suicidal tendencies (Mark 9:22)
9. Screaming (Mark 9:26)
10. Lunacy or insanity (Matthew 17:15)

This spirit threw the boy to the ground, into the fire and into the water attempting to kill him. The spirit had made him deaf and mute. The spirit had torn his body and made him foam at the mouth. It badly bruised him. It caused him to grate his teeth and pine or waste in exhaustion. It made the boy "sore vexed" or extremely sick. It made him crazy.

The word "lunatic" comes from the word "moonstruck." It means "to be crazy, insane, slow, confused." Some have said this was epilepsy. These are all conditions of the brain, conditions that affect how we learn or relate to others. The condition was thought to have been caused by the moon because the attacks were thought to be worse at the change and full of the moon. As the passages teach, it was really caused by a demon. It attacked during this time so as to make others think the moon was the cause.

Why couldn't the disciples cast out the demon? Understanding this is crucial. In Mark chapter 1, Jesus is baptized by John and receives the baptism of the Spirit and begins His ministry. He begins to gather His disciples and travels throughout Galilee and to Capernaum. In Capernaum, He teaches in the temple and does many miracles of healing. Even the demons obeyed and recognized Him.

Mark 1:23-25

"And there was in their synagogue a man with an unclean spirit; and he cried out, Saying, Let us alone; what have we to do with thee, thou Jesus of Nazareth? Art thou come to destroy us? I know thee who thou art, the Holy One of God. And Jesus rebuked him, saying, Hold thy peace, and come out of him."

In Mark 6:4-6 we learned that Jesus could not do "mighty works" in His hometown because of the people's unbelief. The meaning is the same in this situation as it was with the disciples. It's not that the disciples didn't want to. It's not that they didn't have enough power. It's not that they didn't have enough authority. It's not that they hadn't already gone out and preached the gospel and healed the sick. It's not that they hadn't already received the commission and the anointing to preach the gospel and heal the sick, cleanse the lepers and raise the dead and cast out devils. It was because of the unbelief of the boy's father. This is why Jesus referred to the "faithless and perverse generation."

Matthew 17:17

"Then Jesus answered and said, O faithless and perverse generation, how long shall I be with you? How long shall I suffer you? Bring him hither to me."

The word "generation" means the age, the time, the people, the family, the city and the nation. There is something in the generations. There is something in the family, the church, the city, the nation that is keeping this young boy from being healed. Jesus is saying that it is not that My disciples didn't have the power; it's not that I didn't want them to do it. There was something in the generations then, and there still is today.

In Mark 9:21, Jesus asked the father how long the boy had been sick, and the father said since a child or from infancy. In verse 22 the father says, "but if thou canst do anything, have compassion on us, and help us."

This was the desperate cry of a father for his son. "Help, if you can." He did not believe that Jesus really could or would heal his son. We are saying the same thing today when we say "if it be your will." In verse 23, Jesus looked at that father and he said, "If you can believe." In others words, "It's not a matter of 'if' I can, it's a matter if 'you' can believe." But the father was so discouraged and so disappointed and so beat up by the spirit of unbelief and the spirit that made his son deaf, dumb and mute; he wasn't able to believe God. He wasn't able to believe the promise of God.

In verse 24 "the father of the child cried out, and said with tears, Lord, I believe; help thou mine unbelief." Then Jesus cast out the dumb and deaf spirit and the boy was healed. He cast out the spirit and the boy was healed after the father repented for his unbelief. It was the father's unbelief that prevented the disciples from casting the demon out of his son.

Just as unbelief prevented Jesus from doing the works of the Father in Nazareth it prevented the disciples in this passage. Jesus would not have healed the boy either if the father had not repented. The sins of the father are passed on to the third and fourth generation to those who do not believe (Exodus 20:5, Deuteronomy 5:9).

The dumb and deaf spirit blinded the eyes of the father seeking to prevent him from believing. But it was not just the father's sin. It was in the generations. Sometimes we really want to believe that God can and will heal, but the healing does not happen. There is a generational sin of unbelief that must be repented of and broken. Biblical examples of confessing the iniquities of our families and past generations are found in Nehemiah 9:1-3, Daniel 9, and Leviticus 26:40-47.

This is something I have repented of many times in my life. I was raised in a dispensational church that taught that the miracles of Jesus and the gifts of the Holy Spirit ceased when the apostles died. This is a form of godliness that denies the power of God. God does not change. We do. The works that Christ and the apostles did are for today; in fact we are to do greater works than Christ did (John 14:12)

I have heard preachers say, and I have been taught in church, in college, and in seminary that healings, speaking in tongues and other manifestations of the Holy Spirit were of the devil. I Corinthians 12:7 calls the gifts of the Holy Spirit the "manifestations of the Holy Spirit." The visible manifestations are the healings, miracles, prophecies, tongues, interpretations, wisdom, knowledge, and discernment of various kinds. These are the nine gifts of the Holy Spirit listed in I Corinthians 12. It greatly concerns me that anyone could say that these gifts of the Holy Spirit, which were given to us as a promise of His return, are from the devil or that they have passed away. If they have passed away, has our promise of His return also passed away? The Holy Spirit was given to us as a gift from the bridegroom (Jesus) to His bride (the church, which is all believers) in earnest or promise of His return for His bride (II Corinthians 1:22, 5:5).

This sin in our lives, our generations, our churches and seminaries must be repented for and broken. It was the spirit of unbelief that gave power to the deaf and dumb spirit. So the first thing we need to do is get rid of unbelief. Then we can cast out the deaf and dumb spirit that has blinded our eyes, plugged our ears and confused our minds. In doing this, it has stolen our faith because we could not hear or understand the Word of God.

This passage also gives us the answer to the lack of faith. First we repent for our unbelief in our life and in our family, church, schools etc. And then we ask God to help our unbelief. In other words we ask God for His gift of faith that is listed in I Corinthians 12. What an expression of the love of the Father! He will even give us His faith if we will repent for our sin and ask for His faith. What He did for the father and his son in these passages He wants to do for you!

If the Holy Spirit is convicting you for unbelief, why not repent for this sin in your life and in your generations right now? (See the prayer of repentance at the end of this section.)

## WHAT IS 'UNBELIEF' IN TODAY'S CHURCH?

Let me ask a very troubling question. Are there two gospels being preached among Christians today? One is authentic and is supported by the Old and New Testaments, as well as the testimony and experience of the saints throughout church history. One is a counterfeit, a hybrid gospel, a mutation that has been created by ignoring the Old Testament and distorting the New Testament, a mixture of truth and error.

The true gospel calls us to a life of self-sacrifice and self-denial. It produces in us a change of behavior. It is God-centered, emphasizing obedience to the Lord's will.

It produces the fear of the Lord, which Scripture tells us is the beginning of wisdom (Psalms 111:10). We choose to obey because we know that the Father loves us and only wants what is best for each of us. Moreover, it causes us to be different from those of the world.

The true gospel teaches us to love God the Father with all our heart, mind and soul and to love our neighbor as our selves (Matthew 22:37-41).

The other gospel is man-centered, putting the wants and happiness of the person above the will of God. It presents salvation as the means to a happy life, self-fulfillment and mostly as an escape from hell. It emphasizes God's love but down plays obedience to Him. It emphasizes the need to believe correct doctrine but ignores the need to become a new creation in Christ. It produces little or no transformation of the individual, leaving us no different (in behavior or health) than those of the world.

It teaches that man is so depraved that he cannot even exercise his free will to choose. It places all the responsibility on God to choose whom He wishes to save and that Jesus came to save only some. It rejects the responsibility of man, places all responsibility on God and blames others for the consequences of our own actions. This view point teaches that since God is in control nothing can happen to us that He has not approved of thereby making God responsible for every bad thing that has or will happen. Some call this the "blue print" view of how God deals with man. In others words He has planned out everything and nothing can happen that He has not planned for.

The Bible presents a different picture. Ephesians 6:12 teaches that we are in a war and that our enemy is the devil and his powers and principalities not God. If God the Father sent Jesus to destroy all the works of the devil (John 10:10) how can we believe that it is God's will for bad things to happen?

Deuteronomy 30:19

"I call heaven and earth to record this day against you, that I have set before you life and death, blessing and cursing: therefore choose life, that both thou and thy seed may live:"

Joshua 24:15

"And if it seem evil unto you to serve the Lord, choose you this day whom ye will serve; whether the gods which your fathers served that were on the other side of the flood, or the gods of the Amorites, in whose land ye dwell: but as for me and my house, we will serve the Lord."

It would be very difficult to find any chapter in Scripture where people are not being required to make a choice. These two passages are representative of all of Scripture. There are hundreds and hundreds of commands that God tells us to obey for our own good. If it were not possible for us to obey or to even make a choice to obey, why would God command us to make choices, and then punish us for making wrong choices? Is He unfair?

I Timothy 2:4

"Who will have all men to be saved, and to come unto the knowledge of the truth."

II Peter 3:9

"The Lord is not slack concerning his promise, as some men count slackness; but is longsuffering to us-ward, not willing that any should perish, but that all should come to repentance."

John 3:16

"For God so loved the world that He gave His only begotten Son, that whosoever believeth in Him should not perish, but have everlasting life."

These and many other verses simply prove that it is His will to save every person. Jesus died to save every person that He created. Neither God the Father, nor His Son, Jesus the Christ, are respecters of persons (II Samuel 14:14, Proverbs 28:21, Romans 2:11, Ephesians 6:9, Colossians 3:25, James 2:9). If it is all up to God, why have missions programs? Why even have churches if it is all up to Him? If it is God's will that the blood of Jesus is only for some that would make Him guilty of favoritism and thus guilty of sin according to James 2:1-9.

You must choose which message is the true gospel. It is a decision you cannot avoid. You will choose one or the other. If you choose to avoid making a choice you will choose the counterfeit by default. Making the right choice is not easy, for it puts you at odds with Christian relatives and friends and may bring you a "bad reputation." You may be labeled a religious fanatic or a "legalist." You may be accused of "adding" to God's Word. Christians will not understand you and will feel threatened by you, and some will avoid you. They will accuse you of trying to be saved "by works." They may say that you are putting yourself back "under the law." One of the purposes of this book is to provide a compelling reason to make the right choice.

The "blue print" view in reality makes God responsible for everything, good or bad that happens. It teaches that nothing can happen that He has not planned for and therefore approved. Therefore, when a tragedy happens, such as a death or rape, God has allowed it to happen. Some even say that God did it. This view point usually destroys a person's faith in God.

Scripture very clearly teaches that we are in a war, and that bad or evil happens because of the choices that people make. God has chosen to give every person a freewill and in our freewill we disobey. Therefore, God does not always get His will in our lives. This is called a "war fare" view of how God deals with man. Let's keep on studying.

# THE WORKS OF SATAN

In an effort to help each of us make the right choice, let's take a look at the works of Satan and contrast them to the works of Christ that we have already studied. The following is a list taken from Scripture that tells us what the devil is up to:

- Belittling and blaming God the Father; questioning the Father's love (began in Genesis 2).
- Sin-rebellion (Genesis 3:2; II Corinthians 11:3).
- Works of the flesh (Galatians 5:19-21).
- Deceptions, false religions (II Corinthians 11:14; I Timothy 4; Revelation 12:9).
- False doctrines (I Timothy 4; II Timothy 4; II Thessalonians 2; Revelation 13).
- Accusing the brethren (Revelation 12:10).
- All temptation (Matthew 4:3, 13:25; Luke 22:31).
- Persecuting Christians (Ephesians 6:10-18; I Peter 5:8-9).
- To kill and destroy (John 10:10).
- Causing sickness and disease (Matthew 4:23-24, 9:32-33, 15:22; Acts 10:38).
- Causing infirmities (Matthew 8:17; Luke 13:16; John 10:10; Acts 10:38).
- Causing storms (Job 1:18-19; Ephesians 2:2).
- Death (Hebrews 2:14-15).
- Hindering prayers (Daniel 10:12-21)
  (Dake)

James 1:16-17 says, "Do not err, my beloved brethren. Every good gift and every perfect gift is from above, and cometh down from the Father of lights, with whom is no variableness, neither shadow of turning." What is good and perfect about death, disease, temptation, storms etc.? In any way that we believe that God allows (permits or condones) or is the author of any of these things we have fallen into a trap set by the devil. God the Father is the giver of only good and perfect gifts. If it is not good and perfect it is from the devil.

Christ fought against and destroyed evil. He never allowed or willed evil. In every example Jesus was never responsible for evil, He always fought against evil. If our picture of God the Father is focused on Jesus, as it should be, then we must see God fighting evil, not willing it.

The other gospel is producing the Laodicean church described in Revelation 3:15. This bitter fruit has destroyed the fear of God in Christians by teaching them that their past, present and future sins will never come to judgment, that they have nothing to fear on the Day of Judgment except maybe losing a few rewards. Is it true that our past, present and future sins are automatically forgiven if we have accepted Jesus as our Savior?

Scripture teaches that we must forgive others or the Father will not forgive us

(Matthew 6:14-15). The Lord's Prayer teaches that God will forgive each of us in the exact way that we forgive others. We set the standard for our forgiveness. Scripture teaches us that *if* we confess our sins He is faithful and just to cleanse us of all unrighteousness (I John 1:9). What is the practical meaning of these and many other similar verses?

The other gospel has also destroyed Paul's teaching on grace. It has done this by replacing the Scriptural concept of salvation by grace through faith (Ephesians 2:8) with the doctrine of salvation by grace alone, or as some theologians like to put it, salvation by grace, plus nothing. When you remove "through faith" from the Biblical equation, it turns God's grace into nothing more than a license to sin, for it is faith, not unmerited favor, that produces holiness and obedience to God. If we truly believe God, we will show this by our obedience. This is not legalism or putting ourselves back under the law. It is freedom. Grace does not set aside God's requirement to obey. Obedience is still our responsibility. Unbelief is manifested in disobedience.

It has also perverted the Biblical doctrine of the "security" of the believer. This was accomplished by simply ignoring and/or explaining away every portion of Scripture that states it is possible for a believer to fall away from the faith.

But doesn't Scripture teach that we are "eternally secure" in Christ? Absolutely, as long as we are in a vital relationship with Him and as long as we have not turned our backs on Him! As long as we have not chosen to do our own thing while alive on earth. Nowhere does Scripture teach that we are secure regardless of how unfaithful we are to Jesus. The truth is many Christians are in for a rude awakening. The unsaved will not be the only ones weeping and gnashing their teeth on Judgment Day.

We should ask ourselves why there are so many warnings against turning from God in the New Testament if it is not possible to fall away in the first place. Why did the apostles warn us not to fall away (I Timothy 6:9, Hebrews 4:11 and 6:6, II Peter 3:17), or draw back unto perdition (Hebrews 10:39), or fall from grace (Galatians 5:4), or believe in vain (I Corinthians 15:2), if it is not possible to do these things?

The other gospel teaches that the gifts of the Holy Spirit ceased to operate when the original apostles died. This doctrine teaches that the gifts and miracles Jesus and the apostles performed were necessary to substantiate the Scriptures, but now that we have the Scriptures they are not needed any longer. Is this is a form of godliness that denies His power? Scripture commands us to stay away from those who teach or believe this (II Timothy 3:5).

It also teaches a three-part sanctification. First, we are called and set apart by God. Second, it is good to sanctify ourselves in our experience and daily walk in this life, but not required; and third, "ultimate sanctification" or Christ-likeness, which cannot be obtained until we are in heaven. We cannot be "holy as He is holy" or Christ-like in this life. We can only obtain this level once we are in heaven.

Why would God tell us to be Holy as He is holy, to crucify the flesh or to be Christ-like, if it were not possible? Why would He tell us that if we obey Him, we will receive His blessings, and if we do not we will receive curses or punishment, if it were not possible to obey? Has God played a mean trick on us?

In learning what unbelief is, we need to thoroughly study each of these teachings. God does not create impossible situations. In the next section we will take a detailed look at these and other questions as we study through the basic or first principles of Christ.

## THE FIRST PRINCIPLES OF CHRIST

Hebrews 5:11-14

"Of whom we have many things to say, and hard to be uttered, seeing ye are dull of hearing. For when for the time ye ought to be teachers, ye have need that one teach you again which be the first principles of the oracles of God; and are become such as have need of milk, and not of strong meat. For every one that useth milk is unskillful in the word of righteousness: for he is a babe. But strong meat belongeth to them that are of full age, even those who by reason of use have their senses exercised to discern both good and evil."

Just as it was two thousand years ago, believers today are still immature. Most of us are still "dull of hearing," needing to be taught the basic principles of Christianity. We still need "milk" and are "unskillful" in the Word. Those that are "full of age" have become mature by the hard work of using "their senses" to "discern" or thoroughly distinguish good from evil and then do good.

Paul admonished us to "leave" behind the basic principles of the doctrine of Christ. When he says to leave the basic principles of Christ he is not asking us to forget them or deny them. He is saying that having been fully established in them, we should then move deeper into the purposes for which God saved us in the first place.

When we begin grade school we are to learn the "first principles" of mathematics, science or reading. The purpose for learning these skills is for them to be utilized in the affairs of life and to build upon for higher education. While we are in school, they are the focus of our attention. But once we graduate, our focus turns to the concerns of adult life. Though we still use the skills we have learned, they are no longer the focus of our attention.

This is what Paul is talking about. He is saying that as we grow up in Christ, as we press on toward spiritual maturity, the first principles of Christianity will be there for God to utilize in our lives. They will be there as a foundation to keep us grounded in truth. Hebrews 5:14 defines maturity as knowing the difference between good and evil and then doing good.

In our day we have two very serious problems. First, God's people are not going on to maturity. The focus of most believers remains on the basic principles of the faith. Our lives perpetually revolve around the foundational doctrines of the New Testament. What do our denominations argue about? Don't we bicker about how to baptize with water: forward, backward, one time, three times, or sprinkle? We argue whether there really is the baptism of the Holy Spirit, and whether we should lay hands on and pray for the sick, and do we really need to repent for dead works (sin in our lives)? This keeps us in a constant state of spiritual immaturity.

But as bad as this is, we face an even greater crisis, for the first principles of Christianity are being corrupted. The resulting situation is that many of us are choosing to focus our attention on that which is being perverted! Not only are we not going forward in God's purposes, we are actually going backward.

While a person does not have to be a theologian in order to be saved, the reality is that we live in a time of rampant religious deception. We as Christians need to stop looking at all the religious confusion "out there" in the world. Our problem is not the cults and "New Age." The error that really affects us is not the error that comes from outside the churches but the false doctrines within our churches.

It is incredible that so many of us go through life assuming Satan is confined to working his deception out there in the world. But most of the New Testament addresses the activity of Satan inside the various churches of the first century.

The book of Romans addresses both the legalism of the believing Jews and the antinomianism (anti-law) of believing Gentiles, which were causing confusion.

First and Second Corinthians deal with false apostles in the Church. Galatians deals with more legalism brought into that church by other Judaizers.

Second Thessalonians addresses false teachers who were teaching people in that church that the Day of the Lord was at hand. Second Peter deals with false teachers who had come into the Church promoting false liberty. The liberty they were encouraging was the liberty to sin.

Second and Third John deal with the spirit of antichrist that was already at work in the churches. The book of Jude is a direct attack against those that had come into the fellowship and were "turning the grace of God into lasciviousness [sin]." He reminded them of what God did to the angels, Sodom and Gomorrah, Cain, Balaam, Korah and the people of Israel who sinned.

Satan is not a funny little character in a red suit, carrying a pitchfork. He is a fallen archangel, one of the most powerful beings in the universe. He is a master deceiver who knows Scripture better than we do. He comes to us as an angel of light, masquerading as a minister of righteousness, quoting the Word of God freely. He can deceive an entire church if the believers are not diligent. Too many Christians view him as a lion with no teeth or claws. But Paul did not view him this way.

II Corinthians 11:3-4, 13-15

"But I fear, lest by any means, as the serpent beguiled Eve through his subtlety, so your minds should be corrupted from the simplicity that is in Christ. For if he that cometh preacheth another Jesus, whom we have not preached, or if ye receive another spirit, which ye have not received, or another gospel, which ye have not accepted, ye might well bear with him.... For such are false apostles, deceitful workers, transforming themselves into the apostles of Christ. And no marvel; for Satan himself is transformed into an angel of light. Therefore it is no great thing if his ministers also be transformed as the ministers of righteousness; whose end shall be according to their works."

Satan's attack against the Church is not confined to an external, frontal assault. His main activity is covert. He tries to infiltrate the Church and deceive it from within. Paul was afraid for the believers at Corinth. He was afraid they would be duped into receiving another Jesus, another Spirit, or another gospel.

How could Satan achieve this? He did it by sending false apostles and teachers into the Church with a false gospel, accompanied by a false anointing. These men will preach Jesus but it is not the Jesus of Scripture. They will preach a gospel that sounds similar to the true gospel but it will be a counterfeit. They will move under an anointing that passes as the Spirit of God but is really another spirit.

Paul was concerned that the enemy would overcome the Corinthians by moving through ministries who were themselves deceived. Satan goes for the leadership first, for he knows if he can deceive the religious leaders, most of the people will blindly follow them into the same ditch. Do we suppose things have gotten better since Paul's day? In reality they have gotten many times worse. We must have a proper understanding of the Word of God or we, too, will be deceived.

Hebrews 6:1-2

"Therefore leaving the principles [first or basic principles] of the doctrine of Christ, let us go on unto perfection; not laying again the foundation of repentance from dead works, and of faith toward God, of the doctrine of baptisms, and of laying on of hands, and of resurrection of the dead, and of eternal judgment."

Paul is again encouraging us to go beyond the basic principles of Christ and move on to "perfection" in Christ. The word "perfection" means "completion" or "being finished." We have not completed our work or finished the course if we are still in the "first principles" of our faith. Would Paul teach us to "go unto perfection," to complete and finish our faith if it were not possible?

The six "first principles" of Christianity in Hebrews 6:1-2 are:
1. Repentance (II Peter 3:9)
2. Faith in God through Christ (Hebrews 6:1, Romans 3:24-25, 5:1-11,
   I Corinthians 1:18-24, 15:1-8)

3. Baptisms
   (1) Water baptism (Matthew 28:19)
   (2) Spirit baptism (Luke 3, Acts 2)
4. Laying on Hands, when:
   (1) Blessing men (Genesis 48:14)
   (2) Making offerings (Numbers 8:10)
   (3) Ordaining (Numbers 27:18, 23)
   (4) Imparting Spirit (Deuteronomy 34:9)
   (5) Blessing children (Matthew 19:15)
   (6) Healing sick (Mark 6:2, 5, 16:18, Luke 4:40, 13:13, Acts 5:12, 28:8)
   (7) Performing miracles (Acts 19:11)
   (8) Imparting gifts (I Timothy 4:14, II Timothy 1:6, Hebrews 6:2)
   (9) Imparting the Spirit baptism (Acts 8:17-24, 9:17, 19:6)
5. Resurrection of the dead (Hebrews 6:2, I Corinthians 15, I Thessalonians 4:13-16)
6. Eternal judgment (Hebrews 6:2, Matthew 25:46, Revelations 14:9-11, 20:11-15, Isaiah 66:22-24)

Scripture is from God and therefore it is orderly, precise and without contradiction. I have learned to pay attention to the order in which God presents His precepts. There is always a reason for the order in which He taught or ministered. There is always a reason for what He does. These "First Principles" are presented in this specific order for a reason. They show the order and progression of our relationship with Him. First, we must choose to believe or accept His offer and repent; then we have the faith which comes from the hearing of the Word and it grows and matures if we do what the Word teaches; then in obedience to the Word we are baptized in water and Spirit; then as His disciples we can do His works; then resurrection and eternal life with Him.

    Let's examine each of these "First Principles." As it was in the first century, the deception we face today is theological in nature.

## REPENTANCE

For the purposes of this discussion we will be looking at repentance from two aspects. First, the repentance that is necessary for salvation and second, the role that repentance plays in our sanctification or spiritual maturity.

### IS REPENTANCE NECESSARY TO BE SAVED OR JUSTIFIED?

    First, let's define what a Christian is. This may sound too basic but the answer may surprise you. A Christian is a person who is a disciple of Jesus Christ. The Scripture says the disciples were first called Christians at Antioch (Acts 11:26). What is a disciple? Jesus gave us the definition. He said: "if ye continue in my word, then are ye my disciples..." (John 8:31). He also said, "If ye abide in me and my words abide in you… That ye bear much fruit; so shall ye be my disciples" (John 15:7-8).

According to the Scripture then, a Christian is a disciple, and a disciple is one who continues in His word and bears fruit. This being the case, it naturally follows that the person who does not continue in His Word and does not bear fruit is not a Christian.

The fact that repentance is listed first is not an accident because our relationship with the Lord begins with repentance. We must have a Godly sorrow for our sins or we will not turn from them. But many teach that repentance is not necessary for salvation. They claim that salvation is by grace alone and that it is totally unconditional. They are teaching that salvation is by God's choice alone, and that it is totally irresistible. In making these claims they are teaching that man has no responsibility to confess our past, present or future sins. Let's look at what does Scripture teaches:

II Corinthians 7:10

"For godly sorrow worketh repentance to salvation not to be repented of: but the sorrow of the world worketh death."

We must have a Godly sorrow for our sins before we can turn to Him for deliverance. A Godly sorrow for our sins only leads to repentance, and then repentance results in salvation, while a worldly sorrow leads to condemnation.

Luke 13:3

"I tell you, Nay: but, except ye repent, ye shall all likewise perish."

II Peter 3:9

"The Lord is not slack concerning his promise, as some men count slackness; but is longsuffering to us-ward, not willing that any should perish, but that all should come to repentance."

II Thessalonians 2:3-4

"Let no man deceive you by any means: for that day shall not come, except there come a falling away first, and that man of sin be revealed, the son of perdition; who opposeth and exalteth himself above all that is called God, or that is worshipped; so that he as God sitteth in the temple of God, shewing himself that he is God."

There are two major errors taught about the great falling away, or the "apostasia." The first one is that it primarily concerns the unsaved, or professing but phony, Christians. But we need to understand that we cannot fall away from something that we never had. This passage and many other similar ones are written to believers.

The second error is the idea that the "falling away" has to do with abandoning our religious culture and practices. Paul was not saying people will forsake their church programs, spiritual activities and experiences, and return to their former pagan lifestyles. He used the term to signify a departure from the truth. The Greek word *apostasia*, translated "falling away," means a defection from or a forsaking of truth.

Christians are abandoning many of the truths laid out in the Word of God. Some, in their unbelief, are creating a form of godliness that denies His power. Others in their frantic quest for revelation, spiritual experiences and supernatural power, are casting off the restraints of Scripture, going far outside the boundaries God has established for our own protection.

**WHAT IS REPENTANCE?**

One of the most important truths being abandoned is the Scriptural view of redemption. The apostles clearly taught there are requirements for salvation, two of which are repentance and obedience. Go into almost any church and tell the pastor you believe the Scripture teaches that we must obey God in order to be saved and watch his reaction. He will probably reprimand you for thinking you can be saved by works. He will say, "Don't you know you can't earn salvation? We are not saved by what we do, but by what we believe." "You are putting yourself back under the law."

We are told to obey God almost four hundred times in Scripture. Repentance is an act of obedience required by the Old and the New Covenant. Under the Old Covenant the blood of bull and goats covered the sins of the people if they performed the blood sacrifice. I Kings 15:5 is an example of what happens when the sacrifice is not made.

I Kings 15:5

"Because David did that which was right in the eyes of the Lord, and turned not aside from anything that he commanded him all the days of his life, save only in the matter of Uriah the Hittite."

Why would God remember this sin of David long after he was dead? What are God's promises about confessed and unconfessed sin?

Confessed Sins
1. They are blotted out (Isaiah 44:22, Acts 3:19).
2. They are forgiven (Exodus 34:7, I John 1:9, 2:12).
3. They are remitted (Matthew 26:28, Mark 1:4).
4. They are made white as snow (Isaiah 1:18).
5. They are made as wool (Isaiah 1:18).
6. They are cast behind God's back (Isaiah 38:17).
7. They are forgotten (Isaiah 43:25, Hebrews 8:12, 10:17).
8. They are purged away (Psalms 79:9, Hebrews 1:3).
9. They are covered (Psalms 32:1, Romans 4:7).
10. They are put away (II Samuel 12:13, Hebrews 9:22).
11. They are removed as far as the east is from the west (Psalms 103:12).
12. They are cast into the depths of the sea (Micah 7:19).
13. They are washed away (Revelation 1:5).
14. They are taken away (I John 3:5).
15. They are put off (Colossians 2:11).
16. One is saved from them (Matthew 1:21).

17. One is freed from them (Romans 6:7, 16-23, 8:2).

18. One is cleansed from them (I John 1:7, 9).

19. One becomes dead to them (Colossians 2:13, I Peter 2:24).

20. One is quickened from death in them (Ephesians 2:1-10, Colossians 2:13).

Unconfessed Sins

 1. They cause death (Genesis 2:17, Ezekiel 33:8-13, Romans 8:12-13).

 2. They hinder prayers (Psalms 66:18).

 3. They provoke God to anger (I Kings 16:2).

 4. They weary God (Isaiah 43:24).

 5. They separate us from God (Isaiah 59:2).

 6. They testify against us (Isaiah 59:12, Jeremiah 14:7).

 7. They cause God to remember them (Psalms 25:7).

 8. They expose guilt (Psalms 69:5).

 9. They cause God to visit (Hosea 8:13, 9:9).

10. They load us down (II Timothy 3:6, Hebrews 12:1).

11. They cause us to pine away (Ezekiel 33:10, Leviticus 26:39).

12. They cause us to be consumed (Isaiah 64:7, Ezekiel 4:17).

13. They take men away (Isaiah 64:6).

14. They bring punishment (Amos 3:2).

15. They damn the soul (II Thessalonians 2:12).

16. They cause one to be of Satan (I John 3:8).

17. They cause hardening of heart (Hebrews 3:13).

18. They make servants of sin (Romans 6:7-23, John 8:34).

19. They bring reproach (Proverbs 14:34).

20. They cause national judgment (Amos 1:3, 6, 9, 11, 13, 2:1, 4, 6).

21. They cause disease (Deuteronomy 28, Psalms103:3, Mark 2:9, James 5:16).

22. They cause many troubles and calamities in life (Job, Deuteronomy 28, Proverbs 1:27-31).

According to the promises of God, the "matter of Uriah" must be an unconfessed sin. Even though David repented in sackcloth and ashes in Psalms 51 there is not a record of a blood sacrifice. Thus, he did not meet the Old Testament requirement for forgiveness.

David committed another major sin that people rarely remember. He numbered the people after God told him not to (II Samuel 24). This sin is usually not remembered because there was a sacrifice. The sins of Job are also not remembered because in chapter 42, Job and his first three friends performed a blood sacrifice.

Repentance is making a choice to turn away from our sins and sinful life style. Repentance requires that we become actual doers of God's word. The act of repenting or confession and turning from our sin is how we receive forgiveness from God that results in salvation. Then as Christians or disciples of Christ we are required to forgive others and our selves.

Under the New Covenant there are two conditions to receiving forgiveness. The Blood of Jesus is available for the total and final payment for all of our sins, past, present and future, *if* we meet these two conditions. The first is salvation or justification. We must choose to accept the Lord as our savior if we want Him to forgive our sins. Second, as believers we must forgive others and confess our sins if we want our sins forgiven. This is called sanctification. Sanctification is an issue of relationship, trust, and empowerment, not necessarily salvation. Let's look at these conditions in more detail.

## SALVATION — JUSTIFICATION (DECLARED RIGHTEOUS) — BORN AGAIN

This is where contemporary evangelical (dispensational) theology falls flat on its face in several ways. We have been taught that our salvation or justification is all up to God. He will call, predestinate or elect only those that He wants. We are too depraved to make this decision thus it is up to God to choose who He wants. His grace and forgiveness is limited to only those He arbitrarily chooses. Since God is doing the choosing we cannot resist and since it was His choice, not ours, we cannot depart or fall away. We have also been taught that a verbal assent or an agreement with a statement of faith is salvation. Additionally we have been warned that if we teach that obedience is necessary we are teaching salvation through works and then we are putting ourselves back "under the law." Let's look at God's Word.

The first condition in God's Word that we must meet to be forgiven is that we must accept Jesus as the Christ (Messiah) and allow Him to be our LORD and Savior. This is also called justification or imputed righteousness. It means to be declared righteous or born again.

John 3:3

"Jesus answered and said unto him, Verily, verily, I say unto thee, except a man be born again, he cannot see the kingdom of God."

The first step in becoming His sons and daughters is to repent; then we must be born again. We must receive our new nature.

In the Old Testament, the blood of bulls and goats covered the sin until the cross. The Old Testament saint had to perform the sacrifice. The New Testament saint must apply the sacrifice, the blood of Jesus, through forgiveness and repentance. We must do our part; Jesus did His.

The shed blood of Jesus cleanses us from sin if we forgive and confess our sins, but does not remove the power of the sin and death nor the bondage that the sin brings into our lives. The blood pays the price, but it is the power of His resurrection, the power of His Name and the Holy Spirit living in us (the new man or nature), that gives us victory over the works of the devil: the sorrow, guilt, shame, regret, sadness, anger, hatred, bitterness, etc. and death.

This is where the Christian life begins. From here we are told to continue in obedience, sanctify ourselves, abide in Him, overcome, be vessels of honor vs. vessels of dishonor, and be holy as He is holy. This is possible because we have been born again and we have the new nature, the nature of God through the Holy Spirit living in us.

Matthew 3:1-2

"In those days came John the Baptist, preaching in the wilderness of Judea and saying, repent ye: for the kingdom of heaven is at hand."

John didn't come begging the Jews to "make a decision for Christ." He commanded them to repent. He didn't come and bestow salvation on the people. He came and said repent, then you can have the Kingdom. Haggai, Jonah, John the Baptist, Jesus and many others preached the same message. "You must make a decision, you must repent first, and then the Kingdom is at hand or upon you."

Matthew 4:17

"From that time [after His temptation] Jesus began to preach and to say, repent: for the kingdom of heaven is at hand."

Mark 1:14-15

"Now after that John was put in prison, Jesus came into Galilee, preaching the gospel of the kingdom of God, And saying, The time is fulfilled, and the kingdom of God is at hand: repent ye, and believe the gospel."

The message of the Gospels is repentance. Jesus called the people to repent even before He called them to believe. We must choose to repent to become believers.

Matthew 9:13

"I am not come to call the righteous, but sinners to repentance."

Luke 13:3

"I tell you... except ye repent ye shall all likewise perish."

If man is so depraved that he cannot even make a decision why are we commanded to make the decision to repent in so many passages? If it is all up to God to "predestinate, call or elect" only some, why is our decision to repent required? If His grace is irresistible, why are we told to choose repentance? Why do so many refuse to accept Him? The truth is that God has required that we have an active role to play in choosing or denying Him. It is called freewill.

Additionally, James 2:9 says, "...if ye have respect to persons, ye commit sin, and are convinced of the law as transgressors." This verse and many other verses teach that if we are partial or show partiality, we are guilty of sin. If God arbitrarily chooses some and not others, is He then guilty of sin? Absolutely! Since God cannot sin, He cannot be partial. Therefore, this cannot be a true doctrine.

The truth is that God has predestinated, elected and chosen every one that He created. He loves all of His creation. In His great love and mercy and desire for relationship, He chose to give each of us freewill. To claim that He cannot do this is places limits on Him. True relationship is only based in choice. We cannot make someone love us and neither can God. He gave us freewill because He wants to walk in the cool of the day with you.

Repentance is much more than just a change of mind or mental assent. It has to do with a "turning about" of the entire person. A change of mind is only one part of a process that affects the whole man. It must also include the heart, if it is to have any eternal value, because people can accept truth with their minds, yet not let that truth get down into the heart and change them. When the heart of a person is affected by truth, a change of behavior takes place (John 8:31-32). That is why John the Baptist told the Pharisees to bring "fruits meet for repentance" (Matthew 3:8). Proof of genuine repentance was required to discourage a mere profession and outward show. True salvation involves more than the repeating of a few magical words.

II Corinthians 7:9-10

"Now I rejoice, not that ye were made sorry, but that ye sorrowed to repentance: for ye were made sorry after a godly manner, that ye might receive damage by us in nothing. For godly sorrow worketh repentance to salvation not to be repented of: but the sorrow of the world worketh death."

Godly sorrow is a choice that will bring a change in a person's heart and life. Notice the chain-reaction that takes place in an individual that is brought to a place of true repentance. Truth enters the heart and mind and produces a godly sorrow for sin, which in turn produces repentance, which in turn produces salvation. That is why; whenever you see genuine repentance in a person's life you will also find a godly sorrow and also obedience to the Word. The two go hand in hand. Godly sorrow and obedience will always be present, if the repentance is genuine.

James very clearly taught this same message in James 2:14-21, "What doth it profit, my brethren, though a man say he hath faith, and have not works? Can faith save him? If a brother or sister be naked, and destitute of daily food, And one of you say unto them, Depart in peace, be ye warmed and filled; notwithstanding ye give them not those things which are needful to the body; what doth it profit? Even so faith, if it hath not works, is dead, being alone. Yea, a man may say, Thou hast faith, and I have works: shew me thy faith without thy works, and I will shew thee my faith by my works. Thou believest that there is one God; thou doest well: the devils also believe, and tremble. But wilt thou know, O vain man, that faith without works is dead? Was not Abraham our father justified by works, when he had offered Isaac his son upon the altar?"

Jesus also expressed this to Nicodemous in John 3:1-6, "There was a man of the Pharisees, named Nicodemus, a ruler of the Jews: The same came to Jesus by night, and said unto him, Rabbi, we know that thou art a teacher come from God: for no man can do these miracles that thou doest, except God be with him. Jesus answered and said unto him, Verily, verily, I say unto thee, except a man be born again, he cannot see the kingdom of God. Nicodemus saith unto him, how can a man be born when he is old? Can he enter the second time into his mother's womb, and be born? Jesus answered, Verily, verily, I say unto thee, except a man be born of water and of the Spirit, he cannot enter into the kingdom of God. That which is born of the flesh is flesh; and that which is born of the Spirit is spirit."

Nicodemous did not understand because he did not believe he needed to be "born again," since was a Jew. The term "born again" was not a new term to Nicodemous, Jesus or the Apostles. Rather, it was a rabbinic term for a Gentile who underwent a formal conversion to Judaism.

According to Judaism, a Gentile who wants to become a Jew must undergo several ritual requirements. For men, the two main requirements are circumcision and immersion (water baptism). For a woman, immersion itself is the entire conversion ritual. In Jewish thought, a Gentile who converts to Judaism is still a Gentile until he comes up out of the water of the *mikvah* (baptismal water). Going down into the water, the convert is said to die to his old life (Gentile). As he comes up, he is as a newborn child, a new creature (Jewish). The Talmud says that "When he comes up after his immersion, he is deemed as Israelite in all respects" (Yevamot 47b).

In the Jewish culture the term "born again" was already in use. A born again person was a Gentile who had converted to Judaism. It referred to the symbolic death and rebirth the convert underwent as he passed through the waters of baptism. In Judaism, immersion is used as a conversion ritual. The mikvah is regarded as both a grave, in which the immersed dies, and a womb from which the immersed is reborn or "born again." (In the section on baptism I will cover this in greater detail.)

In light of this context we can better understand the conversation between Jesus and Nicodemous. When Nicodemous said "How can a man be born when he is old?" he was really saying "I am already Jewish, How can I convert to Judaism?"

Jesus was teaching Nicodemous that being Jewish, one of God's chosen people, did not make him saved or justified any more than claiming to be God's chosen, predestinated or elect today does. Jesus was teaching that it is not enough to simply be Jewish. To be ethnically Jewish or even to be a convert to Judaism is not adequate for entrance into the Kingdom of Heaven. A spiritual conversion of the heart is the conversion experience that is really necessary.

Jesus said "A man must be born of water and spirit." Jesus was teaching Nicodemous so he could make a choice. We are all faced with this same choice that Jesus demonstrated in this passage. We cannot earn or merit our salvation neither do we have it because we are the "chosen ones." We must choose to accept the gift through our faith (Lancaster 2003, pages 92-97).

It is also very interesting to note from this discussion that there has always been a way to become God's "chosen people." Exodus 12 reveals that a mixed multitude of several million Gentiles converted to Judaism and become Jews, God's chosen, according to the rituals of conversion. God has always kept the door open for everyone. But the Jews messed it up just as we have today. They claimed in Acts 15 that you had to become a Jew in order to be saved. Paul, James and others clearly taught that salvation did not depend on becoming a Jew but upon faith.

Ephesians 2:8-9 says, "For by grace are ye saved through faith; and that not of yourselves: it is the gift of God: Not of works, lest any man should boast." In context the passage teaches that salvation is a gift from God that we cannot earn or merit by the works of converting to Judaism that we should boast that we are the chosen ones. Faith (our choice to believe and obey) is required for salvation and justification just as it was for Abraham (James 2:21, Romans 2:13).

Today some say that we have to be the predestinated or the elect to be saved. In other words we must be the chosen ones. It is just the same argument in different clothes.

The truth is that it is a matter of our hearts and our choices. We only access God's grace through faith (Romans 5:2). (In the section on Faith I will go into this in greater detail.)

## LAW VS. GRACE

This is a great misunderstanding that has created great harm. God's law or precepts have pointed out our sin and demonstrated His grace. In any way that we belittle God's law or imply that it has passed away or that it is just Jewish or Old Testament we have made a huge mistake. Without the Law there could be no grace. The Law defines sin because God loves us and only wants what is best for us. His law tells us the consequences of sin and the benefits of obedience.

Psalms 19:7-11

"The law of the Lord is perfect, converting the soul: the testimony of the Lord is sure, making wise the simple. The statutes of the Lord are right, rejoicing the heart: the commandment of the Lord is pure, enlightening the eyes. The fear of the Lord is clean, enduring for ever: the judgments of the Lord are true and righteous altogether. More to be desired are they than gold, yea, than much fine gold: sweeter also than honey and the honeycomb. Moreover by them is thy servant warned: and in keeping of them there is great reward."

Jesus said in Matthew 5:17-18, "Think not that I am come to destroy the law, or the prophets: I am not come to destroy, but to fulfill. For verily I say unto you, till heaven and earth pass, one jot or one tittle shall in no wise pass from the law, till all be fulfilled."

The Hebrew background of these verses clarifies its deeper meaning. In Rabbinic literature, the Greek words from the Gospel which are translated "abolish" and "fulfill" possess deeper meanings. The word "abolish" means "to interpret incorrectly" and the word "fulfill" refers to interpreting a passage accurately. Jesus is saying that He did not came to destroy or abolish the law as many were doing by improperly interpreting God's Word, but to fulfill it by accurately interpreting it (Young 2007, page 265).

In Matthew 5 Jesus went on to demonstrate this truth by saying several times "Ye have heard... But I say unto you..." He was fulfilling the law by properly interpreting that which had been essentially be abolished or destroyed by the improper interpretations.

With this context in mind let's see what modern theologians have done to God's law.

We have been taught that it was not possible to keep the Law. We have also been taught that if a man did keep the law perfectly, obedience would justify him. Scofield taught that legal obedience to the law was the condition of salvation in the Old Testament, while faith in Christ is the condition of salvation in the New Testament (Scofield Reference Bible, page 1115). Many colleges and seminaries today, in reality, are teaching that there are two ways of being saved or justified.

The Law was never intended to be a vehicle for justification. Yet, this is exactly what dispensationalism teaches, sometimes implicitly, sometimes explicitly. It teaches implicitly that under the Old Covenant there were two ways to obtain salvation (at least theoretically). One way was by "keeping the Law" which, supposedly, no one could ever do. The other avenue was "by faith." Saying it was possible to be justified by keeping the Law, or even that it was theoretically possible to do so, imputes unrighteousness to the Lord, because it casts Him in the role of an unjust tyrant who played a cruel joke on His own people.

Dispensational thought goes something like this: God gave Israel the Law and commanded them to obey it. He said if they obeyed it, He would bless them, but if they disobeyed it, He would curse them, all the time knowing that no one could possibly obey it. Since it was really impossible to obey it in the first place, no one did. So God punished them for failing to obey something that was impossible to obey in the first place! What a twisted image of God!

I have also heard it taught by pastors and seminary professors that it is possible for believers under the New Covenant to be justified by keeping the Law, but it is not possible for a human to do so. Jesus is the only one that could possibly be holy as God is holy since He did not sin. This is often used as a warning not to put yourself "back under the law" and then have to earn salvation verses accepting it as a free gift under grace.

Justification is only available through the blood of Jesus. It is only through the name and blood of Jesus that we can be saved. Salvation is a free gift. There is nothing we can do to earn or merit it. Not even by keeping the law perfectly. The Law was never intended to be a vehicle of justification! It was intended to be the means of sanctification, two totally different purposes. There never has been and never will be two ways to salvation.

Of course, it is true that some Jews and Christians have confused the two and ended up trying to be justified through works. But this was never God's intention. God asks all of us to obey His precepts so that we will be sanctified. It was not wrong for the Hebrew people to strive to obey the Torah. It is not wrong for Christians to obey His precepts. It was only wrong to assume that we can earn or merit salvation.

If God gave the Law of Moses to Israel as a means of justification, knowing in advance that no person would ever actually be able to obey it, then why did He punish Israel for not obeying it? Why does He require obedience today if it is not possible to obey? Did He punish the Jews because they failed to save themselves by their own works?

It was possible to obey the Law. The Bible says people did obey it (Psalms 119:55). Dispensationalism also teaches that Nicodemus and Saul are examples of "perfected Jews." They perfectly kept the law and thus met the Old Testament requirement. As we have already studied in John 3, Jesus clearly teaches Nicodemous that he still needed to be "born again." He still needed a heart change to be justified or born again. God cannot impute righteousness to our account until we are obedient.

In addition, the sacrificial system was designed to provide forgiveness when a person did violate the commandments (Leviticus 16:21-30). This means that even if a person did break the Law, as long as he repented in his heart and brought the appropriate sacrifice, he was still keeping the Law because he was keeping the sacrificial portion of the Law. He was doing what God had commanded. In this the Law was also demonstrating Grace.

The real issue is that we cannot obtain justification through obedience to the law, even perfect obedience. Because in order to stand justified before God, a person has to possess the same kind of holy and righteous nature that God possesses. He has to be as holy as God Himself is. Obedience to the Law, even perfect obedience, could not change man's basic problem, which is that he possessed only one nature, a nature that is contaminated by sin, a nature that is fallen. No matter how well he behaves, no matter what he does, he will never, by his own efforts, be as holy as God. It is only through the New Covenant experience of being born again that we receive a new nature that allows our spirit to become alive to God again.

God never intended to justify His people through keeping the Law. He used their obedience to sanctify them. When He said, be ye holy, He was saying, be sanctified. The way to be sanctified was to obey the Law. Under the Old Covenant, the saints were justified by faith and sanctified by obedience to God; that is, to His Law and the guidance of His priests and prophets. The Law and the Prophets explained and defined what sin was, not in order to condemn everyone to hell, but to show the people how to sanctify themselves.

The Old Testament saints, in essence were looking forward to the cross. They knew that the Messiah was coming to redeem them. After the crucifixion Jesus went to the Old Testament saints in Paradise and finished His work. His blood paid the price for their sins in full, thus they could receive His nature that they had waited so long for in faith. They became "born again" and Jesus escorted them to heaven.

Under the New Covenant, the saints are also justified by faith and sanctified by obedience to God. This is why the Holy Spirit is sent into the lives of the saints. He is our Torah. He is our Law. He is our Priest and Prophet. His task is to show us what God says is sin. He does this so we can sanctify ourselves.

When a person is "born again" he is justified or declared righteous as a legal position by God. We access His grace through faith (Romans 5:2). We need to remember that grace is never alone. Saving grace is always accompanied by faith, which is demonstrated by our obedience and a changed heart. If there is no change, no works, and no evidence of faith, then there will be no justification. If one is not justified they are not saved.

Romans 2:13

"For not the hearers of the law are just before God, but the doers of the law shall be justified."

God applied this same concept to Himself when He was and is justified by His own actions. He always sets the example for us. In the Old Testament, occasionally, it is God who is said to be "justified." This means that His actions and judgments are proved by events to be correct and fair, even if men did not agree or understand.

Job is one of several examples of this. Job claimed that he was innocent and that God was unfair and unjust and demanded a trial. In chapter 38 God granted his request and proceeded to show Job his sin. In chapter 42 Job repented for speaking about things that he had no knowledge and performed the required animal sacrifice and God then restored double what Satan had taken from him (see Part Three).

God was proved to be just by His actions. We also prove that we have been justified by God through our actions. If we do not do the Word of God we will not be justified or saved. This is also taught in Romans 2:7-11, 10:8-21, James 1:21-27, 2:14-26 and I John 1:7.

## SANCTIFICATION:
## REPENTANCE IS NECESSARY FOR SPIRITUAL GROWTH

The second condition to receive forgiveness is about growing in favor with God. It is about becoming a vessel of honor. It is about becoming Christ-like and holy as God is holy. This is not an automatic process. Once again, our active participation is required. If we do not forgive others and ourselves, our heavenly father will not forgive us.

Matthew 6:12

"And forgive us our debts, as we forgive our debtors."

Matthew 6:14-15

"For if ye forgive men their trespasses, your heavenly Father will also forgive you: But if ye forgive not men their trespasses, neither will your Father forgive your trespasses."

There are many other passages that teach the same message, such as the parable of the rich man in Matthew 18. Many references teach that the manner or way we judge others is the manner or way we will be judged. Even the Lord's Prayer teaches us to ask Our Heavenly Father to forgive us as we forgive others.

We need to understand that we are setting the standard by which we will be judged. If we forgive, we will be forgiven. If we do not forgive, we will not be forgiven. The manner in which we judge others is the same manner in which God will judge us.

I John 1:9

"*If* we confess our sins, He is faithful and just to forgive us our sins, and to cleanse us from all unrighteousness."

What happens if we do not confess our known sins? If we do not confess our sins we will live in the shame and guilt and the resulting diseases. This is our choice. God the Father has made a way for us to escape the consequences of our sin if we will repent. The "ifs," "thens" and "buts" of Scripture are very important to study and pay attention to.

James 5:16

"Confess your faults one to another, and pray one for another, that ye may be healed. The effectual fervent prayer of a righteous man availeth much."

When we do not confess our sin, the guilt, shame, regret, sadness, anger, hatred, bitterness, etc., are still in the memory and we are in bondage and held captive by those memories and the pain. If all of our past, present, and future sins were automatically forgiven when we accepted Jesus why would these verses be written to believers and why would the bondage and pain still be there?

II Timothy 2:19-21

"Nevertheless the foundation of God standeth sure, having this seal, The Lord knoweth them that are his. And, Let everyone that nameth the name of Christ depart from iniquity. But in a great house there are not only vessels of gold and of silver, but also of wood and of earth; and some to honour, and some to dishonour. If a man therefore purge himself from these, he shall be a vessel unto honour, sanctified, and meet for the master's use, and prepared unto every good work."

These verses present a great challenge to all of us. Do you want to be a vessel of honor or dishonor? Do you want to be a fit vessel, sanctified (cleansed) and prepared for His assignments? If so, these verses are very plain about what we have to do to accomplish this, we must purge (sanctify) ourselves of all our iniquities or sins. This not an automatic process, we must learn to actually forgive and repent. In my book *Biblical Foundations of Freedom* we teach and demonstrate how to forgive and how to know that we have really forgiven.

God is doing much the same thing with New Testament believers as he did with Old Testament believers, but on a deeper level. He has sanctified us by calling us and setting us apart as his people. He has given us His Spirit, His Word and the example of His Son, so we, like the ancient Hebrews, can sanctify ourselves and fulfill our call as a light to the nations. The only difference between "them and us," is that our light (righteousness) can be the very light of God himself. The Hebrews' light was only a dim (human) representation of that light.

Jesus, our example, was obedient even to the cross. He could have called thousands of angels at any time, but he chose to obey His Father. On the cross He said, "It is finished." What was finished? Among other things, His work as a man was finished. He demonstrated that it was possible to do the works of the Father, and to be holy, as He is holy.

Sanctification is critical because it produces light. Light is not what we "say." Talk is cheap. Light is what we "do." God is not content that we spend our lives talking about light. He wants us to be light. As we become light we will discover that people who would never listen to what we say about God, many times will be affected by how we live in spite of themselves.

In the Hebrew mind set it did not matter what you said, but what you did. Actions speak louder than words. In our Western or Greek mind set we want to write statements of faith and believe that mental assent to these statements is all that is required. This is not how the Hebrew or God looks at things. This is why God teaches us that faith without works (obedience) is dead being alone.

Satan knows better than we do just how important sanctification is in fulfilling our call. He also knows that obedience is the key factor in sanctification. Without full obedience we will never be sanctified (in experience). Therefore, it has been his plan from the beginning of time to convince man that obedience is not important. He convinced Eve of it. He convinced Old Testament Israel of it and he has convinced the New Testament Church of it as well.

The other gospel produces disobedience. It does not cause us to deny the faith or reject the Savior. But it instills a false sense of security in our minds by teaching us that while it is good to obey God, and even profitable, it is not absolutely necessary to obey Him. Thus we become lazy in our relationship with God. We become careless and become easy prey for the whims of doctrine. We are easily deceived because we do not know His precepts. We also miss out on the excitement, authority and power that is found in true obedience to God.

Many are going to wake up one day and realize too late that they made the same tragic mistake Israel did. After being called, chosen and set apart by God, after being brought into a covenant relationship with Him, they allowed themselves to be deceived and refused to sanctify themselves; thus they forfeit their call and destiny as the "chosen people."

Sanctification comes from a Greek word that means "to sanctify something." To sanctify something is to set it apart for God's use. Thus, it is considered holy or sacred. The term is used various ways in Scripture, most often with either objects or people, which have been consecrated to God's use. When referring to people there are two distinct aspects of sanctification: First, separation to God; and second, a separation from sin. Separation to God and separation from sin are absolutely necessary if we are to be truly sanctified and useful to God. Both aspects can be seen in God's dealings with Israel.

Exodus 31:13

"Speak thou also unto the children of Israel, saying, Verily my Sabbaths ye shall keep: for it is a sign between me and you throughout your generations; that ye may know that I am the LORD that doth sanctify you."

Leviticus 11:44

"For I am the LORD your God: ye shall therefore sanctify yourselves ye shall be holy; for I am holy: neither shall ye defile yourselves with any manner of creeping thing that creepeth upon the earth."

Leviticus 20:7-8

"Sanctify yourselves therefore be ye holy: for I am the LORD your God. And ye shall keep my statutes do them: I am the LORD which doeth sanctify you."

The first aspect of sanctification has nothing to do with the present moral condition of the thing or person. It has to do with God's choice. It is God's will that none should perish. He has chosen to set aside all of His creation. The fact that God has chosen to set someone aside for His use does not necessarily mean that the person possesses a holy character. It also does not mean that the person will accept the will of God.

In this sense every Christian has already been sanctified. Yet this does not mean that every Christian has sanctified himself. Just because we have been chosen, set aside and accepted the offer, does not mean that we are exhibiting righteous behavior or living a holy lifestyle. It does not mean that we are in agreement with God and have yielded our freewill to Him.

At large portion of God's word deals with this second aspect of sanctification. It is also a primary concern of Satan. If he cannot prevent people from becoming Christians, he is anxious to see that we neglect our responsibilities. If we are to fulfill the purpose for which we were set aside in the first place, we must sanctify ourselves. We must separate ourselves from every desire, every relationship, every habit, every mind-set, every demon spirit, and every material possession that God declares evil. The person who refuses to do this risks becoming a vessel of dishonor by not overcoming. Worse yet is the risk of being disqualified.

God sanctified the Hebrew people by choosing them and separating them unto His divine purposes. But they were responsible to then sanctify themselves by obeying His statutes. The story of Israel is the story of what happens to a people who have been sanctified (chosen, set aside) by God, but who refuse to sanctify themselves. Though a minority of the people did walk in faith and fulfill their call and destiny, the majority did not. Instead of being a light to the surrounding nations, they blasphemed the name of God wherever they went.

It is this second aspect of sanctification that is God's will for the New Testament Christian (I Thessalonians 4:3-7). It is the primary reason God saved us in the first place (verse 7). It can never be imputed to us, for it must be learned (verse 4) and pursued (I Timothy 2:15, Hebrews 12:14). It is not a legal state but an individual possession that is acquired over time, little by little, as a result of obedience to the Spirit, the Word and following the example of Jesus (Matthew 11:29, John 13:15, Ephesians 4:20, Philippians 2:5). It is not gained by self-will or self-effort, but through the power of the Holy Spirit (Romans 8:13, Ephesians 3:16). However, we are responsible to yield and submit to the Holy Spirit. We can choose to quench the Spirit (I Thessalonians 5:19).

Both the Old and New Covenants were designed to produce sanctification (righteousness and godly behavior). The difference between the two covenants lies in the level or kind of righteousness each was designed to bring forth in the individual. The Old Covenant dealt only with what the New Testament calls our "old man" (Romans 6:6; Ephesians 4:22; Colossians 3:9). That is, it only dealt with our original Adamic nature, for until the Messiah made atonement for sin there was no such thing as a new man or new nature.

Because of the death and resurrection of Christ, it is possible to have the Holy Spirit living in us. This rebirth or "born again" experience makes our spirit alive to God. Old things are passed away and all things are new. We now have the ability to overcome the old nature and the ability to overcome or conquer the law of sin through repentance, forgiveness and in experience through sanctification (Revelation 2-3).

When we become "born again" we have two natures at work in us. This is what Paul was teaching about in Romans. In Romans 6, Paul sets forth the obligations of all people to live a holy life. In Romans 7, he shows why the law is helpless to deliver any man from sin and hell.

In Romans 7, Paul uses the example of a marriage and death to demonstrate that the law could not deliver people from sin. The purpose of the law was to show them their sin and lead them to the one who could deliver them. The law was good and holy, but it did not have the power to set them free. Paul makes a remarkable statement in verse 15, "For that which I do I allow not: for what I would, that do I not; but what I hate, that do I."

Paul is telling us about the war that was going on inside of him between the nature of God and the nature of sin; between two laws, the law of God and the law of sin or Satan.

Romans 7:16-19

"If then I do that which I would not, I consent unto the law that it is good. Now then it is no more I that do it, but sin that dwelleth in me. For I know that in me (that is, in my flesh, [my old nature]) dwelleth no good thing: for to will is present with me; but how to perform that which is good I find not. For the good that I would I do not: but the evil which I would not, that I do."

Paul is teaching that when we sin, we are calling the law of God evil, and the law of Satan good. But when Paul says in verse 17 that, "it is no more I that do it, but sin that dwelleth in me," he recognizes that his old nature is from Satan. It is not part of the original Paul that God made. He is separating the sin from himself and is teaching us to love ourselves but hate the sin. Thus it makes sense when Paul says to crucify our flesh because it is the old nature. He is also stating that we cannot do this on our own.

Romans 7:20

"Now if I do that I would not, it is no more I that do it, but sin that dwelleth in me."

Paul is repeating what he said in verse 17 so it must be important. The sin that "dwelleth" in him is the old nature, the sin nature, or the flesh, which is the nature of Satan. When we become "born again" we receive the Holy Spirit and the nature of God. Our spirit becomes alive to Him and a war begins in us.

Romans 7:21-23

"I find then a law, that, when I would do good, evil is present with me. For I delight in the law of God after the inward man [the new man]: But I see another law in my members, warring against the law of my mind, and bringing me into captivity to the law of sin which is in my members."

All believers will fight this war until Christ returns. We all have a thorn in our flesh, a messenger of Satan, warring against us by buffeting our ears with temptation. But thank God we do not have to do this war in our power. Christ came and destroyed the works of the devil and then sent us to do the same thing in His power. Hebrews 4 tells us about "the rest of God" that comes as we gain victory over the devil (unbelief).

Romans 7:24-25

"O wretched man that I am! Who shall deliver me from the body of this death? I thank God through Jesus Christ our Lord. So then with the mind I myself serve the law of God; but with the flesh the law of sin."

Only Jesus Christ is the deliverer. Paul commanded us to crucify the flesh. We can do this because we have the power of God, the new nature living within us. We can be delivered from the power of the flesh, the old nature or Satan.

With our new nature we can choose to serve the law of God, but with the flesh or old nature we choose to serve the law of sin. This is why sanctifying ourselves and thus becoming mature in Christ is so important. This is why it is so important to know the difference between good and evil.

In reality when the other gospel teaches that we cannot be holy, as God is holy, it is saying that we cannot be mature in Christ. This is why few Christians are mature. This is why few Christians are living a victorious life. This is why most Christians are defeated and are waiting to die to have victory. In reality they have placed their faith in the grave instead of the delivering power of Jesus.

Hebrews 5:11-14

"Of whom we have many things to say and hard to be uttered, seeing ye are dull of hearing. For when for the time ye ought to be teachers, ye have need that one teach you again which be the first principles of the oracles of God; and are become such as have need of milk, and not of strong meat. For every one that useth milk is unskillful in the word of righteousness: for he is a babe. But strong meat belongeth to them that are of full age, even those who by reason of use have their senses exercised to discern both good and evil."

Hebrews defines maturity in Christ as the ability to thoroughly distinguish good from evil. Verse 14 teaches us that those of full age, or mature, by the use of their senses, which is a lot of hard work, discern or thoroughly distinguish good from evil. The mature Christian knows the difference between good and evil and shows his faith by his good works. The mature Christian, through the power of God, does not have to sin. We can be holy, as He is holy. James teaches us to be doers of the Word and to display our faith by our works and obedience.

Before the establishment of the New Covenant there was only one man - the old man. Until the resurrection of Jesus, man was stuck with his original, fallen Adamic nature. God had no choice but to work within the framework of that first nature. The Law of Moses was designed to produce a level of righteousness, which the old man could bring forth. It was not the actual character of God.

The different levels of sanctification produced by the two covenants have to do with our experience, not our position in Christ. It has to do with what we can demonstrate. Old Testament saints received the same forgiveness and imputed righteousness we do. However, they could not experience and demonstrate the righteousness that was imputed to them. Though God's nature was reckoned to them by faith, they were unable to manifest it. They could only experience and manifest human righteousness. The Adamic nature will never be able to bring forth the actual character and nature of God. That is why we are to crucify it. This is why the New Covenant is a new and better Covenant.

John 8:32

"And ye shall know the truth, and the truth shall make you free."

The word, "know" means to personally experience, to know in our hearts. When we personally experience His truth we are truly free. God wants His people to possess and experience His holiness. He does not want us to go through eternity only having the imputed righteousness of Jesus. As wonderful as this is, we must realize that whatever is imputed to us is not really ours by experience; it is only ours legally. God wants us to be able to experience what we have by divine legal right. Under the Old Covenant this was not possible. That is why a "new" and "better" covenant had to be established. The New Covenant is designed to bring forth in us the very character and nature of God!

Test this in yourself. Have you ever had victory over one sin? If so, why not two? Why not three? Why not four? Why not all of them? If it is possible to have victory over the power of the devil in one sin, it is possible to have victory over all sin.

Additionally, the belief that it is not possible to be holy as He is holy, or to have "ultimate sanctification" until we are in heaven, makes God arbitrary and capricious. Why would God tell us to do something if it were not possible? Has He played a mean trick on us? Is our faith in the delivering, saving, transforming power of Jesus, or in a magical change when we die? Is our faith in Jesus, or in the grave?

It also creates an attitude in people that we do not need to strive toward the high calling of God because it is not possible in this life. It creates a defeatist mentality: so why bother, why try? Fatalism and Karma are really the same thing. We can change. We can be Victorious. Grace, God's divine empowerment gives us the power to change and to have victory.

## THE ROLE OF THE HOLY SPIRIT

Most of us do not realize the critical role the Holy Spirit plays in our lives. His task is to purify the Church (all believers). He is more than a comforter, more than a good feeling. He is sent by the Father to lead us (Romans 8:14) and teach us (John 14:26) and guide us into all truth (John 16:13); not only doctrinal truth but life-changing truth. His purpose is to change us and transform us into the image of Jesus Christ through the process of sanctification (II Thessalonians 2:13, I Peter 1:2). Sanctification is accomplished as we allow the Spirit to convict us of the sins we currently practice (John 1:9), so that He can then deliver us from that sin. This takes serious obedience on our part, for the Spirit never forces His will on anyone. As we obey the Spirit, He cleanses us and frees us from the bondage of sin, not only legally, but in experience as well.

It is because the Holy Spirit now lives in us under the New Covenant that we can "be holy as He is Holy." It is through the Holy Spirit in us that we can achieve Christ-likeness in this life. To deny this is to deny the power of the Holy Spirit.

Under the Old Covenant, the people of God could be delivered from the penalty of sin but they could not be delivered from the power of sin. The reason is that the power of sin resides in the fallen, Adamic nature. That is why, even though justification, forgiveness and imputed righteousness were available to all who walked by faith under the first covenant, God still had to institute another, better covenant. Under this New Covenant a new experience, referred to as the "born-again" experience, becomes available to us. As a result, we receive power over the sin nature.

# FAITH

The second foundational principal of our relationship with the Lord is faith. Faith is not just words. It is action. Faith is confidence that God will do what He has said He will. Faith first comes by hearing the Word (Romans 10:17). Then if we choose to believe and do what the Word teaches our faith or confidence will grow. The Scriptural proof that we believe the Word or have faith is our obedience. Actually doing what the Word teaches is counted as faith (James 2:14-26).

The more and more that we choose to believe and actually do what the Word teaches the more our faith (confidence) will grow. This why Scripture commands us not to be just hearers of the Word, but doers (James 1:19-26). In fact Scripture goes so far to say in Romans 2:13 that "...not the hearers of the law are just before God, but the doers of the law shall be justified."

## SALVATION THROUGH FAITH

The Scripture says that the saints of all ages have been justified "by faith." Before the Law was given, Abraham was justified by faith. During the Law, God's people were justified by faith. After the Law (under the New Covenant), we are justified by faith. The same thing is true of forgiveness and imputed righteousness. Before the Law was given, Abraham received forgiveness and imputed righteousness. Likewise, during and after the Law, God's people have received forgiveness and the imputed righteousness of Jesus by faith.

Romans 4:1-7, 11

"What shall we say then that Abraham [before the Law] our father, as pertaining to the flesh, hath found? For if Abraham were justified by works, he hath whereof to glory; but not before God. For what saith the Scripture? Abraham believed God it was counted unto him for righteousness. Now to him that worketh is the reward not reckoned of grace, but of debt. But to him that worketh not, but believeth on him that justifieth the ungodly, his faith is counted for righteousness.

"Even as David [during the Law] also describeth the blessedness of the man, unto whom God imputeth righteousness without works, Saying, Blessed are they whose iniquities are forgiven whose sins are covered. And he [Abraham] received the sign of circumcision, a seal of the righteousness of the faith which he had yet being uncircumcised: that he might be the father of all them that believe, though they be not circumcised; that righteousness might be imputed to them also."

Paul emphasized this truth when making his argument against trying to be justified "by works." To understand this we must understand what "works" Paul was talking about. Much of Romans, Acts 15 and Ephesians 2:8-9 are about how the Gentiles were to be saved. The legalist believed that they must convert to Judaism and become a Jew to be saved. But Paul and others taught that salvation is by faith apart from the work or conversion ritual of baptism and circumcision. When we understand this argument, then we will understand the context of these and many other verses. God has always required obedience to His Word, but He has never required that anyone become a "chosen people" to be saved. This same lie has permeated all of human history. The devil is doing a great job of deceiving.

When we understand what the "works" that Paul was talking about in Romans, Acts 15 and Ephesians 2:8-9 are, then James chapter two will also make sense. No one can be saved by converting to Judaism and becoming a Jew or keeping the Law. But this does not mean that obedience is not required. The "works" that James is talking about is the simple obedience to God's Word. James teaches that if we really believe the Bible then we will actually do what it teaches. It is that simple.

It is important to understand the difference between the Eastern and Western mind sets. The Hebrew thought process was singular. They did not separate thoughts from actions or secular from spiritual. In our Western or Greek mind set we are dualistic. We separate thoughts and actions and secular and spiritual. So we write statements of faith and define true belief as the acceptance of a doctrinal statement. But a Hebrew would only accept actions as the evidence of what someone believed. This is also the view point of Scripture. When James says that faith without works is dead, being alone this is exactly what he is talking about. It is not what you say it is what you do. Actions speak louder than words.

There was never a time when people could be justified by anything other than faith. It was never possible to earn justification, forgiveness or imputed righteousness through obedience to any law or commandment, either in the Old or the New Testament. The Law of Moses was not given as a means of justification. Justification has always been by faith.

This is extremely important, because most Christians believe that forgiveness, justification and imputed righteousness are the central issues of our salvation. According to most believers and most theologians this is what being saved is all about. But, if forgiveness, justification and imputed righteousness are what salvation is all about, and if they have always been available by faith, why was it necessary to establish a "new" covenant? Because forgiveness, justification and imputed righteousness are not the central issues of salvation. The Christian life and experience is far more than just a fire insurance policy. Sadly, this is how most Christians view Christianity.

While forgiveness, justification and imputed righteousness are absolutely necessary and the foundation of redemption, they do not constitute the totality of it, they are just the beginning baby steps or a first principle of our faith. The central issue of salvation or redemption under both covenants is sanctification and doing the ministry of Jesus. Not forgiveness, justification or imputed righteousness. Salvation is just the beginning. Our God is a God of relationships. He desires to fellowship with each of us and He cannot do that if sin is separating us. He wants each of us to be His joint heirs and co-laborers on this earth today and not just hang out until we die (I Corinthians 3:9).

## ARE WE SAVED BY GRACE, WORKS, OR BOTH?

Matthew 7:21

"Not everyone that saith unto me, Lord, Lord, shall enter into the kingdom of heaven, but (only) he that doeth the will of my Father which is in heaven."

Hebrews 5:8-9

"Though he were a Son, yet learned He obedience by the things which He suffered; and being made perfect, He became the author of eternal salvation unto all them that obey him."

Antinomianism is a term which comes from two Greek words, *anti* (against) and *nomos* (law). It is the teaching that "grace" makes Christians free from Law. In other words, we can break God's Law and never be forced to pay the penalty because those who are free from the Law are also free from the consequences of disobeying that Law.

Antinomianism is associated historically with a man named Johann Agricola, who was a student of Martin Luther. Though it has been associated with Agricola historically, antinomianism has been around since Adam and Eve. The first human to be deceived by it was Eve. She believed the serpent when he told her she could disobey God without suffering the consequences. She believed the lie of the devil that God was withholding something good from her. The devil enticed her to disobey and eat of the tree in order to become like God. Adam refused to take responsibility for his wife's sin, and then blamed God for giving him Eve.

In truth, the consequences of our actions cannot be avoided. We will always reap what we have sown. If we do not honor the precepts of God, in His love and discipline, He gives us what we want. He turns us over to our own choices and devices to suffer the fruit of them.

Proverbs 1:29-31

"For that they hated knowledge, and did not choose the fear of the Lord: They would none of my counsel: they despised all my reproof. Therefore shall they eat of the fruit of their own way, and be filled with their own devices."

Romans 1, Deuteronomy 28 and many other passages teach the same thing. We will never escape the consequences of our choices, because God loves us. Suffering the consequences of our choices is evidence of His love. If He did not really care, He would not discipline because discipline is true love. Mankind has always tried to escape the consequences and our responsibilities by blaming God or others.

Modern theologies continue this deception by teaching a false security, which is the most appealing element of antinomianism. It is an extremely effective deception. Six thousand years later, Satan is feeding us the same exact lie and we are still swallowing it!

The early Church was plagued by antinomianism. Much of the book of Romans, and most of Paul's writings were devoted to this issue. Paul spent most of his ministry fighting the deceptions of Jewish legalism and Gentile antinomianism, both of which flourish when we are ignorant of the purposes and the proper relationship between the Old and New Covenants. God plainly teaches us that we must choose and then be responsible for our choices.

Jewish believers were caught up in legalism, so Paul kept reminding them that they were not justified "by works" (obeying the Law) but by faith in the atonement (Romans 3:20, 24). Paul convinced the Jewish believers that Gentiles did not have to convert to Judaism to be saved in Acts 15. Gentile believers were never under the Law, so they did not understand the arguments Paul used to persuade his fellow Jews. They drew false conclusions from his statements against trying to be justified by works. He had to remind them that genuine faith is more than mental assent to truth. Faith produces a change in behavior (Galatians 5:16-26). He had to warn them not to assume that being under grace provides an excuse to continue in sin (Romans 6:1, 15).

Much the same thing happened to Martin Luther. He attacked the legalism of the State (Catholic) Church, which taught that salvation came through the Mass and the performance of rituals, sacraments, penances and indulgences. Luther was battling the legalism that had held the entire civilized world in its grip for over a thousand years. Naturally, just like Paul did at times, he stressed heavily that salvation is by "faith alone."

However, when he said salvation was by faith alone, he did not mean that obedience to God and righteous living was no longer necessary. He was saying that salvation was through faith, apart from the need to convert to Judaism by being circumcised or baptized.

Just as in Paul's day, certain people drew false conclusions from his statements, and started teaching that if we are saved "by grace" we are no longer under any obligation to obey the commandments of God. What this boils down to is that salvation is a mental assent, which has nothing to do with our behavior. Once saved, our future behavior, no matter how evil, will never affect our salvation. "Once we are saved, we are always saved."

The message of the modern-day antinomian is essentially the same as it was 1900 years ago. Today, we have broken it down into easily understood concepts and terms. For example, "you didn't save yourself, God saved you." "You were not saved by what you did, but as a result of believing and accepting what Jesus did for you on the Cross." "If you were not capable of saving yourself by being good, how then could you ever possibly keep yourself saved by being good?" "It is God who must keep us saved just as it was He who had to save us in the first place."

This camp says that we are saved and kept secure solely on the basis of believing what Jesus did for us, that we are saved on the basis of being "predestinated" or chosen by God. Thus, "once saved, always saved."

Is this what Paul really taught? If so, how are we to understand Matthew 7:21, Hebrews 5:8-9, and others like them which state salvation is based on obedience? What shall we do with the Scriptures, which teach clearly that eternal life is the result of individual effort (Galatians 6:8, Philippians 2:12, I Timothy 6:12, 19)? What is the truth? Are we saved and kept secure by what we believe, by what we do, or by God Himself?

James 2:14, 17, 19-22, 24, 26

"What doth it profit, my brethren, though a man say he hath faith have not works? Can faith save him? [The implied answer is no]... Even so faith, if it hath not works, is dead, being alone... Thou believest that there is one God; thou doest well: the devils also believe and tremble. But wilt thou know, O vain man, that faith without works is dead?

"Was not Abraham our father justified by works, when he had offered Isaac his son upon the altar? Seest thou how faith wrought with his works and by works was faith made perfect?... Ye see then how that by works a man is justified not by faith only... For as the body without the spirit is dead, so faith without works is dead also."

Remember, the "works" that James is talking about is the simple obedience to God's Word. James teaches that if we really believe the Bible then we will actually do what it teaches. It is important to understand the difference between the Eastern and Western mind sets. Just as the Hebrew thought process was singular, so should ours be. They did not separate thoughts from actions or secular from spiritual, and neither should we. We separate thoughts and actions and secular and spiritual to our detriment. We write statements of faith and define true belief as the acceptance of a doctrinal statement. But God also looks at what we do, not just what we say. This why the books of Romans (Romans

2:13) and James (chapter 2) teach that we are justified by doing the law and that faith without works is dead being alone. Actions speak louder than words.

Today the issue is the necessity of obedience. Is obedience to anything (including Jesus Himself) mandatory in order to be saved or remain a Christian? The belief that a person must obey anything in order to be saved or remain in Christ is a concept that modern antinomians very strongly reject.

Why? Because they believe that if a person can do something to gain or lose his salvation after coming to Christ, then his salvation was not truly based on grace. It was based on the works or effort of the individual. If sinful behavior can cause us to lose our salvation, then salvation is not an "unmerited" gift but a reward for our performance or works.

Can a person accept Jesus as his personal Savior but refuse Him as his personal Lord and still be saved? Can we believe in Jesus and accept His atonement, yet refuse to obey Him faithfully, and remain eternally secure? Can an individual who says he is a believer, yet continues in sin the rest of his life, still inherit the Kingdom of God? Can a Christian sow sin and reap eternal life? What are the consequences for sin?

Most seminaries, Bible colleges and churches, promote exactly such a position. This is the majority view.

Charles Ryrie, editor of the *Ryrie Study Bible*, says on page 170 of his book, *Balancing The Christian Life*:

> The importance of this question cannot be overestimated in relation to both salvation and sanctification. The message of faith only, and the message of faith plus commitment of life, cannot both be the gospel; therefore, one of them is false and comes under the curse of perverting the gospel or preaching another gospel.

Ryrie believes that "faith plus commitment of life" is the false gospel. But commitment of life is the product of genuine faith! Antinomians speak as if commitment, obedience, transformation and good works are all external additions to faith which, when viewed as absolutely necessary to salvation, turn simple faith into faith plus works.

The truth is, these things are an indivisible part of faith. They are the natural outcome of faith. They come in the same package! Where these are lacking, true faith is lacking. This is why James said that faith without works is dead. Antinomians say faith should have works, but if it doesn't, it really makes no difference; it is still very much alive.

Antinomians wrongly define the necessity of obedience as legalism (performance). Once we accept the idea that obedience equals legalism, deception will automatically follow. Scripture states very clearly that a person can neither receive nor retain salvation as a result of performance.

Herein lays the fatal error of antinomianism. While obedience can be legalism, it is not necessarily always legalism. Obedience can just as easily be the fruit of true faith. The thing that determines whether a person's obedience is fruit or legalism is the condition of his heart and what it is that he is obeying.

Obedience to rituals and traditions of the church, or any religious system, does not equal obedience to God's Word. The obedience that comes as a response to the Holy Spirit in our lives is fruit and the work that proves our faith is genuine. Moreover, obedience perfects faith!

The reason most Christians are not aware that they are under the influence of antinomianism is that those who teach it have been deceived themselves. Antinomianism has been mixed with the true gospel. Many preachers and scholars are not even aware of this mixture themselves. In fact, when confronted with their unscriptural theology, they strongly deny that it is, in fact, antinomianism. However, denying the facts can never change them! Antinomianism may not always be taught explicitly, but it is still implied.

Once we have come to Christ, what must we do? What does the Scripture require? Everyone agrees that Christians should live like Christians, but what if we don't? No one suggests that we should continue to practice sin once we are saved, but what if we do? If our profession of faith has produced no fruit, no change of behavior, no works, will it still keep us in Christ? Those who answer yes have been deceived by antinomianism.

Most Christians would agree that a changed life can and does provide assurance that a person is saved. But few would concede that the lack of a changed life is proof that one is not a genuine Christian. This is because we have been taught that we can have justification and forgiveness without sanctification, that we can have faith without works. We have been so afraid of the lie that we can put ourselves back "under the Law" and have to earn our salvation that we have forgotten that obedience is a blessing and the evidence of true faith.

The faith of antinomianism is a faith that has been emptied of its fundamental essence, which is obedience to God. It has been emptied of the life and vitality of Jesus. What is left is the shell of mental assent. All that is mandatory is that a person "believes" that Jesus is the Son of God and that He died for us. If we do this, we assume we possess genuine faith. Mental assent falls short of God's standard.

James 2:19

"Thou believest that there is one God; thou doest well: the devils also believe, and tremble."

If mental assent were all that God required, then the devils would be saved. We are not adding works to grace; the person who insists that true faith must have fruit is simply trying to reclaim that which antinomians have thrown away. He is trying to restore what they have declared unnecessary, namely obedience, which is the core of Biblical faith.

It is true that no individual can earn or merit justification through good works, but today's antinomians draw the conclusion that good works, commitment of life and obedience need not even accompany genuine faith. But the Scripture states that it is the presence or absence of these very things that determines whether a person's faith is alive (and able to save) or dead (and unable to save).

James said that works perfect faith. They are so vitally linked together we can actually say that we are "justified by works." We are justified by works because works are part of genuine, Biblical faith. Even more than this, works are the proof that the Holy Spirit dwells in us.

Scripture requires us to be doers of the Word of God as proof that we are justified. Romans 2:13

"For not the hearers of the law are just before God, but the doers of the law shall be justified."

It is also equally wrong to claim that our salvation is all up to God. The other gospel teaches that man is so totally depraved that he cannot even choose God. It teaches that since man is so depraved, God the Father mercifully elects some to eternal life apart from any condition or choice in themselves. In doing this God also lets many people perish. He only chooses to save some. The other gospel teaches that the Atonement of Jesus was designed for the salvation of only those whom the Father arbitrarily chooses.

God chose, elected and predestinated every human as we are all created in His image. It is His will that none should perish. We then have the duty and responsibility to choose God or Satan. Understanding this shows us the heart of God. It is not His will that any should perish; neither does he want robots. There is no fellowship with robots. He desires to walk in the cool of the day and have fellowship with each person He created. Love and fellowship only come through the ability to choose. God cannot and will not make anyone love or serve Him; neither can you make anyone love you. He gave us that right to choose, so there could be love and fellowship. This shows us the heart of God.

To say that God elects, chooses or predestinates some and not others is to say that God is a respecter of persons. This would violate His nature and thus make Him a liar, arbitrary and capricious. This is not the God of the Holy Bible.

## THE ROLE OF THE HOLY SPRIT

God sends His Holy Spirit to convict, thus man gains knowledge of good and evil, and God. Additionally, man ate of the tree of knowledge of good and evil in the garden; thus, man came to know good and evil. Satan sends his evil spirits to tempt and condemn, thus we are in the middle of a spiritual war.

The person and work of the Holy Spirit is also ignored in Calvinism, Dispensationalism and Armenianism. It is the Holy Spirit that initiates or convicts all men. It is the Holy Spirit that calls all men. But we all have the ability to say no.

God commands us to choose, this day and every day, whom we will serve: life or death (Deuteronomy 30:19, Joshua 24:15). It would be very difficult to find a single chapter in Scripture where God does not command someone to do something. Our free will and ability to choose is so ingrained in every page of the Scripture, it is incomprehensible to deny it. Our free will is our God-given ability to choose. It is also our responsibility.

If we do not understand our free will and the responsibility associated with it, we will be deceived. Calvinism, Dispensationalism and Armenianism to varying degrees blame or make God responsible for the plight of man. The truth is that He is totally just, fair and righteous in His judgments. He has proven this over and over. We must accept the responsibility to choose and then accept the responsibility for the consequences of our choices. If we blame God or put the responsibility on Him we are wrong. This is the sin of Eve, Adam, Cain, Job and every other human.

The Calvinist, Dispensationalist and Armenians all need to understand the difference between responsibility and merit. Merit has to do with earning salvation through good deeds or righteous living. This is legalism. We can never earn God's salvation. But we have the responsibility to accept or reject the salvation and its conditions that God has offered to us through Jesus.

Martin Luther recognized the subtle poison in antinomianism. He taught his pupils that though salvation is by faith alone, faith itself is never alone. Wherever you find faith, you will also find commitment of life, works of obedience, and a transformed life. In this sense, works may be said to be a condition of salvation, in that they always accompany true faith.

Antinomians confuse merit with responsibility. Scripture says, "Faith cometh by hearing and hearing by the Word of God" (Romans 10:17). That means it is God who makes the first move. The Lord makes faith available to every person. If we choose to respond to the convicting power of the Holy Spirit, He imparts the ability to actually believe. God speaks, we choose; He empowers, we experience faith. This is why the man who brought his son to Jesus for healing cried out in tears, "Lord, I believe; help thou my unbelief" (Mark 9:24). What sense does that statement make? How can a person believe and not believe something at the same time? The man was saying he had chosen to believe but did not have the ability to actually experience what he had chosen. He was asking the Lord to impart that ability. If we choose to believe and repent for our unbelief, like this father did, then the Holy Spirit will give each of His gift of faith (I Corinthians 12).

The choice to believe is our responsibility. The initial offer, as well as the power to experience what we have chosen is found in God. What an expression of His love! If you will repent for your unbelief and ask for His gift of faith He will give it to you!

The fact that the choice is our responsibility does not mean that we have earned, through self-effort and legalistic works, the chance to choose! We can do absolutely nothing to earn the opportunity God presents us. Nevertheless, we are totally responsible for the choice we make. How we respond determines whether or not God will continue to bring us to salvation. If we truly believe, then we will do His Word.

The same holds true after we have been justified, accepted and brought into the New Covenant. On the basis of what Jesus Christ did at Calvary, God created a process, which brings about commitment of life, which causes us to obey Jesus, which begins transforming us into His image. However, we are responsible to respond and yield to that work which He is performing in us. God will not perform this work in us against our free will. How we respond determines whether or not God will keep us secure in Christ. If we do not respond, either we have never actually possessed true, genuine faith, or else our faith has died. In continuing to do His Word and work, our faith will increase into a healthy and powerful faith that can destroy all the works of the devil.

The sacrifice that Jesus made on the cross is for everyone, but there are conditions that must be met to receive it. However, most religious leaders are teaching that in one way or another salvation is unconditional. The notes found on Hebrews 8:8, in the *Scofield Reference Bible,* state that:

> The New Covenant, the last of the eight great covenants of Scripture, is (1) better than the Mosaic Covenant (Exodus 19:5 note), not morally but efficaciously (Hebrews 7:1, Romans 8:3). It is established upon better (i.e., unconditional) promises. It rests upon the sacrifice of Christ and secures the eternal blessedness, under the Abrahamic Covenant (Galatians 3:13) of all who believe. It is absolutely unconditional and, since no responsibility is by it committed to man, it is final and irreversible.

Dr. Scofield is stating that salvation is totally unconditional and irreversible and that we do not play any role in our personal salvation. But when I read my Bible I find many verses that contain "ifs," "thens" and "buts." In fact there are more conditions in the New Covenant than in the Old. There is more on this topic in the section on Eternal Judgment.

James 1:27 says that, "Worship that God our Father accepts as pure and faultless is this: to look after orphans and widows in their distress and to keep oneself from being polluted by the world." True religion or true worship according to the God of the Bible (Abraham, Isaac and Jacob) is to go to work and actually do what God tells us to do. The Greek word translated religion means to worship. We are to take care of the widows and orphans in their time of need and we are to sanctify ourselves. This is the "work" that makes and keeps our faith alive.

Doing what the Bible teaches is true worship. James and Romans both teach that we are saved by doing what the Word teaches. That faith without out works (obedience) is dead. There is no faith without obedience (works). If we are not doers of the Word (works) we have only deceived ourselves (Romans 2:13, James 1:22, 2:24).

Traditionally worship has been defined in terms words such as praise, creeds, or liturgy. In contrast Biblical worship encompasses not only the "fruit of the lips" but also our actions. Obedience, which is the "work" of actually doing what the Bible teaches, is true religion or worship. True faith or worship of the God of the Bible means to bow down to Him and accept His authority in all of our lives: both words and actions. Anything else is another gospel.

## BAPTISMS

Baptism is not originally a Christian practice. It is and was a Jewish practice. In the book of Corinthians Paul is writing to a mixed multitude of believers who were proving to be just as much a challenge to him as the mixed multitude was for Moses in Exodus (Exodus 12). Paul refers to this in I Corinthians 10:1-2, "Moreover, brethren, I would not that ye should be ignorant, how that all our fathers were under the cloud, and all passed through the sea; and were all baptized unto Moses in the cloud and in the sea."

Paul is comparing the crossing of the sea to immersion or baptism. Believers generally practice different ideas about how baptism should be done but for many it is a surprise to learn it is not originally a Christian practice. From the days of Moses, immersion was regularly practiced by all of Israel. Anyone who became ritually unclean needed to undergo an immersion before they could enter the Temple. The priest immersed every day. After a woman completed menstruation, needed to immerse herself. Those who became contaminated in any way (i.e. lepers) needed to go through immersion before they were ritually pure again. In Judaism, immersions are referred to as immersion into a "mikvah." *Mikvah* is a Hebrew word meaning, "gathering of water." A mikvah could be a river, a lake, a spring, or any natural body of water.

In Judaism and Jewish life immersion was and is a practice to cleanse one's self ritually and spiritually. It was also part of the process of conversion. A Gentile who wants to become a Jew must undergo several requirements. For men, the main two were circumcision and immersion. For a woman it is immersion. In Talmud a proselyte is considered to be like a new born child. This is the origin of the term "born again" (Yevamot 48b).

In his book *The Waters of Eden*, Rabbi Aryeh Kaplan comments on the imagery of being born again:

Emerging from the mikvah is very much like a process of rebirth. Seen In this light, we see that the mikvah represents the womb. When an individual enters the mikvah, he is reentering the womb, and when he emerges, he is as if born anew. Thus, he attains a completely new status.

When a person immerses himself in water, he places himself in an environment where he cannot live. Were he to remain submerged for more than a few moments, he would die...Thus, when a person submerges himself in a mikvah, he momentarily enters the realm of the nonliving. When he emerges, he is like one reborn.

Paul understood the death and rebirth imagery of the immersion practice. He then applied the same imagery to those in Christ. In Romans chapter 6 he compares the conversion rite to a believer's immersion into the death and resurrection of Jesus.

Romans 6:3-5

"Know ye not, that so many of us as were baptized into Jesus Christ were baptized into his death? Therefore we are buried with him by baptism into death: that like as Christ was raised up from the dead by the glory of the Father, even so we also should walk in newness of life. For if we have been planted together in the likeness of his death, we shall be also in the likeness of his resurrection."

Paul is using the rabbinic conversion ceremony to teach us about the transformation that occurs when we place faith in Jesus the Messiah. In the rabbinic ritual, the Gentile is said to die to his old life and identity and is considered a new creature or "born again" when he comes up out of the baptismal waters. Paul was using what was commonly understood, to teach that as we place faith in Jesus, we actually do die to our old lives and identities and then we are regarded as new creatures, "born again" and walking in newness of life (Lancaster 2003, pages 92-97).

## BAPTISM INTO CHRIST

Scripture reveals three baptisms for believers. First, into Christ or into His body at repentance, which is the new birth. This is called "one baptism" (Ephesians 4:5), because it is the only baptism that saves the soul and brings one into the body of Christ. The Holy Spirit is the agent to baptize into Christ and into His body (I Corinthians 12:13).

Romans 6:3-7

Know ye not, that so many of us as were baptized into Jesus Christ were baptized into his death? Therefore we are buried with him by baptism into death: that like as Christ was raised up from the dead by the glory of the Father, even so we also should walk in newness of life. For if we have been planted together in the likeness of his death, we shall be also in the likeness of his resurrection: Knowing this, that our old man is crucified with him, that the body of sin might be destroyed, that henceforth we should not serve sin. For he that is dead is freed from sin.

I Corinthians 12:13

"For by one Spirit are we all baptized into one body, whether we be Jews or Gentiles, whether we be bond or free; and have been all made to drink into one Spirit."

Galatians 3:27

"For as many of you as have been baptized into Christ have put on Christ."

Colossians 2:12

"Buried with him in baptism, wherein also ye are risen with him through the faith of the operation of God, who hath raised him from the dead."

## WATER BAPTISM

Second, water baptism after one is saved. The minister is the agent to baptize into water (Matthew 28:19). Christian baptism in water is referred to in many passages (Matthew 28:19, Mark 16:16, Acts 2:38-41, Acts 8:12-16, 36-38, Acts 9:18, Acts 10:47-48, Acts 16:15, 33, Acts 18:8, Acts 19:5, Acts 22:16, I Corinthians 1:13-17, I Peter 3:21).

As you read passages about baptism you will notice several key points about water immersion or baptism:

- On all occasions confession of sins was required and was made before baptism (Matthew 3:8, 11, Mark 1:5, Luke 3:8-14).
- Only believers were baptized after repentance and faith in Christ (Matthew 28:19, Mark 16:16, Acts 2:28, 41, Acts 8:12-13, 37, Acts 16:14-15, 31-33, Acts 18:8, Acts 19:1-7).
- Christ who knew no sin was baptized. Christ submitted to baptism for two reasons:
  (1) To fulfill righteousness (Matthew 3:15)
  (2) To be manifest to Israel (John 1:31)
- Baptism is only a symbol of the death, burial, and resurrection of Christ (I Peter 3:21).
- It's not essential to salvation (II Corinthians 1:13-21). Only faith in the blood of Christ brings remission of sins (Matthew 26:28, Romans 3:24-25, Romans 4:1-25, Romans 5:1-11, Romans 8:2, Romans 10:4-10, I Corinthians 15:1-5, Ephesians 1:7, Ephesians 2:8-9, Galatians 3:19-29, John 3:16, Acts 10:43, Acts 13:38-39, I Corinthians 1:18-21, I John 1:9, I John 5:1).

## SPIRIT BAPTISM: ENDUEMENT WITH POWER FOR TODAY

The third baptism is the baptism of the Holy Spirit, the enduement of power for service. It can take place before water baptism (Acts 10:44-48) or after it (Acts 1:4-8, Acts 2:1-11, Acts 8:12-21, Acts 19:1-7). Christ is the agent to baptize in the Holy Spirit (Matthew 3:11, John 1:31-33).

Once again we are coming to a practice that is plainly taught in Scripture that many believe no longer applies to us today. Let's look at this in more detail.

As we study the Old Testament prophets we learn that they all had a special filling of the Holy Spirit. This relationship could be described as a mantle or covering of God to do His work. They knew without any shadow of doubt that they were sent by God to do His work. Elijah, Elisha, Elihu, Jeremiah, Haggai, Ezekiel, Daniel, Hosea, etc. all were confident in who they were and their mission from God in this life. They did not go out to do the Lord's work until the Spirit sent them. Faith and confidence carry the same meaning. In the New Covenant this mantle or covering is available to every believer.

This "sending" continues in the New Testament. John the Baptist received a special calling or sending from God. His calling was to announce that the Messiah was coming. Jesus Himself said that there was not a greater prophet born of a women than John (Luke 7:28). The verse continues to say that the least in the kingdom of heaven is greater than John.

Jesus did not do any public ministry until he received water baptism and the Baptism of the Holy Spirit. Then he began His three years of public ministry.

Matthew 3:16-17

"And Jesus, when he was baptized, went up straightway out of the water: and, lo, the heavens were opened unto him, and he saw the Spirit of God descending like a dove, and lighting upon him: And lo a voice from heaven, saying, This is my beloved Son, in whom I am well pleased." (Also see Mark 1:10-11.)

"The heavens were opened unto him, and he saw the Spirit of God descending like a dove, and lighting upon him." Did not Jesus already have the Spirit of God? Did not the Holy Spirit already reside in or on Jesus? Of course He did. But it was not time to begin His ministry and the Father was telling Jesus and the world that "this is my beloved Son, in whom I am well pleased." He was announcing to the world that He was sending Jesus in His power and authority to do His works and to destroy the works of the devil. He was also bestowing on Jesus a greater level of authority and power, as a man, to do His works. It is only after His baptism in water and in Spirit that Jesus began His public ministry. As part of His ministry He chose, trained and sent out disciples.

The twelve disciples and the "seventy" were sent out by Jesus to minister under His authority while He was physically with them. They were serving and doing many miracles long before Pentecost but it was under the covering or anointing of Jesus. After He was crucified they were required to wait in Jerusalem until Pentecost. Luke 24:49 says, "Behold, I send the Promise of My Father upon you; but tarry in the city of Jerusalem until you are endued with power from on high" (NKJV). This promise was not about salvation. They were already saved.

John 20:20-23 says, "When He had said this, He showed them His hands and

His side. Then the disciples were glad when they saw the Lord. So Jesus said to them again, "Peace to you! As the Father has sent Me, I also send you." And when He had said this, He breathed on them, and said to them, "Receive the Holy Spirit. If you forgive the sins of any, they are forgiven them; if you retain the sins of any, they are retained" (NKJV).

There are many passages that confirm the disciple's choice to believe in Jesus as the son of God before He was crucified. In this passage, which is after the resurrection, He breaths on them to receive the Holy Spirit. This was their born again experience. This is in direct parallel to the Father's first breathing life into Adam. But this was not the enduement with power to do the Ministry of Jesus promised in Luke 24:49. Pentecost was and is another event (Acts 1-2).

**Salvation to Pentecost**

What happened after John 20 and before the promise of Luke 24 was fulfilled at Pentecost in Acts 2? They all stayed in one place and contended in prayer. They prayed for ten days preparing to receive the promise. The disciples did not just assume the promise Jesus gave them would just happen. They did not just hang out in Jerusalem. Acts 1:14 says, "These all continued with one accord in prayer and supplication..." (NKJV).

The disciples and their families used the ten days to strengthen themselves in the upper room. They strengthened themselves in the Lord, preparing to receive and steward the fulfillment of the promise. They wanted to be worthy and ready. I believe they knew there was going to be a great cost and well as a great reward.

The disciples were not allowed to do the ministry that Jesus had taught them on their own until they received the power of the Holy Spirit at Pentecost. After Pentecost they were sent by the Father in His power and authority to do His works and destroy the works of the devil, just like their Teacher.

This allowed them to go and do the works of the Father in the knowledge and power that they were sent of God. It is the knowing that we know that we are sent and commissioned. If Jesus and the original twelve apostles and the 120 were required to have this "baptism" before they could minister why would we be any different?

Growing in favor with God requires our preparation. We must deal with the issues of our hearts to be able to bear the weight of His glory and power. We must prove ourselves trustworthy and we must learn to trust Him.

We were made to carry His glory. The Christian life is not just about getting saved. We need to go on to perfection and move beyond the basic principles of the faith and learn to live in Heaven's reality now. We are called to be co-labors with Christ to establish His Kingdom on earth as it is in heaven. This begins with ourselves and then others, one life, one person at a time.

## Not a One-time Event

The book of Acts tells us that this baptism was never intended to be a one-time event but as an ongoing series of encounters that enable us to walk in increasing levels of power to fulfill the assignments given to us by God. Some of the same people mentioned in the upper room in Acts 2 are also in the outpouring in Acts 4:29-31.

The indwelling of the Holy Spirit that we receive at salvation is the Spirit of adoption who calls out "Abba Father." But as we grow and mature and come to know the Father and that He wants His will done on earth as it is in heaven now, we should realize that salvation is just the beginning of this relationship. His whole plan centers on the unveiling of His sons and daughters, who will walk in the authority that Jesus received at His baptism. The Holy Spirit did not come only to dwell in us, but also to rest upon us with the same anointing Jesus had in order to release Heaven's answers to all of our problems.

As Bill Johnson says we must learn to "steward" or be faithful with what we have been given. Just as in the parable of the master in Luke 19 who gave each servant a sum of money to invest we must also be faithful with what we have been given. Then we will receive more and more as we prove that we are trustworthy.

## Gifts of the Holy Sprit

It is in this baptism that the gifts of the Holy Spirit listed in I Corinthians 12 are given. I believe that the evidence of the Baptism of the Holy Spirit will be at least one of these gifts. Some teach that the only evidence of the Baptism of the Holy Spirit is the gift of tongues. I do not agree. While it seems that this happened in almost every incident of the Baptism of the Holy Ghost recorded in Scripture, I do not believe that it is the initial or only evidence.

I believe that the greatest gift is listed in I Corinthians 13. In fact, if we do not have this gift we are as sounding brass and a tinkling cymbal. A supernatural love for others is the greatest gift. The greatest gift is the very nature of God; love and charity. If we do not have His nature of love and charity, then we are nothing. Scripture considers love greater than faith and hope (I Corinthians 13:13).

The evidence of the Baptism of the Holy Spirit that I look for is the supernatural manifestation of His nature. If we do not have His nature of Love being manifested through us, we are nothing. His love is never puffed up. His love is to be expressed toward God the Father, our neighbors, and ourselves. If we are in His nature or abiding in Christ, then we love God the Father and others as we love ourselves. We will have the faith and confidence that we are called and sent. We will know that we know that we are sent by God to do His work in His power and authority; to destroy all the works of the devil in His power and authority.

We will know that we have the power to preach the gospel, to cast out demons, that we have his protection, and that the sick will be healed (Mark 16:17-20).

## Receiving

Hebrews 6:1-2 says, "Therefore leaving the principles of the doctrine of Christ, let us go on unto perfection; not laying again the foundation of repentance from dead works, and of faith toward God, Of the doctrine of baptisms, and of laying on of hands, and of resurrection of the dead, and of eternal judgment."

It is time to quit arguing about the basic, first "principles of the doctrine of Christ." It is time to go on to perfection. Paul is plainly referring to more than one baptism when he says baptisms (plural). As we have studied earlier there are many different baptisms. There are many different amounts or measures of all the spiritual gifts. We have also seen that there are many different measures or portions of the Holy Spirit. Why not choose to seek all there is?

Jesus and all His disciples were required to receive this baptism before they could minister in His power and authority. How could it be any different for us? Scripture obviously tells us about the need to receive the Baptism of the Holy Ghost. Let's accept the simplicity of God's Word and chose to be obedient.

Luke 11:13 says, "If ye then, being evil, know how to give good gifts unto your children: how much more shall your heavenly Father give the Holy Spirit to them that ask him?"

Here the Holy Spirit is promised to all children of God who ask. That this refers to the Spirit baptism and full enduement of power for service is clear from Luke 24:49, John 7:37-39, Acts 2:33, 38-39, Acts 5:32, Matthew 3:11, Galatians 3:13-14. All children of God are given the Spirit in a measure at the new birth (John 3:3, 5, Romans 8:9, 14-16, Galatians 4:6). So what is this asking for the Holy Spirit after men become the children of God, if it is not what the disciples received at Pentecost after they had been children of God for several years (Acts 1:4-8, Acts 2:1-16)? So let us simply ask!

We receive the Baptism of the Holy Ghost in the same manner that we receive salvation and forgiveness; by faith. It is administered in two different ways in Scripture; first, by the laying on of hands by another that has it, and second, from God Himself.

Simply pray and ask God for His sending, anointing, calling, commissioning, His baptism in His authority and power. Receive it in faith. Some receive tongues or another gift immediately. Others see the evidence over time. In my opinion the primary evidence of the Baptism of the Holy Spirit is found in I Corinthians 13, a supernatural love for others. Let's continue to grow in favor with the Lord.

A suggested prayer begins on the following page. (For more on this topic see Part Five.)

Prayer

*Our Father in heaven, I come to You to ask for the same anointing and the same power of the Holy Spirit that you anointed Jesus and the Apostles with. I ask for this anointing and power to be on my life this hour. I ask for Your baptism of Your Holy Spirit, in your full power and authority.*

*Father, I receive the anointing and power to do good and to undo all the works of the devil so that unsaved will be saved; that the broken-hearted will be healed; that the oppressed will be delivered; that the yokes will be broken; that those imprisoned will be freed; and that the sick will be healed.*

*Lord, I commend myself into Your hands. Use my life; make me a winner of souls. I commit myself to do Your will in all things, in the name of Jesus, Amen.*

## LAYING ON OF HANDS

Sadly, once again we are in need of "laying again the foundation" of one of God's basic doctrines. Scripture is very clear that we are to practice Laying on Hands when:

(1) Blessing men (Genesis 48:14)
(2) Making offerings (Numbers 8:10)
(3) Ordaining (Numbers 27:18, 23)
(4) Imparting Spirit (Deuteronomy 34:9)
(5) Blessing children (Matthew 19:15)
(6) Healing sick (Mark 6:2, 5, Mark 16:18, Luke 4:40, Luke 13:13, Acts 5:12, Acts 28:8)
(7) Performing miracles (Acts 19:11)
(8) Imparting gifts (I Timothy 4:14, II Timothy 1:6, Hebrews 6:2)
(9) Imparting the Baptism of the Holy Spirit (Acts 8:17-24, Acts 9:17, Acts 19:6)

It is evident from the above verses that Laying on of Hands is a very common Biblical practice. But few practice most of these commands in His Word today. In fact many teach that healing, miracles, the gifts of the Holy Spirit and the Baptism of the Holy Spirit are passed away and no longer are part of everyday Christianity. In this book I am only going to discuss four of these examples of Laying on of Hands; Healing the Sick, Miracles, Imparting gifts, and Imparting the Baptism of the Holy Spirit. The Baptism of the Holy Spirit was discussed earlier.

The more we study history the more we see that it repeats itself. As you read through the Old Testament (Hebrew Scriptures) miracles of many kinds are common.

The Red Sea parted, people were raised from the dead, water and food was created, rain fell, bodies were healed, God's Spirit was passed from one to another, people were set free from bondages and sins were forgiven. There is hardly any miracle recorded in the Hebrew Scriptures that does not have a parallel in rabbinic literature and the New Testament.

There is an interesting similarity between many of the stories in the Hebrew Scriptures and those of the Gospels that is found in the tension between the religious establishment and His prophets. In the Hebrew Scriptures God's miracle workers (prophets) were stoned. In the Gospels, God's miracle workers were crucified or martyred in some way by the religious establishment. Today, once again history is repeating itself.

Faith begins with God the Father. God is good! He sent Jesus the Messiah to demonstrate His goodness. This has not changed today. In fact we need to hear the message of God's goodness more today than ever. The Father demonstrated His sovereignty over all the works of the devil in what He sent Jesus to do.

In the Ministry of Jesus, healing begins with God and His goodness. Jesus demonstrated God's love in every miracle. He pronounced the Father's Grace in each miracle and in forgiving sins. Jesus pronounced forgiveness by enacting God's grace when He healed. Healing faith in the Gospels focuses not upon the problem but upon God, by recognizing His goodness and mercy. Faith in God must never be confused with faith in faith. Jesus taught people to have faith in God and demonstrated His love, goodness and mercy in His actions.

Faith in God and His grace requires a total trust. Faith acknowledges who God is and commits everything into His power. The miraculous healing of the Gospel revealed God's Kingdom. The Kingdom comes in full force when Jesus works a miracle of healing because it is the finger of God (The Holy Spirit) that brings deliverance and openly displays divine sovereignty. God's plan is designed to bring wholeness and healing to every area of an individual's life (Young 2007, pages 35-43).

Sadly this tension has not gone away. The religious establishment is still condemning miracle workers and belittling God by teaching that He tests us with diseases or other calamities. (See Parts Three and Five.)

The entire Bible teaches the message of healing for our spirit, soul and body. The following is only a very brief teaching on healing.

**Healing Is Found in Both Covenants**

Exodus 34:10-11 says: "…Behold, I make a covenant. Before all your people I will do marvels such as have not been done in all the earth, nor in any nation; and all the people among whom you are shall see the work of the LORD. For it is an awesome thing that I will do with you" (NKJV).

Hebrews 2:3-4 says, "how shall we escape if we neglect so great a salvation, which at the first began to be spoken by the Lord, and was confirmed to us by those who heard Him, God also bearing witness both with signs and wonders, with various miracles, and gifts of the Holy Spirit, according to His own will?" (NKJV)

### Healing Is Part and Parcel of His Kingdom

The book of Luke clearly teaches in many passages that the Kingdom of God or Heaven is the power and presence of the Lord. Jesus teaches us that the Kingdom is upon us and we "see and hear" the Kingdom every time His power over the devil is displayed. (For a deeper study see Part Five.)

### The Scope of Healing

Psalms 103:2-3says: "Bless the LORD, O my soul, And forget not all His benefits: Who forgives all your iniquities, Who heals all your diseases" (NKJV).

### All Believers Are Commissioned to Heal

In John 20:21 Jesus says to His disciples, "as the Father has sent me, so send I you." Luke 4:18 is one of many passages that tell us what the Father sent Jesus to do. Let's look at other verses that demonstrate what Jesus sent His disciples to do:

Matthew 10:7-8 says, "…as you go, preach, saying, 'The kingdom of heaven is at hand.' Heal the sick, cleanse the lepers, raise the dead, cast out demons. Freely you have received, freely give" (NKJV).

Mark 6:7, 12-13 says, "And He called the twelve to Himself, and began to send them out two by two, and gave them power over unclean spirits… So they went out and preached that people should repent. And they cast out many demons, and anointed with oil many who were sick, and healed them" (NKJV).

Matthew 28:19-20 says, "Go therefore and make disciples of all the nations, baptizing them in the name of the Father and of the Son and of the Holy Spirit, teaching them to observe all things that I have commanded you; and lo, I am with you always, even to the end of the age. Amen" (NKJV).

### Healing Is in the Atonement

Many passages teach that Jesus came to forgive our sins as well as heal our bodies. Matthew 8:17 and I Peter 2:24 clearly relate the healing to the blood atonement of Jesus as prophesied in Isaiah 53.

Isaiah 53:4-5 says, "Surely he took up our infirmities [Hebrew *choli*: sickness, disease (noun form of *chalah*, to be sick or ill)] and carried our sorrows, [Hebrew *makov*: pain], yet we considered him stricken by God, smitten by him, and afflicted. But he was pierced for our transgressions, he was crushed for our iniquities; the punishment that brought us peace [Hebrew *shalom*: wholeness, body, soul and spirit] was upon him, and by his wounds we are healed" (NKJV).

Matthew 8:16-17 says, "When evening had come, they brought to Him many who were demon-possessed. And He cast out the spirits with a word, and healed all who were sick, that it might be fulfilled which was spoken by Isaiah the prophet, saying: 'He Himself took our infirmities And bore our sicknesses'" (NKJV).

I Peter 2:24 says, "who Himself bore our sins in His own body on the tree, that we, having died to sins, might live for righteousness by whose stripes you were healed" (NKJV).

Acts 4:10 says, "let it be known to you all, and to all the people of Israel, that by the name of Jesus Christ of Nazareth, whom you crucified, whom God raised from the dead, by Him this man stands here before you whole" (NKJV).

## Sozo

Definition: The Greek word *sozo* is translated "save" in English. It means to save, to heal and to make whole in mind, body and spirit.

In the Jewish culture miracles signified the presence of God and were performed by one of His messengers. Jesus used miracles to proclaim who He is and also the active force of the Kingdom and God's will, being done on the earth. This was consistent with His culture. Jesus said in Luke 11:20, "...if I with the finger of God cast out devils, no doubt the kingdom of God is come upon you." The miracles recorded in the Gospels reveal God's Kingdom upon the people. This means now, today! The Kingdom comes in full force when Jesus works a miracle because it is the finger of God that brings deliverance and openly displays divine sovereignty. God's plan is designed to bring wholeness and healing to every area of a person's life.

Today the message is the same. Miracles are still performed by disciples of Christ in the same power of the Holy Spirit and they still demonstrate His Kingdom. Miracles are an example of His will being done on earth as it is in heaven. God is still sovereign. He still has power over all the works of the devil. He still loves all of us and still has our best interest at heart. He has not changed.

Matthew 4:23-24 says, "And Jesus went about all Galilee, teaching in their synagogues, and preaching the gospel of the kingdom, and healing all manner of sickness and all manner of disease among the people. And his fame went throughout all Syria: and they brought unto him all sick people that were taken with divers diseases and torments, and those which were possessed with devils, and those which were lunatic, and those that had the palsy; and he healed them." The Gospel of the Kingdom is the healing of all manner of sickness-spiritual and physical. Jesus said in John 12:47, "...for I came not to judge the world, but to save [sozo] the world [people]."

Luke 2:13-14

This passage says, "And suddenly there was with the angel a multitude of the heavenly host praising God, and saying, Glory to God in the highest, and on earth peace, good will toward men." This verse has three very important parts: 1) "Glory to God in the Highest"; 2) "Peace on earth"; and 3) "Good will toward men."

In this three-fold text we see once again the purpose of His birth and His Messianic task. We also find that physical and emotional healing is part of His Messianic mission.

First, Jesus made every effort to give "Glory to God in the Highest." Jesus constantly defended the Father by saying "if you know me you would have known the Father; I and the Father are one; I only do what the Father has sent me to do; God is love." These and many other statements clearly declare that the Father always has our best interests at heart. Jesus realized that one of Satan's greatest temptations is to belittle and blame God the Father for what he has really done. We will see this same theme in Satan's temptations of Jesus.

Second, "peace on earth" is a universal message for all people that God the Father is sending the Prince of Peace for everyone. The Father sent His angels to proclaim His merciful will for all people. His divine favor is provided for all humanity. Luke 2:10 says, "And the angel said unto them, Fear not: for, behold, I bring you good tidings of great joy, which shall be to all people."

To further understand the meaning of the "good tidings" from the angels, we need to remember the Hebrew meaning of peace. The Hebrew word *shalom* means to bring wholeness and completeness in body, soul and spirit. A "prince" could refer to an official in a government. Government officials are in charge of war. Jesus, however, is not the minister of war. He is the Prince of Peace who brings wholeness and salvation for all the people.

Third, "Goodwill toward men" is the goodwill of God for all who will receive God's divine favor, not just a few. "Goodwill" (Hebrew *ratzon*), appears 56 times in the Hebrew Old Testament and in at least 37 instances, it refers to God's good pleasure. It is His higher purpose for those He created. It denotes God's blessing and His divine favor for all men.

The word "goodwill" possessed a deep meaning for the Jewish people. Not only is the term used in Old Testament passages like Deuteronomy 33:24, but in Jewish literature in the time of Christ it signified God's desire to express His mercy to all humanity. God's will is done when His "good pleasure" is accomplished.

In the Lord's Prayer we are instructed to pray "thy will be done." The word used for "will" is the same term ratzon in Hebrew. Remember it means God's higher purpose and His good pleasure for and to mankind. It expresses what God truly desires for us. He wants people to experience His peace and salvation. The birth of the Messiah means that peace, which is His divine wholeness, is made known to all people. The term "goodwill" in the song of the angels refers to God's divine favor, which is being revealed in the birth of Jesus, the Messiah. The Father sent Jesus to bring "Glory to God in the highest, peace on earth, goodwill toward men." This is also our mission as

His disciples.

Let's go to the Word of God and see the importance of Laying on of Hands when:

## LAYING ON OF HANDS WHEN IMPARTING HEALING AND MIRACLES

Mark 6:2

"And when the sabbath day was come, he began to teach in the synagogue: and many hearing him were astonished, saying, From whence hath this man these things? And what wisdom is this which is given unto him, that even such mighty works are wrought by his hands?"

Mark 6:5

"And he could there do no mighty work, save that he laid his hands upon a few sick folk, and healed them."

Mark 16:18

"They shall take up serpents; and if they drink any deadly thing, it shall not hurt them; they shall lay hands on the sick, and they shall recover."

Luke 4:40

"Now when the sun was setting, all they that had any sick with divers diseases brought them unto him; and he laid his hands on every one of them, and healed them."

Luke 13:13

"And he laid his hands on her: and immediately she was made straight, and glorified God."

Acts 5:12

"And by the hands of the apostles were many signs and wonders wrought among the people; and they were all with one accord in Solomon's porch."

Acts 19:11

"And God wrought special miracles by the hands of Paul."

Acts 28:8

"And it came to pass, that the father of Publius lay sick of a fever and of a bloody flux: to whom Paul entered in, and prayed, and laid his hands on him, and healed him."

## LAYING ON OF HANDS WHEN IMPARTING SPIRITUAL GIFTS

I Timothy 4:14

"Neglect not the gift that is in thee, which was given thee by prophecy, with the laying on of the hands of the presbytery."

II Timothy 1:6

"Wherefore I put thee in remembrance that thou stir up the gift of God, which is in thee by the putting on of my hands."

Hebrews 6:2

"Of the doctrine of baptisms, and of laying on of hands, and of resurrection of the dead, and of eternal judgment."

## LAYING ON OF HANDS WHEN IMPARTING THE BAPTISM
## OF THE HOLY SPIRIT

Acts 8:17-24

"Then laid they their hands on them, and they received the Holy Ghost. And when Simon saw that through laying on of the apostles' hands the Holy Ghost was given, he offered them money, Saying, Give me also this power, that on whomsoever I lay hands, he may receive the Holy Ghost. But Peter said unto him, Thy money perish with thee, because thou hast thought that the gift of God may be purchased with money. Thou hast neither part nor lot in this matter: for thy heart is not right in the sight of God. Repent therefore of this thy wickedness, and pray God, if perhaps the thought of thine heart may be forgiven thee. For I perceive that thou art in the gall of bitterness, and in the bond of iniquity. Then answered Simon, and said, Pray ye to the Lord for me, that none of these things which ye have spoken come upon me."

Acts 9:17

"And Ananias went his way, and entered into the house; and putting his hands on him said, Brother Saul, the Lord, even Jesus, that appeared unto thee in the way as thou camest, hath sent me, that thou mightest receive thy sight, and be filled with the Holy Ghost."

Acts 19:6

"And when Paul had laid his hands upon them, the Holy Ghost came on them; and they spake with tongues, and prophesied."

How can we doubt God's profound and simple Word? Either it is truth or a lie.

## RESURRECTION OF THE DEAD

Mark 12:18

"Then come unto him the Sadducees, which say there is no resurrection..."

They not only denied the resurrection, but also angels, demons and the supernatural (Dake). They believed in a historical Moses but not all his doctrines (Mark 12:18, 19, Acts 4:1, Acts 5:15-17, Acts 23:8). Today there are many who call themselves Christians who believe in a historical Jesus, but do not believe in all His doctrines; One who still works through His disciples doing the works of the Father; One who still performs miracles; One who still gives us power over demons. These same religious leaders claim to believe in the resurrection but do not believe in its power or that they will answer for their unbelief and their sins.

Let's see what Jesus had to say to the Sadducees of His day.

Matthew 22:23-33

"The same day came to him the Sadducees, which say that there is no resurrection, and asked him, Saying, Master, Moses said, If a man die, having no children, his brother shall marry his wife, and raise up seed unto his brother. Now there were with us seven brethren: and the first, when he had married a wife, deceased, and, having no issue, left his wife unto his brother: Likewise the second also, and the third, unto the seventh. And last of all the woman died also. Therefore in the resurrection whose wife shall she be of the seven? For they all had her. Jesus answered and said unto them, Ye do err, not knowing the Scriptures, nor the power of God. For in the resurrection they neither marry, nor are given in marriage, but are as the angels of God in heaven. But as touching the resurrection of the dead, have ye not read that which was spoken unto you by God, saying, I am the God of Abraham, and the God of Isaac, and the God of Jacob? God is not the God of the dead, but of the living. And when the multitude heard this, they were astonished at his doctrine."

Jesus quoted from Exodus 3:6 and 16 when He said "I am the God of Abraham, and the God of Isaac, and the God of Jacob." The Sadducees believed that the books of Moses were the only Scriptures. Christ understood this, and in His desire to reach them, used the Torah to prove His point. If Jesus claimed these three men were still alive several hundred years after their physical death, then all who cease to live among mortals are still alive. The Sadducees believed in eternal annihilation at death, so Christ's answer (that the dead still live and that God is not the God of dead bodies but of living souls) not only refuted the annihilation doctrine, but proved they did not know the Scriptures.

In reality the Sadducees then and today still do not know the Scriptures or the Messiah.

I Corinthians 15:12-24

"Now if Christ be preached that he rose from the dead, how say some among you that there is no resurrection of the dead? But if there be no resurrection of the dead, then is Christ not risen: And if Christ be not risen, then is our preaching vain, and your faith is also vain. Yea, and we are found false witnesses of God; because we have testified of God that he raised up Christ: whom he raised not up, if so be that the dead rise not. For if the dead rise not, then is not Christ raised: And if Christ be not raised, your faith is vain; ye are yet in your sins. Then they also which are fallen asleep in Christ are perished. If in this life only we have hope in Christ, we are of all men most miserable. But now is Christ risen from the dead, and become the firstfruits of them that slept. For since by man came death, by man came also the resurrection of the dead. For as in Adam all die, even so in Christ shall all be made alive. But every man in his own order: Christ the firstfruits; afterward they that are Christ's at His coming. Then cometh the end, when he shall have delivered up the kingdom to God, even the Father; when he shall have put down all rule and all authority and power."

Without the resurrection we have no hope, "we are of all men most miserable." The power of the resurrection, the power of the risen Jesus our Messiah is what puts "down all rule and all authority and power" that opposes Him. If we deny the power of the

Lord to work through us today just as He did two thousand years ago we are denying the power of the resurrection. Therefore, I believe that we are in reality denying the resurrection. (See Part Five, Advancing the Kingdom of God.)

# ETERNAL LIFE OR ETERNAL JUDGMENT?

Scripture teaches two judgments. The Great White throne judgment is for the non-believer. The other is called the Judgment Seat of Christ, at which every believer will stand before Jesus and answer for the good and bad in his life.

Matthew 16:27

"For the Son of man shall come in the glory of his Father with his angels; and then he shall reward every man according to his works."

Romans 14:10

"But why dost thou judge thy brother? Or why dost thou set at nought thy brother? For we shall all stand before the judgment seat of Christ."

I Corinthians 3:11-16

"For other foundation can no man lay than that is laid, which is Jesus Christ. Now if any man build upon this foundation gold, silver, precious stones, wood, hay, stubble; Every man's work shall be made manifest: for the day shall declare it, because it shall be revealed by fire; and the fire shall try every man's work of what sort it is. If any man's work abide which he hath built thereupon, he shall receive a reward. If any man's work shall be burned, he shall suffer loss: but he himself shall be saved; yet so as by fire. Know ye not that ye are the temple of God, and that the Spirit of God dwelleth in you?"

II Corinthians 5:10-11

"For we must all appear before the judgment seat of Christ; that every one may receive the things done in his body, according to that he hath done, whether it be good or bad. Knowing therefore the terror of the Lord, we persuade men; but we are made manifest unto God; and I trust also are made manifest in your consciences."

Galatians 6:7-9

"Be not deceived; God is not mocked: for whatsoever a man soweth, that shall he also reap. For he that soweth to his flesh shall of the flesh reap corruption; but he that soweth to the Spirit shall of the Spirit reap life everlasting. And let us not be weary in well doing: for in due season we shall reap, if we faint not."

Jesus also teaches us this same message in the parable the in Luke 19.

Luke 19:11-27

"And as they heard these things, he added and spake a parable, because he was nigh to Jerusalem, and because they thought that the kingdom of God should immediately appear. He said therefore, A certain nobleman went into a far country to receive for himself a kingdom, and to return. And he called his ten servants, and delivered them ten pounds, and said unto them, Occupy till I come. But his citizens hated him, and sent a message after him, saying, We will not have this man to reign over us. And it came to pass, that when he was returned, having received the kingdom, then he commanded these servants to be called unto him, to whom he had given the money, that he might know how much every man had gained by trading. Then came the first, saying, Lord, thy pound hath gained ten pounds. And he said unto him, Well, thou good servant: because thou hast been faithful in a very little, have thou authority over ten cities. And the second came, saying, Lord, thy pound hath gained five pounds. And he said likewise to him, Be thou also over five cities. And another came, saying, Lord, behold, here is thy pound, which I have kept laid up in a napkin: For I feared thee, because thou art an austere man: thou takest up that thou layedst not down, and reapest that thou didst not sow. And he saith unto him, Out of thine own mouth will I judge thee, thou wicked servant. Thou knewest that I was an austere man, taking up that I laid not down, and reaping that I did not sow: Wherefore then gavest not thou my money into the bank, that at my coming I might have required mine own with usury? And he said unto them that stood by, Take from him the pound, and give it to him that hath ten pounds. (And they said unto him, Lord, he hath ten pounds.) For I say unto you, That unto every one which hath shall be given; and from him that hath not, even that he hath shall be taken away from him. But those mine enemies, which would not that I should reign over them, bring hither, and slay them before me."

Please read these verses again and accept the plain simple meaning from God. We will answer for what we do and don't do. We will stand before Jesus and answer to Him for every unconfessed sin in our lives. If we confess He is faithful and just to cleanse us (I John 1:9), but if we do not then God remembers them (Psalms 25:7) and we will answer for them.

Remember:

Confessed Sins
   1. They are blotted out (Isaiah 44:22, Acts 3:19).
   2. They are forgiven (Exodus 34:7, I John 1:9, 2:12).
   3. They are remitted (Matthew 26:28, Mark 1:4).
   4. They are made white as snow (Isaiah 1:18).
   5. They are made as wool (Isaiah 1:18).
   6. They are cast behind God's back (Isaiah 38:17).
   7. They are forgotten (Isaiah 43:25, Hebrews 8:12, 10:17).
   8. They are purged away (Psalms 79:9, Hebrews 1:3).
   9. They are covered (Psalms 32:1, Romans 4:7).
  10. They are put away (II Samuel 12:13, Hebrews 9:22).
  11. They are removed as far as the east is from the west (Psalms 103:12).
  12. They are cast into the depths of the sea (Micah 7:19).
  13. They are washed away (Revelation 1:5).

14. They are taken away (I John 3:5).

15. They are put off (Colossians 2:11).

16. One is saved from them (Matthew 1:21).

17. One is freed from them (Romans 6:7, 16-23, 8:2).

18. One is cleansed from them (I John 1:7, 9).

19. One becomes dead to them (Colossians 2:13, I Peter 2:24).

20. One is quickened from death in them (Ephesians 2:1-10, Colossians 2:13).

Unconfessed Sins

1. They cause death (Genesis 2:17, Ezekiel 33:8-13, Romans 8:12-13).

2. They hinder prayers (Psalms 66:18).

3. They provoke God to anger (I Kings 16:2).

4. They weary God (Isaiah 43:24).

5. They separate us from God (Isaiah 59:2).

6. They testify against us (Isaiah 59:12, Jeremiah 14:7).

7. They cause God to remember them (Psalms 25:7).

8. They expose guilt (Psalms 69:5).

9. They cause God to visit (Hosea 8:13, 9:9).

10. They load us down (II Timothy 3:6, Hebrews 12:1).

11. They cause us to pine away (Ezekiel 33:10, Leviticus 26:39).

12. They cause us to be consumed (Isaiah 64:7, Ezekiel 4:17).

13. They take men away (Isaiah 64:6).

14. They bring punishment (Amos 3:2).

15. They damn the soul (II Thessalonians 2:12).

16. They cause one to be of Satan (I John 3:8).

17. They cause hardening of heart (Hebrews 3:13).

18. They make servants of sin (Romans 6:7-23, John 8:34).

19. They bring reproach (Proverbs 14:34).

20. They cause national judgment (Amos 1:3, 6, 9, 11, 13, 2:1, 4, 6).

21. They cause disease (Deuteronomy 28, Psalms103:3, Mark 2:9, James 5:16).

22. They cause many troubles and calamities in life (Job, Deuteronomy 28, Proverbs 1:27-31).

When I stand before Jesus they only words I want to hear are well done good and faithful servant. For this to happen I must take responsibility for my life and my choices. When we refuse to accept personal responsibility, we blur the distinction between merit and responsibility, which makes us incapable of accepting the obvious meaning of many verses of Scripture which plainly state that a Christian will reap what he sows and that we can be cut off from God eternally.

Antinomian ministers imply in many ways that Christians can live any way they please and still remain saved because we are saved by unmerited favor (grace), not by how we live. They teach that our salvation is entirely up to God, we have no choice in the matter, and therefore it is also up to Him to keep us saved, no matter what we do. When Christians take this doctrine to its logical conclusion, they live the way they please. When they end up falling away from the faith because of how they are living, these same ministers turn around and claim that they were never really saved in the first place, that's why they fell away. "They only thought they were saved; they only appeared to be saved. Real Christians don't fall away. They persevere until the end."

What they are really preaching is that we can be Christians and lie, cheat, steal, backbite and live just like the world, yet still be saved because we are saved by unmerited favor (Grace alone). We can be Christians and make idols out of our jobs, our families, or our hobbies and pleasures, yet still be saved because we are saved by unmerited favor (Grace alone), not by how we live. There is only one thing we can't do if we are Christians. We can't "fall away" from the faith. If we fall away from the faith, that proves that we were never really saved in the first place; real Christians don't fall away.

Real Christians, according to the antinomians, can drink, smoke, curse, lie, steal and live like the devil; but as long as they made a profession of faith they are "saved by grace." However, if a person should abandon the profession of faith, it just shows that they were never really saved in the first place. They or we just thought they were.

I Timothy 4:1

"Now the Spirit speaketh expressly, that in the latter times some shall depart from the faith, giving heed to seducing spirits doctrines of devils."

"Now the Spirit speaketh expressly, in the latter times some shall depart from the faith...." Why can't we believe this simple statement? The Spirit spoke expressly about these events. He did not just hint or insinuate that some shall depart from the faith in the latter days, He made it crystal clear: some of God's people shall depart from the faith in the last days. This simple truth needs to be repeated over and over again until Christians wake up and start living in the reality of what is happening all around them. We must accept the reality that it is possible for a person who once knew God to end up cut off from Him for all eternity.

I Timothy 6:20-21

"O Timothy, keep that which is committed to thy trust, avoiding profane and vain babbling, and oppositions of science falsely so called: Which some professing have erred concerning the faith. Grace be with thee. Amen."

Matthew 24:10-13

"And then shall many be offended and shall betray one another and shall hate one another. And many false prophets shall rise and shall deceive many. And because iniquity shall abound, the love of many shall wax cold. But he that shall endure unto the end, the same shall be saved."

II Thessalonians 2:3

"Let no man deceive you by any means: for that day shall not come, except there come a falling away first that man of sin be revealed, the son of perdition."

II Timothy 4:3-4

"For the time will come when they [Christians] will not endure sound doctrine; but after their own lusts shall they heap to themselves teachers, having itching ears; And they shall turn away their ears from the truth and shall be turned unto fables."

II Peter 2:1-2

"But there were false prophets also among the people, even as there shall be false teachers among you, who privily shall bring in damnable heresies, even denying the Lord that bought them and bring upon themselves swift destruction. And many shall follow their pernicious ways; by reason of whom the way of truth shall be evil spoken of."

II Peter 2:20-22

"For if after they have escaped the pollutions of the world through the knowledge of the Lord and Savior Jesus Christ, they are again entangled therein overcome, the latter end is worse with them than the beginning. For it had been better for them not to have known the way of righteousness, then, after they have known it, to turn from the holy commandment delivered unto them. But it is happened unto them according to the true proverb, The dog is turned to his own vomit again; and the sow that was washed to her wallowing in the mire."

These are just a few of the many Scriptures that teach we can depart from the faith. Not only does the Word say we can depart from the faith, it predicts that in the latter days some of us will depart from it. It tells us that some will depart from the faith because of deception, while others will wander from the faith through an ungodly quest for religious knowledge. Some will be offended because of persecution and others will have their love for God wax cold because of the abundance of iniquity around them. Some will turn from the truth to fables and heap to themselves ministers who are willing to feed them what they want, while others will be tricked into following false prophets.

Peter was very blunt. He said it is possible to have known the way of righteousness and escaped the pollution of the world by the knowledge of the Lord Jesus Christ, yet turn back to our vomit (sin) like a dog and our mire (the world) like a pig. He says if we do so and are overcome in that state, our latter end will be worse than the beginning. In other words, it would be better to have never known God, than to have known Him and turned away from Him. If you die in that state, your eternal destiny will be worse than the guy who was never saved to begin with! Sobering words!

Can non-Christians really depart from the faith? Can unbelievers really wander from the faith? Can sinners really be carried away from the faith? Such a view is not logical. How can you depart from something you were never really part of in the first place? Can you depart from a house you were never in? Can you wander off a path you were never on? Can you fall from a position you were never in? Can you be carried away from a hope you never had?

It is not possible for a "fake" Christian to depart from a genuine faith! There is no such thing as a "fake Christian." Either he is a Christian or he isn't. To say that those who depart from the faith were never in the faith is a just as foolish as saying that we can live any way we please after we are saved because we are kept by grace. Today's theology is producing a whole generation of believers whose view of redemption is illogical, unscriptural and extremely dangerous. It is also producing generations of "Christians" who are no different than the unbeliever. Divorce, pornography, molestation, alcohol and drug addictions etc. are no different for the "Christian" and the unbeliever. The fruit of the other gospel is evident.

When dispensationalists say that they were never really saved if there is no fruit, or change in life, are they not really adding in the conditions at the back door? Why not be intellectually honest up front?

Dispensationalists often quote John 10:28 to prove "once saved, always saved."
John 10:28
"And I give unto them eternal life; and they shall never perish, neither shall any man pluck them out of my hand."
Let's put this verse in context by quoting the verses before and after.
John 10:26-29
"But ye believe not, because ye are not of my sheep, as I said unto you. My sheep hear my voice, and I know them, and they follow me: And I give unto them eternal life; and they shall never perish, neither shall any man pluck them out of my hand. My Father, which gave them me, is greater than all; and no man is able to pluck them out of my Father's hand."

These verses actually teach that we must do and continue in three things to receive eternal life: 1) Believe, which implies complete and continued obedience; 2) Hear His voice, and be not hearers only, but also doers of His Word (John 10:27, James 1:22-27, 2:9-26); and 3) Follow Christ, not only at the beginning of a Christian experience, but daily and throughout life (John 10:27, Luke 9:23).

A study of the word "pluck" is also interesting. It means to seize, to catch away or up, to pluck, to pull, or to take by force. No man or anything else can take us away from Jesus by force. But we, in our free will, can take ourselves away.

God cannot keep anyone contrary to his will, any more than He kept Lucifer (Isaiah 14:12-14, I Timothy 3:6), angels (II Peter 2:4, Jude 1:6-7), demons (Matthew 8:29), Adam and Eve (Genesis 3, Romans 5:12-21), and all of the rest of us who choose to disobey.

## IMPUTED RIGHTEOUSNESS AND IMPUTED SIN

Psalms 32:2

"Blessed is the man unto whom the Lord imputeth not iniquity, and in whose spirit there is no guile."

We must understand that God imputes righteousness as well as sin. As we have discussed before, this is a very misunderstood precept of Christianity. The following is quoted from the *Dake Study Bible* in the notes on Psalms 32:2:

> Imputation is that act of God in salvation whereby He accounts the believer righteous in Christ because Christ bore his sins and because he has properly repented of his sins and met God's terms of reconciliation (Romans 3:24-31; Romans 4:1-25; II Corinthians 5:14-21; Galatians 3:6-9, 13-14)."

As we have already studied this is also called Justification. Dake continues:

> Some people teach that God cannot impute sin to the believer; that his sins, past, present, and future, are forgiven once and forever without any confession, repentance, and turning from sin to a life of holiness; that God cannot see the sins of the saved that they are not real sins as are the same crimes if they are committed by sinners; that God sees only the penalty that was paid for the sins and He excuses the criminal and counts him as holy as if he had not committed sin; that it is no part of the work of God to improve human nature; that men can be as filthy as a barnyard and as sinful as Lucifer and still be saved; and that whatever sins a saved man commits are never held against him, but they are imputed to Christ without any obligation on the part of the believer. These are some of the most blasphemous and slanderous statements about God and the gospel that could be made.

Dake uses very strong language to describe a very common doctrine in today's church. Then he proceeds to defend his position:

> Redemption Fallacies Refuted:
>
> 1. God cannot and does not impute sins of believers to their account.
>
> The fact is that God cannot do otherwise if believers go back into sin again. Sin has to be imputed where there is a law broken (Romans 5:13; Romans 6:23; Romans 8:12-13).
>
> 2. Christ bore the sins of the saved and they cannot be charged to Him more than once. Even in civil courts a crime cannot be charged to a man twice.
>
> This is only partially true, as it deals with sins that have been forgiven. [But] if the same man commits the same sins again any civil court will charge him with them again-as often as he commits them. So it is with the divine court. A man forgiven of past sins must stop sinning. If he commits the same sins

again… he will be charged with them again. They must be properly confessed and forgiven again or he will pay the death penalty for the new crimes (Ezekiel 18:4, 20-26; Romans 6:23; Romans 8:12-13; I Corinthians 6:9-11; Galatians 5:19-21; II Timothy 2:12).

3. All sins — past, present, and future — are forgiven once and forever.

Christ bore the sins of all men, but one cannot receive forgiveness until sin is confessed. Unconfessed sin cannot be forgiven (Luke 13:3, 5; I John 1:9). If men could not be damned for committing unconfessed sins which Christ has borne, then no man would be lost, for He bore the sins of all (Romans 5:8; Galatians 1:4; I Peter 2:24; I Peter 3:18; Hebrews 2:9). Redemption cannot become effective with anyone who refuses to repent and conform to the whole truth (Mark 16:15-16; Luke 13:3, 5; Acts 2:38; Acts 3:19; I John 1:7, 9). Authors Note: Jesus also teaches in Matthew 6:12, 14-15 that if we do not forgive others He will not forgive us.

4. God cannot and does not see the sins of believers. In fact, their sins are not real sins. All He sees is the blood of Christ that automatically covers sin. A person who is born again cannot commit sin.

These claims deny every principle of divine and human governments. No just government would permit such a program with criminals. No pardoned criminal is told that he will not be held responsible for committing the same crime again; that if he did it wouldn't really be a crime in his case; that it would be automatically forgiven; that the law would never again see any crime he committed; that it would only see the pardon he had received; and that the pardon stipulated absolute freedom from any future punishment, even for the worst of crimes. A government that operated this way would be considered intolerably unjust. Yet this is exactly the kind of government many in the church teach and believe in as divine government. God has repeatedly stated that He will punish every sin, even to every idle word (Matthew 12:37-39; Romans 2:12-16; II Corinthians 5:10; Revelation 20:11-15).

5. It dishonors the blood of Christ to teach that it covers only past sins or only the sins of the faithful. A believer does not have to continue to be faithful to be saved. Sin can never reign over a saved man again, regardless of what he does. He is saved even though he serves sin and Satan. Not one child of God can return to his former state of sin and be condemned. He cannot choose to be saved or lost. God chooses men to be saved and all such are secure in His choice. If a man could choose to be saved or lost then he would be more powerful than God. There is no human element in salvation. All men sin every day. The only difference between the saved and unsaved is that one has accepted Christ and the other has not. Sin is inseparable from one in this life.

In the believer sin is unchanged and unchangeable. Even the unsaved are not condemned for their sins, how much less is this true of the saved. God is able to keep one saved who may be sinning every day. If man's choice governs his destiny, then the sovereign grace of God is subject to the will of man and God Himself ceases to be sovereign.

There is not one Scripture to support these false claims. God does not lose sovereignty through His plan of redemption requiring men to meet His terms or be lost. Obedience to God according to the gospel is the basis of all justification and imputation of righteousness to man. God requires confession of sins (Luke 13:3, 5; I John 1:9), faith (John 3:16; Ephesians 2:8-9), and choice on man's part in conformity to the plan of redemption before He justifies a man (Mark 16:16; Romans 1:5, 16; Romans 3:24-31; Romans 5:1-11; Revelation 22:17). From God's standpoint, redemption is provided for all men and it is His will that all accept Christ and be saved (John 3:16; I Timothy 2:4; II Peter 3:9; Revelation 22:17); but no man will be forgiven who personally refuses to believe and conform to the gospel. When one does obey the gospel, then and then alone sins are forgiven. This is all imputation means in Psalms 32:2; Romans 4:3-13, 22-25; II Corinthians 5:19. No believer has to sin, but if he does it will be charged to him and he will pay the death penalty if he dies in sin (Exodus 32:32; Ezekiel 18:4, 20-26; Romans 6:16-23; Romans 8:12-13; I Corinthians 6:9-11; Galatians 5:19-21; Galatians 6:7-8; II Timothy 2:12; James 5:19-20).

I hope you understand that we have a vital role to play in our salvation and in our sanctification. Our unconfessed sins as well as our righteous acts are charged or imputed to us. Our actions speak louder than any of our words. Please understand that I am not teaching that we lose our salvation if we have any unconfessed sin. I do believe that we will answer for every unconfessed sin at the Judgment Seat of Christ. I do not want to have Him ask me about a sin in my life. I want to hear "Well done good and faithful servant." Thus I choose to repent and forgive and thus deal with each and every sin now. When I repent or forgive I am applying the blood of Jesus to the sin and it is cleansed. The Holy Spirit will reveal what you do not know or remember if you ask.

## THE FRUIT OF RIGHTEOUSNESS: BY THEIR FRUITS YOU SHALL KNOW THEM
Hebrews 12:11

"Now no chastening for the present seemeth to be joyous, but grievous: nevertheless afterward it yieldeth the peaceable fruit of righteousness unto them which are exercised [trained] thereby."

The chastening or discipline of the LORD is found in His laws of reaping and sowing. If we obey there are great blessings, but if we choose to disobey then there is a negative consequence that we bring upon ourselves (Deuteronomy 28). We must always remember that God loves us. He has made rules for us to follow because He loves us, just like we love our children. His rules show us the way to salvation, peace, prosperity, happiness and a fulfilling life. The "narrow gate" is a place of joy and fulfillment, not legalism or drudgery.

Galatians 5:22-23

"But the fruit of the Spirit is love, joy, peace, longsuffering, gentleness, goodness, faith, meekness, temperance: against such there is no law."

As we have seen there is a vast difference between imputed righteousness and actual righteousness. When we believe, God imputes or counts it as righteousness (Romans 4:22-24, James 2:23). The fruit or deeds of righteousness, however, must be displayed or manifested in an individual's life. Producing fruit is a process. It is the result of change. As long as an individual's character remains unchanged, his deeds will never change. Fruit is not what we believe. Fruit is what we do.

The Scripture talks very little about imputed righteousness. By far the emphasis is on actual righteous behavior and godly living. We have reversed the emphasis in our day, so that most preaching remains centered on imputed righteousness or justification. Godly lifestyles are encouraged, but they are not presented as being absolutely necessary to obtain eternal life.

The attitude is that we should live a holy life, but if we cannot (or will not) live such a life, it's not that big a deal because "grace" will pick up the slack. God's goal is to have His righteousness manifested through how we live, and by what we do. It is a drastic mistake to make imputed righteousness, which is an invisible legal state, the focus of salvation. The purpose of the New Covenant has always been to bring God's own righteous character forth in the earth, through the lives of His people.

Is true salvation only a fire insurance policy designed to keep us out of hell? Or is true salvation a close, personal relationship with our LORD and Savior? Only our disobedience separates us from true fellowship with God. Our obedience results in receiving His blessing.

Isaiah 62:1-2

"For Zion's sake I will not hold my peace and for Jerusalem's sake I will not rest, until the righteousness thereof go forth as brightness and the salvation thereof as a lamp that burneth. And the Gentiles shall see thy righteousness and all the kings thy glory: and thou shalt be called by a new name which the mouth of the Lord shall name."

Isaiah 61:11

"For as the earth bringeth forth her bud, and as the garden causeth the things that are sown in it to spring forth; so the Lord God will cause righteousness and praise to spring forth before all the nations."

Why is God looking for actual, tangible, visible righteousness? First of all, it brings Him glory because visible righteousness displays His Kingdom on earth as it is in heaven: "Let your light [conduct] so shine before men that they will see your good works and glorify your Father which is in heaven" (Matthew 5:16). Second, because the fruit (manifestation) of righteousness destroys the kingdom of Satan. Imputed righteousness is invisible; no one can see it! Only manifested righteousness can destroy the works of darkness. The "Works and Ministry of Jesus" are very necessary for today.

Proverbs 4:18

"But the path [way, or conduct] of the just is as a shining light, that shineth more and more unto the perfect day."

Isaiah 60:21

"Thy people also shall be all righteous: they shall inherit the land for ever, the branch of my planting, the work of my hands, that I may be glorified."

Isaiah 61:3

"To appoint unto them that mourn in Zion, to give unto them beauty for ashes, the oil of joy for mourning, the garment of praise for the spirit of heaviness; that they might be called trees of righteousness, the planting of the LORD, that he might be glorified."

Philippians 1:9-11

"And this I pray, that your love may abound yet more and more in knowledge and in all judgment; That ye may approve things that are excellent; that ye may be sincere and without offence till the day of Christ; Being filled with the fruits of righteousness, which are by Jesus Christ, unto the glory and praise of God."

The Spirit of God is creating trees (people) of righteousness that will produce fruits (deeds) of righteousness. The fruit of righteousness must be manifested and displayed in our lives. It does not come automatically. To bring forth His righteousness we must choose to be obedient to His precepts. But unfortunately most of us choose to disobey.

Then in His love for us He turns us over to our own devices in a process that involves chastening and discipline, sometimes even severe discipline (Proverbs 1:29-31). In other words, because He loves us He disciplines us. His discipline is giving us what we asked for in our disobedience. In suffering the consequences for our choices the Holy Spirit convicts us of our sin. God wants and requires His people to possess and manifest His character before the nations. Many times it requires the chastening and correction of the Spirit of God to produce that fruit.

The Scripture says the Kingdom of God is visible acts of righteousness, such as peace and joy in the Holy Ghost (Romans 14:17), healing the sick and casting out demons (Luke 10, 11:20). (See Part Five, Advancing the Kingdom of God.) Scripture says that we must seek first that kingdom and that righteousness (Matthew 6:33). Finally, it says that we only enter that kingdom and righteousness through much tribulation (Acts 14:22). This means actual righteousness is not an invisible legal state. Rather, it is a possession that must be acquired. It is acquired through a lot of hard work and persistence to make the right choices. Unfortunately most of us learn in the school of hard knocks.

Hebrew 5:14 teaches us that discernment comes through the use of our senses, which implies much hard work. We must learn to discipline ourselves. Remember His discipline is evidence of His love. He disciplines us by turning us over to our own devices, our own choices, when we disregard His precepts (Proverbs 1:27-31).

It takes personal discipline, and because we are stubborn, usually tribulation and chastening to convert or change us from self-centered creatures to God-centered creatures. It takes chastening to get self off the throne and let Jesus take control of our lives, our desires and our goals. God is looking for actual righteous behavior and that behavior can never be imputed, either now or later in heaven.

God is bringing forth righteousness in the earth and Satan is trying to destroy righteousness in the earth. Wickedness and unrighteousness perpetuate Satan's kingdom on this planet, but righteousness and holiness destroy that kingdom. Since the Church is the "light" of the world and the only real threat to Satan's kingdom, he has focused his attack on the body of Christ by trying to destroy righteousness within the Church. If he can get God's people to be comfortable with sin, if he can get their focus off of being transformed into godly people, then he has succeeded in putting out the light.

Christians live in absolute confusion regarding the difference between our position in Christ and possessing that position. We do not automatically experience what God has given us through Christ. We experience the vitality of the Christian life as a result of personal interaction with the Spirit and taking personal responsibility to choose to be obedient and sanctify ourselves to God.

Obedience is the key to gaining and possessing what God really has for us. Satan cannot touch the finished work of the Cross. It defeated him. His days are numbered and he knows it. Neither can he touch our position in Christ, for this was accomplished for us by the atonement. The only area Satan has room in which to maneuver is the gap between our position in Christ and the actual possession of that position. This gap is not closed by believing and receiving, or by a positive confession, or by knowing orthodox doctrine. It is closed by one thing alone: obedience. That is why the issue of obedience can never be over-stressed. We must be doers of God's Word (James 1:23, 25).

Romans 2:13

"For not the hearers of the law are just before God, but the doers of the law shall be justified."

Since obedience is the key, Satan's plan has always been to somehow get God's people to disobey Him. Disobedience prevents us from experiencing what is legally ours.

Under the New Covenant we can experience what is legally ours. The New Covenant introduced two new elements of redemption: the new birth experience (born again) and the sanctification of the Holy Spirit. Because we now have His nature in us through the Holy Spirit living in us, we can have power over the sin nature. Satan's goal is to stop us from appropriating or walking in, and manifesting the nature of God through disobedience.

The two theological avenues he uses to accomplish this are legalism and antinomianism. Those who are caught up in legalism cannot possess their position in Christ because they are too busy trying to establish their own righteousness (Romans 10:3).

Those who are caught up in antinomianism cannot possess their position because they think obedience to God is not really necessary. They will not discipline themselves or submit to the precepts of God's Word and then accept personal responsibility for their actions. Instead they choose to blame God for the calamities of life, as Adam and Job did.

They oppose the restraints of the Holy Spirit, restraints that are absolutely necessary in order to bring forth the fruit of righteousness, but which they regard as "legalism." If we really believe that God is love and that He always has our best interest at heart why do we choose to call obedience "legalism" or salvation by works?

Jesus said the church of Laodicea said in their heart, "I am rich and increased with goods and have need of nothing" (Revelation 3:14-22). This description will never fit non-Christian groups like Christian Science, Mormons, and Jehovah's Witnesses. Neither could it be applied to the Eastern Religions and the New Age Movement.

It is Bible-believing Christians who are preaching false security. It is we who think we have it all "by grace." It is we who have rejected the need to submit to the restraints and chastisements of God. God chastises through His laws of sowing and reaping. It is we who have put absolute obedience to God at the bottom of our list of priorities.

The deception that obedience is not required is producing the Laodicean Church of today. We have perverted Paul's doctrine of grace. We should stop and check the condition of our faith. Is it a living faith? Is it producing righteous conduct and obedience to Christ?

Haggai 1:3-5

"Then came the word of the LORD by Haggai the prophet, saying, Is it time for you, O ye, to dwell in your cieled houses, and this house lie waste? Now therefore thus saith the LORD of hosts; consider your ways."

Just as Jesus, the LORD of Hosts said through Haggai to His people thousands of years ago, He is saying the same thing today. We have nice homes with roofs and ceilings but His house lies in waste. Today we are the temple of the Lord and His temple is in waste because of our disobedience to Him (I Corinthians 3:16).

Christians need a better understanding of what being "saved by grace" means. Grace is the greatest transforming power in the universe. But that very power, which should be changing us into God's image, is being presented as the means by which we can avoid that transformation now, yet reap the fruit of transformation in the future. It is being presented as a magical legal process that will make it possible to sow sin today and reap eternal life tomorrow.

We are taught that grace is a legal position that provides us with a continual, unconditional pardon from sin, which cannot be affected by how we live. Such a concept goes directly against Scripture and produces careless, sinning Christians, whose lives are filled with the consequences of the sin, disease, divorce, bankruptcy, anger, bitterness, fear, drugs, addictions, perversions, etc. The proof of this statement is found in the fact that disease, divorce, bankruptcy, anger, bitterness, fear, drugs, addictions, pornography, perversions, etc. etc. are just as rampant in Christians as in non-Christians.

God's grace can do much more than justify and reconcile us to God. This is just the beginning! It also gives boldness (Romans 15:15), imparts riches (Ephesians 2:7), gives power (II Corinthians 12:9), gives endurance (I Corinthians 15:10), gives strength (II Timothy 2:1), teaches us how to live in a godly way (Titus 2:11-12), inspires singing (Colossians 3:16), gives the ability to preach (Ephesians 3:8), gives seasoning to speech (Colossians 4:6) and overpowers sin (Romans 5:20; 6:12-13).

Furthermore, any person may receive God's grace in vain (II Corinthians 6:1), frustrate it in his own life (Galatians 2:21), fall from it (II Peter 3:17), fail of it (Hebrews 12:15), turn it into sin (Jude 1:4), continue or discontinue in it (Acts 13:43), minister it to others (I Peter 4:10) or choose to grow or not grow in it (II Peter 3:18). Once again God has given us a choice.

The current concept of grace as an unconditional, continual pardon of the believer assumes that the change from unrighteous to actual righteous behavior will take place in heaven, after we die. Thus, in reality we have placed our faith in the grave instead of the delivering power of Jesus Christ.

This emphasis on a future transformation in heaven encourages a person to absorb himself in the pleasures and duties of this life. He feels no sense of urgency to focus on the daily transforming work of the Spirit. His focus ends up on his career, family, social status, recreation and a long retirement. Holiness and doing the Ministry of Jesus become a low priority in his life, and Satan has succeeded in putting out his light, regardless of how much he may still talk about God! This is the exact opposite of the message that Jesus taught. He taught that His kingdom was a current event as well as future. (See Part Five, Advancing the Kingdom of God.)

The legal position God has provided for us is imputed righteousness and justification, neither of which are unconditional. Scripture says *if* we walk in the light, then the blood of Jesus continues to cleanse us from all (unknown) sin. It says *if* we confess our (known) sins, then Jesus is faithful to forgive those sins and cleanse us from all unrighteousness (I John 1:7-9). What if we do not confess and turn from known sin? What happens if we refuse to obey or walk in the light God has given us? Will grace save us anyway? Salvation is conditional. The New Covenant contains many conditions. We read them, yet we simply refuse to believe that they mean what they say!

Matthew 7:19

"Every tree [person] that bringeth not forth good fruit [of righteousness] is hewn down cast into the fire.... Not everyone that saith unto me, Lord, Lord, shall enter into the kingdom of heaven; but [only] he that doeth the will of my Father which is in heaven."

Matthew 5:13

"Ye [the saints] are the salt of the earth: but if the salt have lost his savour, wherewith shall it be salted? It is thenceforth good for nothing, but to be cast out to be trodden under foot of men."

Matthew 10:22

"And ye shall be hated of all men for my name's sake: but he that endureth to the end shall be saved."

Romans 8:16-17

"The Spirit itself beareth witness with our spirit, that we are the children of God: And if children, then heirs; heirs of God and joint-heirs with Christ; if so be that we suffer with him, that we may be also glorified together."

I Corinthians 15:1-2

"Moreover, brethren, I declare unto you the gospel which I preached unto you, which also ye have received and wherein ye [currently] stand; By which also ye are saved, if ye keep in memory [hold fast] what I preached unto you, unless ye have believed in vain."

Ephesians 5:3-6

"But fornication and all uncleanness, or covetousness, let it not be once named among you, as becometh saints; Neither filthiness, nor foolish talking, nor jesting, which are not convenient [not fitting]: but rather giving of thanks. For this ye know, that no whoremonger, nor unclean person, nor covetous man, who is an idolater, hath any inheritance in the kingdom of Christ and of God. Let no man deceive you with vain words: for because of these things cometh the wrath of God upon the children of disobedience."

Colossians 1:21-23

"And you, that were sometime alienated and enemies in your mind by wicked works, yet now hath he reconciled in the body of his flesh through death, to present you holy and unblameable and unreproveable in his sight: If ye continue in the faith grounded and settled and be not moved away from the hope of the gospel, which ye have heard and which was preached to every creature which is under heaven; whereof I Paul am made a minister."

Galatians 6:9

"And let us not be weary in well doing: for in due season we shall reap, if we faint not."

Hebrews 3:6, 14

"But Christ as a son over his own house; whose house are we, if we hold fast the confidence and the rejoicing of the hope firm unto the end… For we are made partakers of Christ, if we hold the beginning of our confidence stedfast unto the end."

Are all these conditions meaningless? Will everything turn out fine in heaven if we faint now, if we do not suffer with Jesus today, if we bring forth bad fruit or no fruit? Can we commit adultery, lie, cheat, covet, live in fear, etc. and still inherit the Kingdom of God? Will we be rewarded if we do not do the will of the Father? What if we do not endure to the end? These verses should instill a godly fear in us and motivate us to bring forth godly behavior.

Are we being taught the traditions of men and the doctrines of devils instead of Scripture? God is looking for visible righteousness. This has been His plan from the very beginning and it continues to be His plan.

The question is: Are you a doer of the Word or just a hearer? Are there fruits of His Righteousness in your life?

# THE NEW COVENANT

Hebrews 7:11

"If therefore perfection were by the Levitical priesthood (under it the people received the law), what further need was there that another priest should rise after the order of Melchisedec, and not be called after the order of Aaron?"

Hebrews 8:6

"But now hath he obtained a more excellent ministry, by how much also he is the mediator of a better covenant, which was established upon better promises."

Hebrews 6:1-2

"Therefore leaving the principles of the doctrine of Christ, let us go on unto perfection; not laying again the foundation of repentance from dead works, and of faith toward God, Of the doctrine of baptisms, and of laying on of hands, and of resurrection of the dead, and of eternal judgment."

The New Covenant is often preached about, yet the least understood. It seems that few really grasp its astounding message. In Hebrews, Paul said the New Covenant is better than the Old Covenant because it is based on better promises. Darby, Scofield, Chafer and other dispensational teachers have taught that what made the New Covenant "better" is that it is unconditional.

This is not what Paul was saying or implying. What he was saying is that the New Covenant is better because it is able to bring to perfection or completion God's goal for

His people. If perfection could have been attained under the Old Covenant, there would have been no reason to establish another (better) covenant. What kind of perfection is Paul referring to?

It is very important to keep in mind that forgiveness, justification and imputed righteousness have been available to God's people in every age. The reason this is important is because the New Covenant, the covenant of "grace," is being presented as a covenant of forgiveness, justification and imputed righteousness. But these provisions have always been available to God's people by faith! There is nothing "new" about forgiveness, justification and imputed righteousness. They have been available since the day Adam and Eve sinned in the Garden.

If The New Covenant were simply a covenant of forgiveness, justification and imputed righteousness and if it is also true that what makes it new is that these provisions are now "unconditional," then faith is no longer necessary for salvation. We know that faith has always been the condition upon which justification has been based. So the dispensational teaching becomes illogical. What's new about the New Covenant is that it provides power over sin. It provides deliverance from sin.

The New Covenant introduced two new elements of redemption: the new birth experience (born again) and the sanctification of the Holy Spirit. It is through both of these that we have power over the sin nature.

Under the Old Covenant, God could only forgive sin. He could not impart the power to conquer sin. Why? Because sin goes deeper than just wrong deeds. We are all born with a sinful nature, a nature that has been contaminated with rebellion and disobedience, and a nature that is disposed toward unrighteousness. We are all born with a nature that is drawn to sin.

God has been forgiving man's actions since Adam and Eve. He has been justifying us and imputing His righteousness to our account since the original fall and He could just as easily continue to do so for all eternity.

As thankful as we are for His justification and imputed righteousness, we need more. We need a cure for our disease! Forgiveness, justification and imputed righteousness are not the cure because they do not provide actual deliverance from the power of sin. They only provide deliverance from the penalty of sin. This is why a new covenant had to be established, one that would enable us to overcome all sin (Revelation 2-3).

What mankind needs is a remedy for what causes him to sin in the first place. We need to go to the root of the problem. As long as a person possesses only the old nature that he was born with, regardless of how good or bad a person he might be, he will never be delivered from the power of sin. The purpose of the New Covenant is to deliver us from the fallen nature that causes us to disobey and sin in the first place Romans 7:17, 20).

The New Covenant provides the only antidote for our sickness. That cure is the new birth (John 3:3-6). The born-again experience is actually the regeneration or re-creation of our spirit, which was dead in sin. We are re-born to God and it is His nature within us. In our free will we must learn to yield to our new nature (God) and abide in Him one hundred percent of the time.

Galatians 6:14-15

"But God forbid that I should glory, save in the cross of our Lord Jesus Christ, by whom the world is crucified unto me and I unto the world. For in Christ Jesus neither circumcision [Jew] availeth any thing, nor uncircumcision [Gentile], but a new creature [born again]."

II Corinthians 5:17

"Therefore if any man be in Christ, he is a new creature: old things are passed away; behold, all things are become new."

Ephesians 4:22-24

"That ye put off concerning the former conversation the old man, which is corrupt according to the deceitful lusts; And be renewed in the spirit of your mind; And that ye put on the new man, which after God is created in righteousness and true holiness."

Colossians 3:9-10

"Lie not one to another, seeing that ye have put off the old man with his deeds; And have put on the new man, which is renewed in knowledge after the image of him that created him."

## ABIDING IN CHRIST

Grace (the New Covenant) gives us another nature planted within our regenerated spirit. This is why Paul said we are not free to continue in sin as a result of being under grace (Romans 6:6, 14-15). Grace is not a legal position of unconditional, continual pardon of evil deeds based upon our profession of faith. It is the receiving of a new and holy nature. It has to do with the new man, not the old man.

If we have received a new nature, which cannot sin, why do Christians continue to sin? Because we have not learned to yield to the new nature that has been born in us. The Holy Spirit is our conscience and leads us to learn how to abide in Christ. As we learn to abide we stop sinning.

Romans 6:12-14, 16

"Let not sin therefore reign in your mortal body, that ye should obey it in the lusts thereof. Neither yield ye your members as instruments of unrighteousness unto sin: but yield yourselves unto God, as those that are alive from the dead your members as instruments of righteousness unto God. For sin shall not have dominion over you: for ye are not under the law, but under grace.... Know ye not, that to whom ye yield yourselves servants to obey, his servants ye are to whom ye obey; whether of sin unto death, or of obedience unto righteousness?"

I John 3:6, 9

"Whosoever abideth in him sinneth not: whosoever sinneth hath not seen him, neither known him.... Whosoever is born of God doth not commit sin; for his seed remaineth in him: and he cannot sin, because he is born of God."

Galatians 5:16

"This I say then, Walk in the Spirit and ye shall not fulfill the lust of the flesh."

Once we are born again, we have a choice as to what or who we yield to. We can yield to sin (Satan) or we can yield to righteousness (God). We no longer have to be a slave to the weaknesses of our old man. We no longer have to live in the flesh. We can learn to walk in the Spirit, thus overcoming the power of sin.

It is very important that we understand this truth for we are constantly being told that we still do not have a choice. The standard cliché is, "as long as we are human we will sin." What they are saying by this is that, until we die and go to heaven, sin will continue to have dominion over us. Others teach that it is all up to God to call us, save us and keep us saved. Therefore, they are putting all the responsibility and blame on God. Once again, our theology totally contradicts the Word of God!

Romans 8:2

"For the law of the Spirit of life in Christ Jesus hath made me free from the law of sin and death."

John 8:34, 36

"Jesus answered them, Verily, verily, I say unto you, Whosoever committeth sin is the servant of sin.... If the Son therefore shall make you free, ye shall be free indeed."

Romans 6:17-18

"But God be thanked, that ye were the servants of sin, but ye have obeyed from the heart that form of doctrine which was delivered you. Being then made free from sin, ye became the servants of righteousness."

Galatians 5:1

"Stand fast therefore in the liberty wherewith Christ hath made us free and be not entangled again with the yoke of bondage."

Christians have been made free from the law of sin and death. We no longer have to sin! We no longer have to be a slave to the flesh or Adam's weaknesses. God has made a way of escape. He has given us the cure. Scripture clearly states this truth.

Why not test this in your own life. Have you ever had victory over one sin? If you have had one victory, why not two? Why not three? Why not all of them? If we have ever had victory over one sin, we can have victory over them all.

God has made a way for us to overcome and be free from sin, but it doesn't happen automatically. It must be experienced. Moreover, it is not easy. Possible, yes; easy, no! Why? Because we have an enemy who hates us and wants to destroy us. What makes Satan so dangerous is that he knows exactly how to manipulate and intensify the sinful desires of our old nature. He knows our every weakness, and he knows exactly how to use those weaknesses to destroy us.

Until we have learned to walk in the Spirit all the time, we must deal with our adversary. Until we have learned how to abide in Christ day and night, how to yield to the Holy Spirit one hundred percent of the time, we still have to deal with an enemy who is even more determined to destroy us since we have been snatched out of his kingdom. This is why the Scripture talks about "warfare" and "armor" and "soldiers."

Ephesians 6:11-12

"Put on the whole armour of God, that ye may be able to stand against the wiles of the devil. For we wrestle not against flesh and blood, but against principalities, against powers, against the rulers of the darkness of this world, against spiritual wickedness in high places."

I Timothy 6:12

"Fight the good fight of faith, lay hold on eternal life, whereunto thou art also called and hast professed a good profession before many witnesses."

II Timothy 2:3

"Thou therefore endure hardness, as a good soldier of Jesus Christ."

James 4:7

"Submit yourselves therefore to God. Resist the devil he will flee from you."

I Peter 5:8-9

"Be sober, be vigilant; because your adversary the devil, as a roaring lion, walketh about, seeking whom he may devour: Whom resist stedfast in the faith, knowing that the same afflictions are accomplished in your brethren that are in the world."

Many Christians are being taught that Satan can't hurt them, that being "under the blood" automatically shields them from all spiritual harm. Usually the subject of the devil is simply ignored. If someone does have the audacity to teach demonology they are condemned for giving glory to the devil. We are commanded not to be ignorant of the wiles of the devil. We must know our enemy.

The Bible teaches that Christianity is a "race" and a "war." It is not the means to a happy life, in the flesh, here on earth. We are in a contest and there is a prize to be won (Philippians 3:14). We are in a battle against a very capable and dangerous enemy who is trying to stop us from attaining that prize!

How can we win a race if we don't realize we must run? How can we win a war if we don't even know we must fight? How can we win if we do not know our adversary?

## WHAT IS SALVATION?

The New Covenant is a covenant of transformation. This change is not a by-product of being saved; it is salvation! The New Testament definition of salvation is not forgiveness of sin alone, but forgiveness and deliverance from sin. Not just deliverance from the penalty of sin, but deliverance from the power of sin. This deliverance is not a doctrine but a process. It requires the full cooperation of the believer. We must become a New Creation legally (justification/imputed righteousness) and in our experience (sanctification/actual righteousness).

God's people are not being taught that the goal of the New Covenant (the gospel of grace) is to present every believer "perfect" to the Lord Jesus at His appearing. The Lord has a goal concerning us. That goal is that we be sanctified, purified and cleansed, that we be fully conformed to His image, that we be holy, without blemish, having no spot or wrinkle, that we become vessels of honor fit for His service.

We are being taught that we cannot be holy as He is, until we die and go to heaven. If this is true, where is our faith and hope? If we cannot do what Scripture teaches us to do, what becomes of our faith? Our faith transfers from a Jesus with the power to change and transform us to faith in the grave. Our only victory is to die.

"I wish I could die and get it over with." "I wish Jesus would come and take the pain and suffering." "I am going to kill myself and be with Jesus." "I am tired of this life, I wish Jesus would come and take me home." These are clichés that I often hear. These statements show our inclination to escape from our responsibilities in this life. The fatalist approach is no different than Hinduism and Karma. Jesus never taught us to escape, run or give up. He said "be strong, for I am with you." True Christianity is victory in Jesus today. (See Part Five, Advancing the Kingdom of God.)

Physical death (not Christ in us) is really our hope of glory according to this theology. Have we bought into a lie? Have we been deceived? Has our hope been transferred to the grave?

Colossians 1:27-28

"To whom God would make known what is the riches of the glory of this mystery among the Gentiles; which is Christ in you, the hope of glory: Whom we preach, warning every man, and teaching every man and in all wisdom; that we may present every man perfect in Christ Jesus."

II Corinthians 3:18

"But we all, with open face beholding as in a glass the glory of the Lord, are changed into the same image from glory to glory, even as by the Spirit of the Lord."

Romans 8:29

"For whom he did foreknow, he also did predestinate to be conformed [changed] to the image of his Son, that he might be the firstborn among many brethren."

Ephesians 5:26-27

"That he [Jesus] might sanctify and cleanse it [the church] with the washing of water by the word, That he might present it to himself a glorious church, not having spot, or wrinkle, or any such thing; but that it should be holy without blemish."

If you can grasp the truth that it is possible to be without "spot, or wrinkle, or any such thing," then a whole new mindset, a new paradigm, comes alive. The verses that teach that all things are possible to those that believe come alive. A supernatural hope and joy comes alive. An excitement about the future floods over you. The anointing of God falls fresh and is new and exciting.

We started this book by teaching about unbelief. Only unbelief prevents God from doing His work. I believe that one of the greatest lies of the devil is that we cannot be holy as He is holy. Believing this lie of the devil quenches the Spirit of God faster than anything else does.

Many preachers lament the fact that there is a widespread lack of purity and holiness within their congregations. Is it any wonder? We are not presenting them with the correct hope. We are not giving them a goal to strive for! We do not have to sin!

What separates us from God? What separates us from His love? What separates us from His presence? What steals our peace and joy? It is disobedience and unbelief! If you want to personally experience the truth of all of God's promises, obey Him. Root out all disobedience. Hate the things that God hates. Love the things that God loves.

I John 3:5, 8

"And ye know that he [Jesus] was manifested to take away our sins and in him is no sin.... He that committeth sin is of the devil; for the devil sinneth from the beginning. For this purpose the Son of God was manifest, that he might destroy the works of the devil."

## ETERNAL LIFE

We must understand that we are eternal beings right now, today. We are in our eternity now. Our spirits and souls will live forever. Eternal life is not a concept of the future; it is now and today. The question is not whether you are going to live forever, but where; with God or with Satan? Scripture tells us to choose this day whom you will serve. Eternal life is not some ethereal future paradise. Eternal life is today.

When we allowed Jesus into our lives as our Lord and Savior we accepted the promise of eternal life with Him. We had a choice to accept or reject Him. We also have a choice in what we do with this relationship. We can remain as babes, drift away, not endure, faint, depart or we can choose to develop and grow into the fullness of this relationship with God. The choice is ours. It is God's desire that you choose to love Him as much as He loves you. We will reap what we sow, death or life, abundant relationship with the Father or no relationship.

Jesus came to restore the things Satan stole from us. He came to repair our broken relationship with God the Father. He came to restore us back to God's image. He came to return eternal spiritual and physical life to us. In the beginning we had both. God is giving us the opportunity to reclaim it.

# CONCLUSION

Has this study challenged your thinking? Have you found areas of unbelief in your life? If so I would suggest that you deal with it. The following is a prayer that I have prayed and helped others through many times:

> *Dear Heavenly Father, I repent for the sin of unbelief in my life and in my generations. I repent for every way that I have placed limits on you; I repent for not believing your Word and not sanctifying myself. I repent for not being a doer of your Word; I repent for being caught up in the cares of this world and not putting you first; I repent for being lukewarm toward you; I repent for the false doctrines that I have believed; I repent for believing that you do not heal and that the gifts of the Holy Spirit have ceased; I repent for these sins in my life, in my church, in my schools, in my family and in my generations. Help mine unbelief!*

> *Lord, I forgive myself for the false doctrines that I have believed and those that I have taught others. I release myself from these false beliefs and forgive those taught me.*

> *In the name of Jesus, I cancel all of Satan's authority over me in this issue because God has forgiven me and I have forgiven myself.*

> *Holy Spirit I ask that you impart into my life your gift of faith. Help me to believe and tell me your truth.*

(Listen to the Holy Spirit and see what He has to say to you.)

Please continue to read. Part Two explores the tip of the iceberg of what God has for us on this earth today! There are many testimonies of those who have personally experienced the truth and have been set free.

John 8:32

"And ye shall know the truth, and the truth shall make you free."

If you will become a doer of God's Word, you will personally experience His truth and it will make you free.

PART TWO

# The Works
# Of Christ Today

Mark 16:20
*And they went forth, and preached everywhere, the Lord working
with them, and confirming the word with signs following. Amen.*

## INTRODUCTION

In John chapter 10, Jesus said that if we could not believe Him for who He said He was, then believe on Me because of the works I have done, because I have done the works of The Father. In Mark 9, a father brings his lunatic son to Jesus begging Him to help. He said: "if you can do anything help my son." Jesus replied, "It is not if I can help, but it is whether you can believe. All things are possible if you can believe." Then the father repented in tears for his unbelief. He realized that it was his unbelief that had prevented his son from being healed. He then asked Jesus to help his unbelief. Jesus did so, and healed his son.

The miracle healing power of Jesus is still available today. He has not changed. Neither have the conditions for receiving changed. We must believe and we must obey. Even the demons believe and tremble, but they do not obey (James 2:19).

## THE WORKS OF CHRIST TODAY

I was raised in a church that did not believe that the works of Jesus, the miracles that He did in the gospels, and the miracles recorded in Acts that Jesus did through the early believers, are for today. I was taught in college, and by seminary professors, that the works of Jesus were necessary to substantiate the Scriptures, but now that we have the written Word, miracles are no longer needed and that is why they don't happen anymore or only happen very rarely. These same professors also taught that the gifts of the Holy Spirit recorded in I Corinthians 12 are not for today. Are these accurate statements?

I was also taught the doctrines that we discussed in Part One of this book. I thought they brought me hope and security. Instead they really gave me defeat and hopelessness... a hopelessness that I did not even understand. I was deceived, and I did not know it. I was consumed with sin, and I did not know it.

I became very ill and blamed God for the disease. I thought I was going to die, and in that struggle and crying out to God, I discovered the truth. We serve a risen LORD who has power over sin and Satan and He gave that power to each of us. If we will use that power, we do not have to remain defeated and hopeless. We do not have to cower in the corner afraid of the devil.

## PAUL'S THORN IN THE FLESH

Paul's thorn in the flesh is often given as an example of God choosing not to heal. Many teachers claim that Paul's thorn was an eye disease or another kind of physical ailment. In commenting on II Corinthians 12:11, Dr. Scofield says, "It has been conjectured that Paul's thorn in the flesh was chronic ophthalmia, inducing bodily weakness, and a repulsive appearance."

Commenting on Paul's thorn the Jamieson, Fauset and Brown Commentary says, "Alford thinks it to be the same bodily affliction as in Galatians 4:13-14. It certainly was something personal, affecting him individually, and not as an apostle: causing at once acute pain (as "thorn" implies) and shame ("buffet" as slaves are buffeted)."

Many theologians present these arguments in the attempt to justify their position that God does not heal today as He did in the early church, that the gifts of the Holy Spirit are passed away, or to show that Christians are tested by God with disease. Let's look at some of the passages they use to justify their position.

Galatians 4:13-14 says, "Ye know how through infirmity of the flesh I preached the gospel unto you at the first. And my temptation which was in my flesh ye despised not, nor rejected; but received me as an angel of God, even as Christ Jesus."

The Greek word for infirmity is *astheneia* (GSN-769); it is a want of strength, weakness or frailty of the body. It also means a lack of strength or ability to understand, do great works, restrain corrupt desires, or to bear trials and troubles. It is used in the sense of sickness or disease only two times in Scripture. Neither of these is in reference to Paul.

II Corinthians 13:4 says, "For though He [Christ] was crucified through weakness, yet He liveth by the power of God. For we also are weak in Him, but we shall live with Him by the power of God toward you." The word translated in this passage as "weakness" is also astheneia. Did Christ have a disease that caused Him to be crucified? Of course not! To many humans, He may have seemed to be powerless, weak and defeated. In fact many religions claim the defeat of Christ on the cross. His seeming weakness was His strength, and the same is true of each of us (II Corinthians 12:9-10).

Paul's sufferings were not from sickness, disease, or the curses of personal sin and rebellion which Christ died to free us from. Paul was suffering because of his belief in Jesus the Christ. II Corinthians 11 lists many ways that Paul suffered for his faith. There is not a disease in the entire list.

Another passage used to justify that Paul's thorn was a disease is Galatians 6:11. It says, "Ye see how large a letter I have written unto you with mine own hand." From this verse they draw the conclusion that he could not see well and must have had a disease affecting his eyes and thus he wrote in large letters. As we mentioned earlier Dr. Scofield and others go so far as to claim that Paul had an eye disease that had running sores that were repulsive to look at.

This passage simply means that Paul wrote a large or long letter. To stretch this passage into a "disease" is not consistent with the rest of Scripture. Those that subscribe to this are attempting to justify the dispensational teaching that the miracles that Jesus performed were necessary to validate Scripture. But now that we have the Scriptures, the signs and wonders that Jesus and the believers in Acts did are no longer necessary. This is often used as an example of a time when God refused to heal.

Is this a proper presentation of Scripture? Let's allow Scripture to speak for itself.

II Corinthians 12:7 says, "And lest I should be exalted above measure through the abundance of the revelations, there was given to me a thorn in the flesh, the messenger of Satan to buffet me, lest I should be exalted above measure." This verse simply says that Paul's thorn in the flesh was a messenger of Satan. What is a messenger of Satan? The English word "messenger" is the Greek word *agello* (GSN-32). It is translated "angel" 179 times and "messenger" seven times. It is never translated, nor does it ever mean, disease or physical infirmity. The simple explanation of the thorn in the flesh is that an angel of Satan, one of the spirit beings, which fell with him, followed Paul and buffeted him when he was tempted to become exalted. The word buffet means, "to cuff on the ears." In other words, to tempt with words and thoughts.

The giants of the Old Testament were also called thorns. Paul's thorn should be understood in the same sense. In Numbers 33:55, Ezekiel 28:24, and Hosea 2:6 the same Greek word *skolops* (GSN-4647), for thorn, is found in the Septuagint. Were those giants and enemies of Israel diseases in their sides, or the cause of their wars and other kinds of sufferings?

Paul asked God to remove the thorn three times and God refused. There are two very important reasons why this did not happen. First, this proves that the thorn was not a disease. Every person that came to Jesus for healing was healed. He never refused. Scripture plainly teaches that it is God's will to heal all our diseases (Psalms 103).

Second, it also proves that the thorn was the devil, or one of his evil spirits. Satan will not be bound in hell until the Lord comes again. Until then, the devil has the ability to buffet or tempt us. In our Savior's love and mercy, it is His will that none should perish; thus He will delay His second coming until the time is right.

There is another incredible truth that we need to understand. We all have a thorn in our flesh just like Paul. As believers, each of us is buffeted and tempted by Satan. We may not have received the "abundance of revelations" that Paul did, but we have received great revelation, which is evidenced by our spiritual rebirth.

Another point to be considered is the meaning of the word "flesh." The term "flesh" in Scripture almost always carries a spiritual meaning. When Scripture refers to the body, the word "body" is used. In this passage, the thorn in the flesh was a spiritual attack by Satan against Paul. Satan influenced many to come against Paul in many different ways, because Paul was on the cutting edge for his Lord. It is true that his body suffered, but the suffering was from beatings and imprisonment and not disease. He was suffering for his faith; that is why he could count it all joy.

The argument that Scripture needed to be validated with signs and wonders is also false in that the Scriptures were not new. God has always validated His Word because He has never broken it and never will. God has performed miracles and other signs and wonders since the beginning of time. As humans, made from dust, we still need to see His face of relationship as well as His hand of blessing.

The Scriptures have been in existence for thousands of years. Jesus and other New Testament writers quoted from the Old Testament over a hundred times. In the New Testament there are sixty eight Passages which say "It is written" that quote more than eighteen Old Testament books. Additionally phrases such as "have you not read," "He hath said" or "Scripture hath said" quote the Old Testament many more times.

He came to fulfill the prophecies of the Old Testament Scriptures. There is not a single contradiction between the Old Testament and the New Testament. Everything that is taught in the New Testament is also taught in the Old Testament. God has not changed; we have. To use this as a reason or excuse for not seeing miracles today does not hold water. We must be careful not to build doctrines to support our failures and our presuppositions.

When Paul and Silas were in prison, they sang songs and praised the Lord. They were truly suffering for their faith. In all examples of suffering for our faith, this is the result. But if we are suffering from the consequence of personal sin there is a different result. We find anger, bitterness, blaming God or others for what happened. Self-pity is present in many different ways when we are under the consequence of our own sin.

The signs and wonders and the works of Christ and the believers in Matthew, Mark, Luke, John and Acts are just as important in today's world as they were then. God's purposes have not changed. He still wants His creation to personally experience His manifold Righteousness. God still wants His will done on earth as it is in heaven. When some say that they do not need signs and wonders today, they are usually implying that they are superior in their faith to those that "need" them.

## THE TESTIMONY OF JESUS

There are several verses in Scripture that refer to "the testimony of Jesus Christ" (Revelation 1:2, 1:9, 12:17, 19:10). What is "the testimony of Jesus Christ"?

First, Jesus always defended the Father. He said the Father and I are one; if you had known me you would have known the Father. Second, the testimony of Jesus includes what the Father sent Him to do for us. I believe that this statement applies to His past works, as well as His present and future works. If we deny His works today then are we not denying Him?

II Timothy 3:5 talks about those "having a form of godliness, but denying the power thereof: from such turn away." Why? If we deny His works, we are also denying His blood and His testimony.

The testimony of Jesus Christ is also the Holy Spirit. The Holy Spirit is given to all those who choose to believe as an earnest of the Bridegroom's promise that He will return for His bride and that we will be with Him for all of eternity. II Corinthians 1:21-22 says, "Now he which stablisheth us with you in Christ, and hath anointed us, is God; Who hath also sealed us, and given the earnest of the Spirit in our hearts." II Corinthians 5:5-8 says, "Now he that hath wrought us for the selfsame thing is God, who also hath given unto us the earnest of the Spirit. Therefore we are always confident, knowing that, whilst we are at home in the body, we are absent from the Lord: (For we walk by faith, not by sight:) We are confident, I say, and willing rather to be absent from the body, and to be present with the Lord."

God has also given us the Holy Spirit, the same Sprit that raised Jesus from the dead, to empower us to do the same works that the Father sent Jesus to do (John 20:21).

## THE IMPORTANCE OF OUR TESTIMONIES

In Revelation 12:11 Jesus says, "And they overcame him [Satan] by the blood of the Lamb, and by the word of their testimony; and they loved not their lives unto the death." Why is Jesus Christ placing the word of our testimonies beside His blood in overcoming our enemy? Wouldn't it seem that His blood would be far more important? But in this verse our testimonies seem to have an equal value to His blood in overcoming the devil. Why? Our testimonies are the fruit, or manifestation, of what God has done for us. Our testimonies tell of the manifest righteousness of God.

Is Satan bound in hell yet? Of course not. Do we still need to overcome Satan in our lives today? Yes, we do. Then we still need the blood of the Lamb to pay for our sins; we still need the Holy Spirit to convict and lead us and empower us, and our testimonies to encourage and build faith in each other. The righteousness of God in our lives is a display of His works. James teaches us that faith without works is dead. God teaches us that if we love Him, we are to obey Him. If we obey Him, His works will be displayed through our lives.

In John 10, Jesus says the same thing but in a different way. In verse 30, Jesus says, "I and My Father are one," thus proclaiming that He was the Christ and also God. The Jews then took up stones to kill Him. And Jesus answered them with a question in verse 32: "Jesus answered them, Many good works have I shewed you from my Father; for which of those works do ye stone Me?"

Jesus was saying, I have healed your sick, cast out demons, cleansed lepers, raised the dead, fed multitudes, given sight to the blind and taught you the truth at all times without charge. Is this My reward?

John 10:33-34 says, "The Jews answered him, saying, For a good work we stone thee not; but for blasphemy; and because that thou, being a man, makest thyself God. Jesus answered them, Is it not written in your law, I said, Ye are gods?" Jesus quoted the passage "I said, Ye are gods" from Psalms 82:6: "I have said, Ye are gods; and all of you are children of the most High." Jesus is saying in this passage, children of the most High were called gods, why then should it be blasphemy of Me to claim deity when I am the Son of God and one with God?

Then, in John 10:36, Jesus turns the tables on them and accuses them of blasphemy because they did not believe the Christ and God: "Say ye of Him, whom the Father hath sanctified, and sent into the world, Thou blasphemest; because I said, I am the Son of God?"

The Father sent His son Jesus, and the Jews did not believe Him, thus they blasphemed the Lord. This is what we all do when we do not believe that Jesus is the Christ and when we do not believe His works.

In John 10:37, Jesus again challenges the Jews based on His works: "If I do not the works of my Father, believe Me not." Wendell Smith in his book, *Great Faith*, writes:

> The early church was a miracle church. The lame were healed. The dead were raised. Demons were cast out. Coming under the shadow of Peter, people were healed as he walked by. Handkerchiefs were taken from Paul, placed on the sick, and became the agents of healing to them. God used that mighty first-generation church by multiplying it greatly and sending it to turn the world upside down.
>
> He is going to do it again with the last-day Church of passionate men and women who will believe Him for miracles. Signs will follow those who believe as they lay hands on the sick and see them recover. They will speak with new tongues. They will have power over the Devil and cast out demons. They will raise the dead. The gifts of miracles will be a hallmark of the final generation. Through their faith they will suspend natural laws and perform mighty signs in the name of Christ. Creative miracles will occur. Limbs will grow, blind eyes will open, organs will be regenerated, cancer will be cured, AIDS will be annihilated, and the dead will be raised to life again. There is a generation that God is preparing who will have this kind of faith.

This isn't just for the last days. Throughout history God has always manifested His righteousness in the gift of miracles and healing through faithful servants. In every generation since Jesus Christ there are recorded miracles of all kinds.

Now I want to demonstrate for you miracles in this generation. The manifestation of the Holy Spirit in the gifts of healing and miracles continues today.

First, I want to share my personal experience of God's healing power and how He blessed me in my obedience. Then I will share the testimonies of many others.

## AUTHOR'S TESTIMONY

In February 1997, I injured my neck in an accident. I had severe pain in my right arm and shoulder that began about five days after the accident. I went to a doctor and did physical therapy for a couple of weeks and the pain went away. However, throughout that summer my arm was not right. It seemed weak at times and my balance was off.

Later that year, in October, the severe pain and muscle cramps returned in my arm and shoulder. I went back to the doctor, tried the therapy again and it did not work. From October through December I went to several doctors and tried every therapy you could imagine, including acupuncture. In early December, a surgeon sent me for an MRI on my shoulder; it was negative. He gave me some pain pills and told me to come back in six weeks if it still hurt. He was "too busy" to deal with me at the end of the year rush in his office.

The pain continued and atrophy began in my arm and shoulder. I was really getting scared. I tried to get into several neurosurgeons' offices but I was told there was at least a month's backlog of patients. One of the receptionists suggested that I see a physiatrist.

This type of doctor does electrical conduction testing to find nerve damage. I was desperate and willing to do anything. But I needed a referral, so I lied and gave the name of a doctor I had seen previously for this problem. The doctor did the test and found that the nerve from the seventh cervical vertebrae was damaged.

She sent me for an MRI on my neck. It showed that I had three disks that were ruptured or fragmented and were putting severe pressure on my spinal cord and on the nerve down my right arm. I was lucky not to be paralyzed.

Now, what would I do? To say the least, I was very scared. The physiatrist recommended surgery to remove the disks. Which surgeon? What were the long-term side effects from this kind of surgery? I started to try to get appointments and talk to several doctors. In the meantime my arm was getting weaker and the atrophy more pronounced every day. The physiatrist told me that I would never regain the full use of my right arm. The nerve damage was too severe.

My fear continued to grow. I was prayed for, hands were laid on me, and I was anointed with oil, but I was not healed. I called out to God. Where are you God? Do you really exist?

On January 21, 1998, I had surgery. The surgeon removed the three disks in my neck and fused the vertebrae with bone taken from my hip. I was in the hospital for three days.

When I got home, I found that my problems were just starting. I could not sit in my easy chair. It seemed to make me nervous and I hurt any place that touched the chair. My fingers and toes would burn. The muscles in my hands and arms and feet and legs would cramp. I lost feeling in the tips of my fingers; my feet would get numb, and the sides of my legs would also get numb. I went back to the surgeon. He examined me, and took more x-rays, but could not find anything wrong. In April I had another MRI on my neck. The surgeon again could not find anything that would cause my symptoms.

I was getting worse, and I got more scared when we could not find out what was happening to me. I could not sleep because of fear and pain. The doctor's only help was to give me drugs to dull the pain and cover up the problems. When I read about the side effects from the drugs, I quit taking them. I had never been so sick and so scared.

One doctor thought I had something called arachnoiditis. A couple of days before surgery I underwent a myelogram where a contrast dye is injected into the spinal cord, and then x-rays and a CAT scan are done. The dye can cause arachnoiditis. Arachnoiditis is the inflammation of the arachnoid layer of the sheath that surrounds the spinal cord. Basically a person becomes paralyzed from the point of inflammation. My fear level again multiplied.

In late April, I went to a neurologist. She examined me and told me that I probably had something called peripheral neuropathy, and ordered a several tests. I made the mistake of looking up peripheral neuropathy on the Internet. The symptoms and prognosis are very similar to MS. Needless to say my fear factor again increased and I felt worse. I continued to cry out to God and still no answer.

A friend took me to her pastor where they laid hands on me and prayed, but again I was not healed. This time it was a charismatic pastor. I wanted to cover all the bases.

In early June, I went to the Mayo Clinic in Arizona. After three days of very painful and expensive testing they confirmed what they called small fiber neuropathy. The small nerves in my hands and feet were dying, but they were not able to determine the cause. Their only treatment involved more drugs with horrible side effects.

When you go to doctors and they have no help or encouragement for you, your fear level grows and your symptoms multiply.

I was scared and willing to try anything, so I started to see alternative doctors and practitioners. I tried many different remedies and treatments: acupuncture, acupressure, many Chinese and Taoist modalities, nutrition, herbs, homeopathy, applied kinesiology, NAET, aromatherapy, and many others.

In August, I began to notice that sometimes the pain in my feet would stop at the top of my socks, so I started to buy different socks. I must have bought fifty different pairs, but it did not help. I started to look at what they were made of, and the only common fabric was nylon. I had myself tested to see if I was allergic to it; I was.

This started me down the road to learning that I was allergic to almost one hundred different foods and fabrics. I was allergic to my own saliva. It was these allergies that were causing the numbness, the cramping, the stomach aches, and the nerve damage. I was relieved to know about the allergies, but I wanted to know what was causing the allergies.

Medical doctors' only answer for allergies is to avoid the allergen; they do not know the cause. We live in Alaska and it is cold. How could I avoid almost every fabric? How could I avoid so many foods, and stay alive? It is also very difficult to identify what you are allergic to. Allergies can be very complex in the combinations of foods or fabrics that become allergens.

In late November, my sister told me about a seminar that she had attended, taught by a pastor. My sister and her husband are missionaries with Wycliffe. (This seminar was given at Wycliffe's headquarters in Waxhaw, North Carolina, in July 1998.) The pastor was teaching on something called "The Spiritual Roots of Diseases." I was skeptical. But her testimony of being healed of breast tumors encouraged me to listen.

She shared with me the process she went through of sanctifying herself. The pastor taught that there was a connection between bitterness towards a nurturing female and female cancers and tumors. First, she forgave our mother for things that had happened, and one breast tumor left almost immediately. But the other was not healed. The Lord then reminded her that she was holding bitterness toward her mother-in-law. She then got on her knees before God and forgave her. The other breast tumor also disappeared.

At that point I was a mess. I was hurting so badly, it was cold out and I could not wear my warm winter clothes; I could not eat many foods; I was willing to try anything.

I got the seminar tapes from my sister in early December 1998. As I studied through the teachings my eyes were opened to many things. I took the whole week off from work and pored through the tapes for several hours every day. For the first time, I was beginning to have hope that there might be an answer for me. But I was still very skeptical.

Being from a fundamentalist, dispensational background, the pastor's teaching on healing was not easy to accept, even with my sister's testimony. I had gone to my church's college and earned a bachelor's degree in Bible, psychology and history. I had studied with some of the best-known college and seminary professors in the world. I thought I knew the Scripture, and knew what I was taught was correct.

In the brain fog that accompanied the disease that I had, I was having a hard time understanding the tapes, so I had one of my employees transcribe them into a book. You see, I had to test it, and test it.

Pastor Wright quoted many Scriptures, but he would often not quote the reference. So my wife Patti and I spent hours looking up verses. We studied them, did word studies in the original languages, checked to see if they were in context. We did much of this in early January while we were in Hawaii on vacation. My wife was very understanding, sitting in our room, working away while the sun was shining outside.

The pastor taught that the root cause of my disease was bitterness. He taught that I needed to forgive people for some things that they had done to me in the past. The resentments, anger, and bitterness were destroying my immune system, allowing the allergies to take over. He was also teaching that I had a spirit of fear that was compounding my problems.

In II Timothy 1:7 God says, I have not given you a spirit of fear, but of power, love and a sound mind. This verse was very troubling to me because the only thing that I was ever taught about demons was that Christians cannot have them. But I had been working on the forgiveness issues, really trying to forgive from my heart, as Scripture says, and God was there for me. On January 7, 1998, in the room in Hawaii, I commanded the spirit of fear to go in Jesus' name. I did not understand what I had done, but immediately a weight lifted from me. I could take a deep breath and relax.

Within two days all the allergies were gone. I could eat anything. It took a lot longer to take back all of my clothing. Some of it hurt so badly that I was still afraid to wear it. A pair of nylon dress socks would cause my feet to cramp up into a tight ball with intense pain.

Even though I was mostly healed in January, I was still skeptical. I bought all the medical textbooks that Pastor Wright taught from. I had to see for myself. I had to read it from the textbook to see if he had quoted them accurately and they were.

In March God reminded me of a letter that I had written to Him the prior November. In this letter I cried out to Him. I wrote down all the garbage that had gone on in my life in the last ten years, all the emotional and physical pain that I was in. In the last paragraph I said to God, "All I have wanted to do was serve you. I don't understand why I have this disease, I don't understand why I have all this pain, but I still love you and want to serve you. And if that means living with the pain and dying an early death, I still want to serve you." I wrote this and put it in my Bible. Within two weeks my sister called and told me about Pastor Wright and sent me his tapes.

Later I asked my sister why she had not told me about them last summer. She knew what I was going through. She said that she did not think I was ready to receive and believe them yet. That is why she waited. She was right. I had not fully submitted to God until I wrote that letter.

Wow! What a lesson in our relationship with God.

I am completely healed. I have taken back all my foods; I can eat anything. I have taken back all of my clothes. I can wear my warm winter clothing. My right arm is completely restored. I have full use and strength. All the numbness and neuropathies are healed. God has healed me one hundred percent! Praise God!

I want to share with you what I have learned, because you, too, can be healed. God wants all of us to have a better life. Jesus said, "Come unto me all of you who are heavily laden and I will give you rest." I never understood that Scripture until now. I would like to show you what it really means. God is not a respecter of persons. He does not have favorites. What he did for me He will do for you too.

When I was crying out to God for healing, I searched the Scriptures, I read books. I studied everything I could find. I questioned everything that I had ever believed.

Scripture tells us that God loves us and that He came and died for us in the person of the Lord Jesus. In Matthew, Luke, Mark and John, He healed all the people of all their diseases, and cast out all their evil spirits. The disciples did it, the seventy did it, and the early church did it in Acts. But why couldn't I?

I wanted to know why God said in Psalms 103:3 that He not only forgave us of all our iniquities but He healed us of all our diseases. In the Old Testament they raised people from the dead, people were healed, and many other miracles were done. In the New Testament, I found that we were supposed to have a new and better covenant. In III John verse 2 it says, "Dearly beloved I wish above all things that you prosper and be in good health even as your soul prospers." I Thessalonians 5:23 says, "May the God of Peace sanctify you wholly in spirit, in soul, and in body."

I believe from reading these and other Scriptures that God wants to heal all of our diseases, but why doesn't it happen very often? Most pastors will tell you that they believe that God "can" heal, but less than five percent of those they pray for are healed. Few pastors believe that God "will" heal.

In James 1:5 the Bible says, "If any man lack wisdom, let him ask of God and God will give it to him liberally..." God wants us to seek His wisdom. He wants us to boldly come to the throne and ask Him. God began to show me from the Scriptures that it wasn't that He could not heal. It was that we had to become sanctified in areas of our lives before He would heal. Let's read III John verse 2 again: "Dearly beloved I wish above all things that you prosper and be in good health even as your soul prospers."

My soul was not prospering. My life was full of resentment and bitterness. It was full of the pain from past memories and experiences. To be blunt, my life was full of sin and I did not even realize it. I had become separated from God the Father, others and myself.

Diseases in our lives are the result of a separation from Him and His word in certain areas of our life. Sometimes this is the result of Adam's sin, making this a fallen and cursed world. Sometimes we can suffer because of someone else's sin, but usually it is the result of our personal sin. God would have had to become double minded and would have had to become evil in condoning evil to bless us in our sins. It always has been an issue to do with circumcision of the heart.

A lot of people struggle with the supposed "gap" between Matthew, Mark, Luke, John, Acts and Romans through Jude. After Acts there is little further discussion about healing, so some have said, "Well it passed away because you don't find it." "Healing was only for Christ or the disciples and not for us." I no longer agree with these statements.

The Lord came and He demonstrated the love of God and power over the devil, over sin, and disease. In Matthew, Mark, Luke and John He demonstrated it. His disciples, and the early church, also demonstrated it in Acts. Then from Romans all the way to Jude, you find the teaching to be about sanctification and warning about deception in the church. You can't have Matthew, Mark, Luke, John and Acts until you have applied Romans to Jude. You cannot expect God to bless you if you are disobedient and separated from Him.

Deuteronomy 28 is divided into two sections. The first fourteen verses reveal His blessing for obedience. Verse 15 begins the warning about the consequences of disobedience. It begins with if, then, and but. These are very important words in Scripture. If we obey then God promises to bless us, but if we disobey we will suffer the consequences of our choices.

In His love and mercy He told us what would happen if we disobeyed His laws. God has given us tremendous authority if we accept the responsibility. If we want to be free we must accept the responsibility for what is going on in our lives. Matthew 14-15 says,"For if ye forgive men their trespasses, your heavenly Father will also forgive you: But if ye forgive not men their trespasses, neither will your Father forgive your trespasses.

People ask me, "does God forgive all matter of sin?" No, but He wants to. There are conditions to receiving His forgiveness. First, we must forgive others from our hearts and second, we must confess our sins, past, present and future. I John 1:9 says, "If we confess our sins, He is faithful and just to forgive us our sins..."

Christians, for the most part, believe we are saved by grace alone. But because you are born again and because your spirit has become alive to God, does not mean you have resolved the consequences of sin in your life. Sanctification is a process of identifying the sin or the ways we have become separated from God, others and ourselves.

In Matthew 22:36-40 a lawyer asked Jesus a question: "Master, which is the great commandment in the law? Jesus said unto him, Thou shalt love the Lord thy God with all thy heart, and with all thy soul, and with all thy mind. This is the first and great commandment. And the second is like unto it, Thou shalt love thy neighbour as thyself. On these two commandments hang all the law and the prophets."

The first separation mentioned is from God, His word and His love. Every problem that we have in life is the result of our separation from God and His word and His truth and His love. We become separated through our disobedience and our unbelief.

Religion teaches that God the Father is sitting on the throne, with lightning bolts, waiting to strike you dead if you're "bad" today. That's not what I read in Scripture. He's a loving God who says, "God is love" and "for God so loved the world that He gave...." God the Father is the giver of every good and perfect gift. Jesus said, "You've seen me, you've seen the Father." "I and the Father are one" (I John 4:8, John 3:16, James 1:16-17, John 14:9, John 10:30).

Our understanding of who God the Father is and what His will on earth is should and must be formed by who Jesus is and what He did. If it is not then we have fallen into a trap set by the devil.

Instead Satan has tricked most of us into seeing God the Father in the same manner that we view our earthly fathers. My earthly father was never there for me. He has always been too busy to have time for me. I made my Heavenly Father "guilty" by association. One day God spoke to me and asked how much I love my two sons. As I felt that love, He said, "I love you a billion times more."

Think about the most important person in this world to you. Multiply that by a billion and you will begin to understand His love for you. If you will allow this paradigm shift to happen in your mind, your relationship with God the Father will become real and alive.

Healing doesn't ultimately come from Jesus. It comes from the Father. Jesus says in John 5:19 "...verily, I say unto you, The Son can do nothing of himself, but what he seeth the Father do: for what things soever he doeth, these also doeth the Son likewise." Jesus only did what the Father told Him to do.

James 1:17 says, "Every good gift and every perfect gift is from above, and cometh down from the Father of lights, with whom is no variableness, neither shadow of turning." Our heavenly Father is the giver of every good and perfect gift, period. If it is not good and perfect, it is not from God. Psalms 68:19 says, "Blessed be the Lord, who daily loadeth us with benefits, even the God of our salvation." Even our salvation comes from the Father.

The second separation, listed in the verses from Matthew, is from yourself. Do you know how many people do not like themselves? Do you know how many people struggle with self-hatred, lack of self-esteem, and guilt? It's a massive plague. How can we not love ourselves if God loves us? He's greater than we are. How then can we have the audacity to say we do not love ourselves? If we do, we put ourselves in opposition to God. We make ourselves a god unto ourselves by denying His statement of love, and open ourselves up to the enemy to agree with us. Instead of hearing God speaking to us by His Word, and by the Holy Spirit telling us that we are loved and that we are "okay," we are going to hear this voice coming into our mind telling us how rotten, or stupid, or worthless we are.

We are commanded to love our neighbor as ourselves. How can we love our neighbor or God if we do not love and respect ourselves?

The third area of separation is from others. Each of these areas of separation involves bitterness, resentment or unforgiveness. When you think of someone who has wronged you, do you feel it in the pit of your stomach? You will always remember the individual and what they did to you, but you do not have to carry the emotions of resentment, or bitterness. When we truly forgive from our heart, the emotions such as anger and resentment and the pain they bring into our lives will be gone.

Jesus said that all the law, all the Scriptures, stand on these two commandments. If we do not love ourselves we cannot love others or God. If the Bible is not working for us, we will find the answer in the broken relationships with God, others and self. God says if you love Me, obey Me.

Let me explain to you what happened in my life.

I had a disease called multiple chemical sensitivity, or environmental illness. In this disease I had developed over one hundred allergies. MCS-EI works like this: sometime, somewhere, the person has been terribly hurt. Their heart and spirit have been broken. It involves one or more of the following: verbal or emotional abuse, physical abuse, sexual abuse, or drivenness to meet the expectations of a parent to receive love.

From these situations — whatever they were — anger, bitterness, and unforgiveness develop. As we think about the old hurts our adrenal glands secrete adrenaline and cortisol. Too much adrenaline and cortisol over time destroy the immune system. When the immune system is weak or suppressed, almost any disease can take over. In my case allergies took over.

I started out with just a couple of allergies, and as my fear level increased, the number of allergies increased. I would see a doctor with one or two problems and leave with ten. A spirit of fear can take over your life. It is a vicious cycle. Fear negates faith and as you become more afraid, more allergies develop.

I remember a doctor asking me if my watch was hurting my arm. My watch had a battery and produced a magnetic field. Many people suffer from allergies to lights or electrical fields or magnetic fields. Well, the next day I could no longer wear my watch. It made my wrist cramp with intense pain. That is how powerful our minds are. We can become conditioned to respond in ways that we do not cognitively understand.

When we have strong emotions or thoughts the chemical secretions of our bodies are changed. It started in my mind, but the pain in my body was real. One of the major emotions that we deal with is anxiety and fear. A Biblical definition of anxiety is fear, worry or frustration. Fear is equated in Scripture with unbelief or faithlessness. Thus, fear is the opposite of faith. If we are in fear, we are not in faith. If we are in faith, we cannot be in fear.

## ANXIETY AND FEAR DISORDERS (NEGATIVE EMOTIONS)

Let me share from a medical textbook, *Pathophysiology: The Biological Bases for Disease in Adults and Children*, by Kathryn L. McCantz and Sue E. Huther (2nd edition-Mosby). This textbook teaches that the following organs or systems in our bodies are targets for anxiety and stress related diseases and then lists diseases that anxiety and stress cause. (The words in bold and italics are from the textbook, the others are my comments.)

## Cardiovascular System

- *Coronary Artery Disease.* The Bible says, "In the last days men's hearts shall fail them because of fear" (Luke 21:26). Fear, anxiety and stress are synonyms.
- *Hypertension (high blood pressure).* Fear and anxiety, are the root cause of high blood pressure. The Bible and medical science agree. What we teach is not opposed to medical science. In fact, what I see in the Bible only proves medical science, and medical science only proves the Bible.
- *Stroke and Aneurysms.* Strokes and aneurysms are the result of rage and anger, but behind the rage and anger is also fear. Do you know why people go into rage and anger? First of all, they have a root of bitterness. They are really afraid to deal with issues. Rather than being confronted on an issue and having to deal with it, they just blow up because that is their defensive mechanism. They don't want to be confronted on an issue because they are afraid of men and they are afraid of rejection.
- *Disturbances of Heart Rhythm.* Irregular heart beat and Mitral Valve Prolapse, are the result of anxiety and stress.

## Muscles

- *Tension Headaches.* We rub the back of our necks when we are under stress and tension to relieve the pain. Why not turn to God and deal with the fear and anxiety?
- *Muscle Contraction Backache.* Again anxiety and stress are the issues. I have witnessed many healings when people have repented of the lack of faith in God that is manifested in worry, anxiety and fears, and then learned to trust Him.

## Connective Tissues

- *Rheumatoid Arthritis.* We have found that there is a direct relationship between the tremendous stress of self-hatred and all auto-immune disease. The negative emotion and action of degrading or putting ourselves down, in any way, has a severe consequence in our body. Intuitively, we know that it is wrong to condemn what God said was very good (Genesis 1:31). Thus these negative emotions expressed against us, and the resulting guilt, have a consequence in our bodies. This internal conflict causes the immune system to form antibodies to our own flesh. This is called an auto-immune response that leads to auto-immune diseases.
- *Related inflammatory diseases of the connective tissues.*

## Pulmonary System

- *Asthma*

• *Hay fever.* This medical textbook is teaching that hay fever and asthma are caused by anxiety and stress and not by airborne allergens. We have learned and demonstrated hundreds of times that fear of abandonment and rejection are the two most common causes of asthma. It has nothing to do with breathing, dander, dust, pollen, etc.

## Immune System

• *Immunosuppression or Immune Deficiency.* The over-secretion of cortisol and adrenaline destroy the immune system. When the immune system is weak, almost any disease can invade our bodies.

• *Auto-immune Disease.* In this type of disease, the immune system has become over-active and has formed antibodies to parts of our own body (autoantibodies). It has been discovered that antibodies can be formed to almost any body tissue. We have learned that the immune system attacks the body, as a person attacks themselves spiritually, in self-rejection, self-hatred, and self-bitterness. Guilt, regret, sorrow, and shame are negative emotions that are evidence of self-hatred. The immune system agrees with the mind, and starts attacking its own body. This is a high price to pay for not loving yourself, as Scripture requires (Matthew 22:37-40). Lupus, Crohn's, Diabetes, Rheumatoid Arthritis, and MS are examples.

## Gastrointestinal System

• *Ulcers.* For years the medical community believed that stress and anxiety caused an over-secretion of stomach acids that caused an irritation in the stomach, that eventually caused the ulceration. Recently they have begun to prescribe antibiotics and are telling us that a bacteria or viruses cause ulcers.

People who have ulcers also have compromised immune systems because of the anxiety and stress. When you have a compromised immune system, you don't have the ability to defeat bacteria and viruses. The fear and anxiety come first and the bacteria and viruses show up after the immune system is compromised.

• *Irritable Bowel Syndrome (IBS)*
• *Diarrhea*
• *Nausea, vomiting*
• *Ulcerative colitis*

Anxiety and stress cause every single malfunction in the gastrointestinal tract. The peace of God in your heart, regarding issues in your life, is the cure (with the exception of Crohn's disease, which is an auto-immune disease).

## Genital and Urinary Systems

• *Diuresis*
• *Impotence*
• *Frigidity*

Are all caused by anxiety and fear.

## Skin
- *Eczema*
- *Acne*
- *Dermatitis.* Adolescent acne is caused by fear coming from peer pressure. It is not a genetic or biologic problem by itself, but in most cases the kids are afraid of other kids. That level of fear and anxiety triggers increased histamine secretion. It also increases white corpuscle activity in the epidermis, thus causing acne.

## Endocrine system
- *Diabetes*
- *Amenorrhea*

## Central Nervous System
- *Fatigue and lethargy*
- *Type A behavior*
- *Overeating*
- *Depression*
- *Insomnia*

(McCance 1998)

Dr. Michael D. Jacobson, in his book, *The Word on Health*, explains the negative consequences of excessive adrenaline and cortisol by listing and describing various diseases they cause:

## Detrimental Effects of Excessive Adrenaline
- *Gastric Ulcers.* …Stress induces increased secretion of stomach acid, leading to an increased risk of ulcers. In a recent example, the occurrence of gastric ulcers was noted to increase dramatically in Japanese residents who survived the devastating Hanshin-Awaji earthquake. The presence of another significant disease further increases the likelihood, that stress will cause gastric ulcers.
- *Skin Disorders.* Stress may also play a role in some skin diseases. For example, vitiligo is a disease in which cells lose their pigmentation, causing white blotches to form on the skin. Dr. Morrone and colleagues demonstrated that the onset and progression of vitiligo correlate with increased levels of adrenaline.
- *High Blood Pressure.* A growing body of evidence seems to support the potential connection between stress and high blood pressure. In one study patients who had borderline hypertension, or a family history of high blood pressure, were more likely to have stress-related behavior patterns. In a long-term study involving nearly 3,000 patients, those who had high anxiety or high depression were nearly twice as likely to develop high blood pressure, over time.

**Heart and Circulatory System Damage.**

According to the doctors who discovered the link between personality types and heart disease, the most serious effect of elevated adrenaline, when persistent and unrelenting, is its damage to the heart and arteries. Adrenaline's detrimental effects, include the following:

• *Constriction of Blood Vessels.* ...This can result in spasm of the coronary arteries, reducing blood flow to the heart.

• *Increased Cholesterol Production.* Especially LDL, the "bad" cholesterol, and decreased cholesterol clearance. This results in increased formation of plaque on artery walls.

The evidence that stress raises cholesterol levels is abundant. Accountants' cholesterol levels, have been found to be highest at tax time; medical students registered ten percent higher during examination time; employees fired from their jobs, showed a ten percent drop in cholesterol when they finally secured new work.

But, cholesterol may not be so deserving of all the bad press it has been receiving. Archibald Hart cites evidence that elevated cholesterol does not increase the risk of heart disease unless it is combined with stress.

Simply put, if blood cholesterol levels are high, stress will much more likely, contribute to heart disease. On the other hand, if stress levels are kept low, even high cholesterol will probably not result in heart disease.

• *Plaque Disruption.* ...Two-thirds of all acute coronary events tend to occur when there is only mild to moderate obstructive plaque. The culprit does not appear to be the plaque itself, but the adrenaline surge that precipitates the crisis, which results from anger and rage.

• *Arterial Spasm and Increased Clotting.* Stress depletes magnesium, which results in increased arterial spasm and an increased clotting of platelets.

• *Heart Dysrhythmias.* Adrenaline stimulates the heart to beat faster and more erratically. For example, when given intravenously in amounts to match stressful situations, adrenaline induced episodes of PSVT (a condition in which the heart spontaneously beats extremely rapidly) in patients that were being medicated for this condition. Healthy physicians, when paged while on call in the hospital, showed derangement in their EKG, similar to those seen preceding fatal dysrhythmias. Likewise, when rats and dogs were subjected to acute stress, there was a corresponding destabilization in their ventricular rhythm, as the heart showed signs of increasing injury.

• *Sudden Death.* Most episodes of stress-related sudden death appear to be due to the direct effect of stress upon the heart. For example (in a recent study by Dr. Jacobson), thirty-eight of forty-three cases of stress-related sudden death were attributed to heart problems. This was despite the fact that ninety percent who died from an underlying heart condition during this stress episode had no known prior history of heart disease. Two died of stroke. All of these episodes of stress-related sudden death were witnessed. Fear and anger were the stressful triggers in forty out of forty-three cases, and death occurred without warning in all. This is exactly what happened to Nabal when he heard from his wife that David had come to take his life. "But it came to pass in the morning, when the wine was gone out of Nabal, and his wife had told him these things, that his heart died within him, and he became as a stone" (I Samuel 25:37).

• *Mitral Valve Prolapse.* MVP is a relatively common diagnosis, given to patients who have chest pain, that is not due to coronary artery disease. Such patients are more than twice as likely to suffer from panic disorder or major depression, than are patients who have chest pain due to coronary artery disease. Similarly, another study demonstrated that forty percent of patients with non-cardiac chest pain, met the diagnostic criteria for panic disorder, compared to none of the patients with typical angina.

• *Panic Disorder.* This stress-related disorder is especially common in middle-aged women, and is characterized by rapid heart rate, pressure or burning sensation in the chest, neck, or head, shortness of breath, and a sense of impending doom.

## Detrimental Effects of Excessive Cortisol

The adrenal cortex produces two of the most critical stress hormones, cortisol and DHEA. Cortisol is a steroid hormone, with effects very similar to those of the medication prednisone. It powerfully blocks inflammation, and it suppresses the immune system. On the other hand, DHEA serves to balance out the effects of cortisol. It is believed to have anti-aging effects, to be an immune system booster, and to have important effects on the sex hormones and, therefore, fertility.

Normally, the adrenal cortex increases production of cortisol by about fifty percent with the onset of stress. At the same time, DHEA levels fall off. Once the stress is removed, cortisol and DHEA levels will typically return to the normal range.

However, with prolonged stress, these changes become even more exaggerated. Cortisol rises to nearly 240 percent of normal, and DHEA production drops to near zero. The elevated cortisol, with its prednisone-like effects, along with virtually no DHEA to counteract it, eventually wreaks havoc on a variety of the body's organ systems.

Note that the adrenal glands always produce cortisol, even at the expense of other hormones. This is because cortisol is essential to life. The emphasis here, however, is placed on the negative effects of excess cortisol in response to stress. Its other important functions, are beyond the scope of this discussion.

• *Effects on Hormones.* First of all, cortisol stimulates the conversion of noradrenaline to adrenaline, resulting in increased levels of adrenaline in the blood. This puts the individual at increased risk for all of the problems related to adrenaline excess noted above. Cortisol also blocks the conversion of T4 thyroid hormone to the more active T3 form, so that individuals under stress may develop symptoms of hypothyroidism (even though the thyroid function tests may appear normal).

• *Infection.* Cortisol suppresses antibody production and T-cell activity (both are types of white blood cells). This puts the stressed individual at much greater risk for infections. For example, the risk of the common cold has been found to correlate directly with the level of stress one is experiencing. Selye said: "If a microbe is in or around us all of the time, and yet it causes no disease until we are exposed to stress, what is the 'cause' of our illness, the microbe or the stress? I think both are — and equally so."

Increased risk of infection is of particular concern with surgical patients since, in addition to the exposure of the inner sanctum to germs, surgery itself has been demonstrated to be a potent stressor, depressing the immune system, through dramatically stimulating increased cortisol production.

Louis Pasteur, the first great microbiologist, was constantly challenged by Claude Bernard, who insisted on the body's own homeostasis being more important than the microbe. Upon his deathbed, Pasteur said, "Bernard is right. The microbe is nothing, the soul is everything."

• *Protein Breakdown Increase.* Under the influence of cortisol, protein breakdown increases thirty-eight percent, while the manufacturing of protein drops twenty-eight percent. Together, this translates into a sixty-six percent drop in protein production. Thus, lean muscle is converted to fat, so that individuals with chronically elevated cortisol may develop a "buffalo hump" between their shoulders. A lack of protein, also leads to poor wound healing.

• *Arthritis.* Selye claimed that gout is related to stress. In addition, researchers have indicated that rheumatoid arthritis activity correlates with the degree of emotional stress.

• *Heavy Metal Chelation.* Today, especially in alternative medicine, there is a growing interest in the treatment of heavy metal toxicity with chelation. "Chelation" comes from the Greek root word *chele*, meaning "claw" and refers to the manner in which protein molecules or other substances grab and bind heavy metals in the body. The human body is already designed with an inherent, powerful chelation system, for binding and removing toxic heavy metals. But stress, through elevated levels of cortisol, blocks this process, rendering the stressed individual more vulnerable to heavy-metal-toxicity-related illness.

• *Cancer.* Elevated cortisol also suppresses killer cells, which are critical in the destruction of tumor cells. Giving cortisol to rats with cancer caused their cancer to spread in direct proportion to the amount of cortisol administered. Incidentally, stress also triggers a release of endogenous opiates (morphine like compounds that are found naturally in the body). Studies show that these appear to block immune responses and interfere with the body's ability to reject tumor cells.

The association of stress with cancer has led investigators to identify the personality or behavioral profile of the typical individual who is at an increased risk for cancer. Now referred to as "Type C," such an individual is characterized by denial and suppression of emotions (especially anger), "pathological niceness," avoidance of conflicts, exaggerated social desirability, harmonizing behavior, over-compliance, over-patience, high rationality, and a rigid control of emotional expression. Christians understand that love, joy, patience, kindness and self-control are fruit of the Holy Spirit (Galatians 5:22). The point here is that these characteristics must not be "put on," but come from a sincere, pure heart.

This pattern, usually concealed behind a facade of pleasantness, appears to be effective as long as environmental and psychological homeostasis is maintained, but collapses in the course of time under the impact of accumulated strains and stressors, especially those evoking feelings of depression and reactions of helplessness and hopelessness. As a prominent feature of this particular coping style, excessive denial, avoidance, suppression and repression of emotions and own basic needs, appear to weaken the organism's natural resistance to carcinogenic influences.

These and other findings have led researchers to recommend that more attention should be paid to the manipulation of the psyche in the prevention and management of cancer.

• *Diabetes.* Laboratory animals that are genetically susceptible to insulin-dependent diabetes mellitus, develop this dreaded disease more commonly when they are subjected to stress. And, since cortisol blocks insulin, patients who already have diabetes, have a more difficult time controlling their blood sugars when they are under stress.

George, the leader of a large Christian ministry, has struggled for several years with adult-onset diabetes. Although he has some degree of success controlling his blood sugar with proper diet, it has become clear over the last year or so that the level of his blood sugar is more related to stress than to anything else. He can get up in the morning, have normal blood sugar and eat a healthy breakfast with no sugar or starches. But if he has a stressful morning at work, his blood sugar can easily shoot up one hundred points or more. On the other hand, when he is out of a stressful environment, he tends to have little difficulty keeping his blood sugar under control.

• *Adverse Effect on Sex Hormones: Infertility, Miscarriage.* Cortisol stimulates the conversion of dhea to estrogen in fat cells (especially abdominal fat). Therefore, a woman who is obese and under stress can have blood estrogen levels equivalent to that of a woman in her thirties. This estrogen-dominance picture is consistent with an increased risk of estrogen-related disorders such as cancer, especially of the breast and uterus.

Years ago, Selye reported that stress had a definite negative effect on the reproductive system. "During stress, the sex glands shrink and become less active," and nursing mothers stop producing milk. In addition, monthly cycles become irregular or may even stop altogether. Likewise, in men who are under stress, sperm cell formation is reduced.

In addition, stress increases miscarriages by blocking protective mechanisms and promoting an increased release of the natural inflammatory chemicals that can cause miscarriage.

• *Memory Loss.* In order for us to recall stored information, our brains must be able to make connections at nerve endings called "dendrites." Cortisol "fries" the delicate dendrites in the brain that are necessary for the transfer of information. Therefore, stress can lead to learning disabilities and memory loss problems similar to what Alzheimer's patients experience.

• *Emotional and Mental Illness.* Selye noted that certain breakdown products of adrenaline can cause hallucination, and he proposed that it might therefore play a role in some mental illness. Certainly, stress has been implicated as a cause of depression. As Dr. Jacobson said, "And no wonder, I'd be depressed, too, if I were suffering from infections, protein loss, arthritis, cancer, diabetes, infertility, miscarriages, mental illness, and -what was the other one? Oh yes, memory loss! (Jacobson 2000, pages 164-170) Note: Dr. Jacobson quoted several sources in this quote. Please see his book for the complete references.

## THE NEGATIVE EMOTION OF BITTERNESS

One of the most common negative emotions is our life is Bitterness. Let me explain how bitterness works in our lives.

Ephesians 6:12 says, "For we wrestle not against flesh and blood, but against principalities, against powers, against the rulers of the darkness of this world, against spiritual wickedness in high places." We are not each other's enemy. Our enemy is Satan. Our battle is not with flesh and blood, but Satan and his principalities and powers, and bitterness is one of his major principalities. If we are in conflict with one another, the real enemy is Satan. He is behind the scenes stirring the pot. We must learn to separate others and ourselves from our sins.

When someone violates us, we make him evil along with the evil that he did. We need to be able to separate people from their sin. God didn't create you from the foundation of the world, a sinner. He created you from the foundation of the world as saints and as His sons and daughters forever. Because of sin, we have become separated from Him and each other.

In Romans 7 we find that the apostle Paul also struggled with sin. In verses 15 and 16 he lamented about the things he wanted to do that he didn't; and the things that he did not want to do that he did. Then in verse 17 he said that it was not him, but the sin that dwelt within him. This is an amazing statement.

Paul is separating the new nature, the nature of God that we received when we became "born again," from the old nature, or flesh. Paul understood that he had yielded to his flesh, or old nature, when he sinned. He also understood that the old nature, or flesh, was not him. He was not sin. The flesh, or old nature, is from Satan; thus we are to crucify the flesh, or old nature, daily in our lives. He was still working out his sanctification, his salvation daily. But he was able to separate himself from the sin. He was able to love himself but hate the sin.

Bitterness is a principality. A principality is a ruling demon that has several lesser demons answering to it. Answering to it, giving it protection and providing its armor are: 1) Unforgiveness, 2) Resentment, 3) Retaliation, 4) Anger, 5) Hatred, 6) Violence, 7) Murder (Luke 11:21-22).

In the hierarchy of the principality of bitterness, resentment is worse than unforgiveness; unforgiveness answers to resentment. Retaliation is worse than resentment; resentment answers to retaliation, and so on. Each lower demon protects and provides armor for the next higher demon.

Hebrews 12:14-15 says, "Follow peace with all men, and holiness, without which no man shall see the Lord: Looking diligently lest any man fail of the grace of God; lest any root of bitterness springing up trouble you, and thereby many be defiled." To "follow peace with all men" means to actively seek for peaceful and healthy relationships with others. If we cause trouble, slander, stir up gossip, or are resentful, we are not following peace; we have serious issues to deal with. This Scripture is very clear. If we don't seek peace and holiness we won't see the Lord, because we will have failed to receive God's grace.

Holiness requires removing sin from our lives. I hope we are each at a point where we actively seek after God and His righteousness as our first priority. Our salvation is at stake. Revelation 2 and 3 reveal in clear terms what the Lord has to say to the seven churches. Ezekiel 24 also has much to say to us. These passages were written to believers.

Does Hebrews 12:15 say that we should look casually when we feel like it or when somebody's nice to us? No! It says, "looking diligently." This means active searching; the kind that requires constant effort. Scripture goes on to say, "lest any man fail of the grace of God...."

What does "fail of the grace of God" mean? Galatians 6:1 defines it. It says, "if any man is overtaken in a fault...." What's a fault? A spiritual defect. If another believer is overtaken by a spiritual defect, those who consider themselves spiritually mature are to restore that person in a spirit of meekness. They are to guard against falling into the same spiritual defect, the end result of which will be falling away from faith. This is "the knowledge of God" in this matter.

Romans 2:1 says, "Therefore thou art inexcusable, O man, whosoever thou art that judgest: for wherein thou judgest another, thou condemnest thyself; for thou that judgest doest the same things." Paul says that the very thing of which you accuse another, you are also often guilty: You accuse another of having a spiritual problem but excuse the same problem in yourself. We need to be very careful to build and restore relationships, not to tear them down. Galatians 6:1 says that we are to restore one another in gentleness and love. Galatians 6:2 says to go one more step by bearing a brother's burden. How many of us ever even come close to doing this?

If we ignore this sound advice, we will be contaminated by a demon, and a root of bitterness will spring up to trouble us (Hebrews 12:15). When this root takes hold it not only defiles us, but also branches out to affect everyone around us. It is highly contagious.

Have you spent time with a bitter person? Have you ever been bitter? Are you able to discern bitterness in yourself, or in others?

Usually, when we encounter a bitter person, we cop our own attitude. Bitterness begins to flow from our soul toward them. We play a game of "bitterness ping pong" with them. It becomes my bitterness against their bitterness. We both become defiled. Does this sound familiar? It should. It's a common daily experience.

Bitterness gains its entrance to us first through unforgiveness, the first piece of the armor surrounding bitterness. That evil strongman banks on unforgiveness to be an active part of our life. He counts on us never forgiving others or ourselves so that he can have his place, his habitation, within us. Once taking up a home in us, he can act out his evil nature through us and give his boss, the devil, a victory.

Unforgiveness whispers in our ear, "No, you're not going to forgive them, you don't need to forgive them, there's no way you need to forgive them." Unforgiveness keeps a "record of wrongs" against another person. Satan banks on the spirit of unforgiveness to remind us of the bitterness that somebody else has toward us. Unforgiveness reminds, rehashes, projects and torments us with past negative events. It reminds us of what others have done to us, and what we have done to others.

The strongman, the principality, uses the spirit of unforgiveness to constantly accuse us. But unforgiveness is a smaller entity, a lower spirit. It's just the beginning.

After unforgiveness has done its work, the strongman sends out the spirit of resentment. Resentment builds on the foundation laid by unforgiveness. The record of wrongs ferments, and resentment begins to grow.

Resentment generates a feeling of ill will toward a person who has wronged us. Resentment says, "I don't like Mary," or "I will never forgive Alex," or "I don't trust my neighbors." Resentment constantly reminds us of past events, seeking to stir up negative sentiments that stew and ferment within us.

Unforgiveness formed the first piece of armor to provide protection for bitterness. Now Satan trusts that resentment will gain a foothold. Resentment feeds off of unforgiveness. Resentment is a stronger evil spirit, because unforgiveness supports it. And it is more dangerous than unforgiveness.

Satan employs millions of evil spirits in his attempt to control us. This is why resentment can exist in many people at the same time. It can multiply its growth and so defile us that it can completely take over an individual, a family or a church.

Because of the work of resentment, families and churches become dysfunctional. They maintain their own record of wrongs that generate stronger resentment. One person shares his or her resentment, and soon, everybody is doing the same. Then, the church splits or the family ends up in divorce, and the devil has won a battle in his war against good.

Unforgiveness is like instant replay: replaying the words, voices, sights and sounds of wrong events from our past. Unforgiveness flashes negative thoughts and images of everything someone ever said or did to us. Have you ever had that happen? The accusing spirit continuously replays a record of the evil music of our lives to reinforce itself, so this strongman of bitterness can find a home in us. Resentment adds fuel to the fire.

Resentment and unforgiveness stem from thoughts. They find their homes in our memories.

After unforgiveness and resentment have gained a foothold in our minds, the strongman sends out the spirit of retaliation. Now it's time to get even.

I remember a bumper sticker I saw a few years ago that said, "I don't forgive, I just get even." Retaliation projects these kinds of sentiments: "Bill should pay for what he did to me," or "I am going to make Jane pay for what she said." "I am going to make sure Bob gets what he deserves, if it is the last thing that I do!"

The spirit of retaliation is much more dangerous than the spirits of unforgiveness and resentment. Retaliation's presence shows progressive demonization. Each spirit is much more dangerous than the previous one.

In ministry, when we see someone who wants to "get even," and they say, "Well, they're gonna pay," we know immediately that a spirit of retaliation is speaking. We also know that the spirits of unforgiveness and resentment are present, and we know that the strongman of bitterness is behind it all. We know that this person is harboring a record of wrongs against others or themselves.

When you see evidence of any of these spirits, you know that all the others down the line are present as well. So, if we're going after the spirit of retaliation in ministry, we're going to go after the spirits of unforgiveness and resentment as well.

As we see evidence of higher orders of spirits, we know that the underling spirits are there as well, each reinforcing the one just above it. What reinforces retaliation? Resentment fuels retaliation. What fuels resentment? Unforgiveness. And at the top of this principality is bitterness. (There exists an entire kingdom of evil spirits, and we name each spirit by the word that describes its nature.)

Bitterness is the strongman; he wants to occupy the house. He trusts in his armor (Luke 11:21-22). To help people achieve healing, we have to strip this armor off of them. Bitterness will remain until its entire armor is stripped away. We see this happen over and over again in ministry.

As unforgiveness gains a foothold, then resentment gains a foothold. Next, retaliation gains a foothold. Each of these manifests itself in ways that are progressively worse than the prior spirit.

When retaliation wins its foothold, bitterness sends out anger.

Anger and wrath are outward expressions that remind others that we are not going to forgive them, that we resent them, and that we plan to get even. With anger, we have crossed a line. Anger gives the evil spirit a voice. Unforgiveness, resentment and retaliation can be kept unspoken, eating away at a person's own spirit through self-deception.

Once the line is crossed to anger and wrath, the demons start to show themselves physically. Have you ever seen anger in a person's eyes? It is very real and very observable. This is anger caused by the root of bitterness, because of unforgiveness, resentment and retaliation. Maybe you have experienced this yourself. We all have.

We need to understand, when our anger buttons are being pushed, it is the strongman of bitterness fighting to gain a foothold. He puts on the armor of anger and wrath to protect himself. You have sensed it yourself, when resentments fester over time, anger isn't far behind. Anger and wrath never occur without the first three spirits being in place.

We get angry when a trust has been breached, resulting in hurt. We feel victimized. Then unforgiveness, resentment and retaliation well up and overflow with the fourth spirit: anger and wrath.

After anger and wrath have gained their foothold, hatred moves in. Bitterness gains fuel from unforgiveness, resentment, retaliation, and anger and wrath. Now hatred starts a process of elimination. Hatred says, "I live on this planet and so do you. And one of us has to go and it ain't going to be me." Maybe hatred says, "This church ain't big enough for both of us. I think you'd better leave." Hatred seeks to eliminate the other person.

Retaliation fermented anger on behalf of bitterness. Anger vocalized bitterness, and now comes hatred to act out of bitterness.

Hatred reveals your feelings toward an offender, tells them that they don't belong in your world, and you absolutely hate their guts. Hatred says, "I will do what it takes to get even."

When we observe hatred in someone, we know that anger, retaliation, resentment and unforgiveness are there as well. And we know that bitterness is in the driver's seat, trusting in the armor provided by these lesser evil spirits.

What makes up the armor of bitterness? It is the seven levels of spirits who fall under his principality. Bitterness banks on the fact that when we are finally ready to forgive, unforgiveness will show us a flash card of voices, sights, sounds and smells reminding us of how someone harmed us. Resentment joins in saying, "Now, let me help you really feel it right here, deep inside you."

You may try to argue against resentment saying, "But, I'm trying to forgive Ruthie," but resentment answers, "No, you really resent her." Retaliation joins in, saying, "Yeah, besides you never did get even with Ruthie, did you? She needs to pay for what she did to you."

Anger rears up, saying, "Yeah, and I'm going to go tell Ruthie just what I think, and if I don't tell her, then I'll tell somebody else."

You're getting emotional now, and hatred says, "Yeah, I'm not only going to get even, I'm not only going to retaliate, but I know how to hit her where it hurts. I hate Ruthie."

We see this scenario repeated daily in the lives of families, businesses and churches. This is evidence of how progressively more evil influences break up human relationships and the strongman, bitterness, causes it all.

The sixth level of bitterness is violence. Violence is anger and hatred set into motion. Our emotions erupt into physical or sometimes hate-filled verbal attacks. At this point, we see pots and pans thrown across the room, or punches being thrown. Fights, physical, sexual and verbal abuse are a result.

The seventh and worst spirit in the principality of bitterness is murder. Just as Cain slew Abel because of his bitterness, so we see others murder their children, spouses or friends in a fit of rage. This completes the full cycle of Satan's plan for the use of bitterness.

The spirit of murder includes more than taking someone's physical life. God's Word teaches how we can "murder" someone with our words. Murder starts in the heart, because the ultimate level of the spirit of bitterness is the elimination of someone's personhood. I John 3:15 says, "Whosoever hateth his brother is a murderer: and ye know that no murderer hath eternal life abiding in him."

For me to get well, I had to get the bitterness out of my life. I had to forgive those who had hurt me, those who had wronged me. I had to give all that to God. And I had to cast the spirit of fear out of my life, and replace it with a spirit of joy and spirit of gladness. When I was obedient to Him, He was able to heal me.

When I tell people about God healing me I get three different reactions. First, some look at me and think that I am crazy. They are very skeptical; they don't believe me and think I'm wacko. Second, anger. I can see anger and bitterness in their faces. They are saying "why not me?" "God, why haven't you healed me?" He can. Third, are those that are excited and want to learn more. They see hope. I hope that you will be in the last group!

In Matthew 11:28 Jesus says, "Come unto me, all ye that labour and are heavy laden, and I will give you rest." Hebrews talks about the heavy weights that we carry. The weights are the anger, unforgiveness, resentments and the bitterness. When I gave God all the junk, all the bitterness, all the resentment, all the anger, all the fear, all the hatred, I didn't have to carry it anymore. I don't have to think about it. I don't have to deal with it. I can rest. I can heal. I can have joy, and peace, and God's blessings in my life. I am free of Satan's bondage. My burden became light, and so can yours. Doesn't this sound like a better way?

After I was healed I changed in many ways and others started asking me questions. As I answered them and ministered to them, many others have also received healing from God. Let me tell you about some of them.

# TESTIMONIES OF MANY OTHERS
## Marlene (my sister) written August 15, 2001

"I was healed of breast cysts and lumps by the application of God's Word. Proverbs 4:20-22 says that God's Word is 'life, to those that find them and health to all their flesh.'

"Through the teachings of Pastor Henry Wright about spiritual roots of diseases, I learned that bitterness toward a mother figure could produce breast cancer. I asked the Lord for the truth. I had breast cysts and lumps and I also thought that I had forgiven. The Lord showed me I had a deep, deep bitterness toward a family member. I purposely chose to forgive each action or word that hurt me. With each unforgiveness I dealt with, a lump went away. God and I worked together and, as He revealed hurts, I would forgive and repent of my unforgiveness. Then the lumps and cysts left one by one. I had one lump left and when I dealt with that unforgiveness, it left, and I was totally free of all lumps and cysts.

"About a year later, the lumps started to reappear, I cried out to the Lord, 'What is this?' God told me that the root of bitterness had not been completely dealt with and it was growing. I had allowed unforgiveness to creep back in with its reminder of wrongs. I knew I did not want to return to illness or to the tormentors so I took captive the unforgiveness, resentment, retaliation, anger/wrath, hate, violence, murder, and murder by tongue — all different degrees of bitterness that I was not going to allow to operate. They were not the fruit I wanted. Immediately after this, God spoke and said 'Now, Marlene, get up and call (the person I had bitterness toward) and acknowledge your sin.' As I did this, this person burst out in tears as my confession released her of the bitterness I was holding her in. With that obedience, the principality of bitterness and every part of it was gone. That was over two years ago.

"It is wonderful to live in peace with God, others and myself. I praise God His Word is living and powerful and accurate.

"I also have been healed of sciatic nerve pain, hip joint pain, fever blisters, allergies, and back problems, as I have dealt with other issues in my life."

**Linda**

Linda helped with much of the transcription and editing of the tapes into *A More Excellent Way*. As she worked on the book, she began to understand the lies of the devil that she had believed. Here is her testimony:

"My name is Linda. I am a wife, a mother, and a grandmother. I suffered a toxic mold exposure in the workplace in December, 1988, and was catapulted into the nightmare of MCS-EI, chronic fatigue immune dysfunction syndrome (CFIDS), Hashimoto's thyroiditis (hypothyroidism), and fibromyalgia. I spent years seeking traditional and non-traditional medical help to eliminate or alleviate the symptoms of pain, depression, brain fog, fatigue and loss of motor skills.

"I even went to work as office manager for an alternative doctor who promised me that he could heal my diseases. I spent many thousands of dollars for supplements, vitamin and mineral therapy, allergy elimination treatments, ozone and vitamin IV's, and I did not get well. In fact, I got sicker and had to leave the work environment.

"By 1992, I was on Social Security disability, unable to work, at home, depressed by the circumstances I found myself in, in a brain fog, and experiencing the chronic, severe pain of fibromyalgia.

"I turned to the Lord, and He was waiting. He always is waiting for us to reach out to Him, you know. As my relationship with my God grew stronger, and I listened to Him more, I slowly began to heal. I realized that there was a direct correlation to my obedience — my submission — and my healing, and I was amazed at the changes the Lord was making in my life.

"I declared that my CFIDS had gone into "remission" in late 1996, because it just wasn't there anymore. I made a phone call, and asked to take myself off of Social Security Disability. That was an experience! The Social Security Administration sent me to a psychiatrist because they thought I needed my head examined. After all, I told them I didn't want their money any more! The psychiatrist told me that he had read my medical records thoroughly, and could not figure out why he was seeing me.

"I explained that the Social Security Administration had told me that I was entitled to benefits because my case wasn't scheduled for review for several years, and that obviously they thought I was crazy because I was turning down their money. I also told him that I didn't think the Social Security Administration understood much about integrity, but that as a woman of integrity I could not take their money when I was no longer disabled!

"I guess he got the message through to them because those monthly checks finally quit coming.

"I remained under medical care for fibromyalgia and thyroid disease. In 1996, I fell while carrying my infant grandson in his car seat, and herniated a disc in my lower back. I tried to avoid surgery through physical therapy and an exercise program for over a year. When I couldn't progress past a certain point, I had the back surgery in June of 1997, and began the recovery process with the help, of course, of anti-inflammatory drugs, pain killers, antidepressants and muscle relaxers.

"I was tested for sleep apnea, and it was confirmed. The specialist wanted me to wear a special positive airflow device at night to help me breath. I opted to try a jaw-repositioning device, but it caused me excruciating pain. Instead of those options, I lost forty-five pounds, used two pillows to elevate my head and lungs, and took an herbal sleeping aid.

"I began re-entering the work world in early 1998, doing part-time temporary work through a local agency, and enjoying it very much. I also revitalized a small business of my own that had been basically dormant during my years of brain fog.

"In January of 1999, I got a call from my former boss and long-time friend, Art Mathias. I had gone to work for Art in 1982 when he opened his State Farm office, and even though my employment there ended back in 1988, we've always kept in touch. Art began sharing with me the "good news" of the healing he'd had from God after listening to some tapes his sister had sent him. Of course, I wanted to know more.

"He gave me a copy of the fifteen tapes of the Wycliffe Seminar. I began to listen to them.

"Then, in February 1999, just a month later, I became part of the team that turned Pastor Henry Wright's "Wycliffe Seminar" into the book, *A More Excellent Way*. During those many hours of transcribing and editing, I gained a deeper understanding of spiritual warfare. I clearly saw how the unforgiveness, bitterness, fear and anxiety in my life had directly affected my health, and in some areas, still was affecting me.

"I immediately began putting the Biblical principles Pastor Wright teaches into practice in my own life. Within two months, I weaned myself off ten years of prescription anti-inflammatory, and antidepressant drug therapy, and the herbal remedies I had used to help me sleep.

"In fact, when I heard Pastor Henry say that he claimed Proverbs 3:24 each night, I immediately began doing the same thing. I took a little computer graphic with a cat sleeping peacefully in a wicker chair, and added the Scriptural promise of my Heavenly Father: 'When thou liest down, thou shalt not be afraid: yea, thou shalt lie down, and thy sleep shall be sweet' (Proverbs 3:24). I framed it, and put it on my nightstand. Each night, just as I turn out the light, I read my little Scripture, praise God that I am safe because of Who He Is, and thank Him that my sleep will be sweet.

"Not only have I had awesome sleep, but no matter how late I turn out the light, God wakens me at 5:00 A.M. to spend time with Him before the alarm goes off. I quickly learned to look forward to this morning appointment with my Lord. He provides the energy each day regardless of the shortness of the night, because that "sweet sleep" is incredibly restorative!

"My thyroid function is coming back (and I've had that verified by medical testing). My fibromyalgia is gone. The 'inflammatory' pain from back surgery two years ago, that I'd been told would last up to years, is gone. My allergies are a thing of the past. Gastric reflux is no longer giving me severe, angina-like, chest pain.

"When I do get that pressure in my chest, I know God is telling me to pay attention to my fear and anxiety levels. I meet Him in prayer and we deal with it right then and there! It works!

"I am thrilled to have my health returned, and my energy restored. I praise God for taking me ever deeper into His Word and for His healing! I see the Scriptures each day in new awareness, and see the blessings of obedience, and the healing of the hurting areas of my life. I am learning so much about what God desires from me in my relationship with Him. He continually provides me with the gift of peace - the peace that passeth understanding, which is the joy of the Lord."

Linda's testimony was written several years ago. Today she is well and doing great.

## Beverly

I first started to minister to Beverly in March 1999. She was suffering from panic attacks, asthma, allergies, frequent sinusitis and stomach problems. Beverly had been molested as a child and was a very nervous and fearful person.

As I led her in a process of forgiving those who had hurt her, God healed the emotional pain and her self-worth grew. We prayed and repented for the fears and commanded them to leave. As we worked through the fears and bitterness we began to challenge the allergies.

I asked Beverly to eat something that she had been allergic to. First she was to bless the food, repent for any fear and then eat it. If a reaction started she was then to again repent for fear and in the name of Jesus command the reaction to stop. This was working well and she was taking her foods back.

I will always remember her coming to see me in April or May 1999 and telling me that an allergy was bothering her again. I knew that somehow she had let fear back in. I asked her to repent and then commanded the reaction to stop. It did! From that day on she was a believer, and she has had victory ever since.

As time went on she has been healed of all her diseases, but it does not stop there. Her oldest son was so allergic to mosquito bites that his face would swell to almost double its normal size. He too has been healed.

In June 1999 we started to pray for the salvation of her husband. As he witnessed the power of God in his family over the next year, he decided to accept the Lord as his savior in June 2000. A couple of months later he came to see me asking to be taught how to give a father's blessing to his children. We serve a miracle-working God!

## Catherine

In April 1999, Catherine came to us seeking help for fibromyalgia. The Merck Manual teaches that fibromyalgia is "found mainly in females... particularly likely to occur in healthy young women who tend to be stressed, tense, depressed, anxious, and striving...." Catharine was taking on many responsibilities that were designed for her husband to deal with. She did not feel nurtured and cared for. We worked through these issues in forgiveness of her husband and repentance for her bitterness. In this process she learned and experienced a much deeper relationship with God. Her fibromyalgia disappeared.

## Karen

Karen suffered from an extreme case of Chronic Fatigue. She was so sick that she was confined to a wheel chair, unable even to feed herself. Her parents took her to every doctor in America and England who offered them any hope. I first met her many years ago when she was in high school and witnessed what I have described.

Today she is completely normal and well. She lives on her own and is busy helping others.

## Joan

Joan was one of the most severely abused persons I have ever seen. She is the eldest of five children but grew up with only one sibling. She was raised in foster care. She had contact and lived with her mother at times. When abuse became too bad she was again removed from the home. She was sexually and satanically ritually abused.

I will never forget my first meeting with her at a seminar. On that night almost everyone in the church lined up needing ministry. More than 150 people wanted help. We started ministering to them at 9:00 P.M., and continued until 4:00 A.M. It was wonderful seeing the Holy Spirit work in the lives of these people.

Around 2:00 A.M. there were four people working with Joan and they asked me to help. She sat on the steps leading up to the platform, and I sat down beside her. Pastor Wright had asked people to write down the issues they needed help with. He called it a "yucky pucky" list. Her list was several pages long. I was tired and didn't have my glasses with me and could not read her list, but I easily spotted three large letters: SRA. I thought, "No, this can't be." I asked her, "is this Satanic Ritual Abuse?"

"Yes," she said.

My heart flip-flopped a couple of times. I had never dealt with anything like this before and I asked the Holy Spirit to help us.

"It was not your fault; you were a victim. In the name of Jesus, I release you from all guilt and shame," I said.

She started to sob and all of us held her. Her body started to go rigid and her fingers and hands contorted. I didn't know what to do. I looked at Pastor Wright and he said,

"Cast out the spirit of insanity." I had only done something like this once before when I cast the spirit of fear out of myself. "This can't be any different," I thought. So I said, "In the name of Jesus, I command the spirit of insanity to leave."

Immediately she fell limp. We had to hold her tightly, or she would have fallen off the steps.

In what seemed like several minutes, but was only a few seconds, Joan revived and her hands returned to the rigid and contorted positions they'd been in before. "Well, there must be more to do," I thought.

She refused to look me in the eye, so I gently took her chin and turned her head toward me. Then I commanded all the unclean, foul spirits to leave. Nothing happened.

Then I demanded in Jesus' name that the spirit tell me its name. The most guttural voice I have ever heard said, "hatred."

I was on uncharted ground, but with a holy boldness I commanded "hatred" to leave in the name of Jesus. The voice retorted, "No, I don't have to, I'm justified."

Wow! What a statement! What did it mean? "No, you are not justified; leave her now in the name of Jesus," I demanded.

"She hates everybody," the demon growled.

I ordered the demon to be quiet, and we carefully led Joan through forgiveness of everybody that had ever abused her. It took more than an hour. We commanded the principality of bitterness and all its supporting demons of unforgiveness, resentment, retaliation, anger, hatred, violence, and murder to leave in the name of Jesus. They did.

My wife helped during this session with Joan. As we discussed it later, we felt certain that Joan could not have been a born-again believer. How could a true Christian have resident in her all those demons? I had pondered this after casting the spirit of fear out of myself a few months earlier.

We wondered if we would ever see Joan again, and had no way of contacting her since we only knew her first name.

Joan walked into my office about three weeks later. "Do you remember me?" she asked.

"Are you kidding? Of course I remember you. How could I forget?"

We talked for an hour, and set a follow-up time for continued ministry. I learned to my great surprise that she was definitely a born-again, spirit-filled Christian — I checked that out carefully.

I spent about six hours in ministry with Joan during two different sessions. She had been ritually abused for several years and developed several personalities (DID) along with other problems. God delivered her from them all. Now she has only one God-given personality. Praise God!

My experience with Joan was very important in several ways. I had to examine and adjust my theology several times. She was a born-again Christian occupied by demons that spoke to me through her. Four other people had also heard them. One demon called itself "hatred." The demons obeyed me, just like Jesus said they would. I learned that sometimes demons will not leave if they are, indeed, justified in staying.

Ephesians 4:27 says, "give not the devil a place." The word "place" in Greek means a "right or a room." If demons have a right to indwell someone, they will refuse to leave. Sin justifies their right to refuse to leave.

This incredible lesson has helped me to help others many, many times. Since meeting Joan, I have had several similar experiences with other people. I have learned through God's Word and my own experience that despite being born-again and filled with the Holy Spirit, we are and always will be in a spiritual war until Jesus removes Satan forever.

### Donna

Environmental illness is one of our most common fear and anxiety disorders. People become "allergic to everything." Donna was allergic to literally all foods. She stands five feet, five inches, but weighed just seventy-nine pounds when we first met. She was able only to drink one or two cans of Ensure a day and they gave her extreme stomach cramps. She was able to sleep for only one to two hours at a time. She was in despair ready to die.

Within two weeks of our first ministry session, she was eating more than fifty foods. She had gone from despair to joy as she learned to defeat bitterness and fear. She no longer feared different foods, saying, "I was preparing to die because I could not eat enough to live. I thought I'd only get to enjoy food again in Heaven." Since casting down bitterness and fear, she is able to eat all foods and has regained normal weight. God has restored her health in response to her obedience.

### Barbara

Barbara was our first case of multiple sclerosis. She had suffered with this disease for about three years. It was diagnosed based on the results of an MRI. She was bulimic as a teenager and hypoglycemic since early childhood. Her mother and grandmother also have MS.

In her words, October 27, 2000:

"Art, It has been one year since the Lord healed me from MS. It has been a fantastic year and now we have a new baby daughter. I do notice that if I slip into the old sinful thought patterns a little of the numbness flares. I rebuke it, ask forgiveness and it is gone! Praise the Lord, He is so good!

"Thank you for the work you do. You will never know, until heaven, all the lives you touch.

"God bless you and your ministry, Barbara."

We helped Barbara to gain victory over bitterness toward others and intense self-bitterness. As she worked through this process of repenting and forgiving, her relationship with God skyrocketed.

We also taught her to resist the devil. The numbness and tingling associated with the MS would waken her at night. We taught her to repent of her fear, and in the name of Jesus to command the symptoms to go. She first did this on a Monday night before she went to bed, praying with her husband and commanding the symptoms not to appear. They did not. On Tuesday they did the same thing with the same result. On Wednesday they did not pray and the symptoms returned during the night. They then prayed together and the symptoms left. On Thursday they prayed before bed and there were no symptoms. On Friday they prayed commanding the symptoms to go forever.

As you can see by her testimony she has had victory for over two years.

### Christina

Christina was referred to me by a business associate of mine. She was suffering from anxiety, stress, and many allergies. She was raised as a Catholic until age five and had rarely attended church since. In visiting with her I explained how anxiety, fear, and bitterness caused allergies. I did this from medical textbooks and Scripture. I told her that Jesus was the healer and asked if she wanted to accept Him into her heart. She said "yes."

I thought in my heart "this is too easy," but the Holy Spirit spoke and said, "I have been preparing this heart for a long time." I led her in a prayer accepting Jesus as her Lord. I gave her Scriptures to study, set up a time for a second meeting and she left my office in joy.

The following Monday she came in bouncing off the ceiling in joy and happiness. All the fear and all the allergies were gone. I asked her if she had read the verses that I had given her. A puzzled look came on her face. She asked me, "What is John? What does 3 mean? What does 16 mean?" I was amazed; she did not even know how to use a Bible. I opened a Bible and turned to the table of contents and explained the book to her.

I have found that God will hear non-Christians quicker than believers. There is a different level of accountability based on knowledge.

### Martha

Martha was suffering from allergies and asthma. As we ministered to her we learned that her children and husband were suffering from the same diseases. We usually find the same issues and thus the same diseases in families. This is proof that attitudes, emotions and beliefs cause most of our diseases and problems in life. The sins of the father are passed on to the third and fourth generation.

Martha has been healed and her family is in process.

### Darlene

Darlene suffered from extreme fears, panic and allergies for most of her life. We worked with her once a week over a three-month period of time. She has been free for over two years.

### Lenore

Lenore was suffering from fear, stress, anxiety and fibromyalgia. We worked with her for about three months and she gained victory. Her process has been more difficult because she does not have support from her husband. He does not accept his responsibility and role as a husband as God intended.

Lenore falls back into the fear and anxiety and at times fibromyalgia when she allows the old thought patterns to return. This is the same for all of us. We must always remember that we are in a spiritual war and will be until Satan is bound in hell forever.

### Bridget

In January 2000, Bridget called me asking for help. She had just been diagnosed with ovarian cancer. The result of a CA-125 test was 310. CA-125 is elevated in most patients with epithelial ovarian cancer. The normal range is 0-35.

Bridget is from a Jewish family, and has been a Christian for many years. But her and her family's lives were filled with extreme resentment and bitterness. The entire family harbors every hurt forever. I led her in forgiving her family, especially her mother and sister. As we were obedient to God in forgiving, He responded.

In February her CA-125 test result was 81. In March her test was 19. The two oncologists that she was working with canceled the surgery and pronounced her cancer gone!

### Margaret

I was teaching a seminar in May 2000, and Margaret was in attendance. At one of the meetings, while teaching, I noticed that she was turning red in the face and having difficulties breathing. I watched this for a couple of minutes as the panic was building. Finally she spoke out in fear exclaiming, "I can't breathe." She was going into anaphylactic shock, and a panic attack.

I went to her, put my hand on her shoulder and said to her, "You are safe, you are okay," and then I commanded in the Name of Jesus, that the spirit of fear and trauma to leave her. In about thirty seconds, her breathing returned to normal as the fear left.

After the seminar was over that day, we spent time helping her with her issues and she has been free of panic attacks since.

### David

David is a medical doctor and was suffering with panic attacks and Grave's Disease (hyperthyroidism). He was having great difficulty maintaining his practice because of the fear and anxiety and panic attacks. He chose to undergo a medical treatment that killed his thyroid gland to prevent the over secretion of thyroxin, which was causing his eyes to swell. This creates Hashimoto's thyroiditis (hypothyroidism), which is treatable with synthetic thyroxin.

Killing his thyroid did not stop the panic attacks because they were rooted in fear. In fact, the fear was responsible for the Grave's Disease in the first place. We led him through a process of identifying the fears, repenting for them and commanding the spirit of fear to leave (II Timothy 1:7). In doing this, he gained victory over the fears and panic and is now able to continue being a great doctor.

He must maintain his healing by holding his thoughts captive to the Lord (II Corinthians 10:5), and by maintaining his relationship to God.

## Jack

Jack is an architect who had struggled in his career. He had had severe issues of rejection, abandonment and fear stemming from an abusive childhood. He had always felt inadequate, and his self-esteem had been very poor. At times anger controlled him, creating problems at work.

We led him through a process of forgiving all the people in his past. As God healed his broken heart, and as the pain in the past memories was healed, the anger went away. Today he is a new person, in control of his life through the power of Jesus.

## Mary

Mary has been a friend of ours for about twenty years. Here is her story in her own words:

"I am writing this letter to you because something very profound has happened in my life and I want to share it with you. This will be a long note but I want to give you many of the details. Hopefully by the time I finish writing, you will be able to understand what I have experienced.

"I had a severe wheat allergy for twenty years. About four years ago I developed a condition called multiple chemical sensitivity/environmental illness. I went through my home and removed anything that had any type of fragrance. My basic cleaning supplies were vinegar and water. Makeup was a real problem. Being in a mall was almost impossible. Several times I suffered panic attacks because of smells I encountered. Many times in church I would have to move because of the perfumes people were wearing. After we moved to Arizona things did get better. No panic attacks and a little more tolerance for perfume, i.e. church and shopping.

"Now, let me begin telling you about my journey. It began with a trip to Alaska on Friday, July 28, 2000. Jim had been focused on going to Alaska all summer, so he could do some fishing. We have friends that live in Anchorage. Art and Patti Mathias have been close and dear friends for twenty years.

"We arrived in Anchorage Friday evening. Art and Patti picked us up and we went directly to their home. We talked for about two hours before going to bed. During those two hours I was very distressed. I felt very uncomfortable with Art and Patti. The thoughts that ran through my mind were, 'This is going to be a long ten days.' I was also thinking how much they had changed, and I did not like the change. They were just too-oo-oo different now. If Jim had said, 'Let's go home,' I would have been on the next plane out of there.

"Art gently told me about his healing. I really did not want to hear about it. I knew I had allergies but they were manageable, and I did not want to delve into my past and see what the "roots" might be. Who knows, I might learn something I didn't want to know. Well, by Sunday, I could not stand it. I was feeling so tormented, angry, agitated, and so I challenged Art, 'So you think you can help me!' Of course he said he could.

"We decided to begin the next morning at 7:00 A.M. He gave me a book Sunday evening and asked me to read the chapter on Forgiveness and to start a list of people I needed to forgive. That was not too hard. There were some people I was irritated with so I put them down.

"Monday morning we began with prayer and started working through my list. I am not a writer. So to try and explain to you what happened would be very difficult, but the presence of the Lord and the presence of Satan were so profound. I wept and wept. God showed me things that had happened in my life as a child that I have carried all these years. Satan has lied to me and made me believe things that were not true. When I was in the fifth grade I had a nun who thought I was dumb. She told my parents that I would never progress past the fifth grade. This was a lie I carried with me, but I needed to forgive her, and I did. (At this time, I have almost finished my masters degree.)

"The baggage I had carried because of these lies is incredible. I have considered myself a "normal" well-adjusted person. During that Monday session, God spoke to me and peeled away so many negative feelings. Art and I prayed after each item I had on my list. Then I waited to hear the Holy Spirit speak to me concerning that situation. He revealed so much to me. We spent about two hours working on my list. I was so tired when we finished.

"Tuesday morning came and even though Monday had been so wonderful, I was reluctant to get started again. Satan was whispering in my ear, 'Don't go, don't go.' But of course I did, and once again our session was wonderful. Now we worked on three lists: 'Forgiveness,' 'Forgiveness of myself,' and 'Fears.' I never knew how many fears I had in my life. Once again after each item I prayed and waited to hear the Holy Spirit. The insights from the Holy Spirit have changed my life. During our session Art looked at me and said, 'You will have a ministry in this.' Me of so little faith said, 'Yeah right!'

"During the Monday and Tuesday sessions we addressed my allergies. Now I was thinking, well am I healed of my allergies? So I decided to challenge them. Patti and

I went to craft stores, and a craft mall. I said, 'let's go places that have lots of smells.' We wandered these stores for hours. At times I felt the fear welling up inside of me as I smelled the candles, soaps, potpourri, etc. But now I had tools and I just stopped and prayed and the Fear went away. No no no no no allergy reactions! In fact Patti and I were in a Michael's craft store. We were looking in a bin for some little decorating items. Patti got her Kleenex out and blew her nose. She made a comment about the smells. I said, 'What are you talking about?' Patti pointed to the bin next to us and it was filled with potpourri! I had not even noticed. Praise the Lord!

"The Holy Spirit revealed to me why I was so afraid of smells. When Karen (a friend) and I owned the ribbon business, I became very afraid of the glue gun and what kind of health problems it might cause. I had opened the door for Satan to come in, in the form of fear. Soon I became obsessed with all smells. The Holy Spirit gave me a tool to counter Satan's lie about smells. When I smell a fragrance I think to myself, this is how Jesus smells. I feel very peaceful when I smell a fragrance. I don't plan to fill up my house with smells because I have enjoyed the passing smells so much, and the reminders of Christ's presence in my life.

"The Wednesday session came and went with just as many tears and revelations. Each day we spent an average of two hours per session. Another profound thing is, as I have dealt with each issue in my life, I have forgotten them! If you were to ask me what was on my list I would be hard pressed to remember. All the hurts, fears, and unforgiveness have been erased from my mind.

"On Thursday Art had to go to work early so Patti helped me with the last session, which was on the occult. There was a three-page list of things to look through. The list began with Abortion to Wilheim Reich/Neo-Reichian Body Work, an A-to-Z list. I checked things off that I had tried and once again we went through the list item by item and prayed over each thing. (We really should have done this in the first session.)

"I really did not have too many things checked off. But one item did come up concerning Ayurvedic Medicine. I studied this Medicine when I was taking my herb classes. It is a type of medicine practiced in India. I became very interested in it and applied it. When we came to that one on the list, I became very fearful and agitated. It became very obvious that it was a problem for me. Patti and I stopped and addressed it head on, and then we were able to move along the list with ease.

"So where am I today? I can smell perfume without any problems. I am eating foods without fear. I was amazed at how fearful I was of food. Even drinking a cup of coffee caused some upset for me. I would think, 'Is this causing my cholesterol to go up? What about the creamers I am using, they have palm oil, and sugar.' When I ate, it was a constant dialogue about the food. That is all gone. God gave us food for our bodies. It is not harmful, but Satan had made me think so. How can a person be allergic to a food one day and not another? The food did not change, but I did. Satan told me a lie about that food.

"The victories continue to come forth. I am able to go anywhere I want, smell anything I want, and eat anything I want. The fears and panic attacks are also gone. Wheat was a very big issue for me. I now eat anything I want anytime. If I want wheat three times a day, I eat it. No more analyzing everything I put into my mouth. No more allergy reactions. Everything has been given back to me. My life is fresh and new because I have complete freedom.

"Jim had to laugh the other day because I sat down and ate a Krispy Kream donut. It was hot and freshly made. After every other bite I kept saying, 'yum.' I told him, 'You have no idea how good this tastes. It had been at least twenty years since I have eaten a donut.' Oh, the simple pleasures of life, they are mine again. Praise the Lord for restoring me.

"I can't begin to tell you how freeing this experience has been. I truly feel lighter, smaller, and much more peaceful. Eight hours of intense prayer time has changed my life. I am still working on my lists. Art has taught me how to work through things on my own. Yes my list grows and grows, and each day the Lord shows me another item to add. I no longer dread the list, because I know how much better I will feel after addressing the item. And like I said, after it is prayed for, I don't remember it. So now I no longer relive hurtful situations, hear those accusations about my faults, or feel guilty about past situations. They are gone!"

### Mary testifies about Donna

"Let me share with you a story about a lady I have known for twenty years. She lives in Anchorage. All the time I have known her she has been ill with lots of different food allergies. She finally went to Art in October 1999 because she knew she was dying. She, at age fifty-five was five foot, six inches tall and weighed seventy-eight pounds and could only eat four foods.

"After we moved to Seattle in 1984, she came and stayed with us several times because she was going to a special clinic to try and see what was wrong with her. So, over the course of many years, no one was able to help her and she had tried everything.

"She spent time with Art and dealt with all her fears. Today, she is a happy, healthy woman weighing 120 pounds. Patti saw her in the grocery store a few weeks ago and her grocery cart was full of food. She made the comment to Patti, 'I can eat anything I want!'"

Mary's story does not end here. As we have seen in other testimonies, the sins of the parents are passed on to our children. But thank God, so are our victories. As Mary learned the wiles of the devil, she was able break his hold on her life and now that hold has also been broken on her two daughters, Laura and Melissa.

## Laura

Laura had suffered with PMS since puberty, and was unable to conceive. After hearing of her mother's experience, she contacted me in September 2000.

Laura and I spent several hours on the phone and she made one trip to Anchorage to see me. I have known her since she was a small child. PMS is always rooted in resentment and fear about being a female and how God created the female body to function. Mary's fears had transferred to Laura.

Over a few months we worked through her fears and resentments. As we did this the PMS stopped. Laura now looks forward to this time of the month because God made her body. He made it to function in the manner He chose to cleanse itself and to reproduce.

Last July she conceived and will bring a beautiful baby boy into this world in April 2002!

## Melissa

Melissa had suffered from an extreme case of chronic fatigue for many years. She is now a healthy mother of twins and works as a nurse. I have never ministered to Melissa. She was mostly well before Mary was healed. But her story is interesting because it shows how Satan works overtime to destroy our children. Sometimes we think these kinds of things only happen in homes that are terrible. Not true! Jim and Mary are very good, loving and supportive parents.

Through studying our books Mary learned the cause of chronic fatigue, but she could not understand how it came into Melissa's life. A few months ago, she had the opportunity to ask Melissa some questions. What she learned reveals the extent that the devil will go to destroy our families and us.

Chronic Fatigue is a performance disorder. In the striving to keep others happy, our bodies simply wear out and give up. There are two facets to what happened to Melissa. First, Mary's anxieties and fears about allergies were passed on. Second, Melissa's father Jim is a very successful, outgoing person, and Melissa believed that she could never measure up to such a great dad. She drove herself to compete with her sister and make her dad happy with her. Her body could not endure this kind of pressure and stress.

What a lie of the devil. We do not have to strive to seek anyone's approval including God's. We do need to obey, but that is out of love, not duty or obligation. We always need to remember what God has said about us. If we put the opinions of others ahead of, or in place of, what God has said about us, we are in idolatry.

## Mary testifies about Kate

"Do you remember on that Tuesday when Art told me I would someday have a ministry in this area? I said 'Yeah right!' That afternoon when Art came home from work he handed me a piece of paper and said, 'Here is the first person you are going to help.' I looked at the paper and saw that the people lived in Arizona. Then I looked at the address and found that they live only one block from us! All Art said was that the wife was suffering from Panic Attacks, and told me to call them. They have a business, so there was a toll-free number.

"I spoke to Kate's husband and he told me they had six children, ages nine to two. Kate had had panic attacks for eighteen months. A friend of theirs who lives in Seattle called and gave him Art's phone number in Anchorage. He then called Art, who told him I was there visiting, and I lived in the same town. When I called he was in tears because they had tried so many doctors and his wife was such a mess. There seemed to be no help for her. My first thought was 'I can't do this!' but he said I might be their only hope. So I agreed to talk with them when I got home.

"I called Kate on the Monday after we returned home. We talked about forty minutes and about thirty minutes of the time she cried. Now I was really wondering what I was doing. But I did agree to meet with her. I also gave her a copy of Art's book. So I stepped out in faith and started doing with her what Art had done with me.

"The first couple of times we met she cried and cried; she had so much fear, even fear about fear. We began with occult things, then forgiveness, anger, bitterness and rejection. Since she was so fearful, I wanted to attack that last. I wanted to build a relationship of trust with her.

"We met on a Friday, and we agreed to begin working on her fears on Monday. Sunday afternoon her husband called me and asked if I would walk with her because the day had been very difficult. I agreed and we walked three miles and just talked. I told her I felt this was the storm before the calm. Little did I know that the storm was going to spill over onto me. That evening I felt awful, and during the night I felt as though I had wrestled the devil.

"Monday morning I got up feeling very bad. I had so many doubts about working with her. How could I ever expect to help someone as bad off as her? The thoughts just ran and ran like this. I got my lists out and began to pray over my fears and doubts. After I had addressed all the negative thoughts for about an hour, I felt a wonderful peace.

"She came that evening and we worked on fear. She did so well. There were moments we laughed, moments we cried, and moments we prayed. She is very angry about all the lies Satan has told her. She said that all the anger she has placed on herself should have been placed on Satan. The Holy Spirit has given her many truths and she is feeling great relief from her fears. She can't believe she felt so bad for so long because of fear. Her panic attacks are gone now and all her fears have been resolved."

Mary has continued to work with many others since her healing. When we experience the power and truth of God in our hearts, we are never the same again.

## Sharon

Sharon is another person Mary ministered to, a pastor's wife who had suffered from anorexia and bulimia since she was a teenager. In Mary's testimony she mentioned one thing that turned around Sharon's life. Mary repeated something she learned from *Biblical Foundations of Freedom* and our time together: "Not every thought is your own." When Sharon heard this simple truth, the pieces of the puzzle fit together.

All of her life she had heard a voice saying, "you are bad, it is your fault, you will never amount to anything, you are not good enough." Sharon came to realize that it was Satan saying those things; it was Satan lying to her. That day in her life was September 5, 2000. She has been free of the eating disorders ever since.

I have ministered to Sharon since then, and she is well and doing great. We never know the impact our words have on others for good or bad.

## Susan

Susan is a Native American who was abandoned by her unmarried parents, adopted at age two, sexually abused as a small child and as a teenager by a brother, became promiscuous as a teenager and as an adult, became addicted to drugs and alcohol, and tried to kill herself many times.

It does not take a rocket scientist to figure out why Susan went down the road she did. But it also does not take a rocket scientist to understand and teach the love of our Savior.

We spent several months ministering to and loving Susan. She is now healed of all the physical and emotional abuse. The alcoholism and drug addictions have been healed for over a year. She is a beautiful, wonderful person who is able to maintain healthy relationships with others.

## Kent

In the spring of 2000 Kent and his wife were in Anchorage teaching a seminar. One afternoon they came to visit me at my office and we were discussing what he does. They mentioned that their nine-year-old daughter had asthma and allergies that started shortly after birth.

They asked if could help. I began by asking a few questions. Was your daughter planned for and wanted? He answered that she was the fourth child and that he had not wanted any more children. He said that he had asked God to forgive him. I asked if he had asked his daughter to forgive him. He said no. I asked if the daughter had colic as a baby or had been sick in other ways. Yes, the child had colic and was hospitalized at age two for pneumonia.

I explained that asthma is caused by the fear of abandonment and rejection. These emotions cause the alveoli and bronchial tubes to become rigid, trapping the carbon dioxide. The child, in the womb, had felt the emotions of the parents and the fear and rejection had come to her then. I told them that if they would do four things their daughter would be healed.

First, repent to her for not wanting her. Second, give her a mother's and a father's blessing. Third, command the spirits of fear, rejection, and abandonment to go in the name of Jesus. And fourth, command the asthma to go in the name of Jesus.

I received an e-mail about a month later that said, "I sat down with her and talked it over. Then we prayed as you directed. Hallelujah! No more wheezing and allergies."

I have taught these principles to many parents with the same results.

## Marvin

Marvin called from the east coast in August 2000. He wanted help with allergies and Lyme disease, and his marriage was falling apart. He is Jewish by birth and was not then a Christian.

In August and September, I led Marvin through our ministry on the phone. During this time he accepted Jesus as his Lord and Savior. He also moved to Pleasant Valley and began attending the ministry sessions there. His allergies improved over time until they are now healed.

I lost track of him until July 2001 when I met him in person for the first time at Pastor Wright's Ministry in Pleasant Valley. He was on staff, helping with the teaching and sharing his personal testimony. It was a great joy for me to meet him and see his tremendous growth and joy in the Lord. His relationship with God is beautiful.

## Dorothy

Here is Dorothy's testimony in her own words, written in February 2001:

"I'm not sure when the dominoes started to fall. I remember in 1986 that I temporarily experienced terrible chest pains and high blood sugar due to the stress of a shake-up in my church family. I got better after several months with medication and counseling.

"In 1989 I took a position in my company that put me in a high stress situation with a boss who didn't want to work with me. He emotionally drained me. Within five months I was experiencing tremendous headaches, and then I hurt my back while helping my sister with her new house. I couldn't get back to normal so I went to a doctor who had been recommended to me by several of my family and friends.

"Over the course of the next seven years I re-injured my back two more times. During those years my doctor prescribed various levels of pain medication, muscle relaxers and physical therapy. I would get better but never free from the pain. I became weak and depressed from the lack of energy, physical activity and from not sleeping well. I was constantly frustrated from not being able to do all the things that I had done before. I would spend a whole day just sitting on the couch wanting to get up and go places and do things, but just could not move.

"In 1996 I thought I had gotten my pain under control until, in October, I experienced another painful episode with my upper back. Up until this point my pain had always been my lower back with intermittent pain in my ribs. This was different. I had made and decorated five birthday cakes plus a four-tiered wedding cake, traveled twice, all within six weeks.

"I again thought that this pain would go away on its own, but I found myself back at my doctor's. There was another round of regular osteopathic treatments, pain medication and muscle relaxants. Then came the nine steroid and painkiller injections. Nothing was working so my doctor sent me to a pain specialist for PENS treatment.

"PENS is similar to acupuncture with a little different philosophy. Unlike Chinese medicine where the needles are inserted in meridians, these are inserted in trigger points in relation to nerves and muscles. These needles are inserted, then hooked up to a special unit similar to a TENS unit for electrical stimulation. After about six to eight weeks I was so much better that I decided to have this doctor work with my lower back.

"PENS did not work so we continued to use osteopathic manipulation. I was also sent to a biofeedback specialist, which did not give the results they were hoping to see. I was then sent to a pain counselor to help me deal with this constant pain. During this time my doctor tested me and diagnosed me with fibromyalgia. I was given many articles to learn about this illness, its treatments and how to cope with the pain.

"I was sent to physical therapy for extensive rehab for muscle weakness and to learn proper body mechanics. After going through that, I was able to get into their maintenance program to continue working out for the next two years.

"In December 1998, during a routine visit with my doctor, he decided that I needed to go back to my counselor to deal with some issues in my life (whatever they were). He did believe that there is a mind/body connection with fibromyalgia pain and that coming to terms with those issues could relieve seventy percent or more of my pain.

"After about seven weeks in counseling I began to have minor anxiety attacks, something that I had never known before in my life. At first I was able to hide them from others. Then, while in my counselor's office I had a horrible reaction to what I perceived as a threat and had a major panic attack. It was traumatic and shocking to have a panic attack of this magnitude. For the next three-and-a-half months, my attacks ranged from minor to moderate attacks but were worsening. By the next two months I was having major panic attacks five days out of a week. I was then diagnosed with panic disorder, agoraphobia, and dissociative disorder, and was told to take anti-anxiety medication. I couldn't respond to people or make myself understood. I had tremendous fear, not knowing or understanding what was happening to me. I felt like a child cowering in the corner of a room. Twice my doctor almost placed me in the hospital to get me under control and break the cycle.

"I was tormented physically by the attacks; it took twenty-four hours or more to recuperate. I thought I was losing my mind, and had such deep depression that I wanted to die. Driving home on the interstate I struggled not to drive my car into a bridge pillar. Life had gotten too difficult and I couldn't see any way out. There were times when I just wanted to run away so my husband and my family would not have to see me this way. I saw black in those times of depression.

"The one thing that I tried to remember during those times was that my life was not my own; God gives life and God takes life. Tomorrow might be better, but if I died how would my family explain my death to my dear sweet nephews? God gave me another truth during that time in a child's song. 'Jesus loves me this I know because the Bible tells me so,' I would sing to myself.

"I couldn't eat, sleep or go anywhere for any length of time. Grocery shopping went from being a mundane to a panicky situation and I had to run quick trips.

"I had become non-functional. I stopped attending Bible study at my church, stopped seeing my friends, and limited my time with my family. I took myself off the Ladies Council at my church since I couldn't make decisions anymore. I was not able to make decisions about meals, shopping, planning events, or what I needed to pack for a trip. My doctors grounded me from air travel for several months. My husband either made our simple meals at home, brought dinner home, or we went out to places where I could eat very simply and get out quickly. The only thing that I remember doing during that time was the laundry and making it to my appointments. Most of the time my husband had to make a thirty-minute trip home from work to pick me up for my doctor's appointment. At my worst, I was unable to drive because my energy was extremely low and I couldn't handle the thirty-minute trip to the doctor.

"After seven months of unsuccessful counseling, a specific blood test revealed that I was suffering from severe hormonal imbalance, related to menopause. I started on hormones and was told to give myself a few months to adjust and the panic attacks and other symptoms would fade away. After five months it became evident that there was little improvement with my symptoms and that thought frightened me. I knew then that I was dealing with something big. I again began to realize that I was in spiritual warfare.

"After talking to a friend once again I decided to take her advice and talk to Art. As recommended I ordered the book, *A More Excellent Way*, and went to a seminar to hear Pastor Henry Wright. God gave me the presence of mind to process the information enough to know what was going on in my life, that Satan had set out to destroy my mind and my very life. I knew his ultimate goal for me was death.

"After the seminar, Art and I began a long-distance relationship by phone with him teaching me about Satan's role, who my Heavenly Father really is, and who I am in Christ. Session after session he worked with me to defeat Satan's rule in my life, focusing on forgiveness. It was not always easy. Three months after I had gone to the seminar, I woke up one morning telling myself that I had turned a corner. I was able to get up, dress, and open the curtains in my house, make two road trips, and run errands with very little trouble. I have been able to go on three trips this past fall by air, and be around people, some I didn't know.

"This holiday season, during a day of major cooking for a Thanksgiving meal, I realized I no longer experienced the pain that I always got from standing. I could go from standing for long periods of time to sitting with no special movements and with ease. This Christmas I was able to shop, decorate my home, go to parties, and be around fifteen people at my sister's home on Christmas day.

"I am back to participating in all the activities that I did before, because God has given me back my life. Am I cured of everything? My answer is, not yet. I still have things that God brings to my attention that I need to work on, but He has a plan for my life and because of my deeper relationship with Him, these things will work out according to His time frame.

"I want to thank you for the ministry that you have done in my life in the last year. I can't imagine what my life would be like today if my good friends had not put me in touch with you. I thank God for his awesome ways in leading me to the healing that I have experienced so far."

**Lisa**

In November 2000, I taught a seminar at a small town in the interior of Alaska. During the seminar I met Lisa. She had suffered with severe allergies and multiple sclerosis for several years.

Her healing process began as she worked through the bitterness, hurts, and fears in her life, one by one the allergies were healed. During the week that I was in her town she attended the meetings and I ministered to her during the day. She also assisted me as I ministered to others.

We continued the ministry process by phone for a few more weeks. I ministered to her and gave her insight as she ministered to others. As she worked through her deep insecurities and self-hatred, and ministered to others, God healed her MS. Isaiah 58 teaches us that the "fast of the Lord" is a fast of helping and serving others. As we serve others, then our light breaks forth and our health springs forth.

MS is a terrible disease. At this point in time, we have a fifty percent success rate. We have worked with six MS cases and three have been healed. I often ask myself, why not the other three? I wish I knew the answer. I keep asking God and trusting Him because I know that it is His will to heal everyone. Either this is true or He is a liar.

Part of the answer is found in one of those who lost her healing. She fell back into the same bitterness, complaining, and accusations against others that brought her the disease to begin with. Yes, we can lose our healing. Our thoughts and emotions cause most of our diseases. It only makes sense that if we fall back into those sinful thoughts and emotions, the diseases that they cause would return.

## Pauline

I first began working with Pauline in the fall of 2000. We worked together for about six months. As you read her testimony, you will see that there were many issues that broke her heart. Jesus healed every one. The following testimony is from her letter dated August 2001.

"Problems and disease: Depression, panic attacks, nerves on edge, mood swings, chest pain, shortness of breath, bladder spasms and frequent infections, sinus infections and allergies. Chronic fatigue/fibromyalgia/adrenal exhaustion, insomnia, constipation, memory fog, hypoglycemia, ulcers, frequent bronchitis. Issues of deep sadness and fears from early childhood. Diagnosis of ulcers and stress: late teens. Depression: early twenties, late teens. The rest was building over a period of thirty years of torment.

"Story: My first memories are of when I was two and a half. I was playing on the back of dad's car and he didn't see me. As he started to back up, I fell under the car and he stopped when my brother screamed. I spent the night in the hospital, and I woke in the dark, full of fear, no one could understand my French language. There were feelings of fear, abandonment and lack of trust. I had a dad who was frequently in the VA hospital from World War II injuries, so we had issues of lack of income, and fears of losing him, and not being safe or cared for. I had an older sister who was abusive verbally and physically. My mom lost her dad when she was six and was passed around to different married siblings, so she had problems of her own and struggled to nurture us with affection. She always seemed to be in survival mode; she was very controlling, manipulative and dominating in the home. My dad and mom are very strict. They were strong Catholics and sent me to Catholic school for ten years.

"I was a very quiet, shy, sensitive child. I tried to be compliant, hoping if I was 'very good' there might be someone who would notice and love me. I wanted peace in our home and, with an older brother and sister making waves, I tried to 'disappear' into the background and be 'invisible.' So I secretly longed for love and affirmation, but the 'squeaky wheels got the grease'! I remember deep loneliness and longing from a very young age, and was frequently ill. I was frustrated early on in school that I couldn't quite 'get it.' I always felt on the outside looking in.

"In my last two years of high school I finally got to go to a public school, finding it easier academically at a lower standard, making my own friends, and feeling a sense of value through a boyfriend who was a senior and adored me. He was killed the following year right after my graduation and my life bottomed out. I married the following year, to escape the restrictive home life where everything seemed evil and bad and riddled with guilt. I became pregnant on my honeymoon, and again when the first baby was six months old. I was depressed, without strength or motivation. Finding myself in a lifeless marriage, I started having problems with stomach ulcers, averaging four times a year in the hospital and being put on antidepressants and tranquilizers

"We finally agreed upon separation. Too sick to work, and with no child support I struggled to care for a baby and a toddler in endless days of survival, chastisement and despair. I sought help in all the right places and when those came up empty, I began to look in all the wrong places. I became promiscuous, trying to find hope and love and looking to others for the answers. I was mixing drugs and alcohol and was suicidal. I cried out to God and to priests, but found no answers! I was getting psychological counseling, but no answers or relief. I got a divorce. I found a 'hippie' psychologist who convinced me to let him take the kids so could find work. I lived out of my car, slept on floors, but couldn't maintain enough strength to keep a job. I was slipping into a quicksand of hopelessness! I hated myself, felt inadequate and a failure.

"After two years of this, an aunt and uncle on the children's father's side agreed to help, but only if I would sign off on adoption and promise not to see the kids. Tormented by guilt and a broken heart, within six months I put myself in a state mental hospital. The doctors tried and experimented with every drug they could and I almost had shock treatments to erase my memory, but I got no relief. After five months of this, I had to 'play the game' to get out.

"While in the half-way house, I met David. I got a job and someone rented me a room. David and I lived together for one-and-a-half years and were married. I never wanted kids again! That first year I had sought help again, this time from a 'born-again Catholic,' who poured hundreds of hours into my life and led me to the Lord. Two years later, David found Him too. We did have two children together. But I was in and out of major depression, still with physical problems, never knowing joy, or peace of mind and always tormented in my mind no matter what I tried!

"I found no relief from the self-hatred. Unable to forgive myself, others and God, I could not see clearly what the issues were or how to deal with them. I could not see the lies that had so entangled my life and kept me in bondage. I was in constant pursuit of knowing God, but couldn't get lasting breakthroughs.

"I had another breakdown and my husband had to quit work to care for the kids and me. I went to Christian counseling and deliverance, every teaching I could attend. Our marriage came to a crisis point around year six or seven. We had counseling together and separately. I was getting some healing in my life, and I was no longer the 'needy one.' The dynamics changed: he no longer felt needed. It took one-and-a-half years to begin to mend the marriage. At thirteen years of marriage, we left our 'ideal' Vermont life with the security of a home, two cars, and the 'cat in the yard,' and went into missions full time.

"We were 'living on faith' with little outside support but we were full of enthusiasm to serve God with all our hearts. We got very involved, taking on more responsibilities than were humanly possible. Within six years of serving — traveling to many developing nations for three- to five-month stints with training and outreaches — I had a total physical collapse. Some doctors called it adrenal exhaustion, others called it chronic fatigue. Some thought I had caught a rare virus in the tropics. I was too exhausted to eat, unable to walk across the room without collapsing. It affected all my internal organs. I had no capacity to function mentally or physically. I gave up on the doctors after a while; they seemed to have nothing to offer.

"I tried chiropractic, acupuncture, aromatherapy, herbal medicines, purges, colonics, Christian healing services, psychotherapy, magnets, all kinds of diets, kinesiology, homeopathy, drugs, massage, endless blood work, hair testing, barley green, endless vitamins. Some would help for a while but after six years of a very limited lifestyle and a fortune spent on helps, I began to get much worse again: panic attacks, one illness after another, tremendous fatigue, heart pain, muscle and joint pain, constant overwhelming stress and anxiety, insomnia.

"A friend in the mission had been dealing with environmental illness and had been trying to help me through diet, supplements, and vitamins. She had read *A More Excellent Way* and several months later went with her family for two weeks to Pleasant Valley and they were all healed.

"This was a tremendous testimony. After working with her for eight years, I knew her health issues; I had always been hard pressed to find anything to feed her that she could eat without reacting. I read the book but couldn't think of angers I had not forgiven. My husband took me to Pleasant Valley for two weeks, as I was too ill to travel alone. Within two days I was convicted of so many areas in my heart and wrong thinking, I wondered if I was even saved! I began to improve over a couple of months.

"Then, as I faced major changes and decisions in my life, I began to spiral downward. After two months of constant spiritual, emotional, and physical hell, I called Wellspring Ministries. I've found I needed help walking through all the years and layers of lies, bitterness toward myself and God and others, self-hatred, grief and guilt.

"The results have finally given me freedom, strength, life, hope and a set of tools to filter all the issues and circumstances of life through God's Truth. I now recognize the lies that we agree with that open the door to the enemy's schemes to destroy us and rob our joy and worship of God. The lies bind us and blind us from the truth!

"This ministry was successful because it dealt with the root causes of all my issues. It showed me how our physical, mental, and spiritual parts are connected and how we have power and authority in God to take personal responsibility in our lives over the lies of the enemy! It gave me tools and weapons — a lifestyle of new habits to live a victorious life on the offensive rather than that of a defensive victim of circumstances! With all the training I had gotten in the body of Christ, and the work I'd done in missions, nothing had prepared me to see so clearly and deal so simply with the 'mystery' of our everyday and eternal issues of life! It's no longer a mystery!"

Pauline is like all of us. She thought she had worked through the issues. She had not realized that the emotional pain was actually bitterness. As we went back through all the issues in her life, one by one, she was set free of all the guilt, shame and condemnation. I visited with her in January 2002 and she is totally well.

But as we have seen with others, Pauline's story does not end here. She has a daughter, Angela.

## Angela

As we have seen in other families, Angela's issues were not that different from her mother's. The circumstances are different but the issues are the same. Pauline was caught up in her own emotional and physical challenges and Angela suffered. She felt left out and abandoned by her parents.

I worked with Angela only two times by phone. In these sessions I led her in forgiving her parents and encouraging conversation to build relationship, trust and understanding between them. I taught her parents to ask for forgiveness, explore Angela's feelings, and give Angela a mother's and a father's blessing. Children are very quick to respond to the genuine love and repentance of parents. Angela quickly forgave them.

In January 2002 Pauline spoke about her beautiful daughter and how great their relationship is. She shared how Angela now calls and asks her parents for their advice about decisions in her life. Their relationship is truly restored, healthy and beautiful.

## Dinah

Dinah is a pastor's wife who had suffered from asthma for many years. She was in Anchorage helping Wellspring produce a worship musical in the spring of 2001. Her asthma attacks were associated with stress, especially in the role of a pastor's wife.

She had been through many different inner-healing ministries, received prayer many times, but was never healed even though she believed in healing. I explained the medical and spiritual roots to asthma and led her to work through the bitterness, resentment and fears that came from being a pastor's wife. She was healed in that session and has never had an asthma attack again.

## Erica

Erica is a beautiful young woman who traveled with her parents from the Midwest to Oregon to attend a seminar that I taught in April 2001. She was suffering from severe allergies, PMS and migraines. She was unable to work and was still living at home.

Erica and her family attended the meeting and I ministered to Erica two times during the week of meetings. During the first ministry session, I discovered many deep hurts from childhood and from sexual abuse as a teenager.

I helped her pray through these and other issues. As we prayed, God healed her heart and she experienced tremendous relief. After that first session, she ate her favorite food, ice cream, and experienced none of the usual side effects. That evening at the meeting she was excited and hopeful about the future.

Our second session was the next morning. At the beginning of the session she was doing very well. The migraine from the previous day was gone and the progress in the allergies was miraculous. We had a great session watching God continue to heal her heart and body. At the end of the time I asked her parents, who were waiting in the car, to come in.

Her father came into the room and brought a huge cloud of despair with him. I could feel the weight of it. He sat down and asked for prayer, prayer that God would sell his new truck so he could pay for all the expenses that he was encountering on this trip. I turned and looked at Erica. Her countenance dropped. Guilt and shame flooded through her. She was thinking to herself that it was all her fault, "if only I was a better, stronger person, my father would not have to go through all this."

Within ten minutes the migraine was back with a vengeance, and the allergy symptoms began to recur with an upset stomach. That night at the meetings she was a basket case again.

I relate this story to show you the power of our words, especially the power of Dad's words. There is life and death in what we say to others and to ourselves. Dad was more concerned about himself than about his daughter. He had the power to heal his daughter through his love and compassion, but he did not understand his position and its power. His words put his daughter right back into the guilt and shame that she had carried for years, and thus back into the allergies and migraines.

## Judy

Judy's story is one that vividly portrays the depravity of mankind. In early 2001, Judy was a new Christian, suffering from extreme fears and panic attacks. Her husband had abused her verbally, emotionally, sexually and physically. At this time she was separated from him and struggling through the court system with restraining orders and divorce issues. Some Christians were telling her that she could not divorce and her mom was telling her that she must keep her husband "happy." She was confused and extremely scared. She was afraid of God. She was hearing many different voices in her mind and she was very afraid that she was going crazy.

At first she was very difficult to work with. She could not focus, and would go off on emotional tangents. She expressed extreme worry about the voices and worry about being crazy.

I worked with Judy for about six months. In this time I taught her about Satan and how he puts thoughts into our minds, how we all hear voices. It is normal to hear voices.

This shocked her. As she learned, she was able to distinguish God's voice from Satan's. The fear left, and she was able to accept God's love and to command Satan and his fear to leave.

We spent a lot of time working through bitterness toward others, but especially toward herself. As she learned to love herself, she was able to really love others and God. Today she is a well-adjusted, loving, and caring mom. She has her life together and is experiencing an incredible relationship with our loving heavenly Father. She has personally experienced His truth and it has set her free.

### Rose Ann

In April 2001, Rose Ann called from her hospital room very scared. Her doctor had just told her that her heart was very enlarged and that it was failing. The cardiologist believed that her heart could fail any time and wanted to call in the transplant team. She had given birth to her fifth child, about thirty days earlier, at age forty-two.

Scripture teaches us that in the last days, people's hearts will fail them for fear. Rose Ann was obviously scared; in fact she had lived in fear for many years. As I worked with her I learned that this was really her seventh pregnancy. When she was nineteen and twenty, she had ended her first two pregnancies in abortions.

She knew that God had forgiven her, and she was even a Crisis Pregnancy counselor. In her counseling work she had shared her story with many others, but the regret, guilt, and shame were still there. She had never forgiven herself. She lived in the fear that she would never see her five beautiful children grow up. She did not believe that she was worthy of having them after she had killed the first two.

This constant struggle with regret, shame, guilt and fear was the root cause of her heart problems. The constant stress of the fear and guilt caused her heart to work overtime, and thus become enlarged. The stress also caused an irregular heartbeat.

I worked with her for about three hours in the hospital and by phone. Within two days she improved so much that the doctor released her and told her to come back in six months. I continued to work with her for the next three months and she continued to improve. She was able to care for her children and family, mow the lawn, climb the steps and take care of her garden. She was able to perform all her normal duties.

In October, she returned to the cardiologist for the six-month check up. The echocardiogram showed that her heart was almost normal in size and functioning normally.

When she refused to forgive herself, in reality she was saying that the blood of Jesus was not good enough to pay for her sins. She placed herself in a position of idolatry. She placed herself above Jesus in believing the lie of the devil. As we worked through the issues she was able to receive total forgiveness from God and herself. Jesus took all the regret, shame and guilt, and then a peace and joy flooded her soul. Her heart relaxed and returned to its normal size and function.

We serve a powerful, wonderful God!

Once again the story does not end here. Rose Ann's new baby, Colleen, was experiencing screaming fits and colic.

## Colleen

At age forty-two, neither Rose Ann nor her husband was excited about a fifth child. At first both of them were upset. They both love children and soon got over it. But little Colleen, in the womb, knew that she was not really wanted. In children with colic, asthma, or allergies, we always find issues of abandonment, fear or rejection. They can be as minor as simply not being excited about another child.

All children who were conceived out of wedlock, adopted, or were unplanned for in any way, struggle with fear, abandonment, and rejection issues.

I asked Rose Ann and her husband to repent to the two-month-old baby for not wanting her and then to command the fear, rejection and abandonment to go in the name Jesus. To give to her a mother's and a father's blessing, and in the name of Jesus, command the screaming and colic to stop. I told her that if they would do this, their daughter would be healed.

Rose Ann did this, and the screaming and colic stopped. Her husband did not believe and refused. Colleen continued to scream when he tried to hold her. After a few months, the husband realized the truth and blessed his new baby and now she is well all the time.

## Rick

This is a testimony about another special family. As we have seen, the sins of the father, or family, are passed on to the next generation. The human weakness and character flaws of one generation become the weakness or flaws of the next.

I started working with Rick in February 2001. He was a quiet, unassuming maintenance man. He would rarely look you in the eye. He was a nice person but there was no fire or purpose In his life. He was like a lost puppy with no goal or purpose. He felt set off to the side and forgotten. He had been a pastor for a few years, and now was the maintenance man.

Rick was rejected by his father and scared to death of him. He had never heard the words "I love you" or other words of affection or acceptance from him. Thus, he related to God the Father in much the same way. He never felt he could please God, no matter how much he tried. He believed in God, but did not believe that He was there for him. Rick did not believe that he could ever go to school. He did not believe that he was accepted by others or that he was qualified to be a counselor, which was his heart's desire.

As I led him through our ministry he changed. As Rick was obedient to forgive those who had hurt him and ask God to forgive him, he changed. As he learned who he was in Christ, and that Jesus had a purpose for him, he became confident. He began to hold his head up and look me in the eye. He was no longer ashamed.

Before we were through meeting together, Rick and I began to meet with his wife Trudy.

## Trudy

Trudy was in her early thirties, the mother of four children, and trying to work full time. She suffered from depression, irritable bowel syndrome, mitral-valve prolapse, asthma, allergies, chronic sinus infections, panic attacks, bulimia, hypoglycemia, hypothyroidism, severe headaches and back spasms.

I led Trudy through the ministry while Rick sat with us and prayed. Trudy had been abused as a child. She felt she had to perform to gain acceptance. She was very fearful and carried much bitterness toward those that had hurt her. As we worked through the issues, she too changed. God set her free of the guilt and shame. As she repented for the fears and learned to rebuke the devil, the panic attacks were gone.

We worked together for about three months, and in that time she was healed of everything on the list. But once again the story does not stop there. Rick and Trudy have five children now.

## Rick and Trudy's Children

Rick described his oldest daughter as a little girl who carried shame and rejection. She felt that everything was her fault. She was very teary. She had had colic as a baby and now had asthma. The other three children also had asthma and allergies.

I taught Rick and Trudy to minister to their children. The first three or four years of the marriage had been very rocky with quarreling and fighting. I asked them to repent to their children for the arguing and tension, ask the children for forgiveness, command the fear, rejection and abandonment to leave, give each child a mother's and a father's blessing and then command the asthma and allergies to go in the name of Jesus.

As they did this with each of their children, they too were healed.

God has healed this entire family in many miraculous ways. They walk in a special place and relationship with God. He has healed each person in spirit, soul and body. And now Rick has the dream of his life. He is a counselor teaching others what God did for his family, and what God will do for your family.

## Wayne

Wayne's marriage was falling apart. His business was suffering because of his personal problems, which were caused by his anger. I led him through forgiving everyone who ever hurt him, especially in forgiving himself and receiving God's forgiveness. As we worked through the issues, he learned to love himself. Then he could really love those who were important to him. His family and business are now doing well.

### Sandra

Sandra was raised in an abusive, dysfunctional home. Her brothers, a neighbor, and a grandfather molested her. There were sexual experiences with girls and animals at a young age. She became promiscuous as a teenager and a young adult. Her father and a pastor betrayed her. Masturbation became a large part of her life.

She suffered from extreme jealousy and fear about her husband. She became irate if he would look at another woman, and lived in fear that he would leave her. She did not trust anyone, especially God.

I worked with her for about eight months, leading her through forgiving others and repenting for her sins. As we did this, gradually all the shame, guilt and condemnation left. The jealously and envy are gone. She now trusts her husband and God. Life is entirely different because she is cleansed and free.

### Sandra's Children

All of her children were acting out sexually and masturbating. The oldest is five. In working through this, I discovered a very important point. Young children become involved in this usually in a home where there is a lot of strife, arguing and tension. The dopamine release provides a few moments of security. But guilt soon follows and it becomes a vicious circle. But that was not true in this case.

I discovered that masturbation can be a generational issue. I led Sandra through repentance in her life and in her generations. I led her through a prayer breaking the soul tie that she had formed with herself. I asked her to repent to her children and break the generational curse off them. The spirits of sexual perversion had transferred to her children. But praise God there is victory! The children are now free, and no longer act out.

### Earlene

Earlene grew up in a very abusive home. She was beaten by her father until she was twenty-one, when she escaped into a bad marriage. She lived in fear of her periods because of the severe migraine headaches and cramping. She started menopause in her early forties. She had not had a period for over six years, when she called in June 2001. Severe bleeding had begun about ten days before she called. Her husband is a doctor, and her employer is a neurologist.

She was not wanted by her father. He wanted a boy. Her mother often said, "I hate sex." There was tremendous bitterness in this Jewish home, especially among the females. Earlene carried extreme guilt because her first marriage failed.

I only worked with her for one session, leading her in forgiving and repenting. We carefully worked through the female issues. God healed her bleeding and her migraines that very day. She has been free for over six months.

**Natalie**

"I can remember 'fear' coming into me at the early age of five. I'm not talking a small childhood, 'mommy, I'm scared' fear, but real tangible fear. I can remember laying in bed, at the age of six and seven, and being so scared that I was paralyzed with fear. I would break out in a sweat and lay as still as I could until I fell asleep.

"What caused such fear? Was I beaten, in a broken home or molested? No. It was as simple as being raised in a family where absolutely no sign of weakness was allowed or acknowledged. If I would say something as childish and simple as, 'daddy, I'm scared,' the answer I would get would be, 'you're not scared, go to sleep.' This denial of my normal emotions caused me to go into a depression as I grew older, because there was no outlet for emotions. It became a form of mental abuse. And that's how it started.

"Fear is no respecter of persons, or of circumstances. He's an equal opportunity employer. I've learned through this ministry to listen to those emotions of fear, anxiety, stress, and to repent immediately, as they were the core of my woundedness and illness.

"By the time I was a young teenager, I was completely trapped in a web of lies. You see, I come from a family where how you project yourself to the general public is the key to success, power, and reputation. As I was the only girl, and the youngest of three, and had two very talented brothers, I learned to cover all traces of neediness with a bravado, smile and talent that would fool the best.

"At the age of thirteen I had my first episode of PVT, paroxysmal ventricular tachycardia. You may be familiar with it, as it is very common. I was in gym class at school and suddenly my heart started racing out of control. I was completely unable to bring my heart rate back down and ended up in a cardiologist's office the next day.

This pattern of attacks continued throughout my early years of adulthood, and of course most of you know that the doctors will tell you there's nothing you can do about it. I used to muse, 'it's okay, I can control this.'

"I did not know that the cause of this was deep anxiety. I did get some help in my early thirties with doses of calcium and magnesium, which have a calming effect on the heart muscle, but as I grew older, even this didn't help. It never occurred to me in all of those years, that it was directly related to fear.

"In a family raised with extreme expectations of success, control is the operative word. I was in control all right. By the time I was in my early twenties I was a nervous wreck, but still 'covering.' Thankfully, the Lord intervened in my life at the age of twenty-four and I was gloriously saved. I had a very dramatic salvation experience. Almost an 'on the road to Damascus' experience, like Paul's. As most of us know, the Lord graciously gives us a honeymoon period which, in my case, lasted for about six months. Many times during those months, I ministered to others, slew the 'devil' and thought, 'wow, this is a piece of cake being a Christian.' Don't smile too broadly. As you know, this too passed and the symptoms of PVT and the struggles of life began to train me and teach me.

"At the age of forty-five, I began to have serious attacks of PVT and for the first time I became afraid of them. At this time last March, I went into an attack that lasted five hours. I ended up in the er. The doctors stopped my heart (flatline) for four seconds (a lifetime) and restarted it. As I came back, for want of a better word, the Lord spoke to me and said, 'I'm giving you a new heart.' Trust me.... The next day, the world fell apart for me.

"I knew from the time I'd gotten saved to this moment in my life that the Lord had a marvelous plan for me, a plan to see people set free from demons, addictions, and healed of all sorts of diseases. But here I was, in terrible shape and being asked by a ministry group that I worked with to step down because they felt I was unhealthy.

"I bottomed out. I can remember having a very surrealistic feeling, as if in a dream, that life as I knew it, was out of my control. I had a strong "mood" come over me, that I was not going to fulfill what God had for me. It was very real, very dangerous, very demonic and I knew it.

"I called my best friend. We went to lunch, and we cried out to the Lord for answers. As the Lord promises, He delivered. In our despair we cried out and in His unconditional love, He had already orchestrated an answer. Sitting across from us at lunch was Art and one of his counselors.

"Very timidly, I went over to their table and asked for help. You see, I knew Art as an acquaintance and that he had Wellspring Ministries. I asked him what the source of heart problems were, and he said, 'grief.' That cord struck so close to home, that I immediately went into counseling with him.

"I am free today. The PVT was just a symptom of a much deeper bondage. He has set me free from a mind set of struggle, a believing that the enemy must be fought with a sword, spiritual warfare-style, to an understanding, that freedom comes as we repent, of bitterness, rejections, and jealousies that have taken over our lives. Then the abundant life that He promises us becomes a reality. The enemy is thwarted without really lifting a finger. The weapons of our warfare really are not by might or power, but by His spirit and His authority. I am free now to follow my dream of ministry and to fulfill what the Lord showed me almost twenty-five years ago.

"I really believe that these testimonies you are reading are a part of the spiritual weaponry of the Lord God Almighty. I hope this blesses you. Be healed my friend."

### Evelyn

Evelyn was raised in a mixed racial home. Her white father sexually and physically abused her. She was called a "half-breed" and "nigger" by her father and others in the village. Her brothers, uncles and cousins sexually abused her. Her mother was an alcoholic and Evelyn become "mother" to her siblings.

As Evelyn grew up, she, too became addicted to alcohol and drugs and became bulimic. She was promiscuous as a teenager and a young woman.

Today Evelyn is totally free of all addictions and bulimia and very active in serving the Lord. Again the story does not end here. As a young woman she became pregnant and had a son, Gary.

## Gary

Evelyn resented having Gary. She almost died in the delivery, and was alone and on the street barely able to take care of herself. Gary's biological father has not been part of his life. When I first met her, Gary was thirteen and suffering from asthma. I taught Evelyn and her husband, Gary's stepfather, how to minister to their son. Gary was instantly healed of the asthma in June 2001.

## Jack

Jack is Jewish. His parents were divorced when he was one year old. His biological father also died when he was young. His mother remarried a medical doctor who was very demanding and distant. Jack was adopted by his stepfather at age ten, and then prevented from seeing his birth father. The stepfather belittled Jack and put extreme pressure on him to perform.

Jack suffered from great fears and panic attacks for years. His self-esteem was very low. As he learned who he was in Christ, as he learned his true value, position and authority, the fears and panic disappeared. His business was usually on the edge of not doing well because of his insecurities. Now he is confident and able to attract more and better clients.

## Millie

Millie is a beautiful young woman who was driven to please her parents and God. Her life was one of fear that her family or God would not be happy with her. She suffered from fibromyalgia, chronic fatigue, allergies, irritable bowel and depression. This is a group of diseases that come with this type of personality. The drivenness to please others wears the body out and it crashes.

As we led her through the ministry, Millie learned that it was not her "duty" to please others. She learned to love herself and accept the unconditional love of God and she was healed of all the diseases. Today, Millie is living a victorious life, in victory over the wiles of the devil.

## Jeff and Sara

A young couple preparing to serve God, Jeff and Sara learned about Wellspring and came for help. Even though Jeff was only in his twenties, he had high blood pressure, high cholesterol and allergies. Sara was dealing with anger, resentments and many fears.

No one would have guessed these situations existed. They are both outgoing, friendly and committed Christians.

I met with Jeff and Sara together and led them through the ministry process. In the first session Jeff's nose was running, he was sneezing and could barely talk because his voice was so hoarse. I thought he had a terrible cold, but he informed me it was just allergies. By the end of the first meeting the allergies were gone and they have never come back. Each week I asked him to get his blood pressure checked. By the end of the third week it was normal.

Sara was also set free of lifelong fear and dread that had affected every facet of her life. She was able to forgive situations from the past and accept God's love. The old fears and thoughts that haunted her are gone. She can relax and sit quietly for the first time in her life. If we do not deal with the issues in our lives they will deal with us.

**Bonnie**

Bonnie is a forty-five-year-old Eskimo woman. She was suffering from alcoholism, panic attacks, claustrophobia, dyslexia and dissociative disorder (DID). At times there were vivid external demonic manifestations in words and actions. She had thoughts of suicide, feared that she was going crazy and had many voices in her mind.

Bonnie never knew her father. She was conceived in a "one night fling." Her mother had so many of her own problems that Bonnie became the "mother" of the family. Bonnie is half-white, so she was not accepted in either community. She had a son out of wedlock.

We worked with Bonnie for about six months in our ministry process. Today she has victory. The alcoholism, panic, dyslexia and DID are gone. She now understands who she is in Christ and has learned to resist the devil. She has learned the difference between the devil's voice and God's. She no longer needs any medications.

We taught Bonnie how to minister to her son, and as she did this his self-worth improved. His grades have improved from F's to C's.

Bonnie is now working as a counselor, and we are making plans to minister together in addictions.

**Brenda**

Brenda was suffering from fibromyalgia, chronic fatigue, ulcerative colitis, allergies, candidiasis, memory loss and depression. She was a Mormon for many years. When her husband died a few years ago, she left the Mormon church and became a Christian. Her old friends and her children who remained in the Mormon church rejected her. Brenda was very shy, timid and afraid.

We ministered to Brenda for about six months. During this process she grew tremendously in Christ. As His truth became part of her, she learned that she did not have to be afraid. She learned that there was power over Satan through Christ. She was able to reach out to her children who had rejected her. Some of the relationships have been restored.

The list of her diseases has gradually disappeared and today she is free of all of them.

## Jim

I met with Jim in the summer of 2001 for one session. Here is his testimony in his words:

"My growing up years were not fun times. My first two grades in school were taken in two small country schoolhouses. My parents moved to a farm when I was in the third grade and this was a larger school in a town of approximately nine hundred people. I was picked on all through school even up until I graduated. During seventh grade I had homemade Hawaiian print shirts, gold knit pants and fluorescent pink socks to wear to school. I was picked on because I couldn't wear other popular styles, and was told by students and teachers that I was not good enough.

"I was the oldest of six children. My parents had very little money and only one car. They were very strict when it came to dating and socializing with other kids. I could not date because they might need the car in case of an emergency, and "heaven forbid" I do anything to disgrace my family. If I did go to any functions at church or school, my parents had to approve of what I was going to do, with whom, and had to be home early.

"Because we lived on the farm, there was always a lot of work to do. My dad had two sayings, "a man never cries or shows emotion" and "when the work is done, then you can play," but it seemed that the work was never done.

"I had a bachelor uncle who was a farmer and lived a short distance away. He was also my godfather. Because he had no family to help him with his work I was always sent over to help him around the farm. He was verbally abusive and I would receive little or nothing for my labor. He would constantly tell me I was no good and worthless; there was never any sign of appreciation for what I did. After I was married he actually came to my place while my wife and I were at work and took a load of hay from my barn and never paid for it. One time I asked him to combine some grain for me. He did, but charged me more than he did anyone else. So I had a lot of bad feelings toward him.

"Over the years I became a workaholic. Even after I was married, I would work all the time, trying to prove to myself and other people that I was a good person and not worthless. Over the course of the last couple of years I was working thirty-plus hours per shift sometimes with no breaks for lunch or sleep. At the end of one shift one day, my supervisor came up to me, chewed me out and made the comment that people like me were a dime a dozen. He was upset because I had followed the boss's, instead of his, unwritten policy to solve problems. After that, I really started feeling bad about myself. I had bouts of depression, low or no self-esteem at times. I remember my dad telling me that he loved me once and that was shortly before he passed away. Otherwise I don't remember any love or appreciation for anything I did until I got married and that was from my wife. Practically all my life I always acted happy on the outside, but inside I was a terrible mess. I had a Christian upbringing, thanks to mom, but I could never accept the fact that God could truly love a worthless person like me. I had prayed many times and asked God to help me with my problem, but it seemed He never heard me because nothing happened. I knew I was in bad shape and did not know what to do anymore.

"This last summer my wife and I took a vacation for the first time by ourselves in about thirty years. We visited her sister and family for two weeks in Anchorage, Alaska. While there we went to church with them on Sunday. During the service, the words to one of the hymns were put on an overhead screen with pictures of Jesus standing with open arms, and another where He was embracing someone. When I saw this I actually started to cry, because I wanted Jesus to hold me and love me like in those pictures.

"While talking with my sister-in-law about some of my problems and the Bible, she set up an appointment with Art Mathias at Wellspring Ministries the following Friday after the church service. During my visit with Dr. Mathias, he helped me deal with about forty-five years of bitterness, resentment and unforgiveness in my heart. I thought I had forgiven all the people who had hurt me, but I had not forgiven them from the heart. I had been trying to do things myself without putting all my trust in the Lord. I had to give all those bad feelings totally to God and let Him heal them, which I have done.

"Since that visit, with the help of the Holy Spirit and Art Mathias, my life is completely turned around. I am free of all the things that were bothering me before. I feel so loved by my Savior and can picture myself in his embrace. I have daily devotions, pray much more, and I know He is listening because so many of my prayers have been answered. I now pray with confidence that He will answer my prayers in His own way and His own time and not mine. For the first time in my life I feel close to my Lord, I feel great and know with certainty that some day I will see Him in heaven. I now have a relationship with my Father in Heaven that I had always yearned for but never seemed able to enjoy.

"God has blessed me with so many gifts, a wonderful wife, two sons, two grandchildren and a third grandchild due in four weeks. When I got married, I promised myself that my family would always know that they were very much loved, appreciated and a wonderful gift from God. It is a great day to be alive. I now know that we must put all our trust in the Lord for He is in control."

**Kathy**

In her own words written October 13, 2001:

"I have always had the immune system of a mule. I can count on one hand the number of times in my life that I have taken antibiotics. While others around me were succumbing to the latest flu symptoms, I seldom did. I am a teacher and own a seasonal business. It was common for me to work twelve to sixteen hours a day, seven days a week, for the summer season, take a two-week respite and began in the fall, substituting or tutoring. My business partner said he had never met anyone with such stamina.

"In 1997, I came out of the summer season more bone weary than usual. I chalked it up to the fact that I was getting older. My usual two weeks went by and I wasn't regaining my usual vigor. Before I knew it, January was upon me and I was still having a difficult time bouncing back. In fact I could barely get out of bed by 9:00 A.M. and would be back on the bed napping by 2:00 P.M. My thoughts seemed to escape me often, and I was emotional much of the time. My body began to jump and jerk so badly at night that I kicked my husband off of the bed more then once. I was becoming incontinent. I never felt rested no matter how many hours I slept. I was gaining weight. Being of homesteader mentality, I figured this all would pass and by spring I would be fine.

"When the following May came rolling around I wasn't any better. I had a business to run and I knew I was in no mental, physical or emotional condition to do it. I went to my doctor. I had decided I must be in the throes of menopause and hormones would solve everything. Tests proved that my hormones were a little low and I began hormone replacement therapy. It helped and I began to feel better, but I never did regain my normal stamina. Each season I would increase my hormone level, find some relief and go on.

"The summer of 1998 my brother-in-law was diagnosed with cancer. My husband I began traveling back and forth to Texas to spend time with him. I noticed I was still gaining weight and felt sluggish all of the time. I figured it was stress and southern cooking. 'This too shall pass,' was my motto. In the spring of 1999 when my bother-in-law went into crisis with his cancer, we went to Texas to be with him. We stayed until he passed away. His death was one in a succession of the deaths of close family members that had taken place in the previous eight years. His death seemed to be the one thing that pushed me over the edge. I hadn't lost my faith or the joy of my salvation, but I felt as if the sweetness had gone out of my life. What I didn't realize was that bitterness had replaced it.

"In the spring of 2000, God began to deal with me concerning my own health. I knew something was wrong. I begin to exercise, see a physical and massage therapist, and watch what I ate more closely. I knew I was losing ground health wise but could not understand why. By now my weight was up fifty pounds and there seemed no stopping the weight-gain process. I would try to exercise and every bone in my body would ache.

I thought, 'Boy, Kathy, you really are out of shape.'

"The summer came; I had quit substituting in the winter months, so I should have been rested, ready for summer. But all I could think was, 'How will I ever make it through this summer?' My hours at work had been shortened, I was in the area of my business I loved the most, and the conditions of my working environment were wonderful. My business partner began to say to me things like, 'Kathy, I don't know what you're trying to say half the time. You must concentrate harder.'

"Then, Friday, June 16, 2000, life as I knew it came to a screeching halt. I was trying to talk to my business partner, when I realized that what was in my mind and what was coming out of my mouth were two entirely different things. I left and went to my computer and tried to type out something, but I could not. By this time I was beginning to get scared. I headed for my home and by the time I got through my front door I could not speak at all. I was unable to write a simple phone number that I had known for years. I found my husband and pointed to my lips. He surmised I couldn't speak, called my doctor, and took me to the ER.

"By the time I got to the hospital some of my speech had returned, but very haltingly. They diagnosed my condition as stress, gave me some tranquilizers and told me to sleep for the weekend if I could manage it.

"I was to see my regular doctor on Monday.

"When I entered my doctor's office that Monday, I still felt like I had been run over by a Mac truck. My speech was still not clear and I couldn't hold thoughts for any length of time. I tried to convince her that I needed to have my hormones upped again; after all, it had always brought some relief. If it wasn't hormones, what else could it be? The hospital had ruled out that it was a stroke. She would not do it. My GP was of the opinion that no matter what had caused it, if I had not been able to speak, type or write, then I had experienced some type of neurological incident, and she ordered an MRI. It was scheduled for that afternoon.

"By 6:00 that evening the results had come back and my doctor ordered me back to the hospital. She was alarmed. My brain was 'lit up' with random infarcts, and it appeared that I had been having these 'little incidents' for quite some time. One area of the brain indicated that I had experienced a significant stroke at some point. When it had happened, they couldn't determine.

"The testing began: an EKG, a sonogram of my carotid artery, a second MRI, blood flow tests, and blood screening tests. The findings were minimal. My thyroid was apparently not functioning properly, and my cholesterol had gone from 180 to 280, but other than that, there didn't seem to be a significant reason for me to be having mini strokes. No source could be found.

"In July, I went to Seattle's Virginia Mason Diagnostic Clinic to see if they could find the source. I once again went through an extensive battery of tests, saw a heart specialist, an internist and a neurologist. Initially I was put on Synthroid for my thyroid, and Lipitor to lower my cholesterol, but it was basically a mystery why I had been having such a significant amount of stroke activity. The final blood test ordered was an anticoagulation panel. It would be two weeks before all the results were in. We came home.

"The first week of August arrived and I received a call from my internist at Virginia Mason. The blood work was back and she wanted me to get to my local GP as soon as possible. I needed to be started on Heparin and Coumadin immediately. I had been diagnosed with a blood disorder called Leiden Factor V Mutation. It's cause is genetic and in my case passed to me from both parents. This disorder causes your blood to hypercoagulate. It seems the consistency of my blood was somewhere between sorghum syrup and Elmer's glue. I was a 'stroke waiting for a place to happen,' as she put it and I needed to get help now. I was considered at one hundred percent risk for another stroke. So began my journey of trying to balance Coumadin, taking blood tests daily, then weekly, then monthly until my blood levels were right. In the midst of this I was having headaches daily. This was something that I had never experienced before. I spent the winter of 2000-2001 trying to get well. I could never quite get strong.

"I began an exercise regimen in January 2001, working out forty-five minutes to an hour twice a day. Once again, I took seriously trying to get the weight off that I had gained during the past six years. Nothing happened. In six months I lost less then four pounds and although I seemed to be getting stronger, I still did not 'feel' healthy. I would look at pictures of myself and see that my eyes, instead of looking better, seemed to look worse than the first days after my initial stroke. I was doing everything I knew to do to get better. Nothing seemed to be working.

"As I went into the summer season of 2001, I was very aware that I still was not really healthy. My business partner planned for me to be there as I could, and at first I did fairly well.

My menstrual cycle had been quite irregular. I began to bleed frequently. By the end of June I had bled forty out of fifty days. A sonogram was ordered of my uterus. They found a thickening of the uterine wall and ordered a biopsy of the uterine wall to rule out cancer. Praise God it came back negative. Since hormones upped my chances of clotting by sixty percent, my GP and I decided to lower my hormone level, and change the method of application.

"On July 6th, I physically crashed once again, but this time, I was reduced to being in bed for twenty hours a day. My head hurt so badly that I could not function. No amount of pain medication would lessen it. Friends who visited me during that time left my home concerned that I was not long for this world. My husband was beside himself, always supportive, always looking for answers, but needless to say, very worried.

"We decided I needed to see a hematologist and my GP agreed. This process had gotten more and more complicated and convoluted. Nothing seemed to help. I could not keep my Coumadin levels anywhere near regulated. One time it would be dangerously low, another dangerously high. I was so sick of being sick; I quit answering the question, 'How are you?'

"On July 31st, I traveled to Anchorage to meet with my hematologist. He spent two-and-a-half hours with me, going through every detail of the past six years. I discovered that many of the symptoms I had attributed to hormone loss were also symptoms of stroke. He told me point blank, that if we didn't get this thing under control, that it wasn't a matter of if I would have another stroke, but when. The next one might take my life.

"He took me off the Coumadin, put me on two injections a day of a low-weight molecular heparin called 'Lovenox,' and told me I needed to get off all hormones. I was devastated. I couldn't see how I could live a quality life without hormone replacement, and I had been through the injection route when first diagnosed. All I could remember was how traumatic that had been, and how glad I had been to quit giving myself shots. He said that I might feel so much better I wouldn't mind giving myself shots. I wasn't so sure.

"At this point I received a call from a long-time close friend. She had been having bouts with her heart and had been introduced to a ministry called Wellspring. She had been in therapy since May, and was having some real healing take place. For instance, her allergic response to ice cream disappeared. She urged me to make an appointment for the next week when I was returning to Anchorage for a follow-up visit with my hematologist. I told her no, I was too sick. I couldn't handle one more thing, and I certainly didn't need to go through any great 'spiritual' searching. I just didn't have the energy.

"The next week she accompanied my husband and me to the doctor. She had not seen me in person since May and she was alarmed at the way I looked. She told me later that in her mind and heart she believed she was going to lose her best friend.

"While we were sitting in the doctor's office she asked me again if I would consider going to Wellspring. A week on the heparin had helped me a little; at least I wasn't having the headache all day every day, and something in my spirit said, 'Say yes.' Being healed of the Leiden Factor V. was not my main motivation. As far as I was concerned that wasn't the issue. I went to Wellspring because I knew that my whole system was somehow affected by the obsessive-compulsive behavior I had battled all of my life and that somehow my sickness was also tied to it. I had often said that every addiction existed in my birth family except gambling, and that is because no one lived next door to Reno. It was generational and I knew it. I just didn't know what to do with it. I had been prayed for, prayers of deliverance and healing. I had prayed them myself, but complete freedom had never come.

"For the previous two years something inside of me had cried out 'God, there must be a better way. I am so sick. I am sick of fighting this obsessive-compulsive behavior. If it doesn't come out in eating, it comes out in smoking, or overworking, or biting my nails, or being consumed by a project to the point of unhealthiness. Your Holy Spirit has always kept my obsessive behavior in check, or brought me back when I have strayed, but there must be a better way. Will I have to live with this thing just under the surface for the rest of my life? I am sick and getting sicker, help me.' Somewhere down deep in my spirit I knew it was related to my health issues, but I had no idea how.

"My friend called Wellspring to make an appointment. Art had no openings but, because of his mercy and the concern in my friend's voice, he agreed to meet us for lunch the next day. That day was the day that put hope in my heart for the first time in years. We simply sat at a table and Art began to explain what Wellspring does. The Holy Spirit showed up in a very powerful way. Though this wasn't a 'session,' God used this hour lunch to plant a seed of hope in my heart. There were no openings until August 27. I was dismayed, but as always, God knew what He was doing.

"I went home and began to read the book, *Biblical Foundations of Freedom*. I began to make bitterness lists, against others and against myself. (When I tell people that, most say. 'Kathy, you are the last person I would think of as bitter.' Only those who knew me well knew the bitterness I felt over my brother-in-law's death. It brought about the downward swing in my health. It was the proverbial 'straw,' laid on top of all the other things that I had held in my heart against others and myself, that made the house come tumbling down.)

"I walked into the Wellspring office on August 27. That was the beginning of new life for me. After the first session, I went home to my friend's house to discover that, for the first time in about ten years, the Word of God was alive to me again. My headache went away. (And as of this writing I have never been plagued with it again.) By the second session my eyes were looking different. Two days after that session I took my grandkids to the State Fair. I spent all day with them. It had been the first time in over three years that I could play with them, really enjoy them, and not be absolutely exhausted.

"I had set aside two weeks in Anchorage to see my hematologist and attend as many therapy sessions as I could. My husband came to Anchorage over the Labor Day weekend. He was amazed at my energy level and how I looked. That next week I went back to my hematologist. He told me that at my choosing I could go down to one shot a day. I knew that I was not ready to do that yet. I knew the root of the thing that was killing me was not broken, but that it was close to being exposed.

"Although the Ministry seldom has cancellations, they had two during the time I needed. At my fourth session, the root of all my self-hate and self-bitterness was exposed, repented of, and broken. The obsessive-compulsive spirit was broken. I went through what I call a complete melt down. Praise God, He is faithful.

"I returned home on September 5. I had, and have not felt this healthy in six years. People who see me can't believe the change. Within the first week I lost nine pounds. I did nothing to make it happen except continue to work through the *Biblical Foundations of Freedom*. I know it is because my endocrine system is finally working for me, not against me. On September 11, I went in for my six-month blood work. My thyroid and hormone levels are normal for the first time in three years; before, even with the medication, I could not attain good levels. My cholesterol is great, even though I have been off Lipitor for six months. I look forward to my next set of blood work. I know that as I continue to grow in my healing, things will only get better.

"God is faithful. He will hear your heart's cry. He does heal today. As Art says, 'This isn't rocket science. It is simply putting the principles of God into practice.'

"I feel like the blind man Jesus healed in the Synagogue. When he and his parents were questioned about how his healing had taken place, his answer was this, 'All I know is, once I was blind and now I see.' For me it is, 'All I know is, once I was sick and dying and now I am well.'"

### Corrine

Corrine first called in late August 2001. She was very nervous and upset and angry at many situations in life. She was suffering from depression, reflux, migraines, severe PMS since puberty, and back pain. From August until our last appointment on November 19, I met with her four times. In these four sessions I led her through our ministry process.

At our November 19 meeting she informed me that the PMS was gone, the migraines were gone, the depression was gone and the reflux was markedly better. In August she, had great difficulty reading and comprehending Scripture. She would fall asleep when she attempted to read. Now she was able to stay awake and understand what she was reading. She expressed an excitement for God that had been missing for years. "A song is back in my heart," she said.

### Jenifer

In early November 2001 I received a desperate phone call from Jenifer: "I am having the worst migraine that I have ever experienced. Help!" I knew that somehow she was in guilt and condemnation over a conflict in her life. I asked a few questions at the leading of the Holy Spirit. I soon learned that she was blaming herself for the death of her oldest son when he was twelve. She was also blaming herself for the narcolepsy that her second son was suffering.

I led her through receiving forgiveness from God and in forgiving herself. We commanded the lying spirits from Satan to leave. Within twenty minutes the migraine left. I am writing this more than two months later and it has not returned.

## Janet

Janet is a highly educated nurse practitioner. She had suffered with extreme allergies, pancreatic insufficiency, severe asthma, reflux, excessive weight, mild dissociative disorder, and with tremendous fears. When I explain to medical people how we look at disease, they rarely disagree. They know that the body responds to our thoughts and emotions. But Janet had never made the connection in her body.

Janet worked as an emergency room nurse for twenty years and in a burn unit for six years. In these years she was exposed to many horrifying sights, sounds and smells and she had to perform many painful procedures. She came to believe that she was a mean, cruel person who had no compassion for others. She learned to disassociate to protect herself. She went into many fantasies to escape.

I led her through our ministry, helping her to understand how the devil had lied to her, that it took a very compassionate and loving person to work in a burn unit helping the severely burned. As she learned to love herself, and to deal with the fear and bitterness, the allergies were healed. It was a huge struggle but she is now free from all allergies. The DID is gone. The fear is gone.

She had been hospitalized over twenty-one times with severe asthma attacks. The attacks were so severe that she was given over one thousand milligrams of IV steroids to reduce the swelling so she could breath. At this writing the asthma has been healed for over a year.

She is now experiencing a level of peace and joy and a relationship with God that she never even dreamed of.

## Dorrie

Dorrie is in her forties and single. I began working with her in late August 2001. She was suffering from high blood pressure (158/104), hypothyroidism, diabetes, tachycardia, depression, DID, migraines and weight problems.

Within the first month her blood pressure went down to 132/88, which is in the normal range. Most of her anxiety and stress issues were healed through repentance and forgiveness. The tachycardia was related to stress.

In November 2001 she called me suffering from a huge migraine. In the ensuing discussion I learned that she was disassociating and becoming "Penelope." Dorrie is forty-two and single and has always wanted a husband and a family. As "Penelope" she was courted and sought out by men. She escaped into "Penelope" when the pressures were too great. This brought on a cycle of condemnation and guilt. She knew that it was not right to escape.

I led her through repenting for escaping and the migraine left. She has been severely tempted to go back into "Penelope" but has learned to resist the devil and has victory over the migraines and "Penelope" that was trying to control her life.

Dorrie has victory over the depression as long as she controls her thoughts. If she allows the negative thoughts then she will have a bout of depression until she realizes what is happening. When she realizes that she has given in to Satan, she quickly recovers.

## Joe

Joe's first appointment was on November 1, 2001. In the spring of 2001 he was diagnosed with cardiomyopathy. The arteries coming from his heart were restricted, causing the heart to work too hard, and creating an enlarged heart. The cardiologist told him that he should never run or exercise again. Additionally, all seven of his children were diagnosed with the same disease. His two teenage sons were told that they could not participate in sports. The doctors wanted to send the entire family to specialists on the east coast for a special study. They had never seen this in an entire family.

In the first session, I led Joe in dealing with tremendous bitterness issues from his childhood and from his marriage, which was also struggling. Joe was set free of tremendous guilt, shame and regrets. The freedom was so great that he alternately cried and laughed for over thirty minutes. At the end of the session I asked God to heal his heart and scheduled the next session for November 8.

The next day in my prayer time God spoke to me and told me to lay hands on Joe and pray for healing at our next meeting. He made it very plain that He intended to heal Joe and his entire family. I was astounded at these words from God. It is not often that I hear Him tell me this specifically what is going to happen.

On the day of our next session he came into my office ecstatic. I learned that he and his oldest son had been to the cardiologist two days earlier and the cardiomyopathy was gone! Not only was it gone in Joe but also in his son! So far only Joe and his oldest son have been to the cardiologist to confirm the healing but there are no symptoms manifesting in any of the other children.

I had an appointment with Joe's daughter Sheryl later in November.

## Sheryl

Sheryl was also diagnosed with the heart condition and she had suffered with PMS since puberty. Sheryl began to physically develop at age ten and greatly resented the changes in her body. She hung out a "do not touch" sign in big bold letters. She refused to let anyone hug her, as she was ashamed of her body.

I led her through understanding that she was angry with God for making her body the way He did. I taught her a paradigm shift in her thinking, to look forward to her period, instead of being in fear and resenting what God had created. As she repented for blaming God and made this shift in her thinking the PMS stopped. Sheryl has no remaining symptoms from the heart condition either.

There are many other testimonies that I could tell, but I hope you are getting the point that God does heal today! He has performed all of these miracles in the last two-and-a-half years. What He has done through Wellspring, He can and will do in your ministry and in your life, if you can believe! Mark 9:23 states, "Jesus said unto him, If thou canst believe, all things are possible to him that believeth." I have been diligently asking God about unbelief and He has been telling me, "If all things are not happening, then there is unbelief."

May I suggest that you pray this prayer?

> *Dear Heavenly Father, I believe, help my unbelief.*
> *I repent for all the ways that I have not believed, have*
> *not obeyed, have doubted that you were big enough*
> *to handle my problems, and have been double-minded*
> *(be specific in your life).*
>
> *I forgive myself for believing Satan's lies and I forgive*
> *those that taught me error. In the name of Jesus I cancel*
> *all of Satan's authority over me in unbelief because I am*
> *forgiven and I choose to believe.*
>
> *Holy Spirit, I ask for your gift of faith. Please speak*
> *your truth to me.*

## PROLOGUE

Most of the testimonies that you have just read happened in 2001. I have elected to leave them as they were originally written in this new edition because God has not changed. Since then we have continued to witness healings and miracles almost every day. And as our faith has grown we have seen even greater miracles such as blind eyes and deaf ears healed. This year I have witnessed at least five blind eyes and eight people with deaf ears healed. I have seen MS instantly healed, legs grow, joints healed, backs straightened, broken bones healed and many other incredible works of God. We continue to believe God for more and more. — Dr. Art Mathias, August, 2008.

# PART THREE

# The Book of Job:
# A Lesson in
# Personal Responsibility

## INTRODUCTION

It is traditionally taught that Job was a righteous and perfect man whom God tested with severe calamities. Is this what really happened? Does God really test us in this manner? Those who believe this use Job as an example for their own lives: "I am like Job, God is testing me with this cancer or other calamity, it is a Job thing." Is this a proper application of the book of Job and the nature and character of God?

God is not a respecter of persons. He is always just and fair and righteous. God will not be mocked in His laws of sowing and reaping (Galatians 6:11). If we accept responsibility for our lives then God will provide a way. If we choose to believe and obey, He will provide the power and the authority to defeat the devil in our lives.

If you cannot accept anything I teach about Job, at least remember that Job did not remain sick and defeated. The calamities only lasted a few months and then God restored double what Satan stole when Job repented.

## IS GOD A JUST GOD?

Does God treat people differently? Is He ever arbitrary? Romans 9:15 says that God will have mercy on whom He will have mercy. Is God showing favoritism? Scripture says that God hardened Pharaoh's heart. Does this mean that God is responsible for Pharaoh's disobedience?

What about the sufferings of Paul? He was an apostle, but suffered many things. How could a just and loving God allow it to happen?

What about Job? Many teach that he was a sinless man, yet he suffered greatly. Therefore, they believe, God tests even the godliest believers with calamities similar to Job's. Is this an accurate statement?

Why did God "allow" Hitler to kill millions of Jews? Why did God "allow" Herod to kill thousands of babies when he tried to kill the baby Jesus? Does God allow evil?

These are common questions that we hear often hear in ministry. To answer these, let's first look at who God says He is. What is His nature? What is His character? We must look at the events of Scripture and life, keeping in mind the fact that God cannot and will not violate His nature.

## ATTRIBUTES AND NATURE OF GOD

God is a Spirit. He is invisible. He is immortal. He is eternal. He is infinite in presence (I Kings 8:27); in power (Matthew 28:18); in acts (Matthew 19:26); in time (Deuteronomy 33:27, Psalms 90:2, Isaiah 57:15); in knowledge (Romans 11:33); and in greatness (Psalms 145:3).

He is omnipotent (all-powerful) (Revelation 19:6). God can do all things consistent with His nature and plan, but He cannot lie or act contrary to Himself.

He is a covenant-making God. He has made promises in writing in Scripture that He will keep. He has never violated His precepts and never will. We can depend on Him to do exactly what He said He would.

He is omnipresent. Presence is not governed by physical contact, but by knowledge and relationship (Matthew 18:20, 28:20, I Corinthians 5:3-4). His presence can be realized any place where men know Him and seek Him (Matthew 18:20). His Holy Spirit lives in all that choose to believe.

He is omniscient (all-knowing) as far as His nature, plan, and work are concerned (Romans 11:33). As to free moral agents, God learns certain things about them (Genesis 6:5-7, 11:5-7, 18:21, 22:12, II Chronicles 16:9, Job 12:22, 24:23, Psalms 7:9, 44:21, 139:1-6, Proverbs 24:12, Jeremiah 17:10, Ezekiel 11:5, Zechariah 4:10, II Corinthians 2:10-11, Romans 8:27, I Thessalonians 2:4). God sends messengers, or prophets, on errands to help Him carry on His plan (Daniel 10:13-21, Daniel 11:1, Daniel 12:1, Zechariah 1:7-11, 6:1-8, Matthew 18:10-11, Hebrews 1:14). He permits free moral agents freedom of action as to their conduct and destiny.

He is self-existent (Exodus 3:14, 6:3, John 1:4, 5:26).

He is immutable (unchangeable) (Psalms 102:27, Malachi 3:6, II Timothy 2:13, Hebrews 6:18, James 1:17). He is immutable as to His plan for the highest good of every being and of the universe. His plan includes changing of methods or ways to save as many men as possible. For example, when He fulfilled the law of Moses it was not a change in God's plan, but rather the execution of that plan (II Corinthians 3:6-15, Galatians 3:19-25; 4:21-34, Hebrews 7:11-10:18). When man fell and He had to send Christ, it was simply the fulfillment of the plan (Genesis 3:15, 3:13-14, 4:4-5). This plan was designed to be executed when obedience had been rendered and the terms met. When the terms are not met, it is not failure or change with God, but with man. We must always remember that God has a plan and is not surprised by the events that happen.

He is perfect (Deuteronomy 32:4, Psalms 18:30, Matthew 5:48). If any imperfection is noted in creation or redemption, it is sin and rebellion in free moral agents that have caused it. God does not change His original plan of creation and redemption. He plans to redeem and restore all creation (except those who refuse Him) to perfection (Acts 3:21, Ephesians 1:10, I Corinthians 15:24-28, Revelation 21-22).

God is truth. There is perfect harmony in God's Word. There are not contradictions, just things that we do not understand (Deuteronomy 32:4, John 17:3, I John 5:20).

God is wisdom (Romans 11:33, I Timothy 1:17).

God is love by which He communicates to others His infinite goodness (John 3:16, Romans 15:30, I John 4:8).

He is holy. He is absolutely pure in His nature (Exodus 15:11, Isaiah 6:3, I Peter 1:16).

God is righteous. Righteousness is His holiness in action. All His acts are right (Romans 3:21-31, Hebrews 12:5-12, I John 1:9).

God is faithful. He is absolutely trustworthy (I Corinthians 10:13, II Corinthians 1:20, Hebrews 6:18).

God is merciful, which is divine goodness manifest to relieve His creation of misery and suffering (Romans 12:1-2, II Corinthians 1:2, Titus 3:5).

God is good. His goodness and mercy preserve and extend life (Matthew 5:45, Acts 14:17, Romans 2:4).

God provides providence. God cares for and provides for all creation (Job 38:41).

God is the giver of every good and perfect gift (James 1:17). If it is good and perfect, it is from God the Father. If it is not good and perfect, it is from the devil.

The LORD is the healer of all our diseases (Psalms 103:3).

God desires to have a special relationship with each person of His creation, just like He did with Adam and Eve before they sinned.

God is not a respecter of persons. He does not have favorites (II Chronicles 19:7, Job 34:11-19, Romans 2:11, Ephesians 6:9, Colossians 3:25, James 2:1-10). If He will heal one, He will heal all. His judgments cannot be perverted.

We have listed many of His attributes. If He is not a just God, then He is a liar. If He is not who He has claimed to be, then He is a liar. If He is what He claims to be, then He must be just. Every time we explore what appear to be "contradictions" or "mysteries" in Scripture, we discover a great blessing that has been hidden.

Let's look further into this question by looking at some of Paul's statements in Romans, about Paul's thorn in the flesh, his sufferings, and Job, remembering God's nature. We also need to remember what God the Father sent Jesus to do because He did the works of the Father.

# ROMANS
## Romans 9:13-14

"As it is written, Jacob have I loved, but Esau have I hated. What shall we say then? Is there unrighteousness with God? God forbid."

These questions are answered with "God forbid." There is no unrighteousness with God. He can see the dispositions of Jacob and Esau. He knows their hearts. He knows the fruit of their lives before they actually live them out. He chooses on the basis of what

He knows and can foresee in each one. We also need to understand the word "hate" means to "love less." It does not mean to hate as we understand the word in English. God still loved Esau, but Jacob received His blessings because of his obedience.

There is also the issue of the sin of the parents. Scripture teaches that the sins of the father are passed on to the third and fourth generation (Exodus 34:7). If God sees that one will be continually rebelling against Him and another will not, can He not act accordingly without unrighteousness?

God is not responsible for the acts of Esau or Jacob, the Jews or Gentiles. He had to make the choice of Jacob over Esau because of the acts of the boys and their parents. He set aside Israel, due to her ever-increasing rebellion of more than eighteen hundred years. The only thing left for Him to do is to use the Gentiles to carry out His program (Matthew 21:33-45). The law of sowing and reaping will always apply. We will always reap the fruit of our actions and choices.

Romans 9:15-16

"For He saith to Moses, I will have mercy on whom I will have mercy, and I will have compassion on whom I will have compassion. So then it is not of him that willeth, nor of him that runneth, but of God that sheweth mercy."

Paul is teaching that God is sovereign over His mercy. He has laid down His terms of mercy and compassion, and will not dispense with either until people meet His terms. He will not save one soul without repentance, nor will He damn one soul that will meet His terms. God is a covenant making and keeping God. He is not arbitrary. He has given us His written Word and plainly tells us who He will have mercy on and who He will not. He will always do His part, if we do ours.

Romans 9:17-18

"For the scripture saith unto Pharaoh, Even for this same purpose have I raised thee up, that I might shew my power in thee, and that my name might be declared throughout all the earth. Therefore hath he mercy on whom he will have mercy, and whom he will he hardeneth."

First we need to understand that when the Scriptures says that God hardened Pharaoh's heart the Hebrew word for "harden" means to "strengthen." God strengthened Pharaoh's heart because He did not want him to become stubborn. It is God's will that none perish. The plagues were a contest between God and the gods of Egypt and God's purpose was to show His power and goodness to lead all of Egypt to Him. Pharaoh was a wicked king who resisted God's will. At many points in God's dealings with Pharaoh, he could have submitted and escaped judgment. But he was too stubborn to do so, and therefore God could not do otherwise than punish him for his sins and resistance.

Millions of Jews and gentiles in Egypt accepted God's grace and mercy and followed Him. The "mixed multitude" (estimated 2.5 million gentiles) that left Egypt with Moses were circumcised and baptized the same day they left (Exodus 12).

Romans 9:18

"Therefore hath He mercy on whom He will have mercy, and whom He will He hardeneth."

God hardens on the same grounds as He shows mercy. If men will accept mercy, He will give it to them. If they will not, He turns them over to their own devices, thus hardening themselves. He is only just and righteous in judging them. In our free will, we are privileged to humble ourselves and seek mercy or exalt ourselves and refuse mercy. Mercy is the result of a right attitude, and hardening is the result of stubbornness, or a wrong attitude, toward God. It is like clay and wax in the sun. The same sunshine hardens one and softens the other.

The responsibility is with the materials, not with the sun. The responsibility is yours and mine. We are more responsible than these materials, for we have wills to make proper choices. The only sense in which God hardened Pharaoh was in giving him the occasion or choice to harden his own heart or obey (Romans 13). Such is the choice all of us have to make daily. When we do not listen to the precepts of God, we are then turned over to our own devices to reap what we have sown (Proverbs 1:27-31). The only sense that God hardened Pharaoh's heart is that God gave him a free will. This is known as the Hebrew idiom of permission.

This is exactly what happened to me. I was living in bitterness and fear without even knowing it. It was not God's fault that I was ignorant of my sin. The fear and the bitterness caused me severe physical problems. When I forgave those who had hurt me, forgave myself and cast out the spirit of fear, the LORD took away my guilt and sin and healed my body. He is faithful and just.

Who are we to blame God for our sinfulness? Cannot God deal with us as is necessary (Jeremiah 18:1-17)? God wants to save people who will obey Him, Jews or Gentiles. Is that not His right? If He has to damn those who harden themselves, may He not do so without our criticism? This is very similar to the LORD's response to Job, which we will study later.

## PAUL'S SUFFERINGS

Paul's calling as an apostle, and his relationship with God, was questioned by many people in his day and today because of all the things he suffered. In II Corinthians 11 Paul lists all the ways he suffered:

In more abundant labors (II Corinthians 11:23). Stripes above measure (II Corinthians 11:23). In prisons often for Christ (II Corinthians 11:23). Often at the point of death (II Corinthians 11:23). Five times scourged (II Corinthians 11:24). Three times beaten with rods (II Corinthians 11:25). Once stoned to death (II Corinthians 11:25, Acts 14:19). Three times shipwrecked (II Corinthians 11:25). Twenty-four hours in the sea (II Corinthians 11:25). In journeyings often (II Corinthians 11:26). In perils of water

(II Corinthians 11:26). In perils of robbers (II Corinthians 11:26). In perils by the Jews (II Corinthians 11:26). In perils by the heathen (II Corinthians 11:26). In perils in the city (II Corinthians 11:26). In perils in the wilderness (II Corinthians 11:26). In perils in the sea (II Corinthians 11:26). In perils by false brethren (II Corinthians 11:26). In weariness and pain (II Corinthians 11:27). In watching often (II Corinthians 11:27). In hunger and thirst (II Corinthians 11:27). In fastings often (II Corinthians 11:27). In cold and nakedness (II Corinthians 11:27). Mine infirmities (II Corinthians 11:30). Paul is bragging and counting it all joy the many ways he suffered for Christ. It is critical that we know if we are suffering for our sins or for our faith. Compare the ways you "suffer" to the ways Paul suffered. Are they same types of suffering? If not, maybe we should examine ourselves to see if we are simply reaping the consequences of our sin.

The Greek word for infirmity is *astheneia* (GSN-769); it is a want of strength, weakness or frailty of the body. It also means a lack of strength or ability to understand, do great works, restrain corrupt desires, or to bear trials and troubles. It is used in the sense of sickness or disease only two times in Scripture. Neither of these is in reference to Paul.

II Corinthians 13:4 says, "For though He [Christ] was crucified through weakness, yet He liveth by the power of God. For we also are weak in Him, but we shall live with Him by the power of God toward you." The word translated as "weakness" is also astheneia. Did Christ have a disease that caused Him to be crucified? Of course not! To many humans, He seemed to be powerless, weak and defeated. In fact many religions claim the defeat of Christ on the cross. His seeming weakness was His strength, and the same is true of each of us (II Corinthians 12:9-10).

Paul's sufferings were not from sickness, disease, or the curses of personal sin and rebellion which Christ died to free us from. Paul was suffering because of his belief in Jesus the Christ. Suffering for our stand in our faith is different from suffering for our disobedience. When we are suffering for our faith we are to count it all joy. Even so, God wasn't responsible for the things that caused Paul and others to suffer. Rather, He helped them go through the sufferings heaped upon them by Satan and his agents. When suffering because of disobedience, a wise man would fall on his face before God and repent.

We don't need to experience sickness, disease, poverty, and accidents in order to learn what we should know from God. We have been given examples in the Word to go by: Job, Asa, Hezekiah, Paul and many more. Why not glorify God by learning from these and becoming an example ourselves, of one experiencing God's blessing by being kept from such troubles and sufferings? I have experienced defeat, and I have experienced victory over sin and disease and the works of the devil. Victory is sweet, and defeat is bitter.

# JOB

In almost every discussion that I have with someone about sickness, healing, or the troubles that we experience in life, Job is brought up as an example of a perfect, sinless man who still suffered greatly. Invariably, people will say that even though he was perfect and without sin, "God tested him" and allowed all his possessions and family to be destroyed. Job then is used as an example, or excuse, for what is happening in their lives or those of others.

Are these statements accurate? Are they consistent with God's nature that we have studied earlier? God cannot and will not violate His Word or His nature. Let's study the book of Job with this thought in mind.

Let's begin with a brief overview of Job, and then we will study it in more detail:

Chapters 1 and 2 reveal the dilemma that Job found himself in. They reveal his circumstances, the two attacks from Satan and the arrival of his three friends.

Chapters 3 through 31 contain the three debates between Job and the three friends. Throughout these debates, they condemned Job for his sin but they did not have any answers for him, nor did they defend the LORD. Isn't this where most of us are at today? Do you have answers for the problems in life to share with others? Do you defend God? Or do you blame Him? Some even teach that it is not our responsibility to defend God, that He can defend himself. I strongly disagree. We are to be His ambassadors. We are to represent Him.

In these debates, Job claims to be innocent and blames the LORD for his calamities. In chapter 29 Job laments many things that he no longer has, especially his relationship with the LORD. It is interesting to study this chapter and see the anointing of God that was on Job. Job had a very special relationship with the LORD that he lost. God does not remove His anointing without reason; His judgments are always fair. Remember everything that Job had, he regained twice over when he repented. Never forget that everything that Job had is also available to each of us.

After picturing his past prosperity, glory, honor and relationship with God in chapter 29, in chapter 30 Job describes his present state as one of rejection, persecution, and suffering in body and soul. In chapter 31 Job continues to defend himself and in chapter 32 Job's first three friends quit talking to him because of his self-righteousness and a fourth friend Elihu comes on the scene.

Chapters 32 through 37 are Elihu's response to Job. Elihu was a fourth friend, a young man who did not interrupt his elders to participate in their debates. He listens until he can contain himself no longer. In chapter 32 he begins to speak, claiming that he is speaking as a messenger for the LORD. Was he? Elihu had answers for Job. Elihu also defended the LORD.

Chapters 38 through 41 are the LORD's response to Job. The LORD responds to Job's attack on Him by asking Job 184 questions that he cannot answer. In chapter 42

Job repents, prays for or forgives his first three friends, makes an animal sacrifice, and then the LORD restores double what was taken from him by Satan. The LORD required repentance and a sacrifice from Job and his first three friends but not from Elihu. Why didn't the LORD rebuke Elihu? Was Elihu the LORD's prophet?

Job is an exciting book that has tremendous application for each of us today. Let's study together and see what the LORD has for us.

## CHAPTERS 1 AND 2: JOB'S CALAMATIES
Job 1:1

"There was a man in the land of Uz, whose name was Job; and that man was perfect and upright, and one that feared God, and eschewed evil."

"There was a man..."

This is a statement of historical fact, not a myth. So it is with the statements in Luke16:19-20, "There was a certain rich man... and there was a certain beggar." The word "certain" further confirms the historicity of these men. All three men lived and had the experiences related about them by Jesus Christ, and the author of Job, who was inspired by God. Their stories are not myths, parables, or allegories, any more than any other historical part of the Bible.

"...Job"

He was the third son of Issachar, the son of Jacob (Genesis 46:13, Ezekiel 14:14, 20, James 5:11). Job was a very religious man; he was acquainted with God and religion as it was understood and practiced in those days. He no doubt knew of the many traditions and revelations of God up to that time, being a grandson of Jacob. He was born about 278 years after Noah died, and about 125 years after Shem died. Job was about 70 when he was afflicted, according to some scholars. This would make it only 697 years after the flood.

From this commentary, we can understand how Job could know about the religious beliefs and practices of Shem, Abraham, Isaac and Jacob, their spiritual experiences, and the doctrines they taught.

"...was perfect and upright, and one that feared God, and eschewed evil."

What do these words mean? Does "perfect" mean that Job had no sin? The word translated into English as "perfect" is the Hebrew word *tam* (HSN-8535). Tam is derived from Tamam (HSN-8552), which means "to complete; make full; be entire; to finish." It denotes that in which there is no part lacking to complete the whole.

It does not mean sinless perfection or being without any tendencies to evil, for Job was a human with the usual traits and shortcomings that show up in all humans. All humans have sinned, and if any say that they have not sinned they are calling God a liar (Romans 3:23, I John 1:10). As we study, we will see many different ways that Job sinned.

The fact that Job did sin allows the book of Job to be applied to each of our lives today, because each of us has also sinned. Job did not think that he had sinned; he was righteous in his own eyes as many of us can be today. Let's open our minds and learn from Job, and how he sinned. Our goal in this life should be to become closer and closer to God. We can only do this by removing the sin in our lives that separates us from Him.

In reality, learning that there is sin in our life should be a blessing. Sin is easy to deal with. Jesus our LORD has provided a way of escape. I celebrate when I learn of a sin in my life, because it gives me the opportunity to deal with it and then be closer to my Heavenly Father.

"Upright" is the Hebrew word *tamiyn* (HSN-3477), it means "to be straight." It is translated upright, just, righteous, meet, straight, convenient and equity in various verses.

"Feared God" is the Hebrew word *yare* (HSN-3373), it means "to revere; to have deep respect for God."

"Eschewed evil" is the Hebrew word *cuwr* (HSN-5493), it means "to turn off, decline, depart from, lay away, leave undone, be past, pluck away, put down, rebel against, remove, be sour against, or withdraw from evil in this context."

Job was a good man who loved God, and hated evil. He was well respected by his peers. He was a leader in his community, a good father and husband, who loved his family. But he was also a man, made from dust and at times fallible.

Job 1:2-3

"And there were born unto him seven sons and three daughters. His substance also was seven thousand sheep, and three thousand camels, and five hundred yoke of oxen, and five hundred she asses, and a very great household; so that this man was the greatest of all the men of the east."

"...His substance also was seven thousand sheep, and three thousand camels, and five hundred yoke of oxen, and five hundred she asses..."

Among nomadic people it was customary to estimate wealth by the number of animals owned (Job 42:12, Genesis 13:2, 5, 24:35). The following is an estimate of Job's net worth: 7,000 sheep, $560,000 (at $80 each); 3,000 camels, $3 million (at $1000 each); 1,000 oxen, $800,000 (at $800 each); 500 female donkeys, $250,000 (at $500 each). This totals $4,610,000. Job was also a wealthy man, blessed in the work of his hands.

Job 1:4-5

"And his sons went and feasted in their houses, everyone his day; and sent and called for their three sisters to eat and to drink with them. And it was so, when the days of their feasting were gone about, that Job sent and sanctified them, and rose up early in the morning, and offered burnt offerings according to the number of them all: for Job said, It may be that my sons have sinned, and cursed God in their hearts. Thus did Job continually."

Why did Job continually feel that he must make sacrifices to God for the actions of his children? Some commentators teach that he was simply being a good father. As a father, he simply went through religious ceremonies before God in the hope that He would have mercy on his children.

Job 3:25 says that what Job greatly feared came upon him. Was this one of his great fears? Was Job living in the fear that his children, in their feasting (partying), would sin and curse God? Was this a proper course of action? Why did Job allow his children to participate in this behavior? He had a responsibility to discipline, teach and train up his children. Is being afraid that God would not have mercy on his children a sin? Is this fear actually an insult to God? Were the sacrifices done in obedience or in fear? If they were done in fear, then they would have been an insult to God.

Job 1:6

"Now there was a day when the sons of God came to present themselves before the LORD, and Satan came also among them."

"...there was a day..."

There was a day when angels in heaven came to present themselves before God. This happened twice (Job 1:6, 2:1), implying regular days for angels to do this. In Revelation 12, we also find Satan before God accusing the brethren.

"...sons of God..."

The expression "sons of God" is used five times in the Old Testament, always of angels. In the New Testament, Adam and all Christians are called "sons of God." The scene (both here and in Job 2:1) is in heaven, before the Lord.

"...present themselves before the LORD..."

That is, take their places in worship or other activities as revealed in I Kings 22:19-22, Isaiah 6, Daniel 7:9-14, Zechariah 3:1-2, Revelation 4-5, 12:10, 19:1-10. "LORD" is the Hebrew word Jehovah. As we have studied in "The LORD God Revelation," Jehovah is our Creator, Redeemer, Savior, our Messiah, and the Christ.

"...Satan..."

This is the earliest mention (historically speaking) of Satan by name. Not even in Genesis is he mentioned by name. The time of Job was early in history, for he was the son of Issachar, the son of Jacob (Genesis 46:13). It is clear in Genesis 3 that there was an invisible enemy who caused the fall of man, but in the passage he is shown using the serpent as a tool, the same way that he used Peter (Matthew 16:23). In Job 41, he is symbolized by a great dragon. He is the evil spirit working in the children of disobedience throughout the ages (Ephesians 2:1-3). Here he is named and spoken of as a real person and shown to have access to heaven with power to accuse the brethren and seek their destruction (Revelation 12:9-12). The word Satan means adversary.

"...came also among them."

This shows that Satan has access to God. Good and evil are in the same place at the same time. Additionally, he is called a son of God in this passage. We know that he was created by Jesus as Lucifer (Isaiah 14, John 1 and Colossians 1).

# THE WORKS OF SATAN
Job 1:7

"And the LORD said unto Satan, Whence comest thou? Then Satan answered the LORD, and said, From going to and fro in the earth, and from walking up and down in it."

Satan is not an abstract power, or a being with hoofs, horns, and tail, holding a pitchfork and presiding over a lake of fire. He is not omnipresent because he has to go to and fro in the earth, walking up and down in it seeking whom he may devour. He is also not all-knowing or he would not have to seek; he would know. Let's look at the nature of our enemy a little closer.

Attributes of Satan
1. Satan is a real person (I Chronicles 21:1, Job 1:6-12, 2:1-7, Psalms 109:6, Zechariah 3:1-2, I Peter 5:8-9, Revelation 12:7-12).
2. Jesus dealt with him as with a person (Matthew 4:1-11, Luke 4:1-13).
3. Jesus waged war on Satan as on a person (Luke 13:16, Acts 10:38, I John 3:8).
4. Christ taught that Satan was a real person (Luke 10:18, Revelation 12:7-12, 13:1-4, 20:1-10).
5. The apostles fought with Satan as with a real person (Ephesians 6:10-18, I Thessalonians 2:18, I Peter 5:8-9).
6. The apostles warned men against a personal devil (Ephesians 4:27, 6:11, James 4:7, I Peter 5:8-9).
7. Personal singular pronouns are used of Satan (Matthew 4:7-11, 12:26, Luke 11:18).
8. Personal statements are made to him (Job 1:6-12, 2:1-7, Isaiah 14:12-14, Ezekiel 28:11-17, Zechariah 3:1-2, Matthew 4:1-10, Jude 1:9).
9. Personal conversation is carried on with him (Job 1:6-12, 2:1-7, Isaiah 14:12-14, Matthew 4:1-10, Jude 1:9).
10. Personal descriptions are given of him (Isaiah 14:12-14, Ezekiel 28:11-17).
11. The personal names and titles that are given to him:
    (1) Lucifer (Isaiah 14:12-14)
    (2) The Devil and Satan (Revelation 12:9)
    (3) Beelzebub (Matthew 10:25, 12:24)
    (4) Belial (II Corinthians 6:15)
    (5) The adversary (I Peter 5:8-9)

(6) The dragon (Revelation 12:3-12, 13:1-4, 20:1-3)

(7) The serpent (II Corinthians 11:3, Revelation 12:9)

(8) The god of this world (II Corinthians 4:4)

(9) The prince of this world (John 12:31)

(10) The prince of the power of the air (Ephesians 2:1-3)

(11) The accuser of our brethren (Revelation 12:10)

(12) The enemy (Matthew 13:39)

(13) The tempter (Matthew 4:3)

(14) The wicked one (Matthew 13:19, 38)

(15) That wicked one (I John 5:18)

12. Personal acts and attributes are ascribed to him.

13. He is an angel with a body, soul, and spirit like all other angels (Ezekiel 28:11-17, Revelation 12:7-12).

14. He is described as a most beautiful creature who fell through personal pride over his own beauty (Ezekiel 28:11-17, I Timothy 3:6).

15. He has been seen with a body (I Chronicles 21:1, Job 1:6-12, 2:1-7, Psalms 109:6, Zechariah 3:1-2, Matthew 4:1-11, Revelation 20:1-3).

16. He will be bound physically with a chain and cast into a prison (Revelation 20:1-3).

17. He has a heart (Isaiah 14:12-14), pride (Ezekiel 28:17, I Timothy 3:6), speech (Job 1:6-12, 2:1-7, Matthew 4:1-11), knowledge (Job 1:6-12, 2:1-7, Matthew 4:1-11, Revelation 12:12), power (Job 1:6-22, 2:1-7, Acts 10:38, 26:18, II Thessalonians 2:8-12, Revelation 13:1-4), desires (Luke 22:31), lusts (John 8:44, Ephesians 2:1-3), and many other physical parts, soul passions, and spirit faculties.

18. He goes from place to place in a body like anyone else (Job 1:6-12, 2:1-7, Matthew 4:10-11, Mark 4:15).

19. He has a kingdom (Mark 3:22-26).

20. He has access to heaven (Job 1:6-12, 2:1-6, Revelation 12:9-12).

21. He is a great celestial and terrestrial ruler (John 12:31, II Corinthians 4:4, Ephesians 2:2, 6:10-18).

22. He rules the business, social, political, and religious activities of the majority of mankind.

23. His realm is divided into organized principalities and powers (Daniel 10:12-11:1, Matthew 12:24-30, Ephesians 6:10-12).

24. His subjects are fallen angels, fallen men, and demons of various kinds (Matthew 25:41, John 8:44, James 2:19, I John 3:8-10, Revelation 12:7-12).

25. He is the head of some religions and is a leader in religious affairs (II Corinthians 11:14, 2:9, 3:9).

Satan was created by Christ, along with other beings, principalities and powers in heaven and earth (Job 38:4-7, Ezekiel 28:11-17, Colossians 1:15-18). Several Scriptures tell that he fell through pride over his own beauty (Ezekiel 28:11-17, I Timothy 3:6), and trying to exalt himself above God (Isaiah 14:12-14). In general, his work is to oppose God whenever possible. For this reason, his work varies in different ages and dispensations. In Old Testament times, Satan's great work was to cause the fall of man, usurp his dominion, and try to prevent the coming of the Messiah into the world in order to avert his own defeat. Since he failed in preventing the coming of the Messiah, his tactics have changed to some extent in the New Testament. Now he attempts to persuade us that Jesus is not the Messiah, and offers many false messiahs. If he cannot prevent us from believing, he would have us believe that the works of Jesus Christ were only for the early church and not for today. He wants us to be defeated and powerless in our walk with God. Is this not the condition of the church today?

Job 1:8

"And the LORD said unto Satan, Hast thou considered my servant Job, that there is none like him in the earth, a perfect and an upright man, one that feareth God, and escheweth evil?"

Why would the LORD point out Job to Satan? First, we need to remember that we are finite beings that see through a dark glass. We do not understand His ways. But at the same time, The LORD has made promises to us that He will not violate.

In James 1:1-12 we learn that the testing or our faith is from the devil and not God. In these passages temptation and the testing or trying of our faith are used interchangeably. We know that God has promised us that He will not tempt us. James 1:13-14 says, "Let no man say when he is tempted, I am tempted of God: for God cannot be tempted with evil, neither tempteth He any man: But every man is tempted, when he is drawn away of his own lust, and enticed."

Job was drawn away by his own lust and enticed, just as we are. God was not testing him, Satan was through temptations. Satan claimed that Job would curse God if his possessions were taken away. Satan was tempting Job to curse or blame God. Remember, God cannot and will not tempt mankind.

Did God know that Job had sin in his heart? Did God know that Job would curse himself, and thus the One who created him? Did God know that Job would become full of self-pity and arrogance? Did God know that Job would falsely accuse Him of evil? Was God aware of the fear that Job held in his heart? Since God knows all things, was God simply turning Job over to his own devices to bring him to a deeper and fuller walk with Him (Proverbs 1:24-31)?

God said that Job was righteous, perfect and blameless in different verses. It is very interesting to learn that God has said the same things about every believer. Here are several verses from the New Testament:

Ephesians 1:4

"According as He hath chosen us in Him before the foundation of the world, that we should be holy and without blame before Him in love:"

Ephesians 5:27

"That he might present it to himself a glorious church, not having spot, or wrinkle, or any such thing; but that it should be holy and without blemish."

Colossians 1:22

"In the body of His flesh through death, to present you holy and unblameable and unreproveable in His sight:"

Hebrews 9:14

"How much more shall the blood of Christ, who through the eternal Spirit offered Himself without spot to God, purge your conscience from dead works to serve the living God?"

Jude 1:24

"Now unto Him that is able to keep you from falling, and to present you faultless before the presence of His glory with exceeding joy."

Revelation 14:5

"And in their mouth was found no guile: for they are without fault before the throne of God."

In our previous study of Justification we learned that the Old Covenant believers were justified in the same manner as New Covenant believers. I believe that Job held a legal position that all believers hold, called justification. He was looking forward to the Cross as we look back to it. In God's eyes Job was justified or declared righteous just as we are.

Job held the legal position that all believers hold. This why God can see us as He does in these verses, and also why He called Job "perfect and upright." Job knew about the coming Messiah as well as we know about the Messiah that has come. The great body of Old Testament prophecy relates directly to the coming of the Messiah, beginning with Genesis 3:15. The Messianic prophecies in the Old Testament are too numerous to be quoted. (Compare Micah 5:2, Haggai 2:6-9, Isaiah 7:14, 9:6, 7, 11:1, 2, ch.53, 60:10, 13, Psalms 16:11, 68:18.) Job knew about the coming Messiah, just as we know about Jesus the Christ that has come in the flesh. Job was "Justified" but he was not sanctified in his experience or his daily walk. Job was required to sanctify himself and be holy as God is holy, as are all believers. Job was not without sin. Job was not perfect in his experiences.

God also knew Job's heart, just as He knows your heart. He knew that Job would repent. He knew that Job would purge himself from dead works. The LORD knew the beginning and the end of Job's life. He knew that Job would repent in chapter 42. Our LORD Jesus Christ also knows each believer's heart. Do you know your heart?

Job 1:9-10

"Then Satan answered the LORD, and said, Doth Job fear God for nought? Hast not thou made an hedge about him, and about his house, and about all that he hath on every side? Thou hast blessed the work of his hands, and his substance is increased in the land."

Do we serve God for nothing? Of course not! We serve Him for love and relationship, and in our obedience, His promised blessings (Deuteronomy28). Even Satan is acknowledging that blessings come from God. It is against Satan's nature to bless. The rain (blessings) falls on the just and unjust when they practice the precepts of God (Matthew 5:45).

Job 1:11

"But put forth thine hand now, and touch all that he hath, and he will curse thee to thy face."

When Satan suggested that God put forth His hand and touch Job's possessions, it was really a suggestion that God withdraw His hand of protection so Satan could destroy Job's property. Satan and his evil forces are the agents of destruction, not God. The only sense in which God destroys is to withhold His protection, and thereby turn the individual over to the devil to carry out his work upon that person. The LORD allows us to reap what we sow, to suffer the consequences of our actions so that we will learn and return to His ways. This is His discipline.

This truth is plainly demonstrated in the case of Job. Who was it that destroyed Job's possessions (Job 1:12-19) and afflicted his body (Job 2:7)? The answer is Satan, and this will always be the case in instances of affliction and destruction (Luke 13:16, John 10:10, Acts 10:38). Satan brings about the actual happenings of accidents, sickness, disease, and calamity, and then causes men to think that God brings these things to pass. Thus God is blamed for the work of the devil by millions, even by Christians who should know better. God's work is that of deliverance; Satan's work is that of destruction (John 10:10, Acts 10:38).

Why did God withhold or remove his protection from Job? God's protection is promised when we are obedient, and is removed because of our disobedience (Deuteronomy 28, Proverbs 1:24-33, Galatians 6:7). To teach anything else is to deny the nature, character and righteousness of our loving Heavenly Father.

As we will see as we study further, Job sinned in several ways. This disobedience is what required God to remove His protection. Satan was correct in his accusation of Job. Job had given Satan a place, or a right (Ephesians 4:27). God is a covenant-making God. He could not and did not violate His covenant. Job did.

When Job sinned, and thus disobeyed God, he gave Satan permission to accuse and attack him. In reality it was Job that granted the permission to Satan, through his disobedience (Ephesians 4:27).

Satan can also tempt Christians without cause. Until Satan is removed forever we will always be tempted. It is important to know the difference between good and evil so we can know when whether we are being attacked or tempted in our sin, or if it is a false accusation (Hebrews 5:14). If the attack is with cause, because of sin, then we need to repent and/or forgive in order to cancel Satan's legal claim before we can resist or rebuke him. Later in this study, we will see that this is what Job finally did. If the attack is without cause, then we must rebuke or resist Satan or he will continue (James 4:7). (See Paul's Thorn.)

Satan's theory was that no man serves God without personal material gain. If God withheld such blessings, Satan believed that any man would automatically curse and hate Him. This, of course, is not true, for millions have loved and served God without material gain.

Satan claimed that Job would curse the LORD to His face. The word for curse used here means "to make light of, to make little of, to belittle, to curse by abusing or belittling, to slander." As we study, we will see that this is what Job, in fact, did.

Job 1:12

"And the LORD said unto Satan, Behold, all that he hath is in thy power; only upon himself put not forth thine hand. So Satan went forth from the presence of the LORD."

All that Job had was turned over to Satan. All that was left after Satan had finished his work was one servant out of each calamity, and his wife, who cooperated with the devil (Job 1:11, 15-17, 19, 2:9). But Satan was not allowed to touch Job. Even in our disobedience, God limits the power of Satan in our lives. If He did not, Satan would destroy every human.

Job 1:13-15

"And there was a day when his sons and his daughters were eating and drinking wine in their eldest brother's house: And there came a messenger unto Job, and said, The oxen were plowing, and the asses feeding beside them: And the Sabeans fell upon them, and took them away; yea, they have slain the servants with the edge of the sword; and I only am escaped alone to tell thee."

Satan used six agents on earth to attack Job: The Sabeans (Job 1:15), fire from heaven (Job 1:16), Chaldeans (Job 1:17), the elements (Job 1:19), disease (Job 2:7), an ungodly wife (Job 2:9).

Job 1:16

"While he was yet speaking, there came also another, and said, The fire of God is fallen from heaven, and hath burned up the sheep, and the servants, and consumed them; and I only am escaped alone to tell thee."

"While he was yet speaking, there came also another..."

This emphasizes how quickly calamities came upon Job. Satan intended to overwhelm Job all at once (Job 1:16, 17, 18, 20-22). Satan's tactics have not changed today.

"...fire of God is fallen from heaven..."

This was, perhaps, a great bolt of lightning that would seem to be from God. Even today, men consider storms, lightning, winds and other things causing disaster to be acts of God, not realizing that the devil is the prince of the power of the air (Ephesians 2:1-3).

Job 1:17-20

"While he was yet speaking, there came also another, and said, The Chaldeans made out three bands, and fell upon the camels, and have carried them away, yea, and slain the servants with the edge of the sword; and I only am escaped alone to tell thee. While he was yet speaking, there came also another, and said, Thy sons and thy daughters were eating and drinking wine in their eldest brother's house: And, behold, there came a great wind from the wilderness, and smote the four corners of the house, and it fell upon the young men, and they are dead; and I only am escaped alone to tell thee. Then Job arose, and rent his mantle, and shaved his head, and fell down upon the ground, and worshipped, And said, Naked came I out of my mother's womb, and naked shall I return thither: the LORD gave, and the LORD hath taken away; blessed be the name of the LORD."

Job made several statements in verse 21 that are not accurate: 1) "...and naked shall I return thither." Job could not and did not return to his mother's womb; 2) "...the Lord hath taken away." The Lord did not take away his possessions, Satan did; 3) He "blessed the Lord" for what Satan did.

Job 1:22

"In all this Job sinned not, nor charged God foolishly."

Job 2:10 says, "In all this did not Job sin with his lips." Only God knew his heart, but I believe that Job did sin in his heart. Matthew 12:34 says that out of the abundance of the heart the mouth speaks. As we will see, Job sinned in many ways with his words. This is the only explanation that is consistent with all of Scripture and the nature of God.

Chapter 2 repeats much of what is said in chapter 1. I will not comment on the same issues again.

Job 2:1-3

"Again there was a day when the sons of God came to present themselves before the LORD, and Satan came also among them to present himself before the LORD. And the LORD said unto Satan, from whence comest thou? And Satan answered the LORD, and said, from going to and fro in the earth, and from walking up and down in it. And the LORD said unto Satan, Hast thou considered my servant Job, that there is none like him in the earth, a perfect and an upright man, one that feareth God, and escheweth evil? And still he holdeth fast his integrity, although thou movedst me against him, to destroy him without cause."

"...still he holdeth fast his integrity..."

We will see in later verses that Job falsely accused God with many things.

"...thou movedst Me against him, to destroy him without cause..."

Remember that Job held the legal position of being justified in God's eyes. Also this must be understood as a limitation of Satan's in attack on Job. He had no authority to destroy Job himself (Job 1:11, 2:6). Satan can attack or tempt us with or without cause. But, in any attack or temptation, the LORD is there limiting what Satan can do, even in our disobedience.

Job 2:4

"And Satan answered the LORD, and said, Skin for skin, yea, all that a man hath will he give for his life."

"...Skin for skin, yea, all that a man hath will he give for his life..."

This was evidently a familiar proverb in Job's time, and perhaps refers to bartering by means of skins of animals. A man would give all the skins, everything, he owned for food that would save his life.

Job 2:5

"But put forth Thine hand now, and touch his bone and his flesh, and he will curse Thee to thy face."

Satan now suggested that God allow him to afflict Job physically. He thought that would make Job curse God to His face. Satan cannot see into our hearts. He does not know our thoughts, but the LORD does. Remember the word for "curse" used here, means "to make light of, to make little of, to belittle, to curse by abusing or belittling, to slander." As we study, we will see that this is what Job in fact did.

Job 2:6-7

"And the LORD said unto Satan, Behold, he is in thine hand; but save his life. So went Satan forth from the presence of the LORD, and smote Job with sore boils from the sole of his foot unto his crown."

Again, the LORD limited what Satan could do. This verse also plainly states that Satan brings sickness to men. The following is a list of twenty examples that show that sickness and disease are the work of Satan.

1. Satan smote Job with "sore boils" (Job 2:7).
2. God "turned the captivity of Job" (Job 42:10).
3. Jesus healed a "dumb man possessed with a devil" (Matthew 9:32-33).
4. Jesus healed a blind and dumb man "possessed with a devil" (Matthew 12:22).
5. "If Satan cast out Satan, he is divided against himself... I cast out devils by the Spirit of God" (Matthew 12:26-28).
6. A woman's daughter was "grievously vexed with a devil" (Matthew 15:22).
7. "Jesus rebuked the devil" (Matthew 17:18).
8. A man "had a spirit of an unclean devil" (Luke 4:33).

9. "The devil had thrown him in the midst" (Luke 4:35).

10. A boy had a demon the disciples could not cast out, but as Jesus approached, "the devil threw him down, and tare him" (Luke 9:42).

11. After Jesus cast out the dumb devil, "the dumb man spake" (Luke 11:14).

12. "There was a woman which had a spirit of infirmity eighteen years" and was bent and couldn't straighten herself; Jesus declared that Satan had bound her (Luke 13:11-16).

13. "The thief cometh not, but to steal, and to kill, and to destroy: I am come that they might have life, and that they might have it more abundantly" (John 10:10).

14. "God anointed Jesus of Nazareth with the Holy Ghost and with power: who went about doing good, and healing all that were oppressed of the devil; for God was with Him" (Acts 10:38).

15. Jesus called Paul to turn people "from the power of Satan unto God" (Acts 26:18).

16. Regarding an unrepentant immoral man, Paul said he would "deliver such an one unto Satan for the destruction of the flesh" (I Corinthians 5:5).

17. When Jesus sent the twelve disciples out by twos, "they cast out many devils, and anointed with oil many that were sick, and healed them" (Mark 6:7-13).

18. Jesus commissioned the seventy to "heal the sick"; they returned with joy, saying, "Lord, even the devils are subject unto us through Thy name" (Luke 10:9, 17).

19. Jesus partook of flesh and blood, "that through death He might destroy him that had the power of death, that is, the devil" (Hebrews 2:14).

20. "For this purpose the Son of God was manifested, that He might destroy the works of the devil" (I John 3:8). The works of the devil include demons causing many physical infirmities and sicknesses. In every miracle of healing that Jesus did, He either cast out a demon or forgave sin.

Job 2:8-9

"And he took him a potsherd to scrape himself withal; and he sat down among the ashes. Then said his wife unto him, dost thou still retain thine integrity? Curse God, and die.

"...Then said his wife unto him..."

When his wife saw the loss of their wealth, the death of their sons and daughters, and Job afflicted with boils, she told him to speak the words and curse God.

"...curse God, and die..."

Cursing God is what Job feared his sons would do, so he offered sacrifices continually for them (Job 1:5). Now, his wife urged him to curse God and die. Job's wife was a foolish woman. But as Adam did not set aside Eve's sin in eating of the tree and ate himself, neither did Job set aside or correct his wife. Thus her sin became his sin. Adam, Job and all men have the duty to set aside the sins of their wives and daughters under the Law. This does not apply to sons; they must do this for themselves (Numbers 30:6-8). God has given a remarkable level of authority and responsibility to the man. It is through the sin of one man, Adam, that Satan gained access to the earth (Romans 5:12). This is why Genesis 3:15 says that Jesus would be born of the seed of a woman and not a man.

Job cursed God when he falsely accused Him, and when he cursed the day he was born. Remember to curse means "to make light of, to make little of, to belittle, to curse by abusing or belittling, to slander." We are created in the image of God, and when we curse ourselves we are also cursing Him.

Job 2:10

"But he said unto her, Thou speakest as one of the foolish women speaketh. What? Shall we receive good at the hand of God, and shall we not receive evil? In all this did not Job sin with his lips."

"...In all this did not Job sin with his lips."

The King James Version is plainly teaching that Job did sin with his lips. If this is taken as a statement, it is saying that in all that has happened so far, "did not Job sin with his lips." As mentioned before, we do not know Job's heart. The actions that God permitted were and are only consistent with His nature and Scripture, if Job sinned.

For the sake of argument let's change the punctuation to a question mark at the end of this sentence: "In all this, did not Job sin with his lips?" In changing the punctuation, which has been added by man, we still see that Job did sin with his lips. In this verse Job falsely accuses God of sending evil his way. God cannot do an evil act because He cannot sin. Isn't it a sin to falsely accuse God?

Job 2:11-13

"Now when Job's three friends heard of all this evil that was come upon him, they came everyone from his own place; Eliphaz the Temanite, and Bildad the Shuhite, and Zophar the Naamathite: for they had made an appointment together to come to mourn with him and to comfort him. And when they lifted up their eyes afar off, and knew him not, they lifted up their voice, and wept; and they rent everyone his mantle, and sprinkled dust upon their heads toward heaven. So they sat down with him upon the ground seven days and seven nights, and none spake a word unto him: for they saw that his grief was very great."

They did not know what to say because they did not have any answers for Job. In the debates that follow, they condemned Job but they did not have answers for him. Is this not the state that most of us find ourselves in? We condemn others, ourselves or God, when we should have answers because God has given us answers. We do not have answers because we do not really know our LORD or believe what He has promised.

## CHAPTER 3: JOB'S SIN

In chapter 3, Job's sins become obvious. He sinned with his lips by cursing the day he was born and by blaming the LORD for the calamities in his life.

Job 3:1

"After this opened Job his mouth, and cursed his day."

After his three friends arrived, and after the seven days of silence, Job opened his mouth and cursed the day he was born. We are created in the image of God, and when we curse ourselves we are cursing the One that made us. This is the point in time that Job opened his mouth and began to speak out what was in his heart. Because of Job's words there is no longer any question of what was in his heart. Matthew 12:34 says, "...for out of the abundance of the heart the mouth speaketh."

Job sinned in four different ways when he opened his mouth:

1. In Job 3:1-9 he cursed the day he was born seventeen different ways.
2. From chapter 1:21 to chapter 30:22, Job blamed or accused God seventy-four different ways for his troubles.
3. He became bitter, full of self-pity, wanted to die. He did not resist the devil, nor did he take responsibility for his or his wife's actions.
4. He had fear. Fear is the opposite of faith. In several verses Job describes himself as being afraid and he even blamed God for his terror (chapter 3:25, 31:23).

Job 3:2-20

"And Job spake, and said, Let the day perish wherein I was born, and the night in which it was said, There is a man-child conceived. Let that day be darkness; let not God regard it from above, neither let the light shine upon it. Let darkness and the shadow of death stain it; let a cloud dwell upon it; let the blackness of the day terrify it. As for that night, let darkness seize upon it; let it not be joined unto the days of the year, let it not come into the number of the months. Lo, let that night be solitary, let no joyful voice come therein. Let them curse it that curse the day, who are ready to raise up their mourning. Let the stars of the twilight thereof be dark; let it look for light, but have none; neither let it see the dawning of the day: Because it shut not up the doors of my mother's womb, nor hid sorrow from mine eyes. Why died I not from the womb? Why did I not give up the ghost when I came out of the belly? Why did the knees prevent me? Or why the breasts that I should suck? For now should I have lain still and been quiet, I should have slept: then had I been at rest, With kings and counselors of the earth, which built desolate places for themselves; Or with princes that had gold, who filled their houses with silver: Or as an hidden untimely birth I had not been; as infants which never saw light. There the wicked cease from troubling; and there the weary be at rest. There the prisoners rest together; they hear not the voice of the oppressor. The small and great are there; and the servant is free from his master. Wherefore is light given to him that is in misery, and life unto the bitter in soul"

In these verses Job cursed himself seventeen times, in cursing the day he was born:

1. Let the day perish in which I was born.
2. Let the night perish in which it was said, There is a son born.
3. Let that day be darkness.
4. Let God not regard it from above.
5. Let no light shine upon it.
6. Let darkness and the shadow of death stain it.
7. Let a cloud dwell upon it.
8. Let blackness of the day terrify it.
9. Let darkness seize upon that night.
10. Let it not be joined to the days of the year.
11. Let it not come into the number of the months.
12. Let that night be solitary.
13. Let no joyful voice come therein.
14. Let them curse it that curse the day, who are ready to raise up their mourning.
15. Let the stars of the twilight of that night be dark.
16. Let it look for the light, but have none.
17. Let it not see the dawning of the day.

Do you notice any sins in this list? Is there any self-pity or bitterness? Of course there is. We are made in image of God, and when we curse ourselves we also make light of Him. Job cursed the LORD every time he cursed himself. In these verses Job also complained several times:

1. Because of life's misery.
2. Bitterness of soul.
3. Death better than life.
4. Desperation to end it all.
5. The grave would be a relief.
6. Life is so hedged in.
7. Sufferings and troubles are met day and night.

Take a look at some of the things that you have said when life was not going well. Did you say things very similar to what Job said in these verses? I have.

Job 3:21-25

"Which long for death, but it cometh not; and dig for it more than for hid treasures; Which rejoice exceedingly, and are glad, when they can find the grave? Why is light given to a man whose way is hid, and whom God hath hedged in? For my sighing cometh before I eat and my roarings are poured out like the waters. For the thing which I greatly feared is come upon me, and that which I was afraid of is come unto me."

Job 3:25 says, "The thing which I greatly feared is come upon me, and that which I was afraid of is come unto me..." There are at least two distinct ways of looking at this verse, and both are probably correct. First, when calamity began to befall him, Job feared it would continue; when he heard of the first loss, he feared others would follow. This could have been a short-term fear that only grew out of the calamities. Or secondly, it could also have been a fear that he lived under for many, many years. When we examine "that which came upon him," we will see that it was a long-standing fear that to some degree controlled his life. Either way, this kind of fear is a sin because it is the opposite of faith. If it is not of faith it is sin (Romans 14:23).

What did Job fear? First, Scripture says that he continually feared that his children might curse God. In addition, by looking at what happened, we can also gain insight into what his other fears might have been because what he greatly feared and was afraid of came upon him. In other words, in what or who was Job's faith? When we look at what came upon him, we will have the answer. Job lost all of his worldly possessions, his wealth, his status among men, and his family and his friends. Was he afraid that somehow he would lose these things? Were these more important to him than God? If Job was living in fear, he was living in a form of idolatry. Job plainly admits in verse 25 that he was living in fear. His faith was in the things he was afraid of losing and not in God.

I have found that the things people fear usually come to pass. We will always reap what we sow. Fear and faith are opposite. If we are in fear, anxious or worried about something, we are not trusting in the LORD. If we are in faith, there is no room for fear or worry. Faith and fear are equal; one will always replace the other. Fears become self-fulfilling prophecies, because in fear, we are telling the LORD that we do not trust Him. Therefore fear is a sin. Even though Job loved the LORD, he had placed his faith in the things of this life, not our LORD. Are we any different?

Job 3:26

"I was not in safety, neither had I rest, neither was I quiet; yet trouble came."

Job could not find safety or rest or quiet. Why? I John 4:18 says, "There is no fear in love; but perfect love casteth out fear: because fear hath torment. He that feareth is not made perfect in love."

Job is admitting the torment that comes with fear. If he were in faith, and trusting the LORD, there would not have been this torment. When any of us are trusting in ourselves, in our possessions, or in our position, then we will be in torment and in fear of losing what we are putting our faith in. There is perfect peace if our hearts are stayed on our LORD.

# CHAPTERS 4 THROUGH 31: THE DEBATES AND JOB'S SELF-RIGHTEOUSNESS

These chapters are a record of the conversation between Job and his first three friends. They also record Job's response to the calamities. Job responded by accusing God, claiming that he was innocent and that God was unfair and unjust.

Here is a list of seventy-four different ways that Job falsely accused, belittled or cursed God:

1. "The Lord hath taken away" (Job 1:21). Actually, Satan did this (Job 1:6-19).
2. "Shall we not receive evil?" (Job 2:10). Job was accusing God of sending evil his way. The truth is, God cannot tempt men with evil (James 1:13-16); to do so would make God guilty of sin. We are to pray, "deliver us from evil," not "deliver us from God" (Matthew 6:13).
3. "God had hedged in" — with calamity (Job 3:23). Our LORD is the giver of every good and perfect gift (James 1:16-17); if it is not good and perfect, it is from the devil.
4. The arrows of the Almighty are within me, and their poison drinks up my spirit (Job 6:4). God is the giver of good and perfect gifts, not poisonous arrows.
5. "The terrors of God do set themselves in array against me" (Job 6:4).
6. God scares me with dreams, and terrifies me through visions, "so that my soul chooseth strangling and death rather than life" (Job 7:14).
7. You have "set me as a mark" against You (Job 7:20).
8. You do not pardon my transgressions (Job 7:21).
9. "He breaketh me with a tempest" (Job 9:17).
10. He multiplies my wounds without cause (Job 9:17).
11. "He will not suffer me to take my breath" (Job 9:18).
12. "He fills me with bitterness" (Job 9:18).
13. He destroys the perfect and the wicked (Job 9:22).
14. "He will laugh at the trial of the innocent" (Job 9:23).
15. He has given the earth to the wicked (Job 9:24).
16. He hides the faces of the judges so that they cannot discern right and wrong (Job 9:24).
17. If I made myself ever so clean, yet You will plunge me into the ditch (Job 9:30-31).
18. You oppress and despise me (Job 10:3).
19. You "shine upon the counsel of the wicked" (Job 10:3).
20. You know that I am not wicked, yet You destroy me (Job 10:7-8).
21. You have "poured me out as milk, and curdled me like cheese" (Job 10:10).
22. If I sin, then You mark me and will not forgive me (Job 10:14).
23. You hunt me as a fierce lion (Job 10:16).

24. You renew Your witness against me, and increase wrath upon me (Job 10:17).
25. "The tabernacles of robbers prosper, and they that provoke God are secure, into whose hand God brings abundance (Job 12:6).
26. "Though He slay me, yet will I trust in Him" (Job 13:15).
27. You hide Your face from me and count me as Your enemy (Job 13:24).
28. You write bitter things against me, and make me possess the iniquities of my youth (Job 13:26).
29. You put my feet in stocks (Job 13:27).
30. You destroy the hope of man (Job 14:19).
31. He has made me weary (Job 16:7).
32. He has made desolate all my company (Job 16:7).
33. He has filled me with wrinkles (Job 16:8).
34. He tears me in wrath (Job 16:9).
35. He hates me (Job 16:9).
36. He gnashes upon me with His teeth (Job 16:9).
37. He has delivered me to the ungodly, into the hands of the wicked (Job 16:11).
38. He has "broken me asunder" (Job 16:12).
39. He has taken me by the neck and shaken me to pieces (Job 16:12).
40. He has set me up for His mark (Job 16:12).
41. His archers surrounded me (Job 16:13).
42. He cleaves my reigns (Job 16:13).
43. He does not spare me (Job 16:13).
44. He pours out my gall upon the ground (Job 16:13).
45. He breaks me with "breach upon breach" (Job 16:14).
46. He runs upon me like a giant (Job 16:14).
47. He has done all this for no injustice in my hands (Job 16:17).
48. He has made me a byword of the people (Job 17:6).
49. God has overthrown me (Job 19:6).
50. He has captured me in His net (Job 19:6).
51. He does not hear me (Job 19:7).
52. There is no justice from Him (Job 19:7).
53. He has "fenced up my way that I cannot pass" (Job 19:8).
54. He has set darkness in my paths (Job 19:8).
55. He has stripped me of my glory (Job 19:9).
56. He has taken my crown.
57. He has destroyed me on every side (Job 19:10).
58. He has removed my hope like a tree.
59. He has kindled His wrath against me (Job 19:11).
60. He has counted me as one of His enemies.

61. His troops raise up their way against me, and encamp around my house
(Job 19:12).
62. He has put my brethren far from me (Job 19:13).
63. He has estranged my acquaintances (Job 19:13).
64. The Almighty troubles me (Job 23:16).
65. God has taken away my judgment (Job 27:2).
66. He has vexed my soul (Job 27:2).
67. He has loosed my cord (Job 30:11).
68. He has afflicted me (Job 30:11).
69. He has cast me into the mire (Job 30:19).
70. I cry to You, and You do not hear me (Job 30:20).
71. I stand up and You do not regard me (Job 30:20).
72. You are cruel to me (Job 30:21).
73. You oppose me (Job 30:21).
74. You have lifted me up to the wind and have dissolved my substance (Job 30:22).

All seventy-four of the above statements are false, because it was Satan who took away Job's substance (Job 1:12-19), terrorized him, and did all the other cruel things to him (Job 2:6-7, 42:10). Adam and Eve sinned the same way when Satan tempted them to eat of the forbidden tree. Satan claimed that God was only withholding something good from them. Satan began blaming God for his actions in Genesis 3.

Take another look at this list and examine yourself. Have you made said similar statements? Have you also falsely accused our LORD? In any way that we have belittled, blamed, slandered, or accused our LORD, we have cursed Him. In any way that we have doubted, or not believed Him, we have cursed Him. Why not ask Him to forgive you for your unbelief and ask Him for His gift of faith?

The following is a list of the different ways that Job suffered and some of his responses:

1. Satan "smote Job with sore boils" over his entire body (Job 2:7).
2. Job was in such misery that he cursed the day he was born (Job 3:1-13, 20).
3. He was bitter in soul (Job 3:20, 7:11, 10:1).
4. He longed for death (Job 3:21-23, 7:15).
5. His sighs and roarings "are poured out like waters" (Job 3:24).
6. Job felt that his grief and calamity were "heavier than the sand of the sea"
(Job 6:1-3).
7. Job felt like he had poison arrows stuck in him, "the poison whereof drinketh up my spirit" (Job 6:4).
8. He longed for God to destroy him and cut him off (Job 6:8-9).
9. He said, "I would harden myself in sorrow" (Job 6:10).

10. He felt he had no pity from his friends (Job 6:14).
11. He said his brethren had deceived him (Job 6:15).
12. He said he was "made to possess months of vanity, and wearisome nights" were appointed to him (Job 7:3).
13. Unable to sleep, he tossed "to and fro" all night (Job 7:4).
14. He said, "My flesh is clothed with worms and clods of dust" (Job 7:5).
15. His skin was broken and loathsome (Job 7:5).
16. His days were spent without hope (Job 7:6).
17. He spoke in anguish of spirit, and complained in bitterness of soul (Job 7:11).
18. He was scared and terrified with dreams and visions (Job 7:14).
19. He would choose to be strangled, and wanted death more than his life (Job 7:15).
20. He loathed his life (Job 7:16).
21. He felt he was a burden even to himself (Job 7:20).
22. His wounds were multiplied without cause (Job 9:17).
23. He could hardly breathe (Job 9:18).
24. He said, "I am afraid of all my sorrows" (Job 9:28).
25. He said, "My soul is weary of my life" (Job 10:1).
26. His neighbors mocked and scorned him (Job 12:4).
27. He said, "I take my flesh in my teeth" (Job 13:14).
28. He couldn't hold his tongue from crying out in pain (Job 13:19).
29. His flesh was as a rotten thing, consumed as a moth-eaten garment (Job 13:28).
30. His friends heaped up words against him, and shook their heads at him (Job 16:4).
31. He was filled with wrinkles (Job 16:8).
32. His gall was poured out on the ground (Job 16:13).
33. He said, "My face is foul with weeping" (Job 16:16).
34. The shadow of death was on his eyelids (Job 16:16).
35. He said, "My breath is corrupt" (Job 17:1).
36. His friends had reproached him ten times (Job 19:3).
37. They made themselves strange to him (Job 19:3).
38. He cried out, but felt he wasn't heard by God (Job 19:7).
39. He felt he had no justice (Job 19:7).
40. He had been stripped of his glory (Job 19:9).
41. His crown had been taken away (Job 19:9).
42. He felt he had been counted as an enemy of God (Job 19:11).
43. His brethren and acquaintances were estranged from him (Job 19:13).
44. His kinfolk had failed him (Job 19:14).
45. His close friends had forgotten him (Job 19:14).
46. His household maids and servants treated him like a stranger (Job 19:15-16).
47. He was like a stranger to his wife (Job 19:17).

48. Children despised him (Job 19:18).
49. His close friends abhorred him, and those he loved had turned against him (Job 19:19).
50. His bones were clearly visible (Job 19:20).
51. No one had pity on him (Job 19:21).
52. His friends persecuted him (Job 19:22).
53. He said, "I am afraid, and trembling taketh hold on my flesh" (Job 21:6).
54. He said, "My complaint is bitter" (Job 23:2).
55. He said, "My stroke is heavier than my groaning" (Job 23:2).
56. He was afraid of God (Job 23:15).
57. He said, "My bowels boiled, and rested not" (Job 30:27).
58. He said, "My skin is black upon me" (Job 30:30).
59. He said, "My bones are burned with heat" (Job 30:30).
60. His music was turned to mourning and weeping (Job 30:31).

When we look at a list like this it gives us a very different picture of Job from the one we normally are taught. Did you notice the self-pity, the bitterness, the complaining, the fear, the depression, the despair, the wishing to die, the self-righteousness? Every one of these emotions is a sin. This clearly demonstrates how far Job was from the LORD.

Every one of us, at some time in our life, can have each of these feelings, each of these sins. This very clearly demonstrates how far we are from God. We should take stock and examine our ways, lest we fall into the same trap of spiritual pride and arrogance and fear that Job did. Again it is time to examine ourselves. How have you lived in self-pity? How have you been angry at others, God or yourself? Make a list and repent for each of your sins. Job repented in chapter 42.

Note: Chapters 32 through 37 give Elihu's solution to Job's calamities and problems. We will cover these chapters later.

## CHAPTERS 38 THROUGH 42: THE LORD'S RESPONSE TO JOB AND JOB'S REPENTANCE AND RESTORATION

Only our LORD and Savior has true words of wisdom and healing. Let's take a look at what the LORD had to say to Job.

Job 38:1-3

"Then the LORD answered Job out of the whirlwind, and said, Who is this that darkeneth counsel by words without knowledge? Gird up now thy loins like a man; for I will demand of thee, and answer thou Me."

Instead of vindicating the LORD, Job had falsely accused Him. Job had murmured and complained against the LORD until he became embittered against Him, and finally confused the issue with his feelings. One of the greatest lessons of Job is that we should always clear God of fault, and take responsibility ourselves instead. There is no fault with Him in any of His ways.

In verse 3, the LORD tells Job to gird up thy loins like a man. In other words, quit complaining, blaming others for your problems, and take responsibility for your actions. Then, the LORD proceeds to ask Job many questions that essentially put Job in his proper place. The LORD asks Job a total of 184 questions in the next four chapters.

Job 38:4

"Where wast thou when I laid the foundations of the earth? Declare, if thou hast understanding."

If you are so smart and know all the answers, explain how the earth was created. The LORD asked Job thirty-five questions about creation:

1. Foundations of the earth (Job 38:4).
2. Laying the measures thereof (Job 38:5).
3. Stretching the line upon the earth.
4. Fastening of earth's foundations (Job 38:6).
5. Rejoicing when the cornerstone of the earth was laid (Job 38:6-7).
6. Shutting up of the sea (Job 38:8).
7. Limiting or setting bounds for the sea (Job 38:9-11).
8. Laws of day and night (Job 38:12-13).
9. The springs of the sea (Job 38:16).
10. The depths of the sea.
11. The gates of death (Job 38:17).
12. The doors of the shadow of death.
13. The breadth of the earth (Job 38:18).
14. The dwelling of light (Job 38:19).
15. The dwelling of darkness (Job 38:19-20).
16. Number of Job's days (Job 38:21).
17. The treasures of the snow (Job 38:22).
18. The treasures of the hail (Job 38:22-23).
19. The light and winds (Job 38:24).
20. The watercourse, lightning, thunder, and rains (Job 38:25-27).
21. The origin of rain (Job 38:28).
22. The origin of dew drops.
23. The origin of ice (Job 38:29).
24. The origin of hoary frost (Job 38:29-30).
25. Binding and loosing of Pleiades and the bands of Orion (Job 38:31).
26. Mazzaroth in his seasons (Job 38:32).
27. Arcturus and his sons.
28. The ordinances of heaven (Job 38:33).

29. The dominion of heaven in earth.
30. Control of the clouds (Job 38:34).
31. Sending lightnings (Job 38:35).
32. Wisdom in the inward parts (Job 38:36).
33. Understanding in the heart.
34. The number of clouds (Job 38:37).
35. The bottles of heaven and the dust and clods of earth (Job 38:38).

Job could not answer any of these questions; neither can you or I. Then, the Lord asks Job about things on this earth:

1. Hunting prey for lions (Job 38:39-40).
2. Filling the appetite of young lions.
3. Providing food for ravens (Job 38:41).
4. When wild goats increase (Job 39:1).
5. The hinds calve.
6. The gestation periods of animals (Job 39:2).
7. The time when they travail.
8. Sending wild donkeys out free (Job 39:5).
9. Loosing bands of wild donkeys.
10. Taming a unicorn (Job 39:9).
11. Training a unicorn to work (Job 39:10).
12. Using the unicorn to harrow.
13. Trusting the strength of unicorns (Job 39:11).
14. Winning confidence of unicorns.
15. Trusting unicorns to harvest the crops and bring to the barn (Job 39:12).
16. Giving wings to peacocks (Job 39:13).
17. Giving wings and feathers to the ostrich (Job 39:13).
18. Giving strength to a horse (Job 39:19).
19. Clothing his neck with thunder.
20. Making him afraid (Job 39:20).
21. Flying of the hawk (Job 39:26).
22. Mounting up of eagles (Job 39:27).
23. Instructing the Almighty (Job 40:2).

Job could not answer any of these questions either. Who are we to question God? As I look at my own life I am amazed that I could ever question Him in any way. But I have many times. I have blamed Him and questioned Him in my pride and arrogance. There is truly much to learn from Job, because he was a man just like all of us.

Is the Holy Spirit revealing a time that you have questioned or blamed God? Why not ask Him to forgive you? I have asked Him to forgive me many times.

Job 40:1-2

"Moreover the LORD answered Job, and said, Shall he that contendeth with the Almighty instruct him? He that reproveth God, let him answer it."

Job could not answer any of the LORD's questions. But Job, in his pride and arrogance, had contended with God to instruct Him; had reproved God; had questioned God's judgment (Job 40:8); had condemned God to make himself appear righteous; hid counsel without knowledge; hid or concealed God's counsel (Job 42:3); and had uttered what he did not understand. Job sinned against the LORD in each of these ways.

It is not wise to reprove the LORD. I do not have the wisdom or knowledge to answer Him. When I came to the point in my life when I quit asking "why," questioning the LORD, and decided to completely trust Him, and put Him first, He was there (James 4:8). He was faithful, and taught me how to have victory over the devil. We must always remember that God the Father is the giver of every good and perfect gift. If it is not good and perfect, it is from the devil (James 1:16-17).

Job 40:3-5

"Then Job answered the Lord, and said, Behold, I am vile; what shall I answer thee? I will lay mine hand upon my mouth. Once have I spoken; but I will not answer: yea, twice; but I will proceed no further."

As Job listened to the LORD, he realized the error of his way and began to backtrack. Compare Job's brief answer and attitude here with his bragging in Job 23:1-8. He said that he would fill his mouth with arguments if God would only give him a fair trial. But what did he do after he had the trial? He had nothing to say except that he was vile and didn't know what answers to give God, and he put his hand over his mouth. All Job's former arguments were gone now.

In the first barrage of questions from God, Job was brought to complete silence and acknowledgment of his vileness (Job 40:3-5).

Job 40:6-7

"Then answered the LORD unto Job out of the whirlwind, and said, Gird up thy loins now like a man: I will demand of thee, and declare thou unto me."

After Job had answered Him briefly and confessed his vileness, God continued by commanding him to act like a man and take responsibility for his words and actions. In chapter 40 God commands, requires, challenges or warns Job in thirteen ways:

1. Gird up your loins now like a man: for I will demand of you, and you must answer Me (Job 38:3).
2. He that reproves God, let him answer it (Job 40:2).
3. Gird up your loins like a man: I will demand of you, and declare unto Me (Job 40:7).
4. Deck yourself with majesty and excellency (Job 40:10).
5. Array yourself with glory and beauty (Job 40:10).

6. Cast abroad the rage of your wrath: and behold every one that is proud and abase him (Job 40:11).
7. Look on everyone that is proud, and bring him low (Job 40:12).
8. Tread down the wicked in their place (Job 40:12).
9. Hide them in the dust together (Job 40:13).
10. Bind their faces in secret (Job 40:13).
11. Behold now behemoth (Job 40:15).
12. Behold, he drinketh up a river (Job 40:23).
13. Behold, the hope of him is in vain (Job 41:9).

We all should take God's requirements and warnings seriously. We must remember that He loves and cares for us and that He has only our well being in mind when He warns us or requires us to do something. In Job 40:8-9 God continues by asking Job four questions about himself:

1. About disannulling the judgment of God.
2. Condemning the Almighty that Job might be righteous.
3. Having an arm (power) like God.
4. Being able to thunder with a voice like God.

Once again Job had no answers because he was guilty. In chapter 40:15-24 God describes something He calls the behemoth or leviathan. When you consider how God described it, its powers that are suggested in the questions to Job in chapter 41:1-14, and the use of the word in other passages, I believe that the behemoth or leviathan is Satan.

The Hebrew word for "leviathan" (HSN-3882) refers to a great sea serpent as a symbol of Satan (Psalms 74:14, 104:26, Job 41:1, Isaiah 27:1). The language is also figurative of the defeat of satanic powers. In Revelation 12:1-17, 13:2-11, 16:13-16, and 20:2, Satan is symbolized by a great dragon with seven heads and ten horns, picturing his power over the great world empires.

In chapter 41 God asks Job twenty questions about the behemoth, leviathan or Satan that again he cannot answer:

1. Catching him with a hook (Job 41:1).
2. Catching him by his tongue.
3. Catching him by the nose (Job 41:2).
4. Boring his jaw with a thorn.
5. Making supplications to man (Job 41:3).
6. Speaking soft words to man.
7. Making a covenant with man (Job 41:4).
8. Taking him as a servant.
9. Playing with him as a bird (Job 41:5).

10. Binding him for the maidens.
11. Making a banquet of him (Job 41:6).
12. Dividing him among merchants.
13. Filling his skin with barbed irons (Job 41:7).
14. Filling his head with fish spears.
15. Being afraid of him (Job 41:9).
16. No man able to stand before him (Job 41:10).
17. Repaying him (Job 41:11).
18. Discovering his garment (Job 41:13).
19. Bridling him.
20. Opening his jaws (Job 41:14).

Obviously Job could not do any of these things. God again is pointing out Job's weakness and thus his need for God. Chapter 41 gives the following description of leviathan or Satan:

1. He cannot be taken with a hook like a fish (Job 41:1).
2. His tongue cannot be snared with a rope.
3. His nose cannot be hooked (Job 41:2).
4. Jaws cannot be bored through with a thorn (ring).
5. He does not beg for his life (Job 41:3).
6. He cannot be made a servant of man (Job 41:4).
7. He cannot be tamed (Job 41:5).
8. He is not edible (Job 41:6).
9. He cannot be divided and sold.
10. His skin cannot be filled with barbed irons in taking him (Job 41:7).
11. His head cannot be filled with fish spears in capturing him.
12. In seeking to take him, all that a man can do is to fight him and no more (Job 41:8).
13. The hope of taking him in battle is vain (Job 41:9).
14. Men give up in any fight with him when they see him.
15. No man is so fierce that he can stir him up any more than he can stand against God — and who will dare fight with God (Job 41:10-11)?
16. God alone is not confounded by his parts (limbs), power, and frame (Job 41:12).
17. No man can discover the face of his garment or his skin (Job 41:13).
18. No man can bridle him.
19. No man can open his jaws (Job 41:14).
20. His scales are his pride (Job 41:15).
21. His scales are shut up together as with a close seal.
22. One scale is so near another that no air can come between them (Job 41:16).

23. The scales are joined one to another (Job 41:17).
24. They stick together.
25. They cannot be separated.
26. Light shoots out of his nostrils when he sneezes (Job 41:18).
27. His eyes look like two suns that come up in the morning.
28. Burning torches shoot out of his mouth when it is open (Job 41:19).
29. Sparks of fire leap out when his mouth is open.
30. Smoke goes out of his nostrils when he breathes, as out of a boiling pot.
31. His breath kindles the coals of his mouth into flames of fire (Job 41:21).
32. His neck is exceedingly strong (Job 41:22).
33. Sorrow (terror) is turned into joy (dances) before him.
34. His flesh is not flabby and soft, but solid and firm (Job 41:23).
35. His flesh cannot be moved.
36. His heart is as firm and as a hard millstone (Job 41:24).
37. The mighty are afraid when he raises himself up to attack (Job 41:25).
38. By reason of breakings (destruction wrought by him) the mighty purify themselves (miss the mark and flee in terror).
39. The sword (harpoon) that is put into him cannot hold (penetrate his hard skin, Job 41:26).
40. The spear, dart, and other weapons have no effect on him.
41. He esteems iron as weak straw (Job 41:27).
42. He esteems brass as rotten wood.
43. Arrows have no effect on him (Job 41:28).
44. Sling stones fall off him like stubble (Job 41:28).
45. Darts are also counted as stubble by him (Job 41:29).
46. He laughs at the spear.
47. He walks and lies on sharp stones which have no effect on him (Job 41:30).
48. Sharp pointed stones are as soft to him as clay.
49. Wherever he goes he makes the water to boil like a pot (Job 41:31).
50. He stirs the sea up into foam like a pot of ointment.
51. He makes a foamy path in the water after him (Job 41:32).
52. He makes the deep to appear hoary (white) and foamy.
53. There is nothing like him on earth (Job 41:33).
54. He is without fear.
55. He beholds all high things (Job 41:34).
56. He is king over all the children of pride.

This is no doubt a symbol of Satan as a great dragon, the enemy of both God and man. Certain statements in this description could refer only to a supernatural being, as in

Isaiah 27:1 or Revelation 12. In Job 41:34 he is called "the king over all the children of pride." The Berkeley and Young versions read, "he is king over all the sons of pride." Thus leviathan could be none other than Satan, the spirit that now works in all sons of disobedience and pride (Ephesians 2:1-3).

In Scripture the word "pride" is never used in reference to an animal; it is always used to describe men. So "the children of pride" in Job 41:34 must refer to men and their king is the devil. To interpret this verse as meaning that leviathan is king over all the animals is out of harmony with Scripture. If he is king over all the sons of the proud human race, then leviathan must be Satan.

After this barrage of questions and the after listening to God describe his true enemy Job is brought to complete repentance. Job realizes what has happened. He realizes that he has yielded to the devil, and in chapter 42 he repents.

In Job 42:1, again Job attempts to respond, "Then Job answered the LORD, and said...." In the next six verses Job makes ten statements to the LORD:

Job said, I know You can do everything (Job 42:2). No thought can be withheld from You. I have hidden counsel without knowledge (Job 42:3). I uttered what I did not understand. I uttered things too wonderful for me, which I did not know. Hear what I have to say (Job 42:4). I want an answer from You. I have heard of You by the ear. Now I see You (Job 42:5). I abhor myself, and repent in dust and ashes (Job 42:6).

Job finally saw, and had an understanding of, the LORD that he served. He saw how he had failed. He saw and understood his own pride and arrogance, his fear, his self-pity — his sins. He then repented in dust and ashes.

Job 42:5

"I have heard of Thee by the hearing of the ear: but now mine eye seeth Thee."

Through all of his disobedience he accused God and blamed God for the calamities that he suffered. But in His great love for Job, and all of His creation, God used Job's sin and turned it into good. Now Job finally understands the love and justice of God.

Job personally experienced the truth of our LORD. John 8:32 says, "...we shall know the truth and the truth shall set you free." The word "know" means to personally experience. Job personally experienced God's truth and then obeyed and was set free.

I hope that you understand that we are no different than Job. We all have become separated from God in many ways. How have you blamed God for what you, or Satan, really did? Maybe it is time to do what Job did, and take stock of your ways. How have you sinned against God? Do you have fear in your life? Do you have any spiritual pride or arrogance? Is there any unforgiveness or bitterness in you? Is your trust in your position and possessions, or in God?

When Job recognized his sin, he fell on his face before the LORD. The LORD Jehovah, the Messiah, the Christ, in His grace and mercy forgave Job. He will forgive you also.

Job 42:7

"And it was so, that after the LORD had spoken these words unto Job, the LORD said to Eliphaz the Temanite, My wrath is kindled against thee, and against thy two friends: for ye have not spoken of Me the thing that is right, as My servant Job hath."

The LORD told them that they had not spoken of Him the things that were right, as His servant Job had done in his repentance (Job 42:1-6). He is telling them that they too need to repent. All through the debates between these three friends and Job in chapters 4 through 31, they accused Job of sin, they condemned him, but they did not have answers for his questions, and they did not defend the LORD. Now, the LORD requires repentance and a sacrifice from them for their sins (Job 42:8). The requirement for the sacrifice for sin should not have been a surprise. The LORD made this requirement hundreds of years earlier in Genesis.

This seems to be the condition of most believers, and our churches today. We condemn each other. We do not have answers for the problems of life, nor do we defend our LORD. We deserve the same criticism that the LORD delivered to Job and his first three friends.

Job 42:8-9

"Therefore take unto you now seven bullocks and seven rams, and go to My servant Job, and offer up for yourselves a burnt offering; and My servant Job shall pray for you: for him will I accept: lest I deal with you after your folly, in that ye have not spoken of Me the thing which is right, like My servant Job. So Eliphaz the Temanite and Bildad the Shuhite and Zophar the Naamathite went, and did according as the Lord commanded them: the Lord also accepted Job."

The LORD commanded the three friends (by name) to take animals for a blood sacrifice that was required under the law to cover sin, and go to Job. He commanded Job to pray for them, or in other words forgive them for condemning him without answers. After Job had forgiven his three friends and performed the required sacrifice, "the LORD also accepted Job."

Job 42:10

"And the LORD turned the captivity of Job, when he prayed for his friends: also the LORD gave Job twice as much as he had before."

"The LORD turned the captivity of Job" is an incredible statement. Satan was holding Job captive because of his sin. Jesus, our LORD, came that we might recover ourselves from the captivity of Satan (sin). We do this by repenting of our sins, thus allowing the blood of our Savior to cleanse us. In doing this, we cancel Satan's right to us (II Timothy 2:25-26).

In Isaiah 61:1-3 and Luke 4:18-19 we learn that Jesus came to heal the brokenhearted and to set the captives free. This is exactly what He did for Job, after he repented, or submitted to our LORD. This is what He did for me, and what He will do for you if you are willing to obey and put Him first in your life (Matthew 6:33, James 4:7-8).

Job repented, completed the required sacrifice, and forgave those that accused him. You see, God will not forgive us unless we forgive others (Matthew 6:14-15). Then, the LORD was faithful and just to forgive Job of his sin and cleanse him of all unrighteousness, and in doing so restored double what the evil one stole (I John 1:9, Job 42:10).

There was a fourth friend of Job's named Elihu (Job 32-37). Why wasn't he condemned with the other three friends of Job? Review the earlier verses and you will see that he is not named with Job and the first three friends. He was not required to repent, forgive or sacrifice. Why? Did he do something different? This is a very interesting question. In the answer, we will again see how our LORD looks out for us. Let's go back to chapter 32 and find out what happened.

## CHAPTERS 32 THROUGH 37: ELIHU'S SOLUTION

It is my belief that these five chapters are some of the most important in Scripture. Unfortunately, most teach that Elihu was a false prophet. If you will diligently study, you will find God's answers to life contained in Elihu's responses to Job.

First, who was Elihu? This very important question needs to be answered before we can understand Elihu's response to Job and his three friends. In chapter 42 we find that he was the friend of Job who was not condemned by the LORD. The other three friends along with Job were required to perform a blood sacrifice for their sins. Why wasn't Elihu also required to? Let's look at who Elihu says he is:

Job 32:5-8

"When Elihu saw that there was no answer in the mouth of these three men, then his wrath was kindled. And Elihu the son of Barachel the Buzite answered and said, I am young, and ye are very old; wherefore I was afraid, and durst not shew you mine opinion. I said, Days should speak, and multitude of years should teach wisdom. But there is a spirit in man: and the inspiration of the Almighty giveth them understanding."

These verses show that Elihu was a young man that was angry with Job's other friends because they had no answers. He was hesitant to speak because the others were his elders. He remained quiet, and listened out of respect. As he listened, his anger grew to the point he could no longer constrain the inspiration of the Holy Spirit and then he spoke. He was claiming that the Holy Spirit was speaking through him and giving him understanding. Could this be true?

Job 33:6

"Behold, I am according to thy wish in God's stead: I also am formed out of the clay."

Job 36:1-4

"Elihu also proceeded, and said, Suffer me a little, and I will shew thee that I have yet to speak on God's behalf. I will fetch my knowledge from afar, and will ascribe righteousness to my Maker. For truly my words shall not be false: He that is perfect in knowledge is with thee."

Elihu was claiming that he was a man sent by the Lord in answer to Job's request, with a message of wisdom for Job. He said his knowledge was "from afar." He did not claim that it was his knowledge. His knowledge was from the LORD, the One perfect in knowledge. God had sent many prophets to His people. Could Elihu have been a true prophet of the LORD? Every commentator that I have read claims that he is a false prophet.

In Job 33:23 Elihu also says, "If there be a messenger with him, an interpreter, one among a thousand, to shew unto man his uprightness...." Elihu is again claiming to be the LORD'S messenger. Elihu made these bold statements, and then in chapter 42 the LORD did not reprove him. Additionally, the statements made by Elihu were correct.

I believe that Elihu was a messenger, a prophet of God, sent to Job to show him three very important truths. First, Elihu showed Job his sin. This was the role of the prophet in the Old Testament. It is the role of the Holy Spirit in the New Testament. The manner in which Elihu spoke to Job is also very important, because he spoke the truth in love with the goal to restore, not condemn (Galatians 6:1, Ephesians 4:15). Second, Elihu had answers for Job from God that were provable in Scripture and in His nature. God cannot violate His precepts or His nature. All Christians should have an answer for those that come to us. A study of Elihu's answers is extremely profitable. Third, Elihu always defended God while Satan has always blamed God for what he has done. We are His ambassadors, thus we too are to defend Him. A study of Elihu's defenses of God will profit each of us greatly.

The LORD has used pastors, teachers, prophets, and others all through Scripture to deliver His message. Why wouldn't He do the same thing for Job? God loved Job just like He does you and me and He sent a messenger with a message of healing and deliverance for Job, just as He has done for each of us. I challenge you to find one thing that Elihu said or did that was wrong. Everything that he said was correct. He had answers from God for Job. He defended our LORD God. Furthermore, God did not require that he repent and perform a sacrifice, as He did from Job and the others, thus proving his innocence.

Let's take a look at the message Elihu had for Job:

Job 32:1

"So these three men ceased to answer Job, because he was righteous in his own eyes."

This verse sets the stage for Elihu. Job's three friends were giving up, because Job was self-righteous. In addition, they did not have answers. Without answers, it is difficult to continue. Today most Christians do not know how to help either.

Job 32:2-7

"Then was kindled the wrath of Elihu the son of Barachel the Buzite, of the kindred of Ram: against Job was his wrath kindled, because he justified himself rather than God. Also against his three friends was his wrath kindled, because they had found no answer, and yet had condemned Job. Now Elihu had waited till Job had spoken, because they were elder than he. When Elihu saw that there was no answer in the mouths of these three men, then his wrath was kindled. And Elihu the son of Barachel the Buzite answered and said, I am young, and ye are very old; wherefore I was afraid, and durst not shew you mine opinion. I said, Days should speak, and multitude of years should teach wisdom."

Elihu was a descendant of Buz, the second son of Nahor, who was a brother of Abraham (Genesis 22:20-21). He was a young man that respected his elders and waited for his turn to speak. After sitting through the long tedious debates his righteous anger rose up because Job "justified himself rather than God." Elihu was also angry because Job's friends had no answers but condemned him. In doing this were they not as self-righteous as Job?

Many teach today that we cannot or do not have answers for others. They have made the same mistake that Job's friends did. As we continue to study you will see that Elihu had answers and that his answers were full of compassion and the wisdom of God. A "multitude of years should teach wisdom" but unfortunately that does not often happen. All believers should, also, have answers for others from God.

Job 32:8-9

"But there is a spirit in man: and the inspiration of the Almighty giveth them under-standing. Great men are not always wise: neither do the aged understand judgment."

Elihu is claiming that the spirit of man, when it is truly inspired by the Almighty, is reason enough for anyone to speak. In such instances one does not need to be great, aged, or wise. The inspiration of the Holy Spirit is enough (Job 32:8-9, Acts 3:21, II Timothy 3:15-17, II Peter 1:21). Elihu is also claiming that he is speaking as the Holy Spirit is telling him to.

Job 32:10

"Therefore I said, Hearken to me; I also will shew mine opinion."

After claiming to be inspired by the Holy Spirit, Elihu proceeds to give additional reasons for choosing to speak in verses 11-22.

Job 32:11-22

"Behold, I waited for your words; I gave ear to your reasons, whilst ye searched out what to say. Yea, I attended unto you, and, behold, there was none of you that convinced Job, or that answered his words: Lest ye should say, We have found out wisdom: God thrusteth him down, not man. Now He hath not directed His words against me: neither will I answer Him with your speeches. They were amazed, they answered no more: they left off speaking. When I had waited (for they spake not, but stood still, and answered no more;) I said, I will answer also my part, I also will shew mine opinion. For I am full of matter, the spirit within me constraineth me. Behold, my belly is as wine which hath no vent; it is ready to burst like new bottles. I will speak, that I may be refreshed: I will open my lips and answer. Let me not, I pray you, accept any man's person, neither let me give flattering titles unto man. For I know not to give flattering titles; in so doing my maker would soon take me away."

In these verses he gives these reasons for speaking:

1. I have an opinion (Job 32:10, 17).
2. I waited for your words (Job 32:11).
3. I waited carefully for your reasons while you searched out what to say (Job 32:11).
4. I saw that none of you convinced Job (Job 32:12).
5. None of you answered his words (Job 32:12).
6. I was afraid that in your wisdom you would say that God has shoved Job under and not man (Job 32:13).
7. I am better prepared to answer him than you are, for I am not irritated at remarks said to me (Job 32:14).
8. I will not answer him with your line of arguments. I have the right answers because the Holy Spirit speaks through me (Job 32:18).
9. The spirit within me constrains me. I have a burning desire to answer him; I am like new bottles that have no vent and are ready to burst with the wine in them (Job 32:19).
10. I will speak that I may able to breathe (Job 32:20).
11. I will not show partiality (Job 32:21).
12. I will not use flattering titles to man, for I would sin against God if I did so (Job 32:21-22).

In chapter 32 Elihu has established his authority as being from God and his reasons for choosing to speak. Elihu begins chapter 33 by explaining the manner in which he will speak to Job.

Job 33:1-7

"Wherefore, Job, I pray thee, hear my speeches, and hearken to all my words. Behold, now I have opened my mouth, my tongue hath spoken in my mouth. My words shall be of the uprightness of my heart: and my lips shall utter knowledge clearly. The Spirit of God hath made me, and the breath of the Almighty hath given me life. If thou canst answer me, set thy words in order before me, stand up. Behold, I am according to thy wish in God's stead: I also am formed out of the clay. Behold, my terror shall not make thee afraid, neither shall my hand be heavy upon thee."

Elihu continues to answer Job by imploring him to listen, to hear what he has to say. Then he makes five promises to Job.

1. My words shall be of the uprightness of my heart (Job 33:3).
2. My lips shall utter knowledge clearly.
3. I will answer you in God's stead, according to your wish (Job 33:6).
4. My terror shall not make you afraid; that is, my speaking in God's stead will not overwhelm you like His words if He were speaking (Job 33:7).
5. My hand will not be heavy upon you.

Job had demanded a trial from God and Elihu is preparing Job for the questions that are coming from the LORD. He is preparing Job to meet the LORD, whom Job had been accusing. Elihu is also promising to be kind and gentle with Job. He is promising to share without being "heavy" upon him in condemnation or legalism. This is the manner that we are to deal with each other. Galatians 6:1 teaches us that our attitude toward a fallen brother should be one of restoration, not condemnation. Galatians 6:2 takes this one step further and admonishes us to even carry their burdens.

Elihu is demonstrating God's love and compassion. He is also claiming to be a man, thus equal to Job. Equal in responsibility and in sin. Satan is not creative; he tempts all men in similar ways. All temptation is common to man. Elihu is showing compassion to Job in letting him know that that he is also a man subject to the wiles of the devil. But he is also letting Job know in no uncertain terms that he is sent by God and that his answers are from God, so pay attention.

Job 33:8

"Surely thou hast spoken in mine hearing, and I have heard the voice of thy words, saying...."

Elihu now proceeds to repeat words that he personally heard Job say in his debates with the first three friends.

Job 33:9-13

"I am clean without transgression, I am innocent; neither is there iniquity in me. Behold, He findeth occasions against me, He counteth me for his enemy, He putteth my feet in the stocks, He marketh all my paths. Behold, in this thou art not just: I will answer thee, that God is greater than man. Why dost thou strive against Him? For He giveth not account of any of His matters."

In these verses Elihu lists seven false claims that Job made:

1. I am clean without transgression (Job 33:9).
2. I am innocent (Job 33:9).
3. I have no iniquity in me (Job 33:9).
4. God finds occasions against me (Job 33:10).
5. He counts me as His enemy (Job 33:10).

6. He puts my feet in the stocks (Job 33:11).

7. He marks all my paths (Job 33:11).

Elihu was right in these accusations against Job, because he did claim to be suffering without cause (Job 9:17). Job did say that God counted him as an enemy (Job 13:24). He did say that God had put his feet in stocks (Job 13:27), and looked on all his paths (Job 13:27). It is also true that Job was striving to know the cause of calamities. He was seeking someone he could blame for his problems instead of accepting personal responsibility. Job made all of these, plus many other statements that blamed God.

Job claimed to be without transgression, innocent, and without iniquity. How many of us make the same false claim? We have all sinned, and if we say that we have not, we make our LORD a liar (I John 1:10). How many of us cry out to God demanding an answer for our calamities, when He has already given His answer in His Word?

In verse 13 Elihu asked Job why he had chosen to strive against God in all of his false accusations. We might ask ourselves that same question. Why do we strive with God and blame Him for what we are really responsible. Why do we repeat the sin of Adam and blame others for our sins? Elihu is teaching Job to take stock of his ways, as each of us should also do.

Elihu then proceeds to teach how the LORD deals with man:

Job 33:14-30

"For God speaketh once, yea twice, yet man perceiveth it not. In a dream, in a vision of the night, when deep sleep falleth upon men, in slumberings upon the bed; Then He openeth the ears of men, and sealeth their instruction, That He may withdraw man from his purpose, and hide pride from man. He keepeth back his soul from the pit, and his life from perishing by the sword. He is chastened also with pain upon his bed, and the multitude of his bones with strong pain: So that his life abhorreth bread, and his soul dainty meat. His flesh is consumed away, that it cannot be seen; and his bones that were not seen stick out. Yea, his soul draweth near unto the grave, and his life to the destroyers. If there be a messenger with him, an interpreter, one among a thousand, to shew unto man his uprightness: Then he is gracious unto him, and saith, Deliver him from going down to the pit: I have found a ransom. His flesh shall be fresher than a child's: he shall return to the days of his youth: He shall pray unto God, and he will be favourable unto Him: and He shall see his face with joy: for He will render unto man his righteousness. He looketh upon men, and if any say, I have sinned, and perverted that which was right, and it profited me not; He will deliver his soul from going into the pit, and his life shall see the light. Lo, all these things worketh God oftentimes with man, To bring back his soul from the pit, to be enlightened with the light of the living."

Elihu teaches that God shows His love and desire for man by revealing His will and purpose to man (Job 33:14-18). Elihu taught that if man rejects God's will and purpose in his life and won't listen, the next and final means of God is to let him become sick unto death (Job 33:19-22). Elihu said that if man will turn to God when he is brought low, interpreters, or messengers, prophets or teachers will be sent to him (Job 33:23). Additionally, if mankind will accept God's message and conform to His will, we will be saved and healed (Job 33:24-28).

Isn't this how our LORD deals with us? His laws of sowing and reaping will always be fulfilled. Deuteronomy 28 and many other passages plainly teach that if we obey Him, we will receive His blessings, but if we choose to disobey Him, we will suffer the consequences. Proverbs 1:24-31 tells us that if we do not regard the counsel of our LORD, He will not hear us in the day of our calamity and that He will turn us over to our own devices.

Elihu is plainly teaching that God loves and cares for each person that He created. God does not respect persons nor will He spare us the consequences of our choices because He loves us and wants us to mature, and desires fellowship with each of us. He is teaching that God loves us so much that He sends people, the Holy Spirit and His Word to instruct us in His ways, and that if we will turn from our wicked ways, He will heal us.

These are powerful promises of God. They are God's answers that we all should be prepared to share with others. These are words that I have learned to pay attention to. It is my prayer that you have also learned to heed the word of our LORD.

Elihu explains the purposes of the LORD in His dealings with man:

Elihu is also teaching why God does what He does. God does not spare us the consequences of our sins because it is His intent to change our hearts and our intent to sin and do wrong (Job 33:17). He has given believers a new nature by which we can have power over sin. Elihu is teaching that God wants to keep pride from us to keep our souls back from the pit (Job 33:18). It is through His power, the power of the Holy Spirit living in us, that we can be holy as He is holy. He is teaching that God wants to keep our lives from perishing by the sword in war, and to give to us His Divine enlightenment (Job 33:29-30).

Elihu is defending our LORD. He is telling Job that our God is the giver of every good and perfect gift; that the LORD wants to protect Job and to teach him as a father would teach a son. This is the loving and caring LORD that I know. His message to Job is the message for each of us. God has answers for our challenges and calamities if we will trust and follow Him.

Elihu also explains what happens when we do not obey God:

1. He is chastened with pain upon his bed (Job 33:19).
2. His bones are full of pain (Job 33:19).
3. His life abhors bread (Job 33:20).
4. His soul abhors dainty meat (Job 33:20).

5. His flesh is consumed away (Job 33:21).
6. His bones that were not seen stick out (Job 33:21).
7. His soul draws near the grave (Job 33:22).
8. His life draws near the destroyers (Job 33:22).

Scripture plainly teaches that there are rewards in this life for obedience to God. One of the rewards is mental and physical health. Let's compare some of Jobs afflictions listed above with other passages of Scripture.

Job's bones were full of pain (Job 33:19).

Proverbs 14:30

"A sound heart is the life of the flesh: but envy the rottenness of the bones."

Proverbs 16:24

"Pleasant words are as an honeycomb, sweet to the soul, and health to the bones."

Proverbs 17:22

"A merry heart doeth good like a medicine: but a broken spirit drieth the bones."

The marrow in our bones produces our immune system. If our immune system is weak or suppressed, virtually any disease can overtake us. These verses plainly teach that jealousy and envy are rottenness to the bones; that pleasant words are health to the bones; that a broken spirit dries the bones. Medical textbooks teach the same thing (see *In His Own Image*). Anger and bitterness cause the adrenal glands to secrete too much adrenaline and cortisol. The over production of adrenaline and cortisol suppresses the immune system.

In the first thirty-one chapters Job expressed his bitterness toward God, toward others and himself in many ways. We have learned that all of our problems in life are caused by broken relationships with God the Father, with others (our neighbors) and with ourselves. In Matthew 22, Jesus was asked a question by a lawyer, "Master which is the great commandment in the law?"

Matthew 22:37-40

"Jesus said unto him, Thou shalt love the Lord thy God with all thy heart, and with all thy soul, and with all thy mind. This is the first and great commandment. And the second is like unto it, Thou shalt love thy neighbour as thyself. On these two commandments hang all the law and the prophets."

According to Jesus, all the law and the prophets hang on these two commandments. As we have learned to take Him at His word, and with His help heal these relationships, thousands of people have been healed of broken hearts and broken bodies.

Job was unable to eat bread and meat to sustain his flesh and it was consumed away so that his bones were sticking out (Job 33:20-21). When the immune system is weakened by resentment and bitterness, some of the "B" cells form antibodies to foods and other substances in our environment. These hypersensitive reactions are called allergies.

The second component of allergies is fear. Job was consumed with fear (Job 3:25). I wonder if he had allergies like I did. When I was so sick I was unable to eat most foods and my bones were also sticking out. Also toxic negative emotions destroy cells in the immune system thereby suppressing it. A suppressed immune system opens the door to many diseases.

Proverbs 4:20-23

"My son, attend to My words; incline thine ear unto My sayings. Let them not depart from thine eyes; keep them in the midst of thine heart. For they are life unto those that find them, and health to all their flesh. Keep thy heart with all diligence; for out of it are the issues of life."

Proverbs 15:15

"All the days of the afflicted are evil: but he that is of a merry heart hath a continual feast."

Job 33:22 says that Job's soul was drawing near the grave and his life was near the destroyers. Job had cursed the day he was born seventeen times in the first thirty-one chapters. He wished that he had never been born and that his life would be over. Suicide is an extreme form of self-hatred. When we curse ourselves, wishing we were dead, we also curse God because we are made in His image.

Proverbs 12:25

"Heaviness in the heart of man maketh it stoop: but a good word maketh it glad."

Proverbs 15:13

"A merry heart maketh a cheerful countenance: but by sorrow of the heart the spirit is broken."

Proverbs 18:14

"The spirit of a man will sustain his infirmity; but a wounded spirit who can bear?"

These are just a few of the many verses that draw a direct parallel between sin and disease. Again we find that Elihu's wisdom was not his own but from "afar."

Job 33:31-33

"Mark well, O Job, hearken unto me: hold thy peace, and I will speak. If thou hast anything to say, answer me: speak, for I desire to justify thee. If not, hearken unto me: hold thy peace, and I shall teach thee wisdom."

At the end of chapter 33, Elihu again challenges Job to answer him because he wanted to "justify" him. In other words Elihu wanted to teach Job the error of his ways so that he might be justified or cleansed from his sins. Again Elihu is expressing the purpose that God has in giving us His Word, His prophets and His Holy Spirit. He was teaching Job that we are justified by doing the word of God (Romans 2:13).

In verse 33 he says, "If not, hearken unto me: hold thy peace, and I shall teach thee wisdom." Elihu's graciousness and kindness, the fact that he had answers and his defense of the LORD proves that he had Divine wisdom! Let's all choose to defend the LORD and grow in His wisdom.

Elihu begins chapter 34 by challenging Job's three friends to listen to him and to choose judgment.

Job 34:1-4

"Furthermore Elihu answered and said, Hear my words, O ye wise men; and give ear unto me, ye that have knowledge. For the ear trieth words, as the mouth tasteth meat. Let us choose to us judgment: let us know among ourselves what is good."

The mark of a mature believer is one that knows the difference between good and evil (Hebrews 5:14). Mature believers will also choose to judge themselves for their iniquities so they can stand before the Judgment Seat of Christ, pure vessels, fit for His service (II Timothy 2:19-21).

Job 34:5-9

"For Job hath said, I am righteous: and God hath taken away my judgment. Should I lie against my right? My wound is incurable without transgression. What man is like Job, who drinketh up scorning like water? Which goeth in company with the workers of iniquity, and walketh with wicked men. For he hath said, It profiteth a man nothing that he should delight himself with God."

In verse 5, Elihu begins to remind Job of more of his sins. He accused Job for doing or saying these things:

1. I am righteous (Job 34:5).
2. God has taken away my judgment.
3. I am made a liar though I have proved myself to be right (Job 34:6).
4. I am suffering because of no transgression of my own.
5. Gulping down blasphemy like water (Job 34:7).
6. Associating with workers of iniquity (Job 34:8).
7. Walking with wicked men.
8. It does not profit to delight in God (Job 34:9).

Elihu was correct in each of these statements. Job had committed these sins against both God and man. Elihu reasoned that Job insulted man when he claimed to be righteous, because he had falsely accused his friends of making him a liar. Elihu further reasoned that Job sinned against God by claiming to be righteous. Elihu reasoned that when Job claimed that God had taken away his judgment he was accusing God of being unjust. Thus he was claiming that he was suffering at the hand of God for no sin of his own, which was not the truth. He further reasoned that Job was wrong to say that there is no profit in serving God.

Our LORD is a just God! He will not violate His nature. He will not break His covenant with us. Elihu was correct in defending the LORD, and in accusing Job of grievous sins. Job was belittling or cursing God and calling Him a liar

Beginning in Job 34:10 and continuing through verse 30 Elihu goes into a long vindication of the LORD

"Be it far from God to do wickedness. Be it far from God for Him to commit iniquity. He will render to every man according to his work. He will not do wickedly (Job 34:12). He will not pervert judgment. He is sovereign over all (Job 34:13). He rules the whole world. He has set His heart on man (Job 34:14). He controls man's destiny. He has appointed death for all men (Job 34:15, Hebrews 9:27). He has decreed that all bodies go back to dust (Job 34:15, Genesis 3:19). Some men hate that which is right and therefore have no right to govern (Job 34:17). God is most just. He cannot be charged with wickedness (Job 34:18). He does not respect princes. He does not respect the rich (Job 34:19). All men are the work of His hands. Men soon perish, but He is eternal (Job 34:20). He sees the ways of men (Job 34:21). He sees their goings. None can hide from Him (Job 34:22). He requires only that which is right of man (Job 34:23). No man can charge Him with injustice. He shall break the mighty man (Job 34:24). He will set others in their place. He knows their works (Job 34:25). He turns the disobedient over to their own devices to suffer the consequences in the sight of others (Job 34:26). Because they turn back from Him (Job 34:27). Because they oppress the poor, He hears the cry of the poor and afflicted (Job 34:28). He causes trouble to cease. No man can see Him until He sees fit to reveal Himself. He deals with nations as well as with individuals (Job 34:29). He delivers the people from the reign of the hypocrite (Job 34:30).

Every statement made by Elihu about God is accurate. God is not a respecter of persons. Job had to have reaped what he had sown or God is a liar. There is great peace to be found in this truth. We serve a just and fair God. He is never arbitrary. It would be good for each of us to memorize these statements and make them part of our heart. Remember the LORD will never violate His nature.

Job 34:31-34

"Surely it is meet to be said unto God, I have borne chastisement, I will not offend any more: That which I see not teach thou me: if I have done iniquity, I will do no more. Should it be according to thy mind? He will recompense it, whether thou refuse, or whether thou choose; and not I: therefore speak what thou knowest. Let men of understanding tell me, and let a wise man hearken unto me."

Elihu is saying that it is only just that those who sin against Him be chastened or disciplined (Job 34:31). It is only just that they be made to sin no more. Men should sanctify themselves to learn that which they don't know (Job 34:32). They should be willing to renounce sin and live right. God will be just and will punish all wrong, whether man chooses Him to do so or not (Job 34:33).

Elihu is telling Job that he has been suffering because of his sin and that it is time to repent and not offend any more. Elihu is telling Job that God is disciplining him by giving him what he wants. He has turned him over to his own devices (Proverbs 1:29-31) because he has not followed the knowledge of God. Because God loves Job He will not spare him the consequences of his sins. He is telling Job, that God will "recompense" iniquity whether he likes it or not. Now it is time to speak what you know and be a "wise man and hearken unto me," and repent. Elihu ends chapter 34 with these words:

Job 34:35-37

"Job hath spoken without knowledge, and his words were without wisdom. My desire is that Job may be tried unto the end because of his answers for wicked men. For he addeth rebellion unto his sin, he clappeth his hands among us, and multiplieth his words against God."

"...his answers [are] for wicked men."

In this extremely strong statement Elihu is claiming that Job's responses and answers are without knowledge and wisdom, and that they are those of wicked men. In chapter 42:1-6, Job repents for these exact same things. Can we do less?

Elihu begins chapter 35 by accusing Job of more sins:

Job 35:1-3

"Elihu spake moreover, and said, Thinkest thou this to be right, that thou saidst, My righteousness is more than God's? For thou saidst, What advantage will it be unto thee? and, What profit shall I have, if I be cleansed from my sin?"

He accused Job of saying:

1. My righteousness is more than God's righteousness.
2. What advantage will it be for me to be cleansed from my sin?
3. What profit shall I have if I am cleansed from my sin?

Job never said these exact words in his discourses, but Elihu considered them the essence of what he had said. Job had claimed his own uprightness, maintaining his innocence of any sin that brought the calamities upon him. In doing this, he blamed the LORD for the calamities. In truth, Job's sin opened the door for Satan to deliver the calamities. The truth is that, even in his sin, the LORD restricted what Satan could do to Job. This is a picture of God's grace and mercy that He has for each of us, even in our sins.

Job 35:4

"I will answer thee, and thy companions with thee."

Eliphaz had attempted to answer these same questions in chapter 22 but he was unsuccessful. Elihu then proceeds to give his answers to these three accusations Job made against the LORD. Let's take a careful look at Elihu's answer.

Job 35:5-8

"Look unto the heavens, and see; and behold the clouds which are higher than thou. If thou sinnest, what doest thou against Him? Or if thy transgressions be multiplied, what doest thou unto Him? If thou be righteous, what givest thou Him? Or what receiveth He of thine hand? Thy wickedness may hurt a man as thou art; and thy righ-teousness may profit the son of man."

First, Elihu tells Job, and his friends, that God dwells in the heavens and is much higher than man. "Who are you to question Him?" He asks, "How can you be more righteous than Him?" Elihu is also expressing great wisdom in telling Job to look to the heavens and to the future because this life is very short and we are simply in training for our eternity with God. We need to apply the wisdom of Elihu to our lives.

Then Elihu proceeds to further enlighten Job with Divine wisdom by telling him that neither the sin nor the righteousness of man can affect the LORD's plan or conduct. It only affects man's destiny (Job 35:6). In other words, there is a profit and an advan-tage to be cleansed from sin. If we forgive others and repent for our sins, then we are cleansed of all unrighteousness. We then become vessels of honor and overcomers, fit for His service, qualified to rule and reign with Him forever.

There are great rewards in being cleansed from sin in this life and in the next one. In chapter 42, Job receives a reward in this life because he repented of his sin. The LORD returned to Job double what Satan took. Is our LORD a respecter of persons? Of course not! What He did for Job, He will do for you.

Job 35:9-12

"By reason of the multitude of oppressions they make the oppressed to cry: they cry out by reason of the arm of the mighty. But none saith, Where is God my maker, who giveth songs in the night; Who teacheth us more than the beasts of the earth, and maketh us wiser than the fowls of heaven? There they cry, but none giveth answer, because of the pride of evil men."

Elihu continues to share Divine wisdom. He is teaching that the oppressions of life come from men, not God (Job 35:9-12). That the mighty (men) cause others to suffer. In our choices to sin, men cause the suffering, not God. God never allows evil. We do, in our disobedience to His precepts. This was said because Job had repeatedly accused God of being responsible for his sufferings. Job was guilty of the same sin that Adam and Eve were. Adam blamed Eve and then blamed God for giving him Eve. This has continued ever since.

Elihu vindicated God and reproved Job for his many accusations against Him. Elihu was teaching that man, in his free will, is responsible and must take responsibility for his own actions and the consequences of those actions.

Elihu is telling them the oppressed cry out because of the acts of the mighty. But none cry out to God for relief the right way. They complain to God, but they don't seek Him for wisdom, for deliverance, and for songs in the night, even though they are wiser than beasts and birds (Job 35:9-12).

Doesn't this sound like you and me? We cry out and demand answers from God, just like Job did. Proverbs 26:2 says that the curse does not come without a cause.

Remember, this is our loving LORD that wrote these words. He is telling us that there is always a reason for the curse. If there is a reason, then there must be an answer! That answer is always found on our knees in repentance before the LORD.

Job 35:13

"Surely God will not hear vanity, neither will the Almighty regard it."

God's Divine revelation through Elihu continues. Elihu is saying that the oppressed aren't relieved by God, because their cry is merely an empty petition for relief from personal sufferings, without thought of genuine repentance, love, worship, and faith in a deliverance (Proverbs 1:24-31). We must accept responsibility for our sins and the consequences and deal with them. We must also accept responsibility for the sins of our fathers and confess their iniquities (Leviticus 26:40-45, Nehemiah 1, 9:1-3, Daniel 9).

Job 35:14

"Although thou sayest thou shalt not see Him, yet judgment is before Him; therefore trust thou in Him."

Elihu is urging Job to trust and to have faith in God and His justice, and to trust Him to bring him out of his troubles. God the Father is the giver of every good and perfect gift. He is trustworthy. No one can "see" the LORD when we are accusing and cursing Him. Again, Elihu is defending our LORD.

Job 35:15

"But now, because it is not so, he hath visited in his anger; yet he knoweth it not in great extremity."

But now, since Job was not trusting God for deliverance, believing he was suffering in God's anger, all he did was fight back at the Almighty (Job 35:15-16). Chapter 3:25 says that Job was living in great fear of what might come upon him. I believe that this hurts God more than anything else His children can do. When we live in fear, we are saying that God is the giver of every bad gift. In every fear we are calling Him a liar. Since Job did not trust the LORD, and since Job did not believe the LORD, verse 16 explains the result:

Job 35:16

"Therefore doth Job open his mouth in vain; he multiplieth words without knowledge."

The LORD does not hear us when we do not believe or trust Him, or regard His wisdom and knowledge. James 1:6-7 says, "But let him ask in faith, nothing wavering. For he that wavereth is like a wave of the sea driven with the wind and tossed. For let not that man think that he shall receive any thing of the Lord." Elihu is giving us all tremendous Divine wisdom by which to live our lives.

In chapter 36 Elihu continues his defense of God:

Job 36:1-4

"Elihu also proceeded, and said, suffer me a little, and I will shew thee that I have yet to speak on God's behalf. I will fetch my knowledge from afar, and will ascribe righteousness to my Maker. For truly my words shall not be false: He that is perfect in knowledge is with thee."

Elihu is encouraging Job and the three friends to continue listening to him because he is just beginning to speak on God's behalf. Elihu says that he is:

1. Yet to speak in God's behalf (Job 36:2).
2. Bringing knowledge from afar (Job 36:3).
3. Ascribing righteousness to his Maker.
4. Speaking only the truth (Job 36:4).
5. Giving them and us perfect knowledge.

He says that his knowledge is coming from afar, from God, therefore it is worth listening to. He defends the righteousness of God the Creator. He is speaking the truth and giving perfect knowledge because it is from "afar." It is from God not man. Then Elihu proceeds to defend God.

Job 36:5-25

"Behold, God is mighty, and despiseth not any: He is mighty in strength and wisdom. He preserveth not the life of the wicked: but giveth right to the poor. He withdraweth not his eyes from the righteous: but with kings are they on the throne; yea, He doth establish them forever, and they are exalted. And if they be bound in fetters, and be holden in cords of affliction; Then He sheweth them their work, and their transgressions that they have exceeded. He openeth also their ear to discipline, and commandeth that they return from iniquity. If they obey and serve Him, they shall spend their days in prosperity, and their years in pleasures. But if they obey not, they shall perish by the sword, and they shall die without knowledge. But the hypocrites in heart heap up wrath: they cry not when He bindeth them. They die in youth, and their life is among the unclean. He delivereth the poor in his affliction, and openeth their ears in oppression. Even so would He have removed thee out of the strait into a broad place, where there is no straitness; and that which should be set on thy table should be full of fatness. But thou hast fulfilled the judgment of the wicked: judgment and justice take hold on thee. Because there is wrath, beware lest He take thee away with his stroke: then a great ransom cannot deliver thee. Will He esteem thy riches? no, not gold, nor all the forces of strength. Desire not the night, when people are cut off in their place. Take heed, regard not iniquity: for this hast thou chosen rather than affliction. Behold, God exalteth by His power: who teacheth like Him? Who hath enjoined Him his way? Or who can say, Thou hast wrought iniquity? Remember that thou magnify His work, which men behold. Every man may see it; man may behold it afar off."

Once again Elihu is giving us Divine wisdom in his defense of God. Elihu makes the following statements:

1. He is mighty (Job 36:5).
2. He despises nobody.
3. He is mighty in strength and wisdom.
4. He preserves not the life of the wicked (Job 36:6).
5. He gives right to the poor.
6. He does not withdraw His eyes from the righteous (Job 36:7).
7. He establishes the righteous forever.
8. He exalts them.
9. If they sin and are punished, He reminds them of their sins for which they have been punished (Job 36:9).
10. He opens their ear to discipline (Job 36:10).
11. He commands them to turn from sin.
12. If they obey and serve God, He causes them to spend their days in prosperity and pleasure (Job 36:11).
13. If they do not obey, He causes them to perish by the sword, and they die without knowledge (Job 36:12).
14. He heaps up wrath against hypocrites (Job 36:13).
15. He binds them.
16. He cuts them off in their youth (Job 36:14).
17. He delivers the poor in affliction (Job 36:15).
18. He opens their ears in oppression.

Elihu is giving us God's answers and is eloquently defending our Lord. This is what we should also be doing. There is much that we should learn from Elihu.

Job 36:16

"Even so would He have removed thee out of the strait into a broad place, where there is no straitness; and that which should be set on thy table should be full of fatness."

Elihu now makes an application of his words to Job and his friends. Elihu is saying to Job and his friends that even so, even with all their sins, the LORD would have delivered them if they would obey the LORD. Then Elihu shows them the error of their ways and the LORD's conditions for receiving His blessings:

1. If you had obeyed and served God (Job 36:11-12), then He would have removed you out of the strait into a broad place. And then you would have plenty of food for your table (Job 36:16).
2. But you have suffered the judgment of the wicked (Job 36:17).
3. Judgment and justice take hold of you.
4. God is angry at you, so beware, lest He take you away with His stroke (Job 36:18).

5. If He does, then a great ransom cannot deliver you.
6. He will not esteem your riches (Job 36:19).
7. He will not esteem gold or forces of strength.
8. You should not desire the night, when people are cut off (Job 36:20).
9. Take heed, regard not iniquity (Job 36:21).
10. You have chosen iniquity instead of repentance.
11. God exalts by His power and none can teach Him how to deal with men (Job 36:22).
12. You cannot prescribe for Him what to do (Job 36:23).
13. You cannot charge Him with sin.
14. Remember to magnify His work, which all people can see clearly (Job 36:24).
15. Even you can see it in His dealings with you (Job 36:25).

This is a picture of the grace, love, and mercy of our Lord and Savior. He is always ready to forgive and cleanse us of all unrighteousness if we will repent and turn from our wicked ways. Elihu is giving us God's answers for the calamities in our lives, just as he gave answers to Job. Is it time to consider our ways? Is it time to take heed?

Job 36:21

"Take heed, regard not iniquity: for this hast thou chosen rather than affliction."

Elihu is saying that Job chose to regard iniquity; he chose to complain and accuse God instead of judging himself as we are told to do (II Corinthians 13:5, James 4:8-10). Job declared himself righteous instead of God. He should have examined his thoughts and actions. Job suffered from a common disorder called spiritual pride and arrogance or self-righteousness. In dong this he also refused to accept personal responsibility for his actions.

Elihu is making the point that Job chose to regard iniquity, thus he is suffering the consequence of that choice. This is also true for all of us. We will reap what we sow. It is time to consider our ways. The book of Haggai also gives many reasons why God's blessings are not present.

In Job 36:26 Elihu once again begins a defense of the LORD which continues to Job 37:13. He names thirty-four great works of the LORD:

1. He makes small drops of water (Job 36:27).
2. He pours rain on earth according to the vapor that ascends from earth.
3. He causes the clouds to drop rain upon man abundantly (Job 36:28).
4. He spreads out the clouds for a tabernacle (Job 36:29).
5. He makes thunder in the clouds.
6. He spreads light upon His tabernacle (Job 36:30).
7. He covers the seas with water.
8. He judges the people by means of the clouds, lightning, and thunder (Job 36:31).

9. He gives all things meat in abundance.
10. He covers the clouds with light (Job 36:32).
11. He commands light not to shine by bringing clouds between it and the earth.
12. He manifests the thunder (Job 36:33).
13. He gathers the vapor like cattle.
14. He causes the heart of man to tremble (Job 37:1).
15. He causes it to move out of place.
16. He directs the thunder under the whole heaven (Job 37:3).
17. He directs the lightning unto the ends of the earth.
18. He sends the thunder after the lightning (Job 37:4).
19. He thunders with the voice of Excellency.
20. He thunders in a wonderful manner (Job 37:5).
21. He does great things that man cannot comprehend.
22. He sends snow on earth (Job 37:6).
23. He sends small rain on earth.
24. He sends great rains on earth.
25. He causes man to cease in his activity by the great storms (Job 37:7).
26. He causes the beasts to remain in their dens during the storms (Job 37:8).
27. He sends the whirlwinds from the south (Job 37:9).
28. He sends cold out of the north.
29. He gives frost (Job 37:10).
30. He causes waters to freeze.
31. He dispels the thick cloud (Job 37:11).
32. He scatters the bright clouds to make the skies clear again.
33. He commands the clouds where they should go (Job 37:12).
34. He causes the storms to come, whether for correction of man, for the good of the land, or for mercy to man (Job 37:13).

After Elihu praised the Lord for his wondrous works, he then challenged Job to explain them:

Job 37:14-15

"Hearken unto this, O Job: standstill, and consider the wondrous works of God. Dost thou know when God disposed them, and caused the light of his cloud to shine?"

Obviously, Job could not answer Elihu's challenge. Neither can we. Job repeatedly wanted to argue his case personally before God. He was confident that his innocence would be proven (Job 13:3). It is interesting to notice the similarities between Elihu's challenges to Job and the LORD's challenge in chapters 38-42.

In the balance of this chapter, Elihu tried to show that if Job had a true concept of God he would be so overwhelmed by God's presence that he wouldn't know what to say

(Job 37:19-24). This is true of all of us, also. If we had a true understanding of the character and nature of our LORD, we would never accuse Him of causing the calamities in our lives. We would fall on our faces before Him, as Isaiah did when he saw the LORD in Isaiah 6. This is where we began this study, by studying the nature of our LORD.

In Job 42:5 Job says, "I have heard of Thee by the hearing of the ear: but now mine eye seeth Thee." Job learned the truth about God. He learned that he was wrong to blame God for all that had happened to him. He learned to take personal responsibility for what was happening in his life. He personally experienced the truth of God and then was set free (John 8:32).

Job 37:19

"Teach us what we shall say unto him; for we cannot order our speech by reason of darkness."

We all see through a glass darkly. Who are we to question the LORD? Who are we to say that God is not just when He says that He is? We must always remember that He will never violate His own nature.

Elihu was right; Job was responsible for what happened to him. His trust was not in the LORD, but in his possessions and his position. The things that Job greatly feared, that which he was afraid of, did happen (Job 3:25).

All Scripture is given for our instruction. What should we learn from Job?

Job was like many who think that sickness, disease, calamity and other evils come from God, and that Satan has nothing to do with them. Some declare that sickness, disease and calamities are the heritage of believers, and those who go through them are in the perfect will of God. This is not true. Adam's sin allowed Satan into this world and Satan brought with him disease and death. There will be no disease or death or sorrow in the new heaven and the new earth (Revelation 21:4) because Satan will not be there. Satan brought disease and death with him; they are part of his nature.

As Christians, we must learn to exercise our authority in Christ to destroy the works of the devil. James 4:7 says, "Submit yourselves therefore to God. Resist the devil, and he will flee from you." How often do any of us submit ourselves completely to God? When was the last time you exercised your authority over Satan, and rebuked him in the name of Jesus?

This verse requires believers to do two things: first, submit to God. We do this by being obedient to Him and by forgiving those who have hurt us, and repenting for our sins. Second, we are to resist, or rebuke, the devil. This is also our responsibility. Then, the power of our LORD will make the devil flee. If we do not do our part, the LORD cannot do His part.

It is true that Christians experience tests of faith, persecutions, injustices, and trials of life as Paul did. But these sufferings are not the same as sickness, disease, and the curses of sin and rebellion, from which Christ died to free us (Deuteronomy 28). Even so, God wasn't responsible for the things that caused Joseph, Stephen and Paul or others to suffer. Rather, He helped them go through the sufferings heaped upon them by Satan and his agents. Suffering for our stand in our faith is different from suffering for our disobedience.

God can teach us lessons from any kind of trial. He even uses our disobedience for our good. But He doesn't send trials in order to teach us such lessons. If a son broke the law and went to jail, a father could use the experience as an occasion to teach valuable lessons, but only an ungodly father would lead his son into such troubles just to teach those lessons. God cannot, and will not, tempt us.

As I have mentioned before, in 1997 I seriously injured my neck in an accident. I underwent major surgery in 1998 to deal with the damage to my neck, and after that surgery I became allergic to most all foods and fabrics. I was even allergic to my own saliva. God did not bring this on me, nor did He allow it to happen. The truth is that I allowed it by my disobedience to Him. My disobedience opened the door for Satan to have his way with me. Since I would not listen to God, I was given over to my own way (Romans 1:28, Proverbs 1:24-31). But even in my disobedience, God protected me and used the experience for my good. Job experienced the same thing.

There is a better way. We don't need to experience sickness, disease, poverty, and accidents in order to learn what we should know from God. We have been given examples in the Word to go by: Job, Asa, Hezekiah, David, and many more. There are many testimonies of people in our own day and time that teach the same Godly principles (see Part Two). We can best glorify God by learning from these true life experiences, and becoming an example ourselves. Why not experience God's blessing by being kept from such troubles and sufferings, instead of suffering needlessly?

In the Word of God, provision has been made through the "exceeding great and precious promises" to give us "all things that pertain unto life and godliness" (II Peter 1:3-4, II Corinthians 1:20). To use Job as an excuse for unbelief is foolish, he was a man who sinned. When he repented, the LORD restored to him double what Satan had taken. This fact alone proves the cause of his problems. Sin!

James cited Job as an example of someone who was healed, not one who died of sickness and disease (James 5:11-16). Many people use Job as an excuse for being sick and bodily afflicted, but Job's trial lasted only a few months, and he was healed and set free. He did not stay sick and defeated.

The LORD is described as being full of compassion and mercy, not punishment, or one who inflicts calamity or disease. In the end, the LORD healed and blessed Job materially beyond anything he had experienced before his trial, and such is the plan of God for all men who obey Him, not just Job.

It is clear from Scripture that Job's trouble was from Satan, not God (Job 1:6-19, Job 2:1-7). The LORD was Job's deliverer (Job 42:1-10). He delivered Job from himself. Christ came to heal all that were oppressed by the devil, not oppressed by God (Matthew 8:17, Luke 13:16, John 10:10, Acts 10:38, I Peter 2:24). To follow truth, we should stop blaming God for sickness, pain, poverty, and calamity, and count them as curses (or enemies) of both God and man. Then we should learn to cooperate with God, and look to Him for deliverance and power over sin and Satan.

## DOES GOD ALLOW EVIL?

The New Testament equates God to love, and names Him as light, the rewarder of those who diligently seek Him, the giver of every good and perfect gift, and the beginning and the end. The Old Testament calls our LORD the Creator, Redeemer, Shepherd, Savior, Provider and many other positive names. His names also describe His nature. If His nature consists of these attributes, how can there be evil in the world?

"God allowed this cancer (or other negative event) to happen" is a timeworn cliché. Insurance companies label large storms as "acts of God." Philosophers and theologians ask if God "allowed" Hitler to kill millions of Jews during World War II. Did God "allow" all the male babies under age two in Bethlehem to be murdered by Herod in his vain effort to kill the baby Jesus?

In our ministry we find many people who go through life angry and bitter at God. They blame Him for a family tragedy or personal loss.

Why do so many people see God as arbitrary and capricious, as someone who walks around carrying a big stick ready to punish them? Why are so many people afraid of God?

I have heard pastors, and other Christians confidently say that God in His sovereignty "allows" evil, but He uses it for our good as an opportunity for Him to demonstrate His grace and mercy. This verbal salve is supposed to "make it all better," make it "okay" that God "allowed" evil to happen.

Are any of these statements accurate?

What does the word "allow" mean? According to the dictionary it means to permit or condone, to be responsible for. As parents when we allow our children to do something then we have approved the activity. If God really "allows" evil to happen, doesn't that imply that to some degree He approves or condones it? Wouldn't it make Him responsible for that evil action? Remember God cannot sin and be God. To be responsible for evil requires the commission of a sin. Something is wrong with our human reasoning when we allege that God "allows" evil to happen.

In God's manifold wisdom, He created all of us with a free will. Our free will allows us to choose how to live. We have the option to follow God and His precepts, or Satan, the "god of this world." These are the only two choices we can make.

The ability to choose is valuable to each of us, but in order to choose there must be choices available. Our free will is also very important to our LORD. He wants each of us to freely choose Him as He has already chosen us. This reveals the heart of God. God is Love.

Have you ever been able to make someone love you? Many times in our desire to be loved or part of the group we have done some really stupid things. But no matter what we did or gave away it did not work because love requires an act of our free will. Love is an action and a choice. We can never force anyone to love us. Neither can God.

God wants each of us to choose a love relationship with Him, where we remain faithful to Him. It is the only kind of relationship that has any meaning to it. But remember true love is a choice, therefore there must be choices. This is why the LORD created the tree of the knowledge of good and evil and told Adam and Eve not to eat of it. This is also why the LORD created evil. Isaiah 45:7 says that The LORD created evil. We need to understand that God did not create sin. He only created a choice and when we choose to do evil we are guilty of sin. God cannot sin and never does evil.

God created the law of sowing and reaping, and those who sow sin will, for certain, reap evil. God decreed that misery, wretchedness, sorrow, trouble and distress will result from sin (Galatians 6:7-8). He made these rules because He loves us. As parents we also make rules to protect our children.

People sow their own sin and reap their own evil. The responsibility for both is theirs. God gave the law, and provided penalties for breaking the law. This is His discipline because He loves us and wants to protect us from the results of sin. In light of this, we all should examine what we have been taught, and what we believe. Who is really responsible for evil? We are in our choice to sin.

Scripture is replete with references to the two kingdoms that contest for each person. Satan is called the "god of this world" and the "prince and power of the air" (II Corinthians 4:4, Ephesians 2:2). He heads an earthly kingdom that is constantly tempting and testing each of us.

We also know that God the Father, God the Son, and God the Holy Spirit live in our lives. Jesus sits at the right hand of God in the third heaven, but His spirit lives within us. His throne or temple on this earth is in each and every believer (I Corinthians 3:16). Thus giving us the ability of overcome and defeat every wile of the devil.

Satan's goal is to destroy. He employs clever lies and principalities with their demons to persuade us to participate in evil and sin. God comes to us through the Holy Spirit and His Word, and wants us to embrace the truth and be set free from Satan's power.

The word "fellowship," found in Ephesians 3:9, means a partnership or joint effort. This type of "fellowship" can only happen if both parties voluntarily agree. God wants us to choose to love Him as He has already chosen to love us!

Ephesians 3:9-10

"And to make all men see what is the fellowship of the mystery, which from the beginning of the world hath been hid in God, who created all things by Jesus Christ;

To the intent that now unto the principalities and powers in heavenly places might be known by the church the manifold wisdom of God."

Does this understanding of choosing to love God cast a different light on our relationship with Him? Does this cast a different light on our responsibility to properly exercise our free will?

Everything bad that has ever happened to us on earth was planned in hell, and executed by one of Satan's demons. These bad consequences happen because of one or more of the following three aspects:

First, because this is a fallen and cursed world things will go wrong; bad things will happen. There are "natural" disasters and storms that result from the curse. But these are still the result of sin and Satan. This was a perfect world before Satan's temptation of Adam and Eve led them to sin, and it will be again when God provides the new heavens and the new earth.

Second, in exercising our free will, many people choose to follow Satan and commit evil acts. These evil acts hurt innocent people.

Third, we suffer the consequences of our own sins. These consequences are something "evil" that enters our lives. As a result of our sins, God turns us over to "our own devices" (Proverbs 1:24-31, Romans 1:28). We will reap what we sow.

God never "allows" evil. Mankind allows evil by making wrong choices. If we choose to practice evil, then we alone are responsible for the consequences. We cannot blame God for evil.

God has voluntarily restrained His hand from stopping sin and evil during this age. But, we have a God-given covenant that He will honor. If God chose to come to earth now and destroy sin, some people would perish and it is His will that none would perish. God intervenes only at our request — which is why prayer is so important.

II Corinthians 10:6

"And having in a readiness to revenge all disobedience, when your obedience is fulfilled."

Are you ready to "revenge" all disobedience? When you revenge (i.e., stop being) disobedience then your obedience will be fulfilled. We cannot blame God when we choose to disobey Him. Romans 5:12 says, "...By one man [Adam] sin entered into this world [mankind]..." Sin did not enter this world by God. The verse goes on to say, "all have sinned." Thus, all of us are just as guilty of sin as was Adam. We cannot blame him for our problems since we have the same choice he did.

Romans 5:18-19

"Therefore as by the offence of one [Adam] judgment came upon all men to condemnation; even so by the righteousness of one [Jesus] the free gift came upon all men unto justification of life. For as by one man's disobedience many were made sinners, so by the obedience of one [Jesus] shall many be made righteous."

God the Father loves us so much that He gave His only begotten Son that we might have life! By our disobedience, we deserve death, but His love grants us life if we choose to accept it.

Sowing sin reaps evil. The decision of what to sow — God's good or Satan's evil — is each person's. God never "allows" evil. "Allowing" evil violates His Holy nature. We alone must bear the responsibility for sin and evil. One of Satan's greatest tactics is to blame God for that which he is responsible.

In Genesis 3, we see how Satan falsely blamed God for withholding something good from mankind. If we have been blaming God for some event or attitude in our lives, now is the time to recognize who is really responsible. Our enemy is not God. Our enemy is not ourselves. Paul said in Romans 7:17, "Now then it is no more I that do it, but sin that dwelleth in me." Let's recognize Satan as our true enemy, and stop blaming God and ourselves.

Discernment comes from learning to know the difference between good and evil, and then making the choice to agree with God by doing good. This is the mark of a mature Christian. Let's use Godly discernment to destroy the lies of Satan that give him a foothold in our lives!

The bottom line is that God is Love. All of His acts, even those we don't understand, are motivated by love.

Let's take a look at some of God's promises to each of us:

Psalms 34:9-10

"O fear the LORD, ye his saints: for there is no want to them that fear him. The young lions do lack, and suffer hunger: but they that seek the LORD shall not want any good thing."

Psalms 37:1-8

"A Psalm of David. Fret not thyself because of evildoers, neither be thou envious against the workers of iniquity. For they shall soon be cut down like the grass, and wither as the green herb. Trust in the Lord, and do good; so shalt thou dwell in the land, and verily thou shalt be fed. Delight thyself also in the Lord; and He shall give thee the desires of thine heart. Commit thy way unto the Lord; trust also in Him; and He shall bring it to pass. And He shall bring forth thy righteousness as the light, and thy judgment as the noonday. Rest in the Lord, and wait patiently for Him: fret not thyself because of him who prospereth in his way, because of the man who bringeth wicked devices to pass. Cease from anger, and forsake wrath: fret not thyself in any wise to do evil."

Psalms 84:11

"For the LORD God is a sun and shield: the LORD will give grace and glory: no good thing will He withhold from them that walk uprightly."

Psalms 91:1-12

"He that dwelleth in the secret place of the most High shall abide under the shadow of the Almighty. I will say of the LORD, He is my refuge and my fortress: my God; in Him will I trust. Surely He shall deliver thee from the snare of the fowler, and from the noisome pestilence. He shall cover thee with his feathers, and under His wings shalt thou trust: His truth shall be thy shield and buckler. Thou shalt not be afraid for the terror by night; nor for the arrow that flieth by day; Nor for the pestilence that walketh in darkness; nor for the destruction that wasteth at noonday. A thousand shall fall at thy side, and ten thousand at thy right hand; but it shall not come nigh thee. Only with thine eyes shalt thou behold and see the reward of the wicked. Because thou hast made the LORD, which is my refuge, even the most High, thy habitation; There shall no evil befall thee, neither shall any plague come nigh thy dwelling. For He shall give his angels charge over thee, to keep thee in all thy ways. They shall bear thee up in their hands, lest thou dash thy foot against a stone."

Psalms 103:1-4

"A Psalm of David. Bless the LORD, O my soul: and all that is within me, bless His holy name. Bless the LORD, O my soul, and forget not all His benefits: Who forgiveth all thine iniquities; who healeth all thy diseases; Who redeemeth thy life from destruction; who crowneth thee with loving kindness and tender mercies."

Matthew 7:7-11

"Ask, and it shall be given you; seek, and ye shall find; knock, and it shall be opened unto you: For every one that asketh receiveth; and he that seeketh findeth; and to him that knocketh it shall be opened. Or what man is there of you, whom if his son ask bread, will he give him a stone? Or if he ask a fish, will he give him a serpent? If ye then, being evil, know how to give good gifts unto your children, how much more shall your Father which is in heaven give good things to them that ask him?"

Matthew 8:17

"That it might be fulfilled which was spoken by Esaias the prophet, saying, Himself took our infirmities, and bare our sicknesses."

Matthew 17:20

"And Jesus said unto them, Because of your unbelief: for verily I say unto you, If ye have faith as a grain of mustard seed, ye shall say unto this mountain, Remove hence to yonder place; and it shall remove; and nothing shall be impossible unto you."

Matthew 21:22

"And all things, whatsoever ye shall ask in prayer, believing, ye shall receive."

Mark 9:23

"Jesus said unto him, If thou canst believe, all things are possible to him that believeth."

Mark 11:22-24

"And Jesus answering saith unto them, Have faith in God. For verily I say unto you, That whosoever shall say unto this mountain, Be thou removed, and be thou cast into the sea; and shall not doubt in his heart, but shall believe that those things which he saith shall come to pass; he shall have whatsoever he saith. Therefore I say unto you, What things soever ye desire, when ye pray, believe that ye receive them, and ye shall have them."

Luke 11:1-13

"And it came to pass, that, as he was praying in a certain place, when he ceased, one of his disciples said unto him, Lord, teach us to pray, as John also taught his disciples. And He said unto them, When ye pray, say, Our Father which art in heaven, Hallowed be thy name. Thy kingdom come. Thy will be done, as in heaven, so in earth. Give us day by day our daily bread. And forgive us our sins; for we also forgive every one that is indebted to us. And lead us not into temptation; but deliver us from evil. And he said unto them, Which of you shall have a friend, and shall go unto him at midnight, and say unto him, Friend, lend me three loaves; For a friend of mine in his journey is come to me, and I have nothing to set before him? And he from within shall answer and say, Trouble me not: the door is now shut, and my children are with me in bed; I cannot rise and give thee. I say unto you, Though he will not rise and give him, because he is his friend, yet because of his importunity he will rise and give him as many as he needeth. And I say unto you, Ask, and it shall be given you; seek, and ye shall find; knock, and it shall be opened unto you. For every one that asketh receiveth; and he that seeketh findeth; and to him that knocketh it shall be opened. If a son shall ask bread of any of you that is a father, will he give him a stone? or if he ask a fish, will he for a fish give him a serpent? Or if he shall ask an egg, will he offer him a scorpion? If ye then, being evil, know how to give good gifts unto your children: how much more shall your heavenly Father give the Holy Spirit to them that ask him?"

Luke 18:1-8

"And he spake a parable unto them to this end, that men ought always to pray, and not to faint; Saying, There was in a city a judge, which feared not God, neither regarded man: And there was a widow in that city; and she came unto him, saying, Avenge me of mine adversary. And he would not for a while: but afterward he said within himself, Though I fear not God, nor regard man; Yet because this widow troubleth me, I will avenge her, lest by her continual coming she weary me. And the Lord said, Hear what the unjust judge saith. And shall not God avenge his own elect, which cry day and night unto Him, though He bear long with them? I tell you that He will avenge them speedily. Nevertheless when the Son of man cometh, shall he find faith on the earth?"

Luke 24:49

"And, behold, I send the promise of my Father upon you: but tarry ye in the city of Jerusalem, until ye be endued with power from on high."

John 10:10

"The thief cometh not, but for to steal, and to kill, and to destroy: I am come that they might have life, and that they might have it more abundantly."

John 14:12-15

"Verily, verily, I say unto you, He that believeth on Me, the works that I do shall he do also; and greater works than these shall he do; because I go unto my Father. And whatsoever ye shall ask in My name, that will I do, that the Father may be glorified in the Son. If ye shall ask any thing in My name, I will do it. If ye love Me, keep My commandments."

John 15:7

"If ye abide in Me, and My words abide in you, ye shall ask what ye will, and it shall be done unto you."

John 15:16

"Ye have not chosen me, but I have chosen you, and ordained you, that ye should go and bring forth fruit, and that your fruit should remain: that whatsoever ye shall ask of the Father in My name, He may give it you."

John 16:23-26

"And in that day ye shall ask Me nothing. Verily, verily, I say unto you, Whatsoever ye shall ask the Father in My name, He will give it you. Hitherto have ye asked nothing in My name: ask, and ye shall receive, that your joy may be full. These things have I spoken unto you in proverbs: but the time cometh, when I shall no more speak unto you in proverbs, but I shall shew you plainly of the Father. At that day ye shall ask in My name: and I say not unto you, that I will pray the Father for you."

Acts 1:4-8

"And, being assembled together with them, commanded them that they should not depart from Jerusalem, but wait for the promise of the Father, which, saith He, ye have heard of Me. For John truly baptized with water; but ye shall be baptized with the Holy Ghost not many days hence. When they therefore were come together, they asked of Him, saying, Lord, wilt thou at this time restore again the kingdom to Israel? And He said unto them, It is not for you to know the times or the seasons, which the Father hath put in His own power. But ye shall receive power, after that the Holy Ghost is come upon you: and ye shall be witnesses unto Me both in Jerusalem, and in all Judaea, and in Samaria, and unto the uttermost part of the earth."

Acts 2:38-39

"Then Peter said unto them, Repent, and be baptized every one of you in the name of Jesus Christ for the remission of sins, and ye shall receive the gift of the Holy Ghost. For the promise is unto you, and to your children, and to all that are afar off, even as many as the Lord our God shall call.

Acts 5:32

"And we are his witnesses of these things; and so is also the Holy Ghost, whom God hath given to them that obey him."

I Corinthians 12:1-10

"Now concerning spiritual gifts, brethren, I would not have you ignorant. Ye know that ye were Gentiles, carried away unto these dumb idols, even as ye were led. Wherefore I give you to understand, that no man speaking by the Spirit of God calleth Jesus accursed: and that no man can say that Jesus is the Lord, but by the Holy Ghost. Now there are diversities of gifts, but the same Spirit. And there are differences of administrations, but the same Lord. And there are diversities of operations, but it is the same God which worketh all in all. But the manifestation of the Spirit is given to every man to profit withal. For to one is given by the Spirit the word of wisdom; to another the word of knowledge by the same Spirit; To another faith by the same Spirit; to another the gifts of healing by the same Spirit; To another the working of miracles; to another prophecy; to another discerning of spirits; to another divers kinds of tongues; to another the interpretation of tongues:"

Ephesians 6:10-18

"Finally, my brethren, be strong in the Lord, and in the power of his might. Put on the whole armour of God, that ye may be able to stand against the wiles of the devil. For we wrestle not against flesh and blood, but against principalities, against powers, against the rulers of the darkness of this world, against spiritual wickedness in high places. Wherefore take unto you the whole armour of God, that ye may be able to withstand in the evil day, and having done all, to stand. Stand therefore, having your loins girt about with truth, and having on the breastplate of righteousness; And your feet shod with the preparation of the gospel of peace; Above all, taking the shield of faith, wherewith ye shall be able to quench all the fiery darts of the wicked. And take the helmet of salvation, and the sword of the Spirit, which is the word of God: Praying always with all prayer and supplication in the Spirit, and watching thereunto with all perseverance and supplication for all saints."

Hebrews 2:1-4

"Therefore we ought to give the more earnest heed to the things which we have heard, lest at any time we should let them slip. For if the word spoken by angels was stedfast, and every transgression and disobedience received a just recompence of reward; How shall we escape, if we neglect so great salvation; which at the first began to be spoken by the Lord, and was confirmed unto us by them that heard Him; God also bearing them witness, both with signs and wonders, and with divers miracles, and gifts of the Holy Ghost, according to His own will?"

Hebrews 11:6

"But without faith it is impossible to please Him: for he that cometh to God must believe that He is, and that He is a rewarder of them that diligently seek Him."

James 4:7

"Submit yourselves therefore to God. Resist the devil, and he will flee from you."

James 5:14-16

"Is any sick among you? let him call for the elders of the church; and let them pray over him, anointing him with oil in the name of the Lord: And the prayer of faith shall save the sick, and the Lord shall raise him up; and if he have committed sins, they shall be forgiven him. Confess your faults one to another, and pray one for another, that ye may be healed. The effectual fervent prayer of a righteous man availeth much."

I Peter 5:8-9

"Be sober, be vigilant; because your adversary the devil, as a roaring lion, walketh about, seeking whom he may devour: Whom resist stedfast in the faith, knowing that the same afflictions are accomplished in your brethren that are in the world."

I John 3:21-22

"Beloved, if our heart condemn us not, then have we confidence toward God. And whatsoever we ask, we receive of him, because we keep his commandments, and do those things that are pleasing in his sight."

I John 5:13-14

"These things have I written unto you that believe on the name of the Son of God; that ye may know that ye have eternal life, and that ye may believe on the name of the Son of God. And this is the confidence that we have in Him, that, if we ask any thing according to His will, He heareth us."

These Scriptures clearly show that God is a just God! He cannot and will not violate His nature. If we obey Him, we will receive His blessings. If we choose to disobey, then we are turned over to our own devices (Proverbs 1:24-31, Romans 1:28, Deuteronomy 28).

# PART FOUR

# The More Excellent Way

## INTRODUCTION

In Part One of this book, we studied many very common doctrines, many of which I have believed most of my life. They steal the vitality and life from the Christian life and experience. They produce weak and defeated Christians hanging on until this life is over.

In Part Two, we demonstrated through over sixty testimonies that the dispensational doctrines of cessationism are not correct. God has not changed. His works, miracles and gifts of the Holy Spirit are for today. We demonstrated what happens when we are willing to take personal responsibility for what is happening in our lives.

Part Three taught personal responsibility from the book of Job. If we obey and take personal responsibility for our lives, then God will provide a way. It concerns me greatly that most people use Job as an excuse for not taking responsibility, when in truth it is God's lesson for us in how to be responsible. Elihu's response in chapters 32 through 37 contain the manifold wisdom of God. They contain the answers to our problems. They are some of the most important chapters in all of Scripture.

In Part Four, we will find the balance that God desires for us. In the body of Christ one camp does not believe that the works of Jesus are for today. They have fallen into a form of godliness that denies His power. Another camp teaches that the gifts of the Holy Spirit, or the "anointing," is everything. They are seeking every spiritual experience, power gift and revelation, and many become puffed up in their gifts. Both camps have bought into many dangerous doctrines.

I want to challenge you that there is more, much more. There is "a more excellent way!" God's "More Excellent Way" will lead us into our true purpose that we will discuss in Part Five.

## IS IT ALL IN THE ANOINTING?

I Corinthians 12:31-13:3

"But covet earnestly the best gifts: and yet shew I unto you a more excellent way. Though I speak with the tongues of men and of angels, and have not charity, I am become as sounding brass, or a tinkling cymbal. And though I have the gift of prophecy, and understand all mysteries, and all knowledge; and though I have all faith, so that I could remove mountains, and have not charity, I am nothing. And though I bestow all my goods to feed the poor, and though I give my body to be burned, and have not charity, it profiteth me nothing."

In I Corinthians 12, Paul explains the various gifts, administrations and offices of the Holy Spirit to the Corinthians. Then Paul makes a very profound statement to them. He says there is "a more excellent way" than what they were presently experiencing. He then tells them that this more excellent way is to have "charity." Then he goes on to describe what charity is.

I Corinthians 13:4-7

"Charity suffereth long, and is kind; charity envieth not; charity vaunteth not itself, is not puffed up, Doth not behave itself unseemly, seeketh not her own, is not easily provoked, thinketh no evil; Rejoiceth not in iniquity, but rejoiceth in the truth; Beareth all things; Believeth all things; Hopeth all things; Endureth all things."

Charity is God's love. It is God's nature. Some have wondered why the King James Version translates the Greek word *agape* as "love" in some places and "charity" in others. If you look at all the places the writers of the New Testament use this term, it will become evident that it is used to highlight a particular aspect of God's love. It is used to describe His love in action between the members of the body of Christ.

This is exactly what the Corinthians needed to experience, for they were "puffed up" by their gifts and were using them to exalt themselves over one another. They were dividing into sects because of pride. They needed desperately to experience God's agape love and express it towards one another as charity.

As wonderful and as necessary as the gifts are, they are not the end, but a means to an end. They are not the goal, but tools that help us reach the goal. The goal is to possess the nature and character of God, not just in part, but in its fullness (Ephesians 3:19, 4:13), not just part of the time, but one hundred percent of the time.

A clear distinction is made between the gifts of God — which include all the various manifestations, offices and operations of the Spirit — and the character of God. While they cannot be in opposition to each other, Paul is saying that to have God's gifts but not His nature profits us nothing. Nothing!

It is possible to have the gifts of Jesus yet not possess the image of Jesus. It is possible to have a ministry and not have charity. It is possible to be a preacher and not have charity and love. We can be an apostle or an elder and not have it. We can be an evangelist or a prophet and not have it. It is possible to be a miracle worker or a healer and not have it. Having a gift does not mean that we have become conformed to the image of Jesus. In fact, there are many believers who have been given powerful gifts by the Holy Spirit who act very un-Christ-like.

There are those who parade their gifts across the stage and become Christian celebrities and idols. In this situation there are two issues to deal with. First, if we allow men to become elevated in our minds and look to them for our answers and healing we have fallen into idolatry. It is very easy to fall into the trap of worshipping man, which is idolatry.

The second aspect of this question involves the gifted ones who encourage this in any way, even unintentionally. Our purpose should always be to focus all attention on our Lord and Savior. When you attend a conference, or a church, what name do you see emphasized? Is it the name of Christ embossed into the carpet or the preachers? Whose name is on the billboard? Is Christ glorified on the stage, or is it someone dressed in fancy clothes that the audience is being prepared for?

Some who have gifts of miracles or healing pack auditoriums and perform on stages like entertainers and charge for their services. When I started giving seminars, pastors asked me what my fee was. I was amazed at the prices some individuals demand to come to a church.

Some use the gifts of revelation to reign over others. They use God's gifts to set up religious structures that produce people wholly dependent on them. Many people actually travel from one "prophet" to another seeking another "word" to guide their life for another day. These "words" or "prophecies" become law and many lives are bound and destroyed by these "words" of men.

Other ministries believe that "they" are the only one that can do a particular ministry so they beg and beg for money. They beg and manipulate the listeners in order to get them to support their ministry. If we have to beg people to support our spiritual endeavors, it is because the God we claim to serve is not supporting them. When God calls us to a work, He supports it in every way, including financially. He owns the cattle on a thousand hills, and He owns all the gold and silver. If it is His ministry, He will provide.

We need to understand that it is possible to have awesome gifts, yet act like the devil. All our ministries, all our religious works can be wood, hay and stubble. This is exactly what was happening to the believers at Corinth. The church was full of gifted ones who were striving and bickering and dividing the people over their gifts, trying to decide who was the most important member and who had the most important ministry. Paul warns them that they can have all the gifts operating and still miss the goal of being conformed to the image of Christ.

Should we cast off the gifts then? Should we renounce them or discourage their manifestation? Not at all, the gifts are given by God, for His purpose. The main work of the Holy Spirit is teaching, convicting and transforming us into His image. The gifts are tools that help us attain that goal. But they are only tools. By themselves, without His nature, they will profit us nothing. The gifts are the expression of His righteousness. They are His testimony that we all need to encourage us and give us faith.

Paul is explaining the difference between the anointing of God and the life of God. Gifts are the actions or manifestations of the Holy Spirit operating through human vessels. We do not necessarily have to be walking in actual righteousness in order to be anointed, because it is not "we" who are being manifested, but the Holy Spirit.

The life of God is another issue entirely. This life is not someone else acting through us regardless of the condition we are in. It has to come from within us. It has to be our actions, springing from our new nature. The life of God is not manifested regardless of our spiritual condition; life is the result of our righteous moral condition. If we have allowed God to make us holy, in experience we will have life to manifest. If we have not allowed God to do that work, there will be no life present to manifest. There may be gifts but there won't be life. Gifts are not life; gifts are to help produce life.

God distributes the manifestations of His Spirit to every man, as He wills. The present moral condition of the person really has nothing to do with God's decision. The gifts and calling of God are without repentance (Romans 11:29). This is why our gifts, no matter how great they might be, should never puff us up in the least. What is important is to manifest His nature of love and charity.

This is what Paul was trying to get across to the Corinthians. He was saying: you have all kinds of marvelous gifts working in your church; you have apostles and prophets and teachers and every other gift, but you have nothing because of how you are using the gifts. You are manifesting the nature of the old man, not the new man. Stop focusing on the gifts, and on trying to figure out which one is more valuable. Stop being puffed up by them. Stop using them to exalt yourselves. They profit you nothing without God's nature.

The purpose of salvation is to become a different kind of a person, to be a partaker of the God's nature (II Peter 1:4). Spiritual gifts are only temporary provisions to help us become Christ-like. One day God is going to withdraw the gifts. Then what will we have?

I Corinthians 13:8-10

"Charity never faileth: but whether there be prophecies, they shall fail; whether there be tongues, they shall cease; whether there be knowledge, it shall vanish away. For we know in part, and we prophesy in part. But when that which is perfect is come, then that which is in part shall be done away."

Prophesies, tongues, knowledge, apostles, prophets are going to fail, they are going to cease, they are going to vanish. They are only tools to help us become new creatures. We need to understand the implications of this truth. How many believers' lives are totally wrapped up in their gift or in their ministry? Their whole identity is found in their ministry. (Even our ministries are gifts from the Holy Spirit.) In doing so they are making the ministry or gift their idol. Thus they are ignoring the most important work of the Holy Spirit, redemption, which is being transformed into the image of Christ.

What kind of devastation are some of us are going to face when God puts away our gifts? After a lifetime of using, studying, teaching about and profiting by, and building kingdoms around our gifts, God will put away the gift and say, "What kind of person have you allowed Me to make you? What have you done with My gift?"

I Corinthians 13:11-13

"When I was a child, I spake as a child, I understood as a child, I thought as a child: but when I became a man, I put away childish things. For now we see through a glass, darkly; but then face to face: now I know in part; but then shall I know even as also I am known. And now abideth faith, hope, charity, these three; but the greatest of these is charity."

When I was a child, said Paul, I spoke as a child and thought as a child and played with childish things. But when I became a man I put those childish things away. What "things" is Paul calling childish? Is he saying that the gifts of the Spirit, or the use of them, is childish? Not at all. The "childish things" are not the gifts themselves, but our attitudes towards them. Childish things are our evil desires and pride.

Spiritual maturity is not found in having gifts or by using them. Immaturity is marked by a continual preoccupation with them. Childishness is when we use our gifts to exalt ourselves over the rest of the body and demand that everyone focuses on the gift and on us because we have them.

God wants men who are not preoccupied with themselves or their gifts, men who will act like servants. He wants men who will love the people of God more than themselves. He wants men who use their authority and wisdom to teach people to stand with Christ and not be dependent on a man.

## THE WARNING OF JUDE
Jude 1:4, 11-13

"For there are certain men crept in unawares, who were before of old ordained to this condemnation, ungodly men, turning the grace of our God into lasciviousness, and denying the only Lord God, and our Lord Jesus Christ.... Woe unto them! For they have gone in the way of Cain, and ran greedily after the error of Balaam for reward, and perished in the gainsaying of Core. These are spots in your feasts of charity, when they feast with you, feeding themselves without fear: clouds they are without water, carried about of winds; trees whose fruit withereth, without fruit, twice dead, plucked up by the roots; raging waves of the sea, foaming out their own shame; wandering stars, to whom is reserved the blackness of darkness forever."

Jude wrote to encourage and exhort believers to fight or contend for their faith. In verse 4 Jude warns about ungodly men who have crept in unawares, then proceeds to name many of them from history. In verse 11, he mentions three errors they became involved in: (1) the way of Cain, (2) the error of Balaam, and (3) the gainsaying of Core.

People automatically assume that the people Jude was writing about, the ungodly men, were never really saved to begin with. However, the fact that they were believers at one time is clearly revealed by two of the descriptions Jude gives of them. First, they are called "trees whose fruit withereth...." These were men who at one time produced "fruit." It was not that these men had never produced any fruit at all; it was that their fruit had withered. Unsaved people will never produce any fruit, under any circumstances. These men were believers at one time, but the errors they got entangled in ruined their foundation.

Jude also said they were "twice dead." The usual interpretation of this statement is that they were dead once because they were born in sin and dead again (twice) because at some point they "seemed" to be born again, but then turned back to their evil ways.

There is only one way a person can be twice dead spiritually. They must be dead once (in sin), then received spiritual life (born again), then have that second life slain by returning to their own vomit (II Peter 2).

The first error they got involved in was "the way of Cain." The Apostle John called Cain "the wicked one" and said he murdered his brother because "his works were evil and his brother's righteous" (I John 3:12). Thus, the way of Cain has to do with false or perverted worship and the persecution of those who give God true worship. Cain was rebellious. He knew the proper sin offering was an animal, yet he offered the fruit of his own labor. He chose to serve God his own way, on his own terms. He wanted God to serve him instead of the other way around. When he saw that God had accepted Abel's sacrifice, but rejected his sacrifice, he became bitter and chose to murder his brother.

The way of Cain is the attempt to serve God on our own terms. It is a refusal to let Him purify and cleanse our hearts from wickedness, which eventually leads to the destruction and perversion of our faith. It also represents the hatred that those who follow false or corrupted religion have for those who have a true faith. Inevitably, those who corrupt pure worship will persecute and murder those who stay faithful to God.

You can see the way of Cain in the nation of Israel, when wicked kings and corrupt "prophets" worked together to seduce the people of God into idolatry, and then tried to kill any who remained faithful to God.

The way of Cain was evident in how the Pharisees related to Christ and the people of the day. We see it in history when the faith that was "once delivered unto the saints" began to be perverted by the very leaders of Christianity, who soon became bishops and popes.

We also see it today as some religious leaders seduce the people of God into following a false Jesus, a false anointing or a false unity that is based in social expediency instead of truth. We see it today when religious leaders refuse to accept the gifts of the Spirit and persecute those who do. We see it today when those who have a gift, or ministry, become puffed up in the gift or use of it. Those who corrupt true worship always end up persecuting those who remain faithful to God.

The error of Balaam was covetousness. Balaam was concerned with making money through his spiritual gifts. We involve ourselves in the error of Balaam when we sell the anointing given to us by God. Our spiritual gifts are freely given in order that we might freely share them, not sell them in the religious market place.

Another manifestation of the error of Balaam is today's prosperity message. The "name it and claim it" gospel is being spread all over the world by rich pastors and evangelists who say God wants all Christians to be wealthy. They teach that we must learn to use the "spiritual laws of faith" to acquire this wealth. One of those laws has to do with sowing and reaping. Christians must "sow" money if they want to "reap" money. God does promise to bless us if we bring His tithe into the store house, but this promise should not be used to manipulate (Malachi 3:10). The purpose of giving is to build His kingdom, not to gain personal wealth.

Paul teaches about those who, as the result of seeking material wealth, "have erred from the faith" (I Timothy 6:10). He warned that those who seek to be rich will "fall into temptation and a snare and into many foolish and hurtful lusts which drown men in destruction and perdition" (verse 9). He also instructed Timothy to separate himself from all who say "gain is godliness" because true wealth is spiritual, not material.

Paul calls covetousness idolatry and lists it with fornication, filthiness and uncleanness. He warns covetous believers that they have no "inheritance" in the Kingdom of God (Ephesians 5:3-5). The desire or lust to accumulate material wealth often leads to other forms of sin, such as stealing and lying. Even worse, when we try to gain wealth by using spiritual gifts or faith, we are practicing divination.

The Apostle Paul worked as a tent maker to support his ministry. A workman is worthy of his hire and a teacher is worth double honor according to Scripture. But it is God that provides.

The last error Jude mentions is the gainsaying of Core. In the Old Testament Korah was a Levite of the family of Kohath, the son of Levi and grandfather of Moses. Korah led a rebellion against Aaron's claim to the priesthood. As a result of this rebellion, God caused the earth to open and swallow Korah, Dathan and Abiram, and then He slew those that followed Korah with fire.

Korah was a priest who wanted Aaron's position. He was not really concerned about the people. He wanted the priesthood. He wasn't willing to remain an "obscure" minister. He wanted power and recognition; he wanted to be in the limelight; he wanted to be the leader. He was not satisfied with God's will for his life. Just like Lucifer, he rebelled against the one in charge. Just like Lucifer, he said, "I will ascend... I will exalt my throne... I will be like the most High" (Isaiah 14:13-14).

It's a dangerous thing to not be satisfied with what God gives us, or where He places us. Not only does it show that we think we know better than God concerning what is best for us, it reveals a heart that is covetous and rebellious. It reveals a heart that cannot be trusted with spiritual authority. Matthew teaches us that it is what comes out of the mouth that defiles us. It is what comes out of the mouth that reveals the heart of the man.

God lifts up the humble. If we promote ourselves, it only expresses to others how insecure we really are. If we promote ourselves, in reality we chase people away. We accomplish exactly what we are afraid of.

Scripture teaches that salvation is all about bearing fruit, which represents transformation into the image of Christ. It teaches that we can bring forth different levels of Christ-likeness and that we will be rewarded according to the degree of fruit we allow the Spirit to produce in us. It also warns us that we can end up vessels of "dishonor" in the kingdom if we serve God out of our own wisdom, strength and desires. It also warns us that we can end up vessels of "wrath" if we let our lives be choked by the cares and pleasures of this life, or if we allow the foundation of our salvation to be destroyed by the way of Cain, the error of Balaam, or the gainsaying of Core.

## MODERN DECEPTION

We are to obey the Holy Spirit, who is sent into our lives to show us the will of God and to give us the power and authority to fulfill His will. The Holy Spirit is more than a good feeling, more than a giver of supernatural gifts, more than a manifestation of power. All the gifts and manifestations of the Holy Spirit are the means to a goal, which is to be fully conformed to the image of Christ. This is the most important thing in God's eyes. It takes precedence over evangelism, over church work or ministry, over social reform, and everything else. The most important thing a believer can do is to learn to be led by the Holy Spirit every minute of every day.

Even though all Christians say they are being led by the Spirit, clearly, many of them are not, for they are doing and teaching all kinds of things that cannot possibly originate from God. Therefore, as believers, the most important question we face is: how can we be certain that we are following the right Spirit?

First, we must have a thorough knowledge of Scripture, because the Spirit of God will never contradict or oppose the Word of God. The purpose of the Word is to show us what God is like. It reveals His character, it shows how He deals with His people, and it reveals the destiny and purpose of the body of Christ. It is vital to remember that God cannot and will not violate His nature. When we know His nature and character it will become clear that He is not to blame for the calamities of this life. He is the giver of every good and perfect gift, period. If it is not good and perfect, it is not from God.

The Holy Spirit would never teach us, either directly or through a person, that He wants all Christians to be wealthy. He would not teach us that it is never His will we suffer, or be in need. He would never teach us that doctrine is not important, or that the defense of doctrine is wrong. He would never teach us that spiritual unity is more important than following His truth. He would never teach us that it is "all in the anointing."

He would never teach us that because we are under the covenant of "grace" we will not reap what we sow; that we can live in the flesh (the way of the world) and reap eternal life. God is not mocked; we will reap what we sow (Galatians 6:7). He would never teach us that repentance is not necessary for salvation. He would never teach us that obedience is not required. He would never teach us that we would receive rewards in heaven regardless of how we live in this life. He would never teach us that mental assent or belief in Jesus is enough to save a person. He would never teach us that it is His will only to save some. All these concepts and many others directly contradict the written Word. But all of them are being taught in the body of Christ today! What's going on?

Daniel 11:31-32, 12:11

"And arms shall stand on his part, and they shall pollute the sanctuary of strength, and shall take away the daily sacrifice, and they shall place the abomination that maketh desolate. And such as do wickedly against the covenant shall he corrupt by flatteries: but the people that do know their God shall be strong, and do exploits.... And from the time that the daily sacrifice shall be taken away, and the abomination that maketh desolate set up, there shall be a thousand two hundred and ninety days."

Matthew 24:15-18

"When ye therefore shall see the abomination of desolation, spoken of by Daniel the prophet, stand in the holy place, (whoso readeth, let him understand:) Then let them which be in Judaea flee into the mountains: Let him which is on the housetop not come down to take anything out of his house: Neither let him which is in the field return back to take his clothes."

II Thessalonians 2:3-4

"Let no man deceive you by any means: for that day shall not come, except there come a falling away first, and that man of sin be revealed, the son of perdition; who opposeth and exalteth himself above all that is called God, or that is worshipped; so that he as God sitteth in the temple of God, shewing himself that he is God."

Are we witnessing the beginning of the fulfillment of Daniel's prophecy concerning the removal of the "daily sacrifice" and the setting up of the "abomination of desolation" in the Holy Place? This is what Jesus and Paul spoke about in these verses. Is the Antichrist taking his seat in the temple of God? Remember, we are His temple.

Satan has been working to lead us away from the faith "once delivered to the saints" (Jude 1:3) one lie and one error at a time. Each error or false teaching has a specific purpose. Each has been designed to perfectly fit the errors taught before it. Each lie and error has taken many people further and further away from the truth and prepared them to embrace a counterfeit Christ.

Few Christians understand what is happening today because most of us are ignorant of what the Scripture actually says. We rarely read or study for ourselves. We blindly accept what we are taught. We are required by God to test or prove all things. You are required to test and prove what is being taught in this book. Test it against His Word.

We have been taught that the "abomination of desolation" will be a literal idol, set up in the literal, rebuilt temple in Jerusalem; that the "daily sacrifice" the Antichrist "takes away" when he sets his own image up in the temple, consists of reinstituted Old Testament animal sacrifices; and that this event cannot possibly happen until three and one-half years after believers are removed from the earth in the pre-tribulation rapture.

We have also been taught that once we are "saved," Satan cannot influence us or control us. We have been taught that being "under the blood" makes it impossible to have demon spirits operate in or through our lives. "A Christian cannot have a demon," is a statement that I often hear. The person usually is implying that he cannot even come under the influence of one.

The belief that the abomination of desolation is only a literal event, involving a stone idol and a stone temple three and one-half years after the rapture, and the belief that we cannot be overcome by evil spirits, guarantees that most of God's people will never understand what is happening.

We need to remember who our enemy is. He is the master deceiver. He will promote the obvious to deceive us with the subtle. These two false beliefs have caused most believers to forget that we are that temple. We would never allow abomination of desolation to be set up in the Church. But we have forgotten that we are the church.

## WHAT IS THE ANTICHRIST?

There is much confusion over the term Antichrist. We need to understand that we are not dealing with a strictly physical being. Will there be a human Antichrist? Scripture teaches that there will be many. But we are dealing primarily with a spirit. Some aspects of Antichrist and his work are literal and cannot be interpreted spiritually. Other aspects are spiritual and cannot be interpreted literally. Still other aspects are both literal and spiritual. This can be seen in the following Scriptures.

Revelation 9:2-4, 10-11

"And he opened the bottomless pit; and there arose a smoke out of the pit, as the smoke of a great furnace; and the sun and the air were darkened by reason of the smoke of the pit. And there came out of the smoke locusts upon the earth: and unto them was given power, as the scorpions of the earth have power. And it was commanded them that they should not hurt the grass of the earth, neither any green thing, neither any tree; but only those men which have not the seal of God in their foreheads.... And they had tails like unto scorpions, and there were stings in their tails: and their power was to hurt men five months. And they had a king over them, which is the angel of the bottomless pit, whose name in the Hebrew tongue is Abaddon, but in the Greek tongue hath his name Apollyon."

Revelation 20:1-3

"And I saw an angel come down from heaven, having the key of the bottomless pit and a great chain in his hand. And he laid hold on the dragon, that old serpent, which is the Devil, and Satan, and bound him a thousand years, and cast him into the bottomless pit, and shut him up, and set a seal upon him, that he should deceive the nations no more, till the thousand years should be fulfilled: and after that he must be loosed a little season."

Luke 8:31

"And they besought him that he would not command them to go out into the deep."

The bottomless pit, or the "deep," or the "dry place," are places where spiritual beings are held prisoner. In these verses we see that creatures referred to as "locusts" are set free. These are not actual insects because "they had a king over them." Locusts "have no king, yet go they forth all of them by bands..." (Proverbs 30:27).

We also see that Satan, who is a spiritual being, is bound with a chain (which must also be spiritual) and cast into this pit for a thousand years. In Luke 8, Jesus cast a legion (thousands) of demons out of the man. The demons begged Him not to send them into "the deep." The Greek term for the "deep" is the same term that is translated "bottomless pit" throughout the book of Revelation.

Revelation 11:7

"And when they shall have finished their testimony, the beast that ascendeth out of the bottomless pit shall make war against them, and shall overcome them, and kill them."

Revelation 17:8

"The beast that thou sawest was, and is not; and shall ascend out of the bottomless pit, and go into perdition: and they that dwell on the earth shall wonder, whose names were not written in the book of life from the foundation of the world, when they behold the beast that was, and is not, and yet is."

In these verses, John says that the Antichrist (the beast) ascends "out of the bottomless pit." It should be evident that no human being can ascend out of the bottomless pit. No nation or one world government can ascend out of that pit. No type of religious organization can ascend out of it. The inhabitants of the bottomless pit are spiritual creatures. The "beast" that John saw coming out of that pit was a powerful spirit. At the same time, he also said those who "dwell on the earth shall wonder...when they behold the beast." If people can "behold" it with their physical eyes, it has to assume some kind of physical or material form.

Revelation 13:1, 17:12-13

"And I stood upon the sand of the sea, and saw a beast rise up out of the sea, having seven heads and ten horns, and upon his horns ten crowns, and upon his heads the name of blasphemy... And the ten horns which thou sawest are ten kings, which have received no kingdom as yet; but receive power as kings one hour with the beast. These have one mind, and shall give their power and strength unto the beast."

In Revelation 11, the "beast" is described as an evil spirit coming out of the bottomless pit. In chapter 13, it is described as a political power rising up "out of the sea." We know that, in this instance, the beast does not represent either a spirit or a man because John said it had "seven heads" and "ten horns." Later, the angel explains that the seven heads are "seven mountains." Mountains always represent kingdoms in the Scripture. He also said the ten horns are "ten kings" who will "give their power and strength unto the beast" for one hour. In this instance, the "beast" represents a government. In addition, the words of John are the same words that Daniel used to describe the rise of various world empires (Daniel 7:23). Thus, the single term "beast" represents both a spirit and a political government of some kind.

Daniel 7:20-22

"And of the ten horns that were in his head, and of the other which came up, and before whom three fell; even of that horn that had eyes, and a mouth that spake very great things, whose look was more stout than his fellows. I beheld, and the same horn made war with the saints, and prevailed against them; Until the Ancient of days came, and judgment was given to the saints of the most High; and the time came that the saints possessed the kingdom."

In Daniel, we learn some of the things the Antichrist will do. Daniel sees a "beast" coming up out of the sea, on which are ten horns (political leaders). Among these horns, another horn (leader) comes up and overthrows three of them. We know this is occurring at the end of this age because he says this horn will make war on the saints and prevail against them until God comes to put a stop to it, which is the second coming of Christ. The little horn is a human political leader.

In these passages of Scripture, we have learned that the Antichrist is called a beast, a little horn and a man of sin. We have also learned that he takes on three forms; a spirit, a government and a political leader. We must understand which aspect of the Antichrist we are dealing with when we try to interpret various individual pieces of the end time puzzle.

## THE ANTICHRIST SPIRIT

Some the passages that we just read are not talking about a human Antichrist at all, but about the Antichrist spirit. The word "anti" carries with it two different meanings. It can mean one who fights against, openly, or it can mean one who fights against, covertly, by standing in the place of something or posing as something.

The most obvious manifestation of the Antichrist spirit is outside the Church. It fights against God openly, and is seen in those who are involved in Satanism or other forms of the occult, such as the New Age movement or the Masons. It can also be seen in cults and Eastern religions, and in governments that are based in Communism, Fascism and Socialism.

The least obvious and most dangerous manifestation of this spirit is inside the church. It fights against God covertly, by posing as the Holy Spirit or angels. It is seen in those who are teaching beliefs that are opposed to the Word of God. It is also seen in religious experiences that are directly opposed to, or outside of, the restraints of the written Word.

While many Christians are being deceived by the New Age and other false teachings, most Christians are not being overcome by the Antichrist spirit outside the churches because the manifestation of that spirit is too obvious. However, they are being overcome by the Antichrist spirit inside the churches because it masquerades as the Spirit of God. This should not come as a shock to us because Jesus Himself warned that false Christs would come with such powerful deceptions that all who are exposed to them will be deceived, all except the "very elect."

## FALSE 'CHRISTS' OR FALSE 'ANOINTING'
Matthew 24:23-27

"Then if any man shall say unto you, Lo, here is Christ, or there; believe it not. For there shall arise false Christs, and false prophets, and shall shew great signs and wonders; insomuch that, if it were possible, they shall deceive the very elect. Behold, I have told you before. Wherefore if they shall say unto you, Behold, he is in the desert; go not forth: behold, he is in the secret chambers; believe it not. For as the lightning cometh out of the east, and shineth even unto the west; so shall also the coming of the Son of man be."

When we read that false "Christs" will appear and show great signs and wonders, we tend to think of people, or false prophets. But Jesus said there will be false prophets and false Christs. The term false prophets is a reference to individuals, but the term false Christs has a much wider meaning. It can refer to individuals who claim to actually be Jesus, but it can also refer to a false anointing.

The Greek term *christos*, which is translated "Christ," means "anointed," "to smear or rub with oil; by implication, to consecrate to an office or religious service." In other words, Christ is not the last name of Jesus; it is a description of Him and His office. Jesus the Christ is Jesus the Messiah. Jesus the Christ is Our Anointed Savior.

We have become accustomed to thinking of "Christ" as His last name instead of His office as the anointed One. Therefore, when we read that "false Christs" will come, we automatically think of people. But the term can also be a reference to the anointing itself. Many will come in Jesus' name saying they are anointed (Christ), but Jesus may say that I have never known you (Matthew 7:21-23). We must test and prove all spirits. We must test all anointing.

Why do people run after prophets, true or false, in the first place? They run after them because of the anointing they perceive to be on them. They are seeking to hear the voice of God, or experience the power of God, through those who are (or who claim to be) anointed. They are seeking His hand of blessing, but in many ways avoiding His face of relationship by refusing to take responsibility and study the Word. They are seeking a quick fix, a quick blessing, without obedience and effort on their part.

Jesus' warning has to do primarily with what will transpire at the end of this age. He is warning us that in the last days (today), men who possess real supernatural power will enter the churches and say, "I am Christ" (anointed). They will say, I am anointed by God to preach and prophesy; I am anointed to perform healings; I am anointed to perform miracles. Their deception may be overpowering because they will say all the right words, and do signs and wonders which will look and feel exactly like the real thing.

Jesus said, "if any man shall say unto you, Lo, here is Christ, or there; believe it not. If they shall say unto you, behold, he is in the desert; go not forth: behold, he is in the secret chambers; believe it not." The second coming of Jesus The Christ will not be a secret. Zechariah 14 says that the Mount of Olives will split down the middle. The LORD of Hosts will be coming with His army for all to see.

Scripture warns that the deceptions of the last days will be so strong that many will be deceived. The most devastating deception will be within the church. False Christs will look exactly like Pentecostals, exactly like Evangelicals, exactly like Charismatics.

We must be very careful to test all things. Scripture repeats over and over that we will know them by their fruits. There is only one thing Satan will never be able to counterfeit — the nature of God. I do not believe that it is wise or safe to pursue spiritual power, spiritual gifts, or those who claim to have the gifts and want to impart them to you if they do not bear the fruit of God's nature in their lives and ministries. Spiritual gifts are given by the laying on of hands and also directly from God.

If in doubt, let God himself give you His gifts. The only safe thing to pursue is the nature of God. If the Lord chooses to give us gifts, or power, or revelations, or a ministry in the process, that's fine. We should not reject them. But anybody who goes chasing after power, gifts or the anointing in this hour could easily end up in deception. We must make sure that we are seeking God and His kingdom and not just an experience.

Then, if we add to this time of great deception the false belief that Christians cannot be affected or influenced or controlled by demons, we are ripe for a disaster. Wherever you find God moving in the realm of the supernatural among His people, you will always find Satan moving there as well. Satan is a master counterfeiter. But also remember a counterfeiter only counterfeits the real.

This is why, as you study the history of great spiritual outpourings such as Azuza Street, you will always find excesses. There are always demonic manifestations right alongside the true manifestations of the Spirit. In fact, many of the bizarre manifestations we see happening today were present at Azuza Street as well, but they were not the norm. The majority of those who participated in that outpouring reacted in a Godly way. They repented, they wept, they spoke in tongues, and they began to move in the gifts and ministries clearly taught in Scripture.

We need to be very careful of what passes as a manifestation of the Holy Spirit and we need to be very careful with the intentions of our hearts. If we are seeking these unusual or bizarre experiences, and following after those that have this "anointing," we can easily be deceived. It is easy to fall into the trap of worshipping the experience instead of Jesus. I believe that God can do anything. But I choose to stay within what is clearly taught in Scripture. Some take a couple of verses from Acts and use them to justify the strange and bizarre. Paul was very specific in I Corinthians 12 and Romans 12 what the "manifestations" of the Spirit are.

I choose to teach that we are to be holy as He is; that we are to be Christ-like; that we are to sanctify ourselves; that we are to become overcomers and vessels of honor, by cleansing ourselves of all iniquity. In this we cannot be deceived.

Luke 11:29

"And when the people were gathered thick together, he began to say, This is an evil generation: they seek a sign; and there shall no sign be given it, but the sign of Jonas the prophet."

Some of those seeking these experiences are seeking a sign from God and acceptance from others. If one is "slain in the Spirit" and falls on the floor, if one shakes all over, if one laughs uncontrollably, etc., etc., does this in some way show that they are accepted by God? If a person experiences these things, does it in some way show that they are special and then are looked up to by others? Who do these experiences edify? Do they build up the performing minister, the person, or God?

What was the sign of Jonas (Jonah)? God told him to go and preach repentance to Nineveh. Jonah ran from God and refused to do what he was told to do because he knew that they would repent and God would forgive and not destroy them. Many of us also run from God when He only wants to forgive us. We chose to "escape" into all forms of addictions and sin to cover up the pain when He only wants to heal.

The sign of Jonah was God's grace and mercy that is ours through repentance. This is truly how we personally experience His truth and receive deliverance from bondage. This is truly how we become acceptable in His sight and how we become fit for His service.

When we have been taught and believe that evil spirits cannot affect or influence us once we are saved, in reality this false belief only opens us to deception. This lie causes believers to assume that all supernatural manifestations they experience must be coming from the Holy Spirit. After a while, it becomes unthinkable that God would allow a demon to manifest itself around them or through them. Thus they refuse or do not test the spirits to see whether they are from God (I John 4:1), and therefore they cannot tell the difference between a manifestation of the Holy Spirit and a manifestation of the Antichrist spirit!

I have personally witnessed many supernatural manifestations in born-again, spirit-filled believers that were not from the Holy Spirit. Sometimes, they were very bizarre demonic voices speaking through the person. Sometimes the manifestation was bitterness, rage, jealousy and envy, fear or other manifestation of Satan's nature. Why can we be singing a praise song, or be in prayer, one minute and the next second cursing someone that cut us off in traffic? We all have an old nature, the nature of Satan, which we must overcome.

Today many are experiencing the bizarre and they call it revival. This is not revival! True revival is repenting and getting right with God in every area of our lives. True revival is learning to manifest His nature one hundred percent of the time. True revival is a changed life for God. We must be very careful that the concepts of self-sacrifice and self-denial, obedience and holy living are being abandoned for an "experience." Experiencing God can be one of the most incredible things that can ever happen to a believer. But never forget that Satan will counterfeit our relationship with God if he can.

Today there are tens of thousands running to places seeking a manifestation of the Spirit. We must be sure that it really God's spirit. The Spirit of God lives in each believer. Why must we go to a special place seeking a special experience? We don't. But at the same time God has gifted many teachers, prophets, and others with His gifts and manifestations of His Spirit. I have learned much from attending their meetings. I have greatly encouraged and I have seen things that were counterfeit.

It is very important to remember that we are the temple of the Lord and that we must honor and not defile His temple.

## THE TEMPLE OF THE LORD

The New Testament definition of the temple of God is not a literal temple but a people.

I Corinthians 3:16-17

"Know ye not that ye are the temple of God, and that the Spirit of God dwelleth in you? If any man defile the temple of God, him shall God destroy; for the temple of God is holy, which temple ye are."

I Corinthians 6:17-19

"But he that is joined unto the Lord is one spirit. Flee fornication. Every sin that a man doeth is without the body; but he that committeth fornication sinneth against his own body. What? know ye not that your body is the temple of the Holy Ghost which is in you, which ye have of God, and ye are not your own?"

Ephesians 2:19-22

"Now therefore ye are no more strangers and foreigners, but fellow citizens with the saints, and of the household of God; and are built upon the foundation of the apostles and prophets, Jesus Christ himself being the chief corner stone; in whom all the building fitly framed together groweth unto an holy temple in the Lord: In whom ye also are builded together for an habitation of God through the Spirit."

John 14:23

"Jesus answered and said unto him, if a man love Me, he will keep My words: and My Father will love him, and We will come unto him, and make Our abode with him."

All through the New Testament, believers are called the temple of God. The Old Testament tabernacles and the temples were only a type and shadow of the "body of Christ" in the New Testament. God does not desire a temple made of stone, but a people in whom He can dwell. He desires a people who love Him enough to be totally obedient in all things, so that He can manifest His character and glory through them for all eternity.

The book of Haggai is a picture of what happens when we have not rebuilt the LORD's temple. The LORD, through His prophet Haggai, told the people that they were sowing much, bringing in little; eating, but never having enough; drinking, but not filled; clothed, but with not enough to keep warm; and earning wages which do not meet needs, because they had not rebuilt His house. The message is the same today.

Under the New Covenant, we are His temple. We are to rebuild it by cleansing ourselves of all iniquity. We are to sanctify ourselves to become worthy of His presence and fit for His service.

Zechariah 6:12

"And speak unto him, saying, Thus speaketh the Lord of hosts, saying, Behold the man whose name is, The Branch; and he shall grow up out of his place, and he shall build the temple of the Lord."

John 2:19-21

"Jesus answered and said unto them, destroy this temple, and in three days I will raise it up. Then said the Jews, Forty and six years was this temple in building, and wilt thou rear it up in three days? But he spake of the temple of his body."

The prophet Zechariah said the Messiah would build the temple of the Lord when He arrived. Was he saying that Jesus would build another literal temple? Or was he saying Jesus was going to build a temple made without hands, living and vibrant, one which the gates of hell could not stand against?

Jesus was the first actual human expression of God's temple on earth. He manifested the character and power of God. When people came to Him and asked for healing, advice, eternal life or anything else, He had the answers and the power to grant that request because He was the living temple of God on earth. He was the fullness of God dwelling in man.

This is the plan for the body of Christ. God has no desire to come and dwell in a stone temple ever again. He has made Jesus the Head, the "chief corner stone," of a living temple and through union with Him we constitute the "living stones" (NIV I Peter 2:5) that make up the rest of that spiritual building.

When we accept the fact that we are His temple several ramifications become evident. Only believers are His temple and it is also through believers that the Antichrist will deceive many. This is sobering, but true.

While the Antichrist spirit does manifest itself through unsaved people, the unsaved never are and never can be viewed as "the temple of God." The only people who can be referred to as the temple are those who have genuinely trusted in Jesus Christ for salvation and have been given His Spirit. Only we qualify as the temple of God and only we have the ability to "defile" ourselves through our sin.

II Corinthians 11:4

"For if he that cometh preacheth another Jesus, whom we have not preached, or if ye receive another spirit, which ye have not received, or another gospel, which ye have not accepted, ye might well bear with him."

Paul plainly stated that it is possible for a person who has come to Christ, and received the Holy Spirit, to then receive a "different spirit" as well. He was complaining to the Corinthians about their double standard with regard to him. They were questioning his authority, yet they seemed to be willing to accept the authority of false teachers who were coming into the fellowship and presenting a false gospel and a false Jesus. If Paul did not believe that it was possible for a believer to receive another spirit after conversion, then his words in this passage mean absolutely nothing.

Paul is plainly teaching that believers can have both the Spirit of God and another spirit working in them at the same time. He taught this also in Romans 7. Could this be the "mystery of the iniquity" in II Thessalonians 2:7? It is truly a spiritual mystery how Satan can so deceive God's own children that they mistake his voice for God's voice, his anointing for God's anointing, his power for God's power, his ministry for God's ministry, his revelation for God's revelation, and his spirit for God's Spirit! But it happens every minute of every day.

## THE HIGH CALLING OF GOD
I Corinthians 9:23-27

"And this I do for the gospel's sake, that I might be partaker thereof with you. Know ye not that they which run in a race run all, but one receiveth the prize? So run, that ye may obtain. And every man that striveth for the mastery is temperate in all things. Now they do it to obtain a corruptible crown; but we an incorruptible. I therefore so run, not as uncertainly; so fight I, not as one that beateth the air: But I keep under my body, and bring it into subjection: lest that by any means, when I have preached to others, I myself should be a castaway [disqualified]."

Acts 20:24

"But none of these things move me, neither count I my life dear unto myself, so that I might finish my course with joy, and the ministry, which I have received of the Lord Jesus, to testify the gospel of the grace of God."

Philippians 3:10-14

"That I may know Him, and the power of His resurrection, and the fellowship of His sufferings, being made conformable unto His death; if by any means I might attain unto the resurrection of the dead. Not as though I had already attained, either were already perfect: but I follow after, if that I may apprehend that for which also I am apprehended of Christ Jesus. Brethren, I count not myself to have apprehended: but this one thing I do, forgetting those things which are behind, and reaching forth unto those things which are before, I press toward the mark for the prize of the high calling of God in Christ Jesus."

Paul was not confused about his gifts. His sights were on being transformed into the complete image of Christ. In the Acts passage he said he did not count his life dear to himself so that he could achieve two things: he wanted to finish the ministry he had received from God and he wanted to finish the course or his personal race. He wanted to finish his ministry to the Gentiles. His ministry was a gift from God. He was also determined to fulfill and finish God's plan for him to be transformed into the image of Jesus Christ.

In Philippians, Paul said he had to attain what he was after. He had to work hard to get it. He never taught that he would attain the fullness of Christ automatically or by grace. He never taught that he or any other believer would fulfill their purpose and call regardless of their obedience to God. He never taught that God would make sure we finish our personal race even if we choose not to run it. In fact, he taught just the opposite. He said he brought his body into subjection to the Spirit lest after having fulfilled his ministry he might be "disqualified."

In Philippians, he said he was seeking to apprehend the destiny for which he was apprehended or called by Christ Jesus. God had a plan for Paul's life. He had a course, which was laid out for him from before the foundation of the world. In His mercy and by His grace, God laid hold of Saul, the Pharisee, and showed him what that destiny was. Paul was then responsible to "lay hold" of that destiny. He was responsible to yield to the chastening, transforming work of the Holy Spirit in his life. He was responsible to obey the Spirit.

The apostle Paul was seeking to attain something he called the "high calling." When Paul wrote these words he was already saved, had many gifts, was already recognized as an apostle and had an international ministry. For years he had planted churches, worked miracles, endured great suffering and nurtured the body of Christ. He was one of God's mighty men, a spiritual veteran who was able to defeat Satan's strongholds wherever he ministered. He was shown revelations so spectacular he was not even allowed to share them.

He had vast experience in the deep things of God and did more to further the Kingdom of God than probably any other person in history. Yet he was still laboring to receive a prize, still seeking to "apprehend," still pressing toward something he called the "high calling of God."

What was he still trying to obtain? He was trying to win Christ (Philippians 3:8). He was trying to win the image of Christ. He was seeking to attain full transformation into His likeness. The thing that motivated Paul was the desire "that I might know Him."

Paul has thus defined the goal of the Christian life. Paul's race, your race, my race, and the race of every believer, is to fulfill God's plan for our personal transformation into His image, not later (in heaven) but in this life. Our ministries and gifts are important and necessary but they are not the main goal. If we do not have His nature manifesting through us, we are nothing.

The responsibility of drawing men to God rests on the shoulders of the Holy Spirit and He has never transferred that responsibility to the Church. He has never placed that responsibility on my shoulders or your shoulders. We must learn to let God be God. It is He who convicts and brings people to Himself.

Acts 15:14

"Simeon [Peter] hath declared how God at the first did visit the Gentiles, to take out of them a people for his name."

In one sentence, this verse reveals the whole purpose of the New Testament Church age. God is visiting the Gentiles (nations) in order to "take out of them" a people for His name. Who is taking them out? God is! He is "taking out" all who will follow Him.

We must remember that our main goal and purpose in this age is the internal war to crucify our old nature. We accomplish this by forgiving, repenting and resisting the devil. We must become doers of God's Word. The religious system of today is making the same mistake that the Jews did two thousand years ago. They were looking for an external kingdom. They were looking for a Messiah who would set up a physical kingdom. This is the same thing that most ministries and churches are doing today. They focus on the future literal kingdom and not the internal kingdom, which is personal sanctification.

Our focus should be the same as Paul's. He managed to win thousands of souls while focusing on attaining the high calling of God. We need to understand why God saved us. First, he wants a relationship with each of us, and that comes as we cleanse ourselves of all unrighteousness through repenting and confessing our sins and by forgiving others. As we draw nigh to God by cleansing ourselves, He will draw nigh to us (James 4:8).

It is His desire that none will perish. But He also knows that not everyone will accept Him. Our primary goal must be one of personal sanctification as it was for Paul. Then as we become vessels fit for His service He will give us a ministry and gifts that will bring forth fruit that is gold, silver and precious stones.

## CHRISTIAN REWARDS, ACCORDING TO OUR WORKS

There is no clearer teaching in the entire Word of God than the doctrine of rewards. From Genesis to Revelation, virtually every book states very plainly that every person, saved or unsaved, will be rewarded according to their works.

Even though we read verses that teach we will reap what we sow, that God is going to reward us according to what we have done, most of us do not really believe them. When it comes right down to it we still think we are going to be rewarded by "grace."

The subject of rewards, like sanctification, is usually avoided in our churches. It is implied that all Christians will receive basically the same authority, the same degree of glory, and the same rewards in heaven, based upon our profession of faith. The common belief is that there will not be not any difference between those who are in heaven. The goal is in achieving "heaven" and thereby heaven becomes our reward, and that is all that matters.

But there is a difference, and we need to know what it is, for such knowledge will help eliminate the spiritual lethargy and false security that is the norm in the church.

James 5:7-8

"Be patient therefore, brethren, unto the coming of the Lord. Behold, the husbandman waiteth for the precious fruit of the earth, and hath long patience for it, until he receive the early and latter rain. Be ye also patient; stablish your hearts: for the coming of the Lord draweth nigh."

The coming of the Lord is compared to a farmer who "waiteth for the precious fruit of the earth, and hath long patience for it." God is not trying to evangelize the world. He is not waiting for "revival" to sweep the earth. He is waiting for the precious fruit (saints) to be "stablish" or mature and bring forth fruit. He has been and still is going to the nations and taking out of them a people for His name so they will mature and bring forth fruit.

John 15:16

"Ye have not chosen me, but I have chosen you, and ordained you, that ye should go and bring forth fruit, and that your fruit should remain: that whatsoever ye shall ask of the Father in My name, He may give it you."

Romans 7:4

"Wherefore, my brethren, ye also are become dead to the law by the body of Christ;

that ye should be married to another, even to him who is raised from the dead, that we should bring forth fruit unto God."

Galatians 5:22-23

"But the fruit of the Spirit is love, joy, peace, longsuffering, gentleness, goodness, faith, meekness, temperance: against such there is no law."

John said the "called out" ones are chosen and ordained by God to bring forth fruit. Paul said that we were set free from the Law, not to live in lawlessness or any way we please, but so we could marry the Lord Jesus and bring forth fruit from that marriage. We were not chosen and ordained to evangelize the world. We were chosen to bear fruit.

It is true that as we learn to manifest His nature, the Holy Spirit will use us to reach the unsaved. However, God's focus is not on evangelizing the lost, but on bearing fruit. What is the fruit God "hath long patience for"? Is it religious works? Is it ministry? Is it souls? No. He is looking for the fruit of the Spirit. He is looking for love, joy, peace, longsuffering, gentleness, goodness, faith, meekness and temperance (Galatians 5:22-23). He is waiting for His own image to be fully formed in us. God wants His nature and character manifested on this planet, through His people.

## PARABLE OF THE SEED
Matthew 13:3-9

"And he spake many things unto them in parables, saying, Behold, a sower went forth to sow; And when he sowed, some seeds fell by the way side, and the fowls came and devoured them up: Some fell upon stony places, where they had not much earth: and forthwith they sprung up, because they had no deepness of earth: And when the sun was up, they were scorched; and because they had no root, they withered away. And some fell among thorns; and the thorns sprung up, and choked them: But other fell into good ground, and brought forth fruit, some an hundredfold, some sixtyfold, some thirtyfold. Who hath ears to hear, let him hear."

Jesus is teaching the people about fruit. The seed is the word of God, the sower is the Lord, and the ground is the hearts of men, which are like soil. The earth is a picture of the hearts of men. Our different characteristics and dispositions are represented by the four kinds of ground. The first three types of ground either do not bear any fruit at all or bear fruit that does not last. All those who claim to be "in" Christ and part of the "vine" should be producing some kind of fruit.

God is a fruit inspector. He comes to His vineyard looking for that fruit so He may prune the branches. He does this in order to get even more fruit (John 15:1-6). Everything is geared to and focused on getting the most possible fruit from the branches. His attitude towards those who are not producing any fruit is grim (Luke 13:6-9). Jesus tells us plainly what will be done with every branch that has failed to produce any fruit at all;

they will be "hewn down and cast into the fire" (Matthew 7:19).

It needs to be emphasized again that the fruit God is looking for is not religious accomplishments. The fruit He is looking for is the fruit of the Spirit, which is His Divine nature. Fruit equals character: the character of God. Fruit equals image: the image of Christ. As long as our lives have yielded fruit, in any degree, we are part of the family of God. We are part of the Church and members of the body of Christ.

However, we will not all bear the same degree of fruit. Some will be more faithful to God than others. Some will allow God to do a deeper work of sanctification in their lives and will bring forth a hundredfold fruit. Others will hold certain areas of their lives back from the Lord, thus only producing thirtyfold or sixtyfold fruit. The person who brings forth a hundredfold fruit will bear the full image of Christ. Those who bring forth sixtyfold fruit will only bear sixty percent of that fullness. Those who bring forth thirtyfold fruit will only bear thirty percent of that fullness.

There are varying degrees of transformation we can experience as believers. We do not automatically bring forth a hundredfold fruit just because we believe in Jesus. We are not automatically transformed into the fullness of His image simply because we have accepted Him as our personal Savior, or have been baptized in the Spirit, or die and go to heaven. The issue of how much fruit we produce has nothing to do with being saved or lost, unless we have produced no fruit at all. It has to do with how much of the image of Christ we bring forth in our lives.

## VESSELS OF HONOR AND DISHONOR
II Timothy 2:19-21

"Nevertheless the foundation of God standeth sure, having this seal, The Lord knoweth them that are His. And, Let everyone that nameth the name of Christ depart from iniquity. But in a great house there are not only vessels of gold and of silver, but also of wood and of earth; and some to honour, and some to dishonour. If a man therefore purge himself from these, he shall be a vessel unto honour, sanctified, and meet for the master's use, and prepared unto every good work."

The Apostle Paul said, in God's "house" there will be "vessels of honor" and "vessels of dishonor." Both kinds of vessels are in God's house; they all belong to God. Once again, we are not discussing eternal punishment or salvation. If Paul wanted to compare the saved with the unsaved he would not have used the term dishonor. He would have referred to a third kind of vessel, which represents those who are lost and called vessels of wrath (Romans 9:22).

Paul is not comparing vessels of honor with vessels of wrath; he is comparing vessels of honor with vessels of dishonor, both of which are God's people. Both will be in God's house. He is warning believers that in the coming kingdom, believers will experience different spiritual states, some honorable, some not so honorable.

Vessels of wood and earth, or of wood, hay and stubble, represent the old nature, while gold and silver represent the nature of God. Paul is telling us that though we are all God's people, we are not all going to necessarily be honorable vessels in the Kingdom of God. Both our rewards, and what kind of vessel we end up becoming, are not going to be based on our profession of faith. They are not going to be based on unmerited favor. They are going to be based on how much of God's image we have allowed Him to work in us.

Those who have allowed the Spirit of God to cultivate them, and prune them until they bring forth a hundredfold fruit, will have greater rewards and more honor than those who only bring forth sixtyfold fruit or thirtyfold fruit.

The Bible does not teach that we will all be equal. It teaches just the opposite. It mentions three levels of fruit and two kinds of vessels. Jesus also said that in His kingdom some will be called great and others would be called least (Mat. 5:19). Again, the contrast is not between the saved and the unsaved. Both the great and the least will be in the same kingdom.

## GREATEST OR LEAST IN HIS KINGDOM
Matthew 5:19

"Whosoever therefore shall break one of these least commandments, and shall teach men so, he shall be called the least in the kingdom of heaven: but whosoever shall do and teach them, the same shall be called great in the kingdom of heaven."

Is there any reason not to accept Jesus' words at face value? Would it be unreasonable to assume that, if there are those who will be the "greatest" and those who will be the "least," there will be others who will fall somewhere in between?

What determines who will be great and who will be least? Obedience; not doctrine, not confession, not justification, not forgiveness, not imputed righteousness, not grace, not love, not mercy, not church attendance, not spiritual knowledge or revelation, not gifts and ministry, not evangelism. To be called great in His Kingdom we must obey His commands and precepts and teach others to also obey. In obeying Him we will do what Jesus did while He was on the earth. He came to set the example for us (John 20:19-23).

## DEFILED GARMENTS
Jude 1:22-23

"And of some have compassion, making a difference: And others save with fear, pulling them out of the fire; hating even the garment spotted by the flesh."

Revelation. 3:4

"Thou hast a few names even in Sardis which have not defiled their garments; and they shall walk with me in white: for they are worthy."

Revelation 16:15

"Behold, I come as a thief. Blessed is he that watcheth, and keepeth his garments, lest he walk naked, and they see his shame."

Here we have another distinction between God's people. This time, it is between those who keep their garments clean and those who defile them by yielding to sin. Jesus said of those who keep their garments clean, "they shall walk with me in white." Revelation 16:15 says that those who do not keep their garments will walk naked, exposing their shame. Again, the issue is not between eternal damnation and eternal life. It is between those believers who will be granted the right to walk with the Lord in white, and those believers who will walk naked because of their carelessness in this life.

There is a visible distinction between believers. This is the only possible way to interpret the Lord's words, unless we maintain that the distinction He is making is between believers and unbelievers. If this were the case, we must conclude that every Christian who defiles his garment will be cast into the lake of fire. If this were true, there would be no one in heaven. It is possible to manifest varying degrees of Christ's likeness, and thus experience different levels of reward.

In different states, or levels of spiritual maturity, it is also possible to have different levels of closeness or relationship to the Lord, which is exactly what Jesus was describing in Revelation 3:4. This is true in our future relationship with Jesus and well as here on earth today. Not all those who followed Him shared the same degree of closeness to Him two thousand years ago. Why would we think it would be different today or in heaven?

The Lord had a number of groups following Him, some closer than others. Those furthest away were the multitudes who followed Him to get healing for their various physical diseases. They were seeking a supernatural manifestation. A little closer to Him was a large group of disciples that followed Him for a season, most of whom turned back because they could not handle what He said about eating His flesh and drinking His blood (John 6:66). A little closer to Him was an inner circle of twelve disciples who lived and walked with Him throughout His entire ministry. These twelve had a much more intimate relationship with the Master. To them Jesus explained His mission.

Among that inner circle of twelve there existed an even smaller, more intimate, circle of disciples: Peter, James and John. These three men were shown things that the rest of the twelve were not. Finally, among the three there was one (John), who laid his head on the bosom of Jesus at the Last Supper and who stood by Him at His crucifixion. John refers to himself as "the disciple whom Jesus loved" four times in his Gospel. This shows that he had the closest relationship of all with Him.

We need to realize that our place in His Kingdom will be determined by what kind of person we have allowed God to make us. We have to break free of the mind-set that all believers will get the same rewards. It is totally unscriptural and goes against every principle of God's justice and equity. God is not a respecter of persons; He rewards all according to their works.

There are different groups of believers within the family of God. There are wise and foolish virgins, the greatest and least, vessels of honor and of dishonor, and those who keep their garments clean and those who defile them. There are spiritual babes (I Corinthians 3:1, I Peter 2:2), little children, young men and fathers in the family of God (I John 2:13-14). There are also overcomers and non-overcomers.

# OVERCOMERS
Revelation 2:7

"He that hath an ear, let him hear what the Spirit saith unto the churches; To him that overcometh will I give to eat of the tree of life, which is in the midst of the paradise of God."

Revelation 2:11

"He that hath an ear, let him hear what the Spirit saith unto the churches; He that overcometh shall not be hurt of the second death."

Revelation 2:17

"He that hath an ear, let him hear what the Spirit saith unto the churches; To him that overcometh will I give to eat of the hidden manna, and will give him a white stone, and in the stone a new name written, which no man knoweth saving he that receiveth it."

Revelation 2:26-28

"And he that overcometh, and keepeth my works unto the end, to him will I give power over the nations: And he shall rule them with a rod of iron; as the vessels of a potter shall they be broken to shivers: even as I received of My Father. And I will give him the morning star."

Revelation 3:5

"He that overcometh, the same shall be clothed in white raiment; and I will not blot out his name out of the book of life, but I will confess his name before my Father, and before His angels."

Revelation 3:12

"Him that overcometh will I make a pillar in the temple of my God, and he shall go no more out: and I will write upon him the name of my God, and the name of the city of my God, which is new Jerusalem, which cometh down out of heaven from my God: and I will write upon him My new name."

Revelation 3:21

"To him that overcometh will I grant to sit with Me in My throne, even as I also overcame, and am set down with My Father in His throne."

In the book of Revelation, Jesus challenges the members of the seven churches of Asia to overcome. There is no way to explain away the fact that Jesus is not challenging unsaved people to become believers. He is challenging Christians to be overcomers. Some use a verse in I John to teach that overcoming means to become a Christian.

I John 5:4

"For whatsoever is born of God overcometh the world: and this is the victory that overcometh the world, even our faith."

This is the first step in becoming an overcomer. Many read this verse and stop there. Let's not forget the context of this passage.

I John 5:2

"By this we know that we love the children of God, when we love God, and keep his commandments."

We prove our faith by being obedient. This is the same message that James taught when he said I will show you my faith by my works. Faith is never alone; it will always be accompanied by proof, which is obedience to His commandments. We overcome Satan by becoming born-again, thus acquiring the new nature of Christ and also by being obedient. We overcome Satan by the blood of the Lamb and the word of our testimony.

If having faith equals overcoming, then why did the Lord challenge those who already possessed faith to overcome? If being born-again equals overcoming, why was the Lord challenging the churches to overcome? Was He telling John that none of the people in these churches were actually believers? If being born-again equals overcoming, these passages can mean only one thing: Jesus was telling the people in those seven churches that they were not really saved. It is far easier and more accurate to accept the simple truth that faith is never alone; obedience is always required.

What Jesus is really saying is that not all Christians will overcome. After we have been born again, after we have been baptized in the Spirit, after God has given us gifts and ministries, we still must overcome. It means that we can be a genuine believer and not overcome. It means that some Christians will overcome and some will not overcome. It means that those who do not overcome will not partake of all the rewards listed in these verses.

Overcoming means to conquer, overcome, prevail, and to get the victory. Revelation 2 and 3 reveal the great rewards that are promised to those that overcome. These rewards include:

• Eating of the tree of life.
• They will not be hurt in the second death.
• They will eat of hidden manna.
• They will be given a white stone.
• In the stone a new name will be written.
• They will be given power over nations.
• They will rule the nations with a rod of iron.

• They will be given a morning star.
• They will be clothed in white raiment.
• I (Jesus) will not (never) blot out his name from the book of life.
• I (Jesus) will confess his Name before the Father and angels.
• I (Jesus) will make him a pillar in the temple.
• He will go out no more.
• I (Jesus) will write upon him the name of My God (the Father).
• I (Jesus) will write upon him the name of the city of God, New Jerusalem.
• I (Jesus) will write upon him My new name.
• He will sit with Me in My throne.

While we do not understand what all these mean, some of them are incredible. Old Testament judges had both a black stone and white stone. If the person was guilty he received a black stone. If the person before him was innocent, the judge gave him the white stone to carry as proof that he was declared innocent. Jesus also gives a white stone to those that overcome. And He will write upon us, or the stone, the name of God the Father to show to Whom we belong. He will also write upon us the name the city, New Jerusalem, to show where we belong. He will write in the stone, or upon us, our new name, the secret name that only Jesus knows and has for each member of His bride. We are the living stones that His kingdom and His temple are truly being built upon.

Two of these rewards are about escaping judgment. This can create confusion if we believe that those who do not overcome are not saved and will face eternal punishment. But as we have seen there are Christians who do not overcome. Let's look at these two rewards.

The first statement is that those who overcome will not "be hurt in the second death." We know that the second death is the lake of fire. So the implication is that those who do not overcome will be cast into the lake of fire. It is dangerous to draw implications from Scripture instead of accepting the face value of the words. But this is how most scholars and commentators interpret this verse. Jesus was not implying that the non-overcomer will be cast into the lake of fire (second death). He was saying that they would not be hurt by it, two totally different concepts.

The Greek word for "cast into" is *ballo*, which means "to throw, more or less violently." The Greek word for "hurt" is *adikeo*. It means "to be unjust, hurt, injure, be an offender, or do or suffer wrong."

In both Greek and English, the two words convey two totally different concepts. If John understood Jesus to mean that those who fail to overcome will be cast into the lake of fire, he would have written *ballo*. He used this word many times in Revelation to describe what was going to happen to Satan, the False Prophet, the Beast and those who are not saved. He intentionally wrote *adikeo* because that is what Jesus meant.

To be hurt by the lake of fire means just that, to be hurt by it. It does not mean to be cast into it.

Will it hurt to find that your life's work for Jesus was burned as wood, hay or stubble? Will that not create gnashing of the teeth and weeping? Obviously, we do not know for sure what this means, but we must believe that it is possible to be hurt by, yet not cast into, the lake of fire because the Lord said it was possible. The result of not overcoming is not necessarily eternal punishment.

The second statement that confuses people is, "I will not blot out his name out of the book of life." Again, it is dangerous to draw conclusions; let's accept the face value of the words. Jesus does not say that those who do not overcome will be removed from the book of life.

There are various meanings and applications of the Greek, which is translated "not" in this verse. The exact meaning must be determined by the context of the entire verse. In this instance, it would be better translated "never." He that overcometh, I will never blot his name out of the book of life. There is great security for those who chose to be overcomers. Those who chose not to overcome still run the risk of giving up their faith and thus have their name blotted out of the book of life.

## WHAT ARE WE TO OVERCOME?

The challenge to overcome was to believers. Christians who overcome will receive spectacular rewards. The real question is, what are we to overcome? What was Jesus telling all these churches to overcome? What is He telling each of us to overcome? He was telling the churches to overcome the issues that they were facing at that time. Each local church was facing their own particular set of tests and temptations.

Jesus said the Church at Sardis was spiritually dead. To have the Lord Jesus declare that we are spiritually dead is not a pleasant thought. Even though the church enjoyed a good religious reputation, only a few people out of the entire assembly had not "defiled their garments" to such an extent that they had died spiritually.

Jesus said to this church, "He that overcometh the same shall be clothed in white raiment, and I will not blot out his name out of the book of life" (Revelation 3:5). Those who overcome the temptation to defile their garments are promised white robes. Those who overcome the spiritual death will never again be in danger of having their names blotted out of the book of life. But those who do not recover themselves from spiritual death are in danger of being blotted out. The believers in these churches were being challenged to overcome the things that were hindering them from bringing forth a hundredfold fruit. He was challenging them to overcome everything that would keep them from bringing forth one hundred percent of the image of Christ.

As believers today, we are to do the same thing. We are required to overcome all the sin that has defiled our lives. If we purge ourselves of all iniquity, we will be called a vessel of honor fit for His service. We are to overcome and purge ourselves from all bitterness, self-bitterness, jealousy and envy, rejection, fear, unbelief, occult activities and any other form of disobedience. If we fail to overcome all sin and temptation we will lose some rewards, but not necessarily all of them. Each and every believer will be rewarded for those things over which we have gotten victory. Conversely, we will not be rewarded for those things which have gotten the victory over us. If there is no victory at all, then there is no life and no salvation.

As it was with the believers in the seven churches, so it is with believers today. The believers in the Church at Philadelphia with their "little strength" will be made pillars in the Temple of God if they overcome. The believers in the Church at Pergamos are promised hidden manna if they overcome the temptation to "eat things sacrificed unto idols." The believers in the Church at Smyrna, who are suffering and being persecuted and will be put to death, are promised a "crown of life" and that they will not be hurt by (the second) death if they overcome, if they remain faithful till the end.

To the believers in the Church at Laodicea, a spectacular reward is promised. This church was lukewarm and on the verge of being spewed out of Christ. It is much easier for the Lord to reach a cold heart than a lukewarm heart. We are warned in Scripture about a church or a people that has a form of godliness that denies his power (II Timothy 3:5). I believe that this church (people) is in danger of being cut out of the Vine completely, not a pleasant place to be at all.

They were promised a seat in the Throne if they can overcome being spiritually lukewarm. This reward applies to us too. Spiritual lethargy is the order of the day. The message to this church is the message to today's church. It is time to get serious about our relationship with the LORD or we are in danger of being spewed out of Christ.

In short, being a Christian does not guarantee us these rewards. They have to be earned. They are rewards for faithfulness, not for conversion, and they are not free. Forgiveness, justification and imputed righteousness are free, but Christian rewards are not. In order to receive them, we must do more than believe and accept Jesus, we must overcome. We must obey Him.

## OVERCOMERS WILL RULE THE NATIONS
Revelation 2:26-29

"And he that overcometh, and keepeth my works unto the end, to him will I give power over the nations: And he shall rule them with a rod of iron: as the vessels of a potter shall they be broken to shivers: even as I received of My Father. And I will give him the morning star. He that hath an ear, let him hear what the Spirit saith unto the churches."

One of the rewards for overcoming is to rule with Jesus on this planet during the Millennium and for all eternity. This is not a reward for being born again or baptized in the Spirit. It is not a reward for having been given gifts and ministries or for soul winning. It is a reward for having struggled against and won the victory over our old nature, over the sin in our lives, over everything that hinders us from manifesting His nature one hundred percent of the time.

Many believers today are making the same mistake that the Pharisees did two thousand years ago. Jesus did not come to set up an external, physical kingdom in this age. This age is about an internal kingdom. It is about the war between our flesh and our new man. It is about overcoming the flesh, the old nature. It is about overcoming the works of the devil in our individual lives.

Believers today are attempting to build external, physical kingdoms through churches, ministries, gifts and spiritual warfare. Again some of these are good but they should not be our primary focus.

In this age we do not have authority over the devil in the heavenlies, or over nations. Even Jesus, while he was on the earth, did not rebuke Satan from nations or the heavenlies. He cast demons out of individuals only. He then gave us the same authority that He was given by the Father.

When we enter into war against principalities that rule over nations or territories we have exceeded the authority given to us by Jesus. I believe that Satan loves for us to enter into this type of prayer or warfare for two reasons. First, it opens the door for him to attack us at a deeper level. Most of those that are seriously involved in this type of "spiritual warfare" are suffering from many illnesses. If you doubt this, check it out and you will find that I am right. I cover this topic in greater detail in my booklet Intercessory Prayer and John Paul Jackson has written a book called Needless Casualties of War that deals with this issue in detail.

Second, it takes our focus off our true calling and purpose of becoming Christ-like one hundred percent of the time. What does this type of warfare really accomplish? What are the fruits? I see only negative fruit.

Scripture teaches us to confess (Nehemiah 9, Leviticus 26) for the sins of our nations and generations. We are to take responsibility for these sins and confess them, not cast out the devil; then He will restore our land.

We have been given total authority over the devil in our lives and in the lives of those that we minister to. This life, this age, is a time of preparation to be His kings and priests. It is a time of preparation to learn how to rule over the nations in an actual physical government and kingdom when the LORD of Hosts (Jesus) returns with His army (all believers).

Isaiah 61:1-2

"The Spirit of the Lord God is upon me; because the Lord hath anointed me to preach good tidings unto the meek; He hath sent me to bind up the brokenhearted, to proclaim liberty to the captives, and the opening of the prison to them that are bound;

To proclaim the acceptable year of the Lord, and the day of vengeance of our God; to comfort all that mourn."

Luke 4:18-20

"The Spirit of the Lord is upon me, because He hath anointed me to preach the gospel to the poor; He hath sent me to heal the brokenhearted, to preach deliverance to the captives, and recovering of sight to the blind, to set at liberty them that are bruised, To preach the acceptable year of the Lord. And he closed the book...."

"The day of vengeance of our God" was not the reason that Jesus became the Christ in His appearance on this earth as a man. He purposely stopped reading in middle of a sentence, and left those words out when He read the prophecy of Isaiah in the synagogue, because that was not His purpose during this age.

Jesus is our example. We are to do the same things that the Father showed Him to do. Jesus came to preach the gospel (repentance), to heal the brokenhearted, deliver those held captive by Satan, to heal the blind, to heal the bruised and broken. Why do we think we should do anything else? Are we to worship and serve God on our terms or His? Remember the "way of Cain."

The responsibilities and rewards of the next life will be based on what we learn and overcome in this life. The "day of vengeance," the day for actual physical, external war against the devil is coming.

## PREPARING FOR WAR
I Corinthians 14:7-8

"And even things without life giving sound, whether pipe or harp, except they give a distinction in the sounds, how shall it be known what is piped or harped? For if the trumpet give an uncertain sound, who shall prepare himself to the battle?"

Paul is teaching us to seek the greater gift of speaking in a known language versus speaking in an unknown tongue so that we will not give an uncertain sound and thus be unprepared for battle. Folks, there are many "uncertain sounds" in today's world. We are to seek the greater gifts. This passage tells us what the greater gift is and that the purpose is not to gather more gifts but to be prepared for the battle.

In Israel, the ram's horn (shofar) was blown to signify the start of specific events. It was sounded when the cloud or the pillar of fire, which rested over the tabernacle, started moving. It was sounded as a defensive alarm, warning the cities of an attack. It was also sounded to gather together the tribes to prepare for war. And it was used to signal the actual start of the battle.

The day of vengeance (the Second Coming) is not going to be a party or a vacation. The vast majority of Christians are waiting to be whisked away into paradise, after which they will begin a long spiritual vacation and party. But that is not what Scripture teaches.

When Jesus came the first time it was to proclaim the acceptable year of the Lord, to bring forgiveness and reconciliation. But when He comes the second time it will be a day of vengeance.

Isaiah 2:12, 13:6, 9, 13

"For the day of the LORD of Hosts shall be upon every one that is proud and lofty, and upon every one that is lifted up; and he shall be brought low... Howl ye; for the day of the LORD is at hand; it shall come as a destruction from the Almighty... Behold, the day of the LORD cometh, cruel both with wrath and fierce anger, to lay the land desolate: and He shall destroy the sinners thereof out of it... Therefore I will shake the heavens, and the earth shall remove out of her place, in the wrath of the LORD of Hosts, and in the day of his fierce anger."

Jeremiah 46:10

"For this is the day of the LORD God of Hosts, a day of vengeance, that He may avenge Him of his adversaries: and the sword shall devour, and it shall be satiate and made drunk with their blood: for the LORD God of hosts hath a sacrifice in the north country by the river Euphrates."

Joel 1:15, 2:1

"Alas for the day! for the day of the LORD is at hand, and as a destruction from the Almighty shall it come... Blow ye the trumpet in Zion, and sound an alarm in my holy mountain: let all the inhabitants of the land tremble: for the day of the LORD cometh, for it is nigh at hand."

Amos 5:18, 20

"Woe unto you that desire the day of the LORD! to what end is it for you? the day of the LORD is darkness, and not light. Shall not the day of the LORD be darkness, and not light? even very dark, and no brightness in it?"

Obadiah 1:15

"For the day of the LORD is near upon all the heathen: as thou hast done, it shall be done unto thee: thy reward shall return upon thine own head."

Zephaniah 1:7, 14

"Hold thy peace at the presence of the LORD God: for the day of the LORD is at hand: for the LORD hath prepared a sacrifice, He hath bid His guests... The great day of the LORD is near, it is near, and hasteth greatly, even the voice of the day of the LORD: the mighty man shall cry there bitterly."

Lest you miss the significance of these passages we need to understand that the LORD of Hosts is Jesus Christ. The Day of the LORD is the day that Jesus returns. The Day of the Lord is not going to be a party. It is going to be a day of darkness, gloom, war, bloodshed and destruction. The reason is simple; this time, the Messiah will not be coming to bring reconciliation to the world, but judgment. He will be coming to avenge and execute the wrath of the Father. This is also taught in the New Testament.

Romans 2:4-6

"Or despisest thou the riches of his goodness and forbearance and longsuffering; not knowing that the goodness of God leadeth thee to repentance? But after thy hardness and impenitent heart treasurest up unto thyself wrath against the day of wrath and revelation of the righteous judgment of God; Who will render to every man according to his deeds."

II Thessalonians 1:7-9

"And to you who are troubled rest with us, when the Lord Jesus shall be revealed from heaven with his mighty angels, In flaming fire taking vengeance on them that know not God, and that obey not the gospel of our Lord Jesus Christ: Who shall be punished with everlasting destruction from the presence of the Lord, and from the glory of his power."

Hebrews 10:26-27

"For if we sin wilfully after that we have received the knowledge of the truth, there remaineth no more sacrifice for sins, but a certain fearful looking for of judgment and fiery indignation, which shall devour the adversaries."

Jude 1:14-15

"And Enoch also, the seventh from Adam, prophesied of these, saying, Behold, the Lord cometh with ten thousands of his saints, To execute judgment upon all, and to convince all that are ungodly among them of all their ungodly deeds which they have ungodly committed, and of all their hard speeches which ungodly sinners have spoken against him."

Revelation 6:15-17

"And the kings of the earth, and the great men, and the rich men, and the chief captains, and the mighty men, and every bondman, and every free man, hid themselves in the dens and in the rocks of the mountains; And said to the mountains and rocks, Fall on us, and hide us from the face of Him that sitteth on the throne, and from the wrath of the Lamb: For the great day of His wrath is come; and who shall be able to stand?"

Obviously this day is not going to be a party. The question is, where will we be, and what will we be doing on the day of vengeance? We believe that we will rule and reign with Christ but we refuse to believe that we are part of His army on this day. We have been taught that we will be taken out or "raptured." Is this what Scripture really teaches?

Psalms 50:3-5

"Our God shall come, and shall not keep silence: a fire shall devour before Him, and it shall be very tempestuous round about Him. He shall call to the heavens from above, and to the earth, that He may judge his people. Gather my saints together unto Me; those that have made a covenant with Me by sacrifice."

Zechariah 14:5

"And ye shall flee to the valley of the mountains; for the valley of the mountains shall reach unto Azal: yea, ye shall flee, like as ye fled from before the earthquake in the days of Uzziah king of Judah: and the LORD my God shall come, and all the saints with thee."

I Thessalonians 3:13

"To the end He may stablish your hearts unblameable in holiness before God, even our Father, at the coming of our Lord Jesus Christ with all his saints."

Matthew 24:30-31

"And then shall appear the sign of the Son of man in heaven: and then shall all the tribes of the earth mourn, and they shall see the Son of man coming in the clouds of heaven with power and great glory. And He shall send His angels with a great sound of a trumpet, and they shall gather together His elect from the four winds, from one end of heaven to the other."

Regardless of our view on the rapture, Scripture is crystal clear on four points: (1) Jesus is coming again, (2) He is going to come on the day of vengeance, (3) He is going to come with His saints and (4) together they are going to execute the judgment that is in God's heart.

Revelation 19:5-8

"And a voice came out of the throne, saying, Praise our God, all ye His servants, and ye that fear Him, both small and great. And I heard as it were the voice of a great multitude, and as the voice of many waters, and as the voice of mighty thunderings, saying, Alleluia: for the Lord God omnipotent reigneth. Let us be glad and rejoice, and give honour to Him: for the marriage of the Lamb is come, and his wife hath made herself ready. And to her was granted that she should be arrayed in fine linen, clean and white: for the fine linen is the righteousness of saints."

In the book of Revelation, the Day of the Lord is connected closely with the marriage of the Lamb. Believers are the Bride of Christ. We are His wife, and He is our Husband. The marriage is not the beginning of a party, but the beginning of a war. Immediately after John heard the voice of many waters announce that the marriage of the Lamb is come, he saw heaven opened. The following is a description of what he saw.

Revelation 19:11-16, 19-21

"And I saw heaven opened, and behold a white horse; and He that sat upon him was called Faithful and True, and in righteousness He doth judge and make war. His eyes were as a flame of fire, and on His head were many crowns; and He had a name written, that no man knew, but He Himself. And He was clothed with a vesture dipped in blood: and his name is called The Word of God. And the armies which were in heaven followed Him upon white horses, clothed in fine linen, white and clean. And out of His mouth goeth a sharp sword, that with it He should smite the nations: and He shall rule them with a rod of iron: and He treadeth the winepress of the fierceness and wrath of Almighty God. And He hath on his vesture and on His thigh a name written, KING OF KINGS, AND LORD OF LORDS."

"And I saw the beast, and the kings of the earth, and their armies, gathered together to make war against Him that sat on the horse, and against His army. And the beast was taken, and with him the false prophet that wrought miracles before him, with which he deceived them that had received the mark of the beast, and them that worshipped his image. These both were cast alive into a lake of fire burning with brimstone. And the remnant [of the armies] were slain with the sword of Him that sat upon the horse, which sword proceeded out of his mouth: and all the fowls were filled with their flesh."

First, John sees the "wife" of the Lamb, believers prepared and ready for the marriage. Then he sees the same people as an "army." This is also consistent with the verses that describe the LORD of Host coming with His army, the hosts or believers. This is not going to be an ordinary wedding and it will not be followed by an ordinary marriage supper.

Revelation 19:16-18

"And He hath on his vesture and on His thigh a name written, KING OF KINGS, AND LORD OF LORDS. And I saw an angel standing in the sun; and He cried with a loud voice, saying to all the fowls that fly in the midst of heaven, Come and gather yourselves together unto the supper of the great God; That ye may eat the flesh of kings, and the flesh of captains, and the flesh of mighty men, and the flesh of horses, and of them that sit on them, and the flesh of all men, both free and bond, both small and great."

The marriage is followed by the Great Supper of God, which is followed by a great battle. Blessed are those who are called to this supper. There is going to be a war between the saints, with Jesus as the Commander and Chief, and the kings of this earth, with the beast as their commander and chief. There are going to be real casualties and thousands of people are going to die.

The marriage of the Lamb, which is the return of the Lord, is the coming of Jesus "with" and "in" His saints to execute judgment and vengeance. Heaven was not rejoicing because the party had started. It was rejoicing because, she who was "drunken with the blood of the saints," she who has butchered God's people throughout the centuries, was finally about to be judged.

After the King, with His army, has subdued the nations, then peace can be established on this planet. After the rebellion is put down, then the nations of the earth can be brought into submission to the authority of God, which will bring peace and blessing. Jesus is not going to do all this alone. He is preparing a body who will rule with Him. He is preparing kings and priests to serve with Him.

Priests "shepherd" people, they provide spiritual protection for them, and they care for them. Kings "rule" people. They exercise authority and judgment. They decree punishments and wage war. God is raising up an army in this age and teaching them how to war against His enemies. He is teaching this to each believer as we learn to destroy the works of the devil in ourselves. He is training us how to stand against and overcome the powers of the devil in our individual lives. We are being trained by the Holy Spirit to be warriors.

At the sound of the "last" trumpet, when the call goes forth to "meet the Bridegroom," will you be ready to follow King Jesus into battle? Jesus is the commander and chief and we are His army and we will carry out the vengeance against evil that is in the Father's heart. Together we will subdue His enemies, set up the everlasting Kingdom on this planet, and rule the nations with a rod of iron. Are you prepared for battle? Are you allowing the Holy Spirit to cleanse you of all iniquity?

The rewards of the Christian life are not only in the next life. In Part Two were the testimonies of over sixty people that received a great reward in this life for being obedient. God's laws of sowing and reaping apply to our situations in this life just as they do to the next one. If we obey Him, then we will receive His blessings (rewards), but if we chose to disobey Him, then we will receive the blessing of the one we chose to obey instead. The "blessing" of Satan is one I choose to miss out on.

This is where the issue of preparation becomes vital. We do not become experienced soldiers instantly. Nor do we automatically become rulers. These things must be learned. We must be trained; we must learn how to do battle. The ability to wage war and govern cannot be automatically transferred to us. It is a skill acquired through the school of this life. It takes time. Those who have not been equipped to rule will never be granted the authority to rule.

II Timothy 2:3-5

"Thou therefore endure hardness, as a good soldier of Jesus Christ. No man that warreth entangleth himself with the affairs of this life; that he may please Him who hath chosen him to be a soldier. And if a man also strive for masteries, yet is he not crowned, except he strive lawfully."

Timothy presents certain qualifications for a good soldier of Christ. A good soldier does not entangle himself with the affairs of this life. We must always remember that we are eternal beings and that this life is as a blade of grass, it withers and fades very quickly. Our focus must remain on the eternal. Our career, finances, businesses, churches, ministries, gifts etc. all take a back seat to our relationship with the Lord.

A good soldier does not take shortcuts and try to do things his way. A good soldier strives lawfully. He does it God's way and then the work is truly gold, silver and precious stones, not wood, hay and stubble. A good soldier puts his hand to the plow and goes to work diligently to learn to manifest the nature of God one hundred percent of the time.

In order to be a king or a priest in the next age we need to be trained and qualified.

The training and qualification come through a process of judging ourselves, listening to the Holy Spirit and cleansing ourselves of all iniquities. Our thoughts and emotions must be brought to the subjection of Jesus (II Corinthians 10:5). We must be ready to revenge all disobedience in our lives that our obedience might be fulfilled (II Corinthians 10:6).

We must be made new creations, creations that are capable of manifesting the whole range of God's character, not just the meekness and the longsuffering, but His complete image. That image includes judgment and discernment. Hebrews 5:14 tells us that mature believers know the difference between good and evil, and do good. It is the process of sanctification that qualifies and trains us to be His kings and priest. Are you willing to let God try your heart for any wicked way?

Psalms 139:23-24

"Search me, O God, and know my heart: try me, and know my thoughts: And see if there be any wicked way in me, and lead me in the way everlasting."

Jeremiah 17:9-10

"The heart is deceitful above all things, and desperately wicked: who can know it? I the Lord search the heart, I try the reins, even to give every man according to his ways, and according to the fruit of his doings."

Will you give permission to God to try your heart for any wicked way? The heart is deceitful and desperately wicked. You cannot trust it. Most people believe that they are righteous and perfect just like Job thought he was. The truth is that we are all desperately wicked.

It is my prayer that each of you reading this book will allow God to search your heart. It is my prayer that each of you will take this Christian life seriously. Jesus is our only hope. What else is there?

II Corinthians 10:4

"For the weapons of our warfare are not carnal, but mighty through God to the pulling down of strong holds."

We can be strong because He is with us. We do not, nor can we do this war in our own power. The good news is that we have His power and His weapons, with which to fight, available for our use, right now! Hallelujah!

In His work on this earth Jesus gave us an example of how to live and how to do His ministry. When we are willing to accept this and then actually do what He taught us to do we will find the true purpose for our lives. Part Five teaches us what we should be doing every day. It explains what the purpose of our lives is and how to accomplish our destiny.

# Advancing the Kingdom of God: The Purpose of the Christian Life

"We must get rid of the idea that Jesus is coming to rescue His church. That lie has dislocated many generations of revolutionaries from their purpose in the same way a joint is pulled out of place. It has put the Church into a defensive posture of occupation to protect what we have instead of positioning ourselves for the purpose of increase. The strategy of occupation for the purpose of advancement and increase is an absolute Kingdom principle. Ask the man who buried His talent in order to protect it." (Johnson, 2006)

## INTRODUCTION

In Matthew 6:9-10 Jesus instructs His disciples to pray "...Our Father which art in heaven, Hallowed be thy name. Thy kingdom come. Thy will be done in earth, as it is in heaven." I know we have all prayed this hundreds of times but do we really believe or even understand what we are praying? God is revealing His purpose for each of us.

A few years ago I read what I considered to be a very radical thought: that His will should actually be done on earth today as it is in heaven. Bill Johnson's book, *When Heaven Invades Earth* (2003), challenged me greatly. But today, after several years of actually experiencing His will being done in the lives of thousands of people, it does not seem so radical. My experiences over the last few years have led me to another realization which may even be more radical. When His will is being done, His Kingdom is present and upon us! Let's keep studying and I will demonstrate this truth.

Dispensationalists claim that the Kingdom will not appear until the millennium, at the end of the present church age. Many dispensationalists also teach that there are two kingdoms: one on the earth for the Jews, and another in heaven for the Church. The "kingdom now" movement believes that the Kingdom of heaven is established on earth by human efforts which make it possible for the second coming. Most Christians, in one way or another, believe that the Kingdom refers to a distant future event that only takes place after we die or the Lord returns. Who is right?

In trying to answer these questions, several more questions come to mind. Why would we be instructed to pray that His Kingdom come if this is not what He meant? What is the Kingdom of God or heaven? What does the Kingdom actually look like? What is His will in heaven? What does Scripture mean when it says the Kingdom is upon you? If the Kingdom is "upon" us, is that evidence of His will being done on earth as it is in heaven? Are the Kingdom and His will the same thing?

I want all of us to understand what Jesus is teaching us in His prayer and to learn to put His instructions into practice in our everyday lives. As we work through this study we will see the answers to these and many other questions.

The Kingdom must be important because Jesus commanded us in the Lord's Prayer to pray that it come. Jesus also commanded us not to worry about the things of this life but to seek His Kingdom first. Matthew 6:33 says, "But seek ye first the kingdom of God, and his righteousness; and all these things shall be added unto you."

We are commanded to repent to get ready for it. Matthew 4:17 says, "From that time Jesus began to preach, and to say, Repent: for the kingdom of heaven is at hand." Repentance, which is the process of sanctification, is what opens the door to His Kingdom. "From that time" means from the time that Jesus started His ministry He taught people to repent and to forgive to prepare for the Kingdom. As we will learn, "at hand" means that it is present and upon us now.

The terms Kingdom of God and Kingdom of heaven are synonymous. In reverence and respect for God, Hebrew people would usually not say "God" and would substitute "Lord" or "heaven."

So what is the Kingdom? Why does Jesus talk about it so much? Why is it so important? The answers to these questions will also explain why it is so misunderstood and counterfeited. I believe that we can answer these questions by looking at what Jesus was sent to do, what He actually did, what He trained His disciples to do, and by His commissioning and sending of His disciples. We will also look at what He said "the Kingdom is like" in His parables.

The Kingdom message of Jesus is taught throughout the Bible. But for the purposes of this chapter I have chosen to look at how the Kingdom message is taught in the prophecies of His birth, His actual birth, His baptism, His temptations, His ministry, how He discipled others, and in His parables.

We will be following the life and ministry of Jesus primarily through the book of Luke. I have chosen to teach primarily from Luke to shorten the teaching. If I chose to use all of the Scripture references related to His Kingdom and His will it would take several volumes to cover the subject.

As we study together I believe that this chapter demonstrates what this book is all about and why we are on the earth. Advancing His Kingdom on earth as it is in heaven is our purpose. Let's go to His Word and see how this plays out.

## THE KINGDOM MESSAGE IN PROPHECY

The coming of the Messiah was and is an eagerly awaited event. Two thousand years ago the Jewish people were living under the bondage of Rome and were desperately looking to be rescued from Rome in the same way that Moses rescued them from Egypt. In this time of bondage there was a great deal of speculation about what the reign of the Messiah would be like. In Jewish thought it was as if there must be two different Messiahs: one that would come and rescue them from the bondages of Rome, and another that would suffer and die for them. In their desperate circumstances most could not understand a suffering Messiah, but looked for one that would rescue them from their current living conditions.

An example of this is found in John the Baptist. Luke 7:19 says, "And John calling unto him two of his disciples sent them to Jesus, saying, Art thou he that should come? Or look we for another?" This seems strange since earlier in Scripture John baptized Jesus and recognized Him as the person who would bring about a change in the world. But now he has begun to doubt whether Jesus was the coming one. Perhaps he should anticipate someone else?

John's skepticism concerning the ministry of Jesus was rooted in Jewish messianic expectations. The issue really involved defining and understanding what the Messiah was to do. John and many others of his day anticipated the coming of a deliverer — but not quite like Jesus. It was thought that the anointed one would be more like King David than a suffering servant. Jesus was not the one that they expected since they were looking for a "general" to re-establish the political kingdom of King David. But if a person seeks a healer of needy people, like the servant of the Lord from Isaiah, then he or she will not be disappointed.

Jesus sent His answer back to John in Luke 7. Luke 7:22 says, "Then Jesus answering said unto them, Go your way, and tell John what things ye have seen and heard; how that the blind see, the lame walk, the lepers are cleansed, the deaf hear, the dead are raised, to the poor the gospel is preached."

Jesus answered John by quoting prophetic passages from Isaiah 29:18-19, 35:3-6, and 61 about His coming and what He was sent to do as the Messiah. Jesus is plainly telling John that the Father sent Him to be a healer in body, soul and spirit.

Isaiah 61:1 says, "The Spirit of the Lord God is upon me; because the Lord hath anointed me to preach good tidings unto the meek; he hath sent me to bind up the brokenhearted, to proclaim liberty to the captives, and the opening of the prison to them that are bound." This passage confirms the message and work of the Messiah in His first coming.

Verse 2 confirms His work for the second coming. This is what John and the others were looking for. Isaiah 61:2 says, "To proclaim the acceptable year of the Lord, and the day of vengeance of our God..." Jesus further explains this in Luke 4.

Luke 4:17-21 says, "And there was delivered unto him the book of the prophet Esaias. And when he had opened the book, he found the place where it was written, [18] The Spirit of the Lord is upon me, because he hath anointed me to preach the gospel to the poor; he hath sent me to heal the brokenhearted, to preach deliverance to the captives, and recovering of sight to the blind, to set at liberty them that are bruised, [19] To preach the acceptable year of the Lord. [20] And he closed the book, and he gave it again to the minister, and sat down. And the eyes of all them that were in the synagogue were fastened on him. [21] And he began to say unto them, this day is this scripture fulfilled in your ears."

Did you notice in verse 19 that Jesus did not repeat all of Isaiah 61:2? He did not proclaim "the day of vengeance of our God." This will be His purpose in His second coming (Luke 21:20-27). All Christians and Jews are looking for the same thing in His future return!

The Jews were not wrong to look for a deliverer; they just misunderstood how He chose to deliver them. Let's not make the same mistake. The Word of God is very clear as to the purpose, work and message of the Messiah. The Father gave Jesus two major tasks to accomplish. First, He came to redeem all of mankind. He could only do this by proclaiming the Gospel, demonstrating His power over Satan, and by becoming the sacrifice for our sins. His second task is that of the Righteous Judge. These two purposes are clearly taught in many Old Testament passages. What many people have misunderstood is that He will accomplish both of these tasks but at different times. His first coming enables us to set up His Kingdom in our hearts and lives, what I call the internal Kingdom. At His second coming He will establish His literal Kingdom and establish His righteousness for all people.

The book of Haggai is a beautiful prophetic picture of His Kingdom and how it is to be expressed in each of our lives. The people of Israel had not rebuilt the temple of the LORD and the LORD's prophet was warning them. Haggai 1:2-6 says, "Thus speaketh the LORD of Hosts, saying, this people say, the time is not come, the time that the LORD's house should be built. Then came the word of the LORD by Haggai the prophet, saying, is it time for you, O ye, to dwell in your cieled houses, and this house lie waste? Now therefore thus saith the LORD of Hosts; consider your ways. Ye have sown much, and bring in little; ye eat, but ye have not enough; ye drink, but ye are not filled with drink; ye clothe you, but there is none warm; and he that earneth wages earneth wages to put it into a bag with holes."

Haggai is telling Israel that since they have not rebuilt His temple they were suffering as a result of their disobedience. Haggai continues the warning in verses 9-11, "Ye looked for much, and, lo, it came to little; and when ye brought it home, I did blow upon it. Why? saith the LORD of Hosts. Because of mine house that is waste, and ye run every man unto his own house. Therefore the heaven over you is stayed from dew, and the earth is stayed from her fruit. And I called for a drought upon the land, and upon the mountains, and upon the corn, and upon the new wine, and upon the oil, and upon that which the ground bringeth forth, and upon men, and upon cattle, and upon all the labour of the hands."

We know that in the New Covenant we are the temple of the LORD (I Corinthians 3:16). The application for each of us today is to do the same thing. We rebuild our temple by cleansing ourselves of all iniquities (II Timothy 2:19-21) to become vessels of honor fit for any work Jesus would ask us to do. When we purge our selves of sin our broken hearts are also healed. Jesus heals our broken hearts when we choose to forgive and repent.

Haggai continues to teach that as the people chose to obey the LORD, the LORD proclaimed that He was with them and that they should not be afraid. Haggai 2:7 also prophecies that the LORD "...will shake all nations, and the desire of all nations shall come: and I will fill this house with glory, saith the LORD of hosts." The LORD of hosts is Jesus. Jesus is also the "desire of all nations" who will come and bring peace. The Hebrew word for "peace" is *shalom* which means to be whole and complete in body, soul and spirit. Only the Prince of Peace can bring complete healing in our body, soul and spirit. This is the message of the Kingdom. It is also our purpose and destiny.

This same message is told in His birth.

## THE KINGDOM MESSAGE IN THE BIRTH OF JESUS

There are so many prophecies in the Old Testament about the coming Messiah that no one has ever been able to count them. The first one is found in Genesis 3:15. His birth is told in countless prophecies and by angelic visitations.

Luke 2:13-14 says, "And suddenly there was with the angel a multitude of the heavenly host praising God, and saying, Glory to God in the highest, and on earth peace, good will toward men."

In this threefold text, "Glory to God in the highest," "peace on earth," and "good-will toward men," we see once again the purpose of His birth and His Messianic task.

First, Jesus made every effort to give "Glory to God in the highest." Jesus constantly defended the Father by saying "if you know me you would have known the Father; I and the Father are one; I only do what the Father has sent me to do; God is love" and many other statements that clearly declare that the Father always has our best interests at heart. Jesus realized that one of Satan's greatest temptations is to belittle and blame God the Father for what Satan has really done. We will see this same theme in Satan's temptations of Jesus.

Second, "peace on earth" is a universal message for all people that God the Father is sending the Prince of Peace for everyone. The Father sent His angels to proclaim His merciful will for all people. His divine favor is provided for all humanity. Luke 2:10 says, "And the angel said unto them, Fear not: for, behold, I bring you good tidings of great joy, which shall be to all people."

To further understand the meaning of the "good tidings" from the angels, we need to remember the Hebrew meaning of peace. The Hebrew word *shalom* means to bring wholeness and completeness in body, soul and spirit. A "prince" could refer to an official in a government. Government officials are in charge of war. Jesus, however, is not the minister of war. He is the Prince of Peace who brings wholeness and salvation for all the people.

Third, "goodwill toward men" is the goodwill of God for all who will receive God's divine favor, not just a few. "Goodwill" (Hebrew *ratzon*), appears 56 times in the Hebrew Old Testament and in at least 37 instances, it refers to God's good pleasure. It is His higher purpose for those He created. It denotes God's blessing and His divine favor for all men.

The word "goodwill" possessed a deep meaning for the Jewish people. Not only is the term used in Old Testament passages like Deuteronomy 33:24, but in Jewish literature in the time of Christ it signifies God's desire to express His mercy to all humanity. God's will is done when His "good pleasure" is accomplished.

In the Lord's Prayer we are instructed to pray "Thy will be done." The word used for "will" is the same term *ratzon* in Hebrew. Remember it means God's higher purpose and His good pleasure for and to mankind. It expresses what God truly desires for us. He wants people to experience His peace and salvation. The birth of the Messiah means that peace, which is His divine wholeness, is made known to all people. The term "goodwill" in the song of the angels refers to God's divine favor, which is being revealed in the birth of Jesus, the Messiah. The Father sent Jesus to bring "Glory to God in the highest, peace on earth, goodwill toward men." This is His Kingdom and our message and mission as His disciples.

## THE KINGDOM MESSAGE IN THE BAPTISM OF JESUS

After His birth He lived a normal life of a child learning at the hands of His father, Joseph. He learned to be a carpenter and He was thoroughly schooled in the Hebrew Scriptures. As Jesus grew into an adult there came a time for Him to be about His heavenly Father's business. His baptism is the beginning of that time. I have always found the order that events are presented in Scripture to be of extreme importance. We need to learn to do His ministry in His order and in His way. Let's continue to follow the events in the life of Christ in the Book of Luke.

Before Jesus preached and demonstrated the Kingdom there was a commissioning service. In Luke 3:22 Jesus was baptized in water and spirit. The Spirit of the Lord in the form of a dove descended on Jesus. This signified the beginning of His ministry. The Spirit of the Lord anointed, sent, commissioned, and empowered Him to do the work of the Father.

Luke 3:21-22 says, "Now when all the people were baptized, it came to pass, that Jesus also being baptized, and praying, the heaven was opened, and the Holy Ghost descended in a bodily shape like a dove upon him, and a voice came from heaven, which said, Thou art my beloved Son; in thee I am well pleased."

Some have taught that Jesus was baptized to be purified of sin. If this were true, He could not be God, or the Messiah. John's baptism required that first the person turn from sin and then be baptized with a pure heart. Repentance prepared the way for baptism. In that regard the pure life of Jesus was not a hindrance but rather a prerequisite for John's baptism.

There are two reasons for His baptism. First, in the conversation between John and Jesus in Matthew 3:15, Jesus says that He must "fulfill all righteousness." In other words, obedience is required. Jesus had to obey every command in the Torah or He would have been guilty of sin. He had to do everything the Father told Him and sent Him to do or He would have sinned.

Second, it was time for Him to be about His Father's business and the Father wanted to empower, send and commission Him. Luke 3:21-22 says, "...the heaven was opened, and the Holy Ghost descended in a bodily shape like a dove upon him, and a voice came from heaven, which said, Thou art my beloved Son; in thee I am well pleased."

There are several powerful points that we need to understand in this passage. First, Jesus did His ministry on this earth as a man and not as God. Scripture teaches that Jesus set aside His position and power as God and became fully a man. Philippians 2:6-7 says, "Who, being in the form of God, thought it not robbery to be equal with God: But made himself of no reputation, and took upon him the form of a servant, and was made in the likeness of men."

This has been a major point of contention since the first century. First century Gnostic Christians argued that Jesus could not be contaminated by the material world. Gnostics taught that Christ could not be spiritual and at the same time have any direct contact with the material world because they believe that matter (the physical world) is evil. So they invented the idea that Jesus Christ actually was two beings. There was a spirit called Christ who descended to rest on the material man named Jesus; though they functioned as one being, their personalities or nature never mixed. Christ's spirituality (He was still God) was preserved because he never actually merged with the material man Jesus (man or flesh).

Today scholars call this Docetism. But Docetism and Gnosticism, in one form or another, are still alive and well. This dual nature of Jesus Christ is still being taught in most of our churches. The argument that Jesus was a man but did His miracles as God is just another version of Docetism and Gnosticism that has extreme implications that affect how we live the Christian life.

The argument that Jesus had two natures, both man and God while He was on the earth, leads to the conclusion that His miracles could only be performed by Him (God) and the original twelve apostles since they were with Him. It leads to the belief that the earthly ministry of Jesus has no bearing on today; that the ministry of Jesus was not an example for each of us to follow.

Dispensationalists divide the earthly ministry of Jesus into two parts, two completely separate messages, one to the Jews and one to the Church. They believe that Jesus preached an earthly (material) kingdom to the Jews and when they rejected Him, He then preached a spiritual kingdom to the Gentiles (Church).

The key element to this argument is that the Church has absolutely nothing to do with Israel or any covenant in which Israel is involved. Therefore, everything in Jesus' earthly ministry that dealt with repentance, obedience and anything Jewish, are part of the New Covenant dispensation offered to the Jews. They believe that this is the gospel of the Kingdom. Since the Church is under the dispensation of Grace they believe we must ignore all those portions of Jesus' earthly ministry — where He taught obedience to the Torah and repentance — and accept everything dealing with faith, love and grace.

The dispensational argument continues to teach that in the second coming Jesus will set up a literal (material) kingdom on the earth that is for Jews only, while Christians (the Church) will continue to reign with Him in Heaven in a spiritual kingdom. The dispensational argument is just a rehash of Docetism and Gnosticism, and is just as incorrect. This argument has also led to the belief that God has two plans of salvation, one for the Jews (keeping the Law, i.e. material) and another for the Church (Grace, i.e. spiritual). The Bible is very clear that there is only one way to God. We are saved by grace through faith, which requires a change of heart (spiritual) and faith (obedience, i.e. material) (Knight 2007, pages 161-163).

Another fallout from the emphasis on the spiritual over the material is found in physical healing. This viewpoint led to the belief that our physical (material) bodies are not important, so healing is no longer necessary, because it is all about a spiritual relationship. If this were the belief of Jesus, then He would not have healed and taught others to do the same thing. Jesus created both the spiritual and material. Both are from Him and important to Him.

The Apostle John was confronting these same false arguments and beliefs in the first century and he had a very strong response in these passages:

I John 4:1-3

"Beloved, believe not every spirit, but try the spirits whether they are of God: because many false prophets are gone out into the world. Hereby know ye the Spirit of God: Every spirit that confesseth that Jesus Christ is come in the flesh is of God: And every spirit that confesseth not that Jesus Christ is come in the flesh is not of God: and this is that spirit of antichrist, whereof ye have heard that it should come; and even now already is it in the world."

II John 1:7

"For many deceivers are entered into the world, who confess not that Jesus Christ is come in the flesh. This is a deceiver and an antichrist."

As these verses teach, the antichrist spirit has been in the world (mankind) for a long time. Jesus while He was on the earth cannot be both God and man; it is not possible to have it both ways. Remember Philippians 2:6-7 says, "Who, being in the form of God, thought it not robbery to be equal with God: But made himself of no reputation, and took upon him the form of a servant, and was made in the likeness of men." As you can see, this has great implications on our faith and our future. Which gospel will you choose?

Second, "the Holy Ghost descended in a bodily shape like a dove upon him." Since Jesus chose to take on the form of a man, He needed the empowering and indwelling of the Holy Spirit, just as we do, to accomplish the will of the Father. He did the ministry that the Father sent Him to do in the power of the Holy Spirit. The same Spirit that raised Jesus from the dead is the power that we also need to do His ministry (Romans 8:11).

Acts 10:38 says, "...God anointed Jesus of Nazareth with the Holy Ghost and with power: who went about doing good, and healing all that were oppressed of the devil; for God was with Him."

In Luke 4:18-19 Jesus says, "The Spirit of the Lord is upon me, because he hath anointed me to preach the gospel to the poor; he hath sent me to heal the brokenhearted, to preach deliverance to the captives, and recovering of sight to the blind, to set at liberty them that are bruised, to preach the acceptable year of the Lord."

As these verses plainly teach, God was with Jesus in the form of the Holy Spirit that was upon Him. Jesus did the work the Father sent Him to do in the power of the Holy Spirit. This example and promise is for each of us because we can do the same things that Jesus did because the same Spirit can also be upon each of us (John 20:19-22).

Additionally, if Jesus did the work of the Father as God then He could not be our Faithful High Priest. Hebrews 2:14-18 says, "Forasmuch then as the children are partakers of flesh and blood, he also himself likewise took part of the same; that through death he might destroy him that had the power of death, that is, the devil; And deliver them who through fear of death were all their lifetime subject to bondage. For verily he took not on him the nature of angels; but he took on him the seed of Abraham. Wherefore in all things it behoved him to be made like unto his brethren, that he might be a merciful and faithful high priest in things pertaining to God, to make reconciliation for the sins of the people. For in that he himself hath suffered being tempted, he is able to succour them that are tempted."

Again let me ask you which gospel are you going to choose? Jesus came to give us an example to follow in every way. Jesus did what the Father sent Him to do in the power of the Holy Spirit and then trained and sent disciples to do the same things. Let's learn to follow Him in all that He taught and demonstrated.

Third, Jesus was proclaimed and brought forth by the Father, "Thou art my beloved

Son; in thee I am well pleased." The Father is announcing, commissioning and sending Jesus. He is saying "you are my son, the chosen; today I have brought you forth."

This voice from heaven was very significant in the view of the rabbis and teachers of the day. It was prophetic of the coming Messiah and also signaled the return of the prophetic to God's people. Isaiah 11:1, Isaiah 42:1-5, Isaiah 48:16 and Isaiah 61:1 are all passages proclaiming that the Spirit of the Lord would rest upon the Messiah. The same message carried into the New Testament in Luke 4:16-18, Acts 10:38 and I John 5:7.

The rabbis of the day taught that since the death of the last prophets, Haggai, Zechariah and Malachi, the Holy Spirit had departed from Israel. They believed that God would send another prophet like Moses who would renew the Spirit and bring about the redemption of the people. The Father is announcing the Messiah, His Son, the return of the Holy Spirit and His redemption.

It is interesting to note that before His baptism in water and in the Spirit Jesus did not do any public ministry that is recorded in Scripture except to speak in the temple at age twelve. It was only after being filled with the Spirit and being brought forth by the Father that He began His ministry. I believe that this is an example that we all need to follow. Jesus needed the empowerment for service by the Holy Spirit just as we do.

God has spoken, Jesus is made known and His work begins. At His baptism Jesus is empowered by the Spirit to fulfill His Messianic work. He came as a minister who would preach the Gospel, heal the broken hearted, cast out demons and heal the sick. He advanced and demonstrated the Kingdom of God in His teachings and in His work. Then He chose disciples, trained and sent them to do the same things. Are you seeing a pattern develop?

## THE KINGDOM MESSAGE IN THE TEMPTATION OF JESUS

As we continue to study through Luke the next event is the temptation of Jesus. Luke 4:1-2 says, "And Jesus being full of the Holy Ghost returned from Jordan, and was led by the Spirit into the wilderness, being forty days tempted of the devil...."

We should not be surprised that Satan would not like what had just happened and that he would do all that he could to derail God's plan. In this event we see the reality of Satan, the reality of the spiritual war and His power over the devil. We also see that Satan still does the same thing over and over again. His primary goal is to destroy our relationship with God the Father.

Satan is not asking Jesus to prove that He is the Son of God. This was affirmed at His baptism. The temptations are about the Father and His purpose. The three temptations focus on the nature of the Father and the identity of the only One worthy of worship and love. These temptations prove crucial for revealing the mission and work of the Messiah. They reveal the presence of His Kingdom on the earth.

We must realize that these temptations are real. Jesus could have failed. Sometimes it is wrongly claimed that Jesus could have turned the stone into bread; or that He could have received the rule of this world from Satan; or that He would have been saved by the angels if He had taken the suicidal jump from the pinnacle of the temple. Nothing could be further from the truth. The temptations were very real tests that had the potential to undermine the redemptive work of the Messiah. Satan is the master deceiver and did all he could to undermine God's plan. If it were not possible for Jesus to have failed, then Christianity is a hoax. As we stated above He could not be our Faithful High Priest if this was not real.

Satan was tempting Jesus to worship him and recognize his power. Such acts would have denied the Father and Scripture. Only God is worthy of worship. Satan tells Jesus that by defying God He will achieve a good purpose. Does this sound familiar?

The first temptation was about God's provision. Luke 4:2-3 says, "Being forty days tempted of the devil. And in those days he did eat nothing: and when they were ended, he afterward hungered. And the devil said unto him, if thou be the Son of God, command this stone that it be made bread." Satan is saying, "Since you are the Son of God, command this stone to be bread."

God had sustained Jesus during His fast. To accept Satan's challenge would have said that God's provision was not adequate. Jesus realized the deception and answered, "It is written, that man shall not live by bread alone, but by every word of God" (Luke 4:4). God sustained Jesus just as He did the people of Israel in the desert.

The second temptation is about the sovereignty of God. Luke 4:5-7 says, "And the devil, taking him up into an high mountain, shewed unto him all the kingdoms of the world in a moment of time. And the devil said unto him, all this power will I give thee, and the glory of them: for that is delivered unto me; and to whomsoever I will I give it. If thou therefore wilt worship me, all shall be thine."

Once again Satan plays the part of the master deceiver with partial truths. The devil promised Jesus all the kingdoms of the world if Jesus would just worship him. According to Daniel, only God has the authority over His creation (Daniel 2:20-22, 4:17, 25, 32-36, 5:23-31, 7:13-17). God alone is the King of the universe, not Satan. And as we see in the conversation between Satan and God in Job 1 and 2, the authority of the devil is limited.

Satan lied! Satan cannot give what belongs to God. Adam was only given dominion, not ownership of the earth. Satan could not give what he did not have. The real nature of this test was to deny the Lordship of God and to enter into idolatrous worship of the devil. Once again Jesus responds to a temptation with Scripture: Luke 4:8, "…Get thee behind me, Satan: for it is written, Thou shalt worship the Lord thy God, and him only shalt thou serve." Jesus knew His Scriptures and quoted from the Torah (Deuteronomy 6:13, 10:20).

The third temptation involved the purpose of His first coming. Luke 4:9-11 says,

"And he [Satan] brought him to Jerusalem, and set him on a pinnacle of the temple, and said unto him, If thou be the Son of God [since you are the Son of God], cast thyself down from hence: For it is written, He shall give his angels charge over thee, to keep thee: And in their hands they shall bear thee up, lest at any time thou dash thy foot against a stone."

As we have mentioned before, there was an ongoing argument about what the reign or the Kingdom of the Messiah was to be like. The Zealots, on one hand, believed that God's reign and Kingdom would be established through military resistance and active political involvement. They were looking for deliverance from Rome. Jesus, on the other hand, preached a message of healing through applying the message of the Gospel. This is a deliverance of a different type. This is a deliverance from the bondage of Satan. This was really a temptation to short-cut God's plan. God wants everyone to be healed in body, soul and spirit. This is far more important than a literal Kingdom. This same temptation has continued today in several ways.

The Father intended Jesus to come and preach the Gospel of repentance and forgiveness, heal broken hearts, cast out demons, and heal the sick. Jesus understood this when He did not proclaim the day of vengeance in Luke 4:18-19. His first coming is about the inner (spiritual) Kingdom and freedom from sin and disease. Overcoming, today, prepares us to rule and reign with Him at His second coming, which will be a literal (material) Kingdom for all believers.

In this temptation Satan brings Jesus to Jerusalem and places Him on a pinnacle of the temple, and then quotes Scripture attempting to entice Jesus into accepting the easy way to success. Satan reasons that if Jesus would cast Himself down from the lethal height, God would save Him and the people would flock to His movement. After all, the promises of the Psalms say that the angels will shield Him from all harm. Psalms 91 speaks of divine protection under God's wings of refuge in the sanctuary. Satan quotes a portion of Scripture to entice Him to jump. But as is always the case, the devil only tells part of the story. He omitted the reference in Psalms 91:11 which states, "In all thy ways," which should be understood to mean in the normal or natural ways in which a human walks. Suicide is not a normal or natural way. He also left out the commands in the Torah against suicide.

Once again Jesus responds with Scripture. His words affirm the character and nature of God and human responsibility. Luke 4:12-13 says, "...It is said, Thou shalt not tempt the Lord thy God." Jesus was God's representative just as we should be. Then Satan departed from Him for a season. This was not the last time that Jesus was tempted.

This temptation really centered on the nature of the work of Jesus. Jesus came to die on the cross for our sins. He came to give us power over all the works of the devil. He came to give us freedom and healing. He came to give us eternal life. If He had obeyed Satan and tried to set up an earthly kingdom, all of humanity would have lost

His redemption. Jesus was not fooled. He knew why He was on the earth. He knew and understood the full plan of God. He knew that He had come to die and become the offering for all of our sins. His blood is the only true payment for sin and redemption of mankind. Hebrews chapter nine is very clear that the blood of bulls and goats was only a temporary covering.

There are many very important lessons for all of us in these temptations because they have not stopped. These same temptations come to us in many other forms. Let's keep our eyes open and not be fooled by the wiles of the devil that repeat and repeat. The devil is still trying to prevent the manifestation of His Kingdom. The devil is still trying to prevent God's will being done on earth as it is in Heaven.

## THE KINGDOM MESSAGE IN THE MINISTRY OF JESUS

After the time of temptation Jesus returns home and begins to do what the Father sent Him to accomplish on this earth. The Father sent Jesus to proclaim His Kingdom and His will on the earth as it is in heaven. Luke 4:14-16 says, "And Jesus returned in the power of the Spirit into Galilee: and there went out a fame of him through all the region round about. And he taught in their synagogues, being glorified of all. And he came to Nazareth, where he had been brought up: and, as his custom was, he went into the synagogue on the Sabbath day, and stood up to read."

Next, in Luke 4:17-19 we see what was prophesied in Isaiah 61 come to pass. We see why Jesus was anointed and what He was sent by God the Father to do.

In verse 17 Jesus is handed the book (the Torah) and He opens it to Isaiah 61 and reads:

"The Spirit of the Lord is upon me, because he hath anointed me to preach the gospel to the poor; he hath sent me to heal the brokenhearted, to preach deliverance to the captives, and recovering of sight to the blind, to set at liberty them that are bruised, to preach the acceptable year of the Lord."

Here we learn that God the Father is sending His only son, Jesus, to preach the Gospel to the poor; He taught and demonstrated who He was and that we needed to repent and forgive so He could pay the price for our sins. The Father sent Jesus to heal the broken hearted; to heal the places where our hearts are hurt and bruised from the events in life. The Father sent Jesus to teach us that we do not have to be held captive by Satan, that we can actually be overcomers. The Father sent Jesus to heal the blind, the sick, raise the dead and to preach that today is the day of salvation, body, soul and spirit.

Luke 4:20 says, "And he closed the book, and he gave it again to the minister, and sat down. And the eyes of all them that were in the synagogue were fastened on him." He closed the book and purposely did not finish reading Isaiah 61:2 which says, "...and the day of vengeance of our God...," because the day of vengeance is the purpose of His second coming.

Then Jesus makes an astounding statement in verse 21, "...This day is this scripture fulfilled in your ears." Jesus was proclaiming that He is the Messiah. All those present fully understood what He was saying and that they must make a decision. Is this really the Messiah that they had all looked and longed for? Each of us is faced with the same decision. What will you decide?

In the next few verses of Luke 4 we see that there is a cost in doing what the Father sends us to do. Luke 4:28-29 says, "And all they in the synagogue, when they heard these things, were filled with wrath, And rose up, and thrust him out of the city, and led him unto the brow of the hill whereon their city was built, that they might cast him down headlong."

They rejected Jesus and threw Him out of the temple. This did not stop Him. He simply went to those that would listen. As we continue to follow the Scripture, we see Jesus actually doing what the Father sent Him to do.

## THE KINGDOM MESSAGE IN HIS MINISTRY OF MIRACLES

Christians have greatly misunderstood the purpose of His miracles partially because we do not understand the Jewish culture and background of His miracles. Christians usually teach that Jesus used miracles to substantiate that He was the Christ, and since this was accomplished we no longer need the miraculous. This doctrine called Cessationism teaches that the miracles of Jesus were for then and not today.

The Jewish view of the world embraced and longed for miracles. The Old Testament Scriptures tell of one miracle after another. In times of need they always turned to God for a miracle. The Jewish people strongly believed in the sovereignty of God who is good and who works miracles to save and help His people.

In the Jewish culture miracles signified the presence of God and were performed by one of His messengers. Jesus used miracles to proclaim who He is and also the active force of the Kingdom and God's will being done on the earth. This was consistent with His culture. Jesus said in Luke 11:20, "...if I with the finger of God cast out devils, no doubt the kingdom of God is come upon you." The miracles recorded in the Gospels reveal God's Kingdom upon the people. This means now, today! The Kingdom comes in full force when Jesus works a miracle because it is the finger of God (the Holy Spirit) that brings deliverance and openly displays divine sovereignty. God's plan is designed to bring wholeness and healing to every area of a person's life.

Today the message is the same. Miracles are still performed by the disciples of Christ in the same power of the Holy Spirit and they still demonstrate His Kingdom. Miracles are an example of His will being done on earth as it is in heaven. God is still sovereign. He still has power over all the works of the devil. He still loves all of us and still has our best interest at heart. He has not changed.

Matthew 4:23-24 says, "And Jesus went about all Galilee, teaching in their synagogues, and preaching the gospel of the kingdom, and healing all manner of sickness and all manner of disease among the people. And his fame went throughout all Syria: and they brought unto him all sick people that were taken with divers diseases and torments, and those which were possessed with devils, and those which were lunatick, and those that had the palsy; and he healed them." The Gospel of the Kingdom is the healing of all manner of sickness, spiritual and physical. Jesus said in John 12:47, "...for I came not to judge the world, but to save the world [people]." The Greek word *sozo* is translated "save" in English; it means to save, to heal and to make whole, body, soul and spirit.

Let's continue our study in Luke.

After Jesus was kicked out of Nazareth He goes to Capernaum and Luke 4:31-32 says that He "taught them on the Sabbath days. And they were astonished at his doctrine: for his word was with power." Jesus did not just teach or talk about things; He actually did what He taught. This is His example for us to follow.

As we continue to follow the Ministry of Jesus, let's take a look at what happened in just one day. This day in the life of Jesus begins in Luke 4:33-35: "And in the synagogue there was a man, which had a spirit of an unclean devil, and cried out with a loud voice, saying, Let us alone; what have we to do with thee, thou Jesus of Nazareth? Art thou come to destroy us? I know thee who thou art; the Holy One of God. And Jesus rebuked him, saying, Hold thy peace, and come out of him. And when the devil had thrown him in the midst, he came out of him, and hurt him not."

As Jesus taught He demonstrated His words with power by casting out a demon. He demonstrated His power over Satan. Then He left the synagogue and went to another divine appointment.

Luke 4:38-39 says, "And he arose out of the synagogue, and entered into Simon's house. And Simon's wife's mother was taken with a great fever; and they besought him for her. And he stood over her, and rebuked the fever; and it left her: and immediately she arose and ministered unto them."

Once again He demonstrated the power of God and His Kingdom by healing the sick. Then as the sun was setting, Luke 4:40-41 says, "Now when the sun was setting, all they that had any sick with divers diseases brought them unto him; and he laid his hands on every one of them, and healed them. And devils also came out of many, crying out, and saying, Thou art Christ the Son of God. And he rebuking them suffered them not to speak: for they knew that he was Christ."

Wow! What a day of ministry! What a day of proclaiming and demonstrating God's Kingdom and His will being done on earth as it is in heaven! Jesus taught and demonstrated repentance, deliverance and healing. Once again, remember that He came to be an example for each of us.

## THE KINGDOM MESSAGE IN HIS MINISTRY OF DISCIPLESHIP

Then in Chapter 5:1-11 we see Jesus choosing disciples. He wanted others to do His ministry. Then as He has others with Him to learn, He continues the work that the Father sent Him to do. This is a pattern that Jesus repeated several times. At first He had the disciples go with Him to learn and then He sends them on their own. Jesus knew that His time on this earth was to be very short. Therefore one of His major goals was to raise up disciples so that they could continue His work. By training others He demonstrated that His work was to be repeated over and over again. In fact in John 14:12 He even said that His disciples would do greater works!

Next in chapter 5, with His first disciples with Him, Jesus heals a leper and a man with the palsy. In healing the palsy, Jesus makes an astounding statement to the man He healed. Luke 5:20 says, "… Man, thy sins are forgiven thee."

Needless to say this caused the religious leaders great consternation. Jesus knew what was in their hearts and said:

Luke 5:22-24

"But when Jesus perceived their thoughts, he answering said unto them, What reason ye in your hearts? Whether is easier, to say, Thy sins be forgiven thee; or to say, Rise up and walk? But that ye may know that the Son of man hath power upon earth to forgive sins, (he said unto the sick of the palsy,) I say unto thee, Arise, and take up thy couch, and go into thine house."

Jesus is making it very plain that He has the power to forgive sin and that there is a connection between sin and disease. We are also told in James 5:16 to "confess our faults [sins] to one another so that we may be healed."

Next Jesus chooses another disciple, Levi. Levi made a great feast in his own house and there were a great number of publicans that sat down with them. But the scribes and Pharisees murmured. Luke 5:30 says, "But their scribes and Pharisees murmured against his disciples, saying, Why do ye eat and drink with publicans and sinners?"

We need to understand the culture. In the Hebrew culture it was customary to be open and discuss and challenge what was being taught. It is and was part of their way. As we in our western culture read passages like this one we tend to think that Jesus was angry and against the Pharisees. While He challenged their hypocrisy He was also a Pharisee. Their doctrines were much as His own. With this in mind we can understand His response.

Luke 5:31-32

"And Jesus answering said unto them, They that are whole need not a physician; but they that are sick. I came not to call the righteous, but sinners to repentance."

Then the Pharisees responded by questioning Him again about His disciples and how they fasted. Jesus explained that there was no reason to fast since they were with the bridegroom.

The Pharisees were really unhappy that they had not been chosen to be His disciples. So in the next few verses Jesus taught through two parables to explain why He chose who He did.

Luke 5:36-39 says, "And he spake also a parable unto them; No man putteth a piece of a new garment upon an old; if otherwise, then both the new maketh a rent, and the piece that was taken out of the new agreeth not with the old. And no man putteth new wine into old bottles; else the new wine will burst the bottles, and be spilled, and the bottles shall perish. But new wine must be put into new bottles; and both are preserved. No man also having drunk old wine straightway desireth new: for he saith, The old is better."

Jesus was using these two common examples from their daily lives to teach in a way that would be very clear. The new cloth, or His words, would only ruin the old garment. His new wine, or His teachings, would only spoil the old bottle or vessel (person) since they were not teachable. They were stuck in their ways and unwilling to grow and learn. It has and always will be about the issues of our hearts. They fully understood why he chose the disciples He did. Jesus wants followers that will do as He teaches. Jesus says "if you love Me, obey Me." Are you willing to obey? We must do His ministry in His way, and in His order (Young 1998).

This was the same message that Jesus had for Nicodemous in John 3, when He told him that he had to be born again. It is not about our position or race; it is about the condition of our hearts.

With this in mind we need to also realize that not everyone shall enter into His Kingdom. In Luke 14 Jesus tells another parable.

Luke 14:16-24

"Then said he unto him, A certain man made a great supper, and bade many: And sent his servant at supper time to say to them that were bidden, Come; for all things are now ready. And they all with one consent began to make excuse. The first said unto him, I have bought a piece of ground, and I must needs go and see it: I pray thee have me excused. And another said, I have bought five yoke of oxen, and I go to prove them: I pray thee have me excused. And another said, I have married a wife, and therefore I cannot come. So that servant came, and shewed his lord these things. Then the master of the house being angry said to his servant, Go out quickly into the streets and lanes of the city, and bring in hither the poor, and the maimed, and the halt, and the blind. And the servant said, Lord, it is done as thou hast commanded, and yet there is room. And the lord said unto the servant, Go out into the highways and hedges, and compel them to come in, that my house may be filled. For I say unto you, That none of those men which were bidden shall taste of my supper."

As you review these excuses it becomes obvious that they are invalid. Who would buy a piece of ground without looking at it? Who would buy oxen without knowing that they would work together? Who could not bring his new wife?

In Matthew 25 Jesus also uses two more parables to teach that He has called everyone, but not all will answer His call. In the parables of the foolish virgins some are not ready. And in the parable of the talents some are not faithful.

Jesus has been faithful to teach and do what the Father has sent Him to do. He has raised up disciples and trained them and now it is time to send them out on their own.

Luke 10:1-3 says, "After these things the Lord appointed other seventy also, and sent them two and two before his face into every city and place, whither he himself would come. Therefore said he unto them, The harvest truly is great, but the labourers are few: pray ye therefore the Lord of the harvest, that he would send forth labourers into his harvest. Go your ways: behold, I send you forth as lambs among wolves."

This makes a total of eighty-two disciples so far that Jesus has trained and sent out to be preachers and healers. Eighty-two people that He has trained to do the Ministry of Jesus.

As He sent them He gave them these instructions:

Luke 10:8-9 says, "And into whatsoever city ye enter, and they receive you, eat such things as are set before you: And heal the sick that are therein, and say unto them, The kingdom of God is come nigh unto you."

What does "The Kingdom of God is come nigh unto you" mean? First, it means that the Kingdom is now. It is not only a future event. It is present today. But what is the Kingdom? Could it mean that when His power is displayed in healing the broken hearted, casting out demons, and healing the sick, that we are experiencing His Kingdom? Could it mean that as we are obedient to do His ministry that the will of the Father is being done on earth as it is in heaven? Could it be that the Kingdom of God is present when the ministry the Father sent Jesus to do is actually being done? Yes!

Let's look at this concept further.

Luke 10:17 says, "And the seventy returned again with joy, saying, Lord, even the devils are subject unto us through thy name."

The seventy were excited to actually be doing the ministry of Jesus. At Wellspring Ministries this is what we see happening every day. It is so fulfilling and exciting to watch God heal the broken and bruised, set the captives free and heal the sick. Jesus joined in with their happiness by responding: "I beheld Satan as lightning fall from heaven" (Luke 10:18).

Jesus saw Satan fall from heaven as the seventy were destroying the works of the devil in person after person, in the power of the Holy Spirit. Then Jesus continued His rejoicing in verse 21 by spending time with the Father.

Luke 10:21-22 says, "In that hour Jesus rejoiced in spirit, and said, I thank thee, O Father, Lord of heaven and earth, that thou hast hid these things from the wise and prudent, and hast revealed them unto babes: even so, Father; for so it seemed good in thy sight. All things are delivered to me of my Father: and no man knoweth who the Son is, but the Father; and who the Father is, but the Son, and he to whom the Son will reveal him."

After celebrating with the Father, Jesus turned to His disciples and privately said to them, "Blessed are the eyes which *see* the things that ye *see*: For I tell you, that many prophets and kings have desired to *see* those things which ye *see*, and have not *seen* them; and to *hear* those things which ye *hear*, and have not *heard* them" (Luke 10:23-24, emphasis added).

Do you understand how great a privilege it is to be able to do the ministry of Jesus? Jesus tells us in verse 24 that many prophets and kings have wanted to see what they saw and heard on this ministry trip but never did. Jesus taught about the Kingdom of God or Kingdom of Heaven in many passages and in this passage and others He even talked about hearing and seeing His Kingdom.

It is hard to imagine that a spiritual realm such as the Kingdom of God could be perceived by one of our senses. Yet Jesus made this connection by stating that we can "see" and "hear" the Kingdom. This brings us to the obvious question: How do we hear or see His Kingdom?

## SEEING AND HEARING THE KINGDOM

Let's review Luke 10. In this chapter Jesus sends the seventy out on a mission trip. He tells them to go and preach His Gospel and to heal the sick. At their return in verse 17 they were very excited, as they did the Ministry of Jesus, and even the demons obeyed them. Jesus joined in their excitement in verse 18 by saying "I beheld Satan as lightning fall from heaven." As the seventy were doing the Ministry of Jesus, Jesus saw Satan fall from heaven. Wow!

Then in verses 21 and 22 Jesus rejoices in the Spirit with the Father and then turns to His disciples in verses 23 and 24 says "blessed are those that see and hear."

The disciples "heard" the Kingdom message from Jesus as He taught them the Gospel of forgiveness and repentance that heals the broken hearted, breaks bondages, casts out demons, heals the sick and raises the dead.

They "saw" the Kingdom of God when they actually "did" His ministry. When we forgive and repent, and in His name cast out demons and heal the sick, we "see" His Kingdom.

In Luke 9 and 10 Jesus sent the twelve disciples. As they extended the Ministry of Jesus, their work, too, was characterized by "seeing" and "hearing." In every town they entered, they taught forgiveness and repentance, cast out demons and healed the sick and then declared: "The Kingdom of God has come near you [that is, arrived]!"

In Luke 11:20, Jesus said, "But if I with the finger of God cast out devils, no doubt the Kingdom of God is come upon you."

Jesus continually taught about the Kingdom of God, which is the message of restoration and salvation. We need to understand that the central theme of His message is that the Kingdom is upon us. It is present now when we do the work the Father sent Jesus to do.

Here are a few more verses that demonstrate the reality of the presence of His Kingdom:

Matthew 12:28

"But if I cast out devils by the Spirit of God, then the kingdom of God is come unto you."

Mark 1:15

"And saying, The time is fulfilled, and the kingdom of God is at hand: repent ye, and believe the gospel."

Luke 10:9

"And heal the sick that are therein, and say unto them, The kingdom of God is come nigh unto you."

Luke 16:16

"The law and the prophets were until John: since that time the kingdom of God is preached, and every man presseth into it."

Luke 17:21

"Neither shall they say, Lo here! or, lo there! for, behold, the kingdom of God is within you."

Romans 14:17

"For the kingdom of God is not meat and drink; but righteousness, and peace, and joy in the Holy Ghost."

I Corinthians 4:20

"For the kingdom of God is not in word, but in power."

What an exciting truth we can actually experience. We can actually see and hear His Kingdom now by simply doing what the Word teaches us to do. We must learn to be doers of the Word and not hearers only.

## THE KINGDOM MESSAGE IN THE PARABLES OF JESUS

Jesus does not define what His Kingdom is like as a dictionary would, but He gave us many simple and powerful parables. These word pictures are better than any dictionary could ever be. As the saying goes, "A picture paints a thousand words."

In human history there has been and will continue to be controversy as to what Jesus was teaching. Most of us choose to look at a passage through our own presuppositions and theological positions. Dispensationalists claim that the Kingdom cannot appear until the millennium. They believe that it is only a future event and that we cannot be a part of it until we die or Jesus returns. Others in what some call the "kingdom now" movement believe that we have to establish the Kingdom through human effort which makes it then possible for the second coming to happen.

Others teach that the Kingdom is very much a future event. It was operating and advancing during the ministry of Jesus, but it was only a taste of what is to come.

But what did Jesus teach? As we study what He said "the Kingdom is like" we will see an entirely different view. Jesus taught that the Kingdom of heaven is a powerful force in the world that brings healing and wholeness. Jesus defines the Kingdom from His present experience rather than from and an end time or future view point. Furthermore He expected His disciples to continue to advance and do the work of the Kingdom. This is an entirely different mindset than we see taught by most people today.

In Luke 13:18-21 Jesus says, "...Unto what is the kingdom of God like? And whereunto shall I resemble it? It is like a grain of mustard seed, which a man took, and cast into his garden; and it grew, and waxed a great tree; and the fowls of the air lodged in the branches of it. And again he said, Whereunto shall I liken the kingdom of God? It is like leaven, which a woman took and hid in three measures of meal, till the whole was leavened."

In these two parables Jesus uses powerful word pictures to illustrate His message concerning the Kingdom of heaven. In these parables He teaches what the Kingdom is really like and demonstrates its progressive growth. Let's study these further.

First, both parables are supernatural. It is a miracle when a tiny seed can grow into a tree. It is a miracle when a little leaven in the dough causes it to grow into a large loaf of bread. Second, both parables are also illustrating a steady and continuous process. The major theme in both of these parables is this miraculous growth. The idea of a sudden change in a present situation is not present. Jesus clearly teaches that there is a day of judgment, but He never connects the future judgment with the concept of the steady growth of God's Kingdom. There is much more to His Kingdom than a single event.

I was raised on a farm and mustard bushes were common. The same was true of the agricultural society in Israel in the day of Jesus. Mustard seeds are about the size of grain of salt. These very small seeds grow into a bush where birds roost and build nests. The mustard plant will grow in good soil or rocky and poor soil. It is so tenacious that it will grow in the foundation stones of buildings, on rocky hillsides and other places where it rarely is watered. It is so strong that it will move large rocks as it grows. It is a tenacious plant that will take root and grow anywhere. The mustard seems to have an internal power source because it requires very little nourishment from its environment. The only thing that will kill it is a willful act to pull it out of the ground. Are you getting a picture of what His Kingdom is like?

The message of growth in the first parable in this passage is reinforced by the second parable. Once again Jesus uses an illustration that everyone is familiar with. Baking bread is something that was common for families in His day to do. Everyone who ever baked bread would be familiar with leaven and how the action of the leaven entirely permeates the dough.

Some have misunderstood this passage because leaven is also used as a negative illustration. Paul warns how a "little leaven leavens the whole lump" (Galatians 5:9). He also warns to "cleanse out the old leaven that you may be a new lump" (I Corinthians 5:7). During the Passover all leaven is to be removed from the home and is likened to sin.

However the picture created in this parable is completely positive. The process of fermentation and growth of the leaven is compared to the growth of the Kingdom of God. Several examples in Jewish literature demonstrate that a word picture can be used either for a positive or a negative meaning.

The Torah, or Word of God, is compared to leaven. The power of the Word of God is compared to the actions of leaven. rabbis taught that if one would just keep themselves involved in studying the Bible, the leaven of the Torah, its inner force and power, would bring them back to God. The Word of God possesses a compelling or irresistible force.

Peace is also compared to leaven. Peace is sought by almost everyone and the permeating power of peace in the world is compared to leaven in the dough. It is this same imagery that Jesus uses to illustrate another supernatural process that occurs when His disciples submit their wills to God and allow Him to spread redemption through them.

The fact that leaven is used in both positive and negative terms emphasizes the fact that we have free will to choose either God's way or Satan's way.

Modern teachers have sometimes missed the message of the Kingdom of God. It is not only about a future age. The Kingdom is not heaven in the sense that someone dies to enter in. It is not the church or a denomination. It is not up to human leaders to establish or maintain. It is not a political ideology or program.

The Kingdom comes by and through God. It is a divine force in the world that brings healing and salvation. Therefore Jesus did not define the Kingdom as only being in the future. He viewed the reign and Kingdom of God from His experience in the present. Exodus 15:19 describes God's reign as being forever and ever after the miracle of the exodus.

According to the Gospels, Jesus teaches that the Kingdom of God is: (1) God's reign among people who have chosen to obey Him; (2) manifested in the ministry of Jesus in preaching the Gospel, healing broken hearts, casting out demons and healing the sick; and (3) found in the people who have become disciples of Jesus. In the mind of Jesus the Kingdom of God is repeatable because He taught His disciples to continue His work of healing the world. The Kingdom of God was a strong force in their personal lives which is experienced today in the lives of His disciples.

# CONCLUSION

The Kingdom is a present reality for those people who choose to obey the teachings of Jesus, to accept God's redemptive power in their lives, to become disciples of Jesus and to bring His message of redemption and healing to a hurting world. The Kingdom is here when we choose to do His will on earth!

The Kingdom of God or the Kingdom of Heaven is an active force. We see and hear the Kingdom when His divine presence is at work in our everyday lives. The Kingdom of God is displayed when the ministry of Jesus is being accomplished. The Kingdom is "upon" us when the Gospel is preached, when demons are cast out, when the sick are healed and when the dead are raised. The Kingdom of God is God's Word in action.

This active force is from an internal power, the Word and the Holy Spirit, rather than an external power. We can only do His work by knowing His Word and with the indwelling power of the Holy Spirit. Only in the power of the Holy Spirit we learn to break forth seeking His Kingdom.

The King James Version of Matthew 11:12 says, "And from the days of John the Baptist until now the kingdom of heaven suffereth violence, and the violent take it by force."

In the NIV, Matthew 11:12 says, "From the days of John the Baptist until now the kingdom of heaven has been forcefully advancing, and forceful men lay hold of it."

The meaning of this passage is "From the days of John the Baptist until now, the Kingdom of heaven breaks forth and those breaking forth are earnestly pursing it."

Those that are "breaking forth" are those that understand His Kingdom. They have experienced His healing of their broken hearts. They have experienced the release of Satan's bondages. They have cast out demons and healed the sick. They understand that today is the day of the Lord and that in His power we can be free and then be His disciples and instruments to free others. We have learned that we can see and hear His Kingdom. We have learned that His will is being done on earth as it is in heaven when the powers of the devil are being defeated in our lives and in others. We have learned that His Kingdom is present. It is upon us when these things are happening.

Then, those who have broken forth with the Kingdom of heaven pursue the principles of God's reign with all their might. They possess an intensity for the work of the Lord. The rule of God is sought in every part of their lives. They become subjects of the King, accepting the yoke of the Kingdom of heaven and seek to see the redeeming power of healing, deliverance and His love penetrate a world full of hurting people in need of God.

This is the call and ministry of Wellspring. Will you join with us in doing the Ministry of Jesus? Will you join with us in advancing and breaking forth God's Kingdom on the earth? Will you join with us, in the power of the Holy Spirit to see that God's will is done on earth as it is in heaven?

If so, we all need the same power and authority that the Father gave to Jesus. Remember that Jesus did not do any public ministry, he never preached, healed the brokenhearted, cast out demons, or healed the sick until He was anointed and sent by the Father.

If it was good enough for Jesus, isn't it good enough for us?

Can we ask the Father to do the same for us?

May I lead all of us in a prayer accepting His yoke and anointing?

## Prayer

*Our Father in heaven, I come to You to ask for the same anointing and the same power of the Holy Spirit that you anointed Jesus and the Apostles with. I ask for this anointing and power to be on my life this hour. I ask for Your baptism of Your Holy Spirit, in Your full power and authority.*

*Father, I receive the anointing and power to do good and to undo all the works of the devil so that the unsaved will be saved; that the brokenhearted will be healed; that the oppressed will be delivered; that the yokes will be broken; that those imprisoned will be freed; and that the sick will be healed.*

*Lord, I commend myself into Your hands. Use my life; make me a winner of souls. I commit myself to do Your will in all things, in the name of Jesus, Amen.*

Some call the Book of Acts the Second Book of Luke because it tells the story of how the disciples of Jesus continued to advance the Kingdom of God.

Please read Acts again with this concept in mind. The Book of Acts tells just the beginning of the story. The rest of the story should be told through the life of every disciple of Jesus until He returns.

# Bibliography

The Holy Bible, containing the Old and New Testaments. The Authorized King James Version.

Bivin, David. *Understanding the Difficult Words of Jesus*. Destiny Image, 1994.

Bivin, David. *The New Light on the Difficult Words of Jesus*. En-Gedi, 2005.

Campbell, Wesley. *Welcoming a Visitation of the Holy Spirit*. Creation House.

Dake, Finnis Jennings. *Dake's Annotated Reference Bible*. Dake Publishing.

Dake, Finnis Jennings. *God's Plan for Man*. Dake Publishing.

Humberd, R.I. *The Dispensations*. R.I. Humberd.

Jacobson, Michael. *The Word on Health*. Moody.

Johnson, Bill. *When Heaven Invades the Earth*. Treasure House, 2003.

Johnson, Bill. *Dreaming with God*. Destiny Image, 2006.

Knight, Alan. *Primitive Christianity*. A.R.K. Research, 2003.

Knight, Alan. *Spirit of Antichrist*. A.R.K. Research, 2007.

Kraft, Charles H. *I Give You Authority*. Chosen, a division of Baker Book House Co.

Gerstner, John H. *Wrongly Dividing the Word of Truth*. Soli Deo Gloria Publications.

Lancaster, Thomas D. *Restoration*. First Fruits of Zion, 2005.

Lancaster, Thomas D. *King of the Jews*. First Fruits of Zion, 2006.

Lancaster, Thomas D. *The Mystery of the Gospel*. First Fruits of Zion, 2003.

Mace, Dan. *Unmasking Dispensational Theology*. Dan Mace.

Mace, Dan. *The Mystery of the Iniquity*. Dan Mace.

Mathias, Arthur. *Biblical Foundations of Freedom*. Wellspring Publishing, 2001.

Mathias, Arthur. *In His Own Image*. Wellspring Publishing, 2003.

McCance, Kathryn. *Pathophysiology, The Biological Basis for Disease in Adults and Children*. Mosby.

Ryrie, Charles. *Balancing the Christian Life*. Moody Bible Institute.

Smith, Wendell. *Great Faith*. City Bible Publishing.

Scofield, C.I. *Scofield Reference Bible*. Oxford: Oxford University.

Strong, James. *The Exhaustive Concordance of the Bible*. Thomas Nelson.

*The World Book Dictionary*. Doubleday & Co., Inc.

Thompson, Bruce. *The Walls of My Heart*. Crown Ministries International.

Wright, Henry. *A More Excellent Way*. Pleasant Valley Publications.

Young, Brad H. *The Parables*. Hendrickson, 1998.

Young, Brad H. *Jesus the Jewish Theologian*. Hendrickson, 1995.

Vine, W.E. *Vine's Expository Dictionary of Biblical Works*. Thomas Nelson.

# Wellspring Ministry Resources

BOOKS

*In His Own Image — We Are Wonderfully Made*

Is there a connection between our thoughts and health? This question has been asked for thousands of years. In this book, Dr. Mathias explains the connection between negative emotions (sin) and disease. It is written from the viewpoints of psychology, medicine and Scripture and is highly documented with over 180 clinical studies. These clinical studies from psychology and medicine clearly demonstrate how negative emotions destroy our immune system. Medicine and psychology can identify the connection between the mind and body but they leave out the "things of the Spirit." Only God has the ability to bring closure and heal the broken heart and broken body. The spiritual roots of more than 200 diseases are discussed.
$24.95 + shipping.

*Biblical Foundations of Freedom — Destroying Satan's Lies with God's Truth*

Dr. Mathias teaches how to have victory over bitterness, jealousy, envy, rejection, fear, and the occult by aligning our lives with the Word of God. This book teaches our ministry method. Also available in Spanish.
$24.95 + shipping.

*Biblical Foundations of Freedom — Study Guide*

This study guide workbook is designed to review the book *Biblical Foundations of Freedom*. Perfect for Bible Study groups. Also available in Spanish.
$9.95 + shipping.

*The Continuing Works of Christ*

Dr. Mathias teaches the reality of unbelief and that the works of Jesus are for today; shares testimonies of those healed through applying principles from God's Word to their lives; teaches personal responsibility from the book of Job; and teaches being holy as God is holy in preparation for the last days.
$24.95 + shipping.

SEMINARS

For information or to schedule a *Biblical Foundations of Freedom* seminar or *How to Minister to Others* seminar, taught by Dr. Mathias, contact Wellspring Ministries of Alaska at (907) 563-9033.

*Biblical Foundations of Freedom Seminar*

Dr. Mathias has traveled to many churches presenting the truths found in *Biblical Foundations of Freedom* in this four-day seminar. Those who attend learn how to have victory over bitterness, self-hatred, anger, jealousy and envy, fear, and the occult in their lives. Organizations and individuals experience the love of the Father, and healing in their lives. The syllabus contains all the Power Point slides and will greatly enhance your study.

| | |
|---|---|
| MP3-CD | $ 20.00 + shipping |
| DVD | $120.00 + shipping |
| Syllabus | $ 10.00 + shipping |

*How to Minister to Others Seminar*

Dr. Mathias provides training for those who desire to minister to others. It is our premise that all believers are ministers of the Gospel. We do not need to be "professionals" to be His ministers. This seminar is designed as a practical, hands-on approach and includes a workbook. The workbook asks many insightful study questions that will help you grow.

| | |
|---|---|
| MP3-CD | $ 20.00 + shipping |
| DVD | $120.00 + shipping |
| Workbook | $ 10.00 + shipping |

PERSONAL MINISTRY SESSIONS

Trained staff provide personal and telephone ministry sessions.
Call (907) 563-9033 to schedule appointments.
E-mail: akwellspr@aol.com
Website: akwellspring.com

*Please check our website often, as we continually
update our ministry and information.*

www.akwellspring.com

# Order Form

To order these books, please use this convenient order form, or call (907) 563-9033 or order from our online store: www.akwellspring.com.

| ITEM | QUANTITY | PRICE/EACH | TOTAL |
|---|---|---|---|
| *The Continuing Works of Christ* | _____ | 24.95 | _____ |
| *In His Own Image—We Are Wonderfully Made* | _____ | 24.95 | _____ |
| *Biblical Foundations of Freedom* | _____ | 24.95 | _____ |
| *Biblical Foundations Study Guide* | _____ | 10.00 | _____ |
| *Fundamentos Bíblicos de Liberación* | _____ | 24.95 | _____ |
| *Fundamentos Bíblicos Guía para Estudiar* | _____ | 10.00 | _____ |
| *Biblical Foundations of Freedom Seminar* | | | |
|   MP3-CD | _____ | 20.00 | _____ |
|   DVD | _____ | 120.00 | _____ |
|   Workbook | _____ | 10.00 | _____ |
| *How to Minister to Others Seminar* | | | |
|   MP3-CD | _____ | 20.00 | _____ |
|   DVD | _____ | 120.00 | _____ |
|   Syllabus | _____ | 10.00 | _____ |
| | | SUBTOTAL | _____ |
| | | POSTAGE & HANDLING | _____ |
| | | TOTAL | _____ |

Please print name clearly as it appears on your VISA or MasterCard credit card:

NAME _____

ADDRESS _____

CITY _____ STATE _____ ZIP _____

CREDIT CARD NUMBER _____ EXP DATE _____

SIGNATURE _____ PHONE _____

POSTAGE & HANDLING CHARGES:

| | |
|---|---|
| 1-2 Items | 5.00 |
| 3-4 Items | 10.00 |
| 5-6 Items | 15.00 |
| 7-10 Items | 20.00 |

THE ABOVE CHARGES ARE FOR DOMESTIC ORDERS.
PLEASE CALL OR EMAIL FOR SHIPPING & HANDLING
CHARGES ON INTERNATIONAL ORDERS.

THIS ORDER MAY BE MAILED OR FAXED TO:

**Wellspring Ministries of Alaska**
PO Box 190084
Anchorage, AK 99519-0084

fax (907) 243-6623